Y0-BDU-597

9-27

Foreign Policy and U.S. National Security

edited by
William W. Whitson

Published in cooperation
with the BDM Corporation

The Praeger Special Studies program—
utilizing the most modern and efficient book
production techniques and a selective
worldwide distribution network—makes
available to the academic, government, and
business communities significant, timely
research in U.S. and international economic, social, and political development.

Foreign Policy and U.S. National Security
Major Postelection Issues

Praeger Publishers   New York   Washington   London

PRAEGER SPECIAL STUDIES IN INTERNATIONAL POLITICS AND GOVERNMENT

Library of Congress Cataloging in Publication Data
Main entry under title:

Foreign policy and U.S. national security.

   (Praeger special studies in international politics
and government)
   Bibliography: p.
   Includes index.
   1. United States—Foreign relations—1945-
—Addresses, essays, lectures. 2. Security, Inter-
national—Addresses, essays, lectures. I. Whitson,
William W.
JX1417.F67   327.73   76-2070
ISBN 0-275-56540-8
ISBN 0-275-85700-X student ed.

JX
1417
.F67

PRAEGER PUBLISHERS
111 Fourth Avenue, New York, N.Y. 10003, U.S.A.

Published in the United States of America in 1976
by Praeger Publishers, Inc.

All rights reserved

© 1976 by Praeger Publishers, Inc.

Printed in the United States of America

Perhaps the story is apocryphal. . . . In 1967, a senior official in the Defense Department allegedly told the President, "Mr. President, you are pursuing a highly costly, inefficient, no-win policy in Vietnam. I believe that we can change that to a very cost-effective no-win policy." Allegedly, the President exploded, "For God's sake, how about a victory?" "Sorry, Mr. President, that's not systems analysis. We deal in adjectives, not nouns!"

After World War II, American leaders were soon driven to distasteful recognition of the fact that "unconditional surrender" could not continue to serve as the "noun" of peace. Despite the propensity of many leaders, still euphoric over Allied victory, to answer all doubters with "We won the war, didn't we?" within five years after the end of the war, "containment" of Soviet aggressiveness and "international Communism" had become the new "noun." For the next twenty-five years, approximately, the world was divided into two armed camps as leaders appended to that "noun" adjectives pertaining to economic and military assistance, embargoes, alliances, and appropriate declaratory policies designed and sustained to foster containment--and "security."

In late 1974, some of us at BDM Corporation* concluded that the noun "containment" no longer even approximated the realities of either the existing security environment or of American global security policies. Yet, the search for a new "noun" was obviously being obfuscated by a host of influences: the heavy hand of bureaucratic precedent, both in perceptions and in style; the intellectual and emotional pain associated with redefining ends, contrasted with the relative pleasure of tinkering with means (the old ends, presumably, being "good enough for government work"); corporate and private self-serving advantages of prevailing defense budget allocations, contrasted with risks of substantial loss associated with a new definition of America's global security goals; and the confusion of domestic priorities and values, reflected in a post-Vietnam ennui with international causes, mounting unemployment, runaway inflation, and the Watergate syndrome, the loss of faith in national leadership.

---

*The BDM Corporation, with headquarters in Vienna, Virginia, is a full-service consulting and professional services company with 15 years' experience in the analysis of major public policy questions such as theater and strategic security; communications; command and control; terrorism and many other issues addressed in this book.

LIBRARY
ALMA COLLEGE
ALMA, MICHIGAN

This book does not promise easy definition of the new "noun."
Nor does it presume to address all major issues associated with the
"noun," whether it be "containment," "detente," perhaps "survival,"
or some other simple word that distills complexity down to its essentials. But the book does represent the end of an eighteen-month
dialogue among scientists and scholars associated with the BDM effort to identify the security policy issues of highest priority for the
new administration and Congress in 1977. In order that these issues may be perceived in their proper context, several chapters are
addressed to the total "security environment," with particular emphasis on those trends that appear to be redefining that environment,
whether we like them or not. Each issue chapter, then, aims at a
relatively simple explanation of the issue, how it evolved, and what
serious students think should be done about it.

In short, this is not a book about "what should be done." It is
a book about alternative answers to the salient security policy problems of the late 1970s. In sum, it is an attempt to articulate the
challenge to the next round of Executive and Congressional leaders,
whose responsibility it will be to find the new "noun"--somewhat before the new "noun" finds them.

CONTENTS

LIST OF TABLES AND FIGURES

PART

I

INTRODUCTION

Educated by twenty-five years of Cold War to look at national security and security policy in terms of certain values, attitudes, and presumed roles for the superpowers, major powers, and small powers, men and women destined for leadership in the Legislative and Executive branches after January 1977 will be searching for a new vision of international stability. Theirs will be an enviable task, because it will be unique and may be accomplished during their tenure of office. But it will also be painful, because the deep and bitter disagreements are disagreements of purpose and ends, not simply techniques and means. Chapter 1 reminds the reader of certain trends that cannot be ignored--indeed, should be exploited in defining American security policy options for the final decades of the twentieth century.

CHAPTER 1

THE GLOBAL SECURITY ENVIRONMENT OF 1977: SECURITY CONCEPTS FOR NATIONAL LEADERSHIP
William W. Whitson

In recent years, "national security" has been overused and misused as a rationale for various domestic and foreign policies of dubious value. However, the current (1976) erosion of its sanctity in the popular mind is probably less the consequence of disillusionment with those policies and more the expression of its transient meaning. Despite their yearning for permanent "national interests," "national goals," and "national security," leaders must learn to live with the sorry fact that national security cannot be measured. Ultimately, national security is a mood, a sensing, a subjective phenomenon whose interpretation may reflect a herd instinct in one era and the charisma of a single leader in the next. It is thus a subject for political debate, not strictly military net assessment.

This book and this chapter will offer no magic formula for insulating political and military leaders from the essentially psychological definition and significance of national security. But it will attempt to clarify trends among the major components of the image of security--or insecurity. These components are ends, issues, and means. Stated somewhat less conventionally, confusion among leaders about America's priority value-goals ("detente?") is a guarantee of "insecurity," of hysterical and unbalanced perception of issue priorities, and of policies of drift. Conversely, a consensus about purposes and national role (containment) provides leaders and planners with criteria (rightly or wrongly, for "the long term") for assessing issues and designing relevant short-term policies.

In the aftermath of Vietnam, American leaders were confronted by a popular abandonment of the Cold War consensus about the American role as the defender of Wilsonian principles of self-determination and nonaggression. Such words as "detente," "coexistence," and "parity" reflected American disillusionment with the role of world

3

policeman. For the purpose of this book, it is unnecessary, if not
futile, to search for the date when thoughtful Americans began to
entertain serious doubts about their Cold War role. Take your pick:
the Soviet hydrogen bomb (1954)? Sputnik (1957)? the Cuban missile
crisis (1962)? the debate about defending the United States with an
anti-ballistic missile (ABM)? the "loss" of Vietnam (1975)? But it
is very clear that by early 1976, thoughtful Americans had not yet
reached a working consensus about America's new world role.

Under the circumstances, it was hardly surprising in 1975 to
find widely divergent views among American leaders about the importance to American interests of foreign--and even domestic--
crises. One longed for the good old days when the "Communist
threat" was a clarion call for action, almost without regard to price.
By 1975, Americans, whether because of domestic unemployment,
political maturity, or sheer ennui, had acquired a tolerance for international tension that would have shocked the most experienced
(jaded?) analyst on the (now defunct) Board of National Estimates in
CIA. A quarter-century of Cold War struggle on countless political
and military battlefields apparently had exhausted many Americans'
idealism--as well as their willingness to funnel their tax dollars into
remote causes in remote countries. While some few seasoned observers might argue that the "threat" was growing, leaders in both
the Legislative and the Executive branches could find no consensus
about its precise nature.

Given these doubts about American priority goals and roles,
and threats deserving the most attention, we may sympathize with
leaders in the Ford administration who were charged with mobiliz-
ing and deploying American power not only to cope with real and
imagined threats, but also to convey to adversaries and allies alike
an image of credibility, of American resolution, technical capability, and political wisdom. Little wonder that some American leaders
seemed to have lost their sense of humor in these trying times. . . .

Indeed, the efforts to find some new equilibrium among ends,
issues, and means, when all three components of the image of national security were "in transition," promised questionable political
rewards when so few people seemed to care. By 1976, proponents
of great causes, great crises, and great weapons systems were
facing an American electorate whose collective will to tilt foreign
windmills had reached the nadir of post-World War II enthusiasm
and confidence. Congressional determination to curb Executive
power (a) to embark on foreign adventures, (b) to misrepresent foreign threats and crises in CIA and other information channels, and
(c) to spend lavishly on advanced weapons systems sustained endless
confrontations between Congress and the Executive branch regarding
Executive privilege.[1] Where was the vision, the elan, the sense of
purpose, and--most of all--the money to get America on the move again

POLITICAL ROLES: KEY TRENDS IN A TIME
OF CLASSIC TRANSITION

Between 1972 and 1976, the roles of superpowers, major regional powers, and smaller countries crossed a watershed of historic significance for the nation-state system. In popular geopoliti-
cal terms, the bipolarity of the Cold War distribution of political
power was no longer a reliable basis for calculating the significance
of an issue and the probable behavior of one of the superpowers. Indeed, during these years Chinese leaders conducted a public and re-
vealing debate over whether the superpowers were in fact in conten-
tion--or in collusion. [2] From a 1971 consensus among Chinese leaders that the superpowers were conspiring against China, by 1975,
public Chinese statements in the United Nations argued for the inevitability of war between the United States and the Soviet Union. [3]
At the same time, other Chinese leaders were telling Third World
leaders that superpower collusive attempts to exploit Third World
resources should be resisted. This confusion about superpower relations among their former allies and adversaries reflected worldwide confusion about "detente"--a term without boundaries.

For security policy planners among America's allies, the term
implied many things, some good, many not so good. In the latter
category, superpower avoidance of military confrontation loomed as
the central disturbing fact of the new era. From American strategic
superiority in the 1950s, when American generals and admirals, and
even political leaders, seriously contemplated massive retaliation
and nuclear war, American planners had moved to an acceptance of
"parity" and a certain dread of confrontation between superpower
nuclear forces. (See Chapter 16 for a detailed analysis of Strategic
Arms Limitation Talks [SALT] as the salient issue of security policy
dividing the two superpowers.) Whether or not they could afford to
fight a controlled conventional war remained debatable. But detente's
implied commitment to avoidance of nuclear war prompted American
military planners to search for a new concept of nuclear targeting,
whereby strategic weapons would still be employable against selected
targets in a context of highly controlled exchanges of nuclear strikes.
The notion of limited nuclear options continued to be debated in 1976
among a few sophisticated observers of superpower strategies. But
the focal lesson for lesser powers seemed to be that traditional alliance systems could no longer rely on the superpowers for nuclear
support in the event of a limited war. In those terms, the superpowers seemed to be moving toward some form of mutual accommodation, if not collusion, in controlling the utility, and perhaps the
proliferation, of nuclear weapons. (See Chapter 17 for our analysis
of nuclear proliferation.)

How far might such accommodation proceed? If the trend toward superpower interpretation of military non-confrontation, at least in nuclear warfare and possibly in conventional warfare, continued, would that principle assume primacy over more traditional American principles of self-determination, the sanctity of sovereign boundaries, and strict adherence to treaty commitments?

No leaders could answer these questions with confidence in 1976. But since major and minor regional powers could no longer be sure of superpower support in "limited" local conflict, the phenomenon of proxy wars (even for the purpose of testing contending superpowers' military doctrine and equipment) could conceivably disappear. Thus, local leaders were forced to face the prospect of greater responsibility for their own regional security systems, a prospect that would transfer from the superpowers the stabilizing role that had permeated almost every conflict situation for the past twenty-five years.

The prospect of greater superpower constraint in intervention in local conflicts underscored their cautious search (after 1975) for roles and ground rules whereby that constraint might be guided. Building on the first principle of military non-confrontation between the superpowers, their behavior toward regional and national conflicts might be expected to deviate surprisingly from traditional Cold War patterns. Indeed, as a corollary of the first principle of the new era (and the new "noun" for American security policy), both superpowers could share a common interest in isolating regional conflict in order to avoid the possibility of uncontrolled escalation of tensions and military investments in the process of transferring a regional issue to another region--where superpower ground rules and interest would, presumably, be substantially different.

Should this corollary (their joint quarantine of regional conflict) of superpower roles become an accepted principle, its implementation in practice could find superpowers (whether deliberately or inadvertently) supporting and even arming former Cold War adversaries. Such behavior would footnote the Chinese accusation that the superpowers are actually conspiring to exhaust the Third World in a series of local wars, perhaps inspired and inflamed by ancient animosities but fueled by superpower arms exports. (See Chapter 19 for an analysis of international arms trade.) In 1972, and thereafter, rumors in Congress of American postwar aid to North Vietnam matched the clear disdain of the new Cambodian leadership (in 1975) for the USSR. In October 1975, rumors of Soviet resumption of diplomatic relations with Israel were matched by rumors of American military assistance to Egypt and the probability of such assistance to Jordan.

Such dramatic shifts in superpower roles within regions could lead to a third principle of superpower behavior in the new era: the principle of the local standoff. While superpower export of arms to both sides of a regional conflict might appear destructively collusive to Chinese (and many other) observers, the constructive and stabilizing rationale of such behavior could be a local application of the lesson learned by superpowers during a twenty-five-year strategic arms dialogue: no one can win. If local adversaries, well-armed by both superpowers, could calculate no clear rewards and very clear economic and political punishments for continued warfare, the principle of mutual standoff could become the basic rationale for armed "peace," and the greatest stimulus to conflict resolution by nonviolent means.

Lest the reader deride these ideas too hastily, it is worth reflecting on the same principles applied to the problem of domestic crime and the issue of gun laws. One school argues that an armed populace is a deterrent to crime. Another argues that the widespread availability of arms encourages crime. In oversimplified terms, that difference in viewpoint lies at the core of the current debate between the superpowers about the ground rules for behavior in an emerging security environment of greatly increased subnational civil strife and intraregional wars.

Should trends in superpower behavior, whether by plan or by accident, reflect the working of those three principles (superpower conflict-avoidance, quarantine of regional wars, encouragement of local standoff), then a fourth trend would receive significant reinforcement: the increasing responsibility and power of major regional states. By late 1975, observers of the emerging international security environment were devoting increasing attention to the fact or promise of contention between major regional contenders for influence: Iran versus India in the subcontinent and the Persian Gulf; Indonesia versus the new Vietnam in Southeast Asia; China versus Japan in Northeast Asia; Brazil versus Venezuela in South America; Saudi Arabia and Egypt versus Israel in the Middle East.

In each major region, increasingly dominated in power-political terms by the bilateral (in some cases trilateral) relationships between such major powers, "stability" in the new security environment could become primarily dependent on intraregional elite perceptions of those relationships; not superpower relationships (which could become increasingly discounted because of their unreliability in local crises).

While superpower planners may be loath to relinquish Cold War illusions of grandeur, influence, and routines, the practical consequence of their relative impotence, both perceived and self-imposed, must be the inspiration for regional powers to experiment with new, regionally oriented routines and institutions for accommodating tensions and resolving conflict. Brazil's interest in the possible consequences of war between Chile and Peru (for a detailed analysis of Latin American issues, see Chapter 13); Indonesian concerns with incipient "people's wars" in Malaya, Burma, and the Philippines (see Chapter 9 for an analysis of critical issues in Southeast Asia); and Sino-Japanese concern for a revived Korean War, on the one hand, and the Soviet threat, on the other (Chapters 10, 11, and 12 examine different aspects of Northeast Asia) all suggest a new era of conferences aimed at more systematic and routine debate by regional economic and political groups, both formal and informal: OPEC (Organization of Petroleum Exporting Countries), ASEAN (Association of Southeast Asian Nations), and the Asian Development Bank. At the same time, regional groups inspired primarily by the Cold War between the superpowers (SEATO [Southeast Asia Treaty Organization] comes immediately to mind) may be expected to wither--unless their raison d'être is deliberately altered by the members, determined to assert their greater responsibility for their own affairs.

It is in the context of probable superpower and major regional power roles that the roles of minor powers should be examined. The emerging new security environment, and its evolving set of new perceptions and ground rules, must anticipate a heady and destabilizing new round of nationalism, marked by bitter internal conflict between a frustrated younger generation and the men who won the first round of anticolonial revolutions during and following World War II. The difference between this and the earlier outpouring of national adolescent energy is likely to be the absence of substantial superpower financial and military support, at least in the form of grant aid. Congressional and popular American disillusionment with the political payoff for twenty-five years of economic and military assistance seems destined to grow and to discourage small powers from successful blackmail tactics similar to the techniques employed by American allies during the height of the Cold War. However, smaller powers may well discover new sponsors and a new rationale for grant economic and military aid: the emerging system of intraregional contention among major regional powers.

On the one hand, some regional powers will be able to manufacture the transportation, communications, and weapons systems required by a growing coterie of intraregional satellites (Iran, Brazil, India, and Japan come immediately to mind). On the other hand, all regional major powers will generate financial surpluses with which to supply new protégés with necessities--perhaps even to include self-respect, status, and a sense of security, not only from intraregional adversaries but also from superpower "exploitation." For trends in minor power behavior, it is especially instructive to watch United

Nations debate over the "New Economic Order" and redistribution of the world's goods and services, for the obvious benefit of the Third and Fourth Worlds. It is also instructive to recall that small countries facing bankruptcy in 1975 as a result of their energy bills were still gracious toward OPEC, presumably in the expectation that major regional powers would soon shoulder responsibility for making things right.

In addition to their dependence upon new allies among major regional powers for support in intraregional feuds, minor powers may be expected to involve major regional powers in a new round of domestic strife. The consequence of a new generation of leaders facing the worldwide political issue of succession, in a context of economic deprivation and a very slow revival of world production and trade, is likely to be domestic civil wars, riots, and terrorism; perhaps the most disturbing and destabilizing feature of the early stages of the emerging international security environment. (1975 events in Portugal, Angola, Spain, Lebanon, and Ireland suggest the trend. Figure 1.1 shows statistics from one study on warfare.) This increasing incidence of subnational strife will surely encourage both regional powers and superpowers to reexamine their priorities and roles in each case. In some cases, the incentives for adventurism may be almost too inviting to resist--despite countervailing ground rules of superpower behavior. Thus, this trend suggests that the chief source of tensions between the superpowers may well be issues, opportunities, and crises in third countries--not direct bilateral superpower relations.

In addition to the phenomenon of shifting roles among superpowers, major regional powers, and minor powers, brief comment about a new set of actors is required. It seems increasingly likely that the midwife of the new international security environment may well be nonsovereign organizations, principally transnational criminal, terrorist, and corporate organizations. Sharing their ability to transfer resources among states without regard to the interests of either the nation-state system or any particular state, these participants in the international security environment prospered during the 1950s and 1960s by accommodating to, rather than confronting, prevailing Cold War folkways. By the 1970s, however, their interests increasingly seemed to require or encourage defiance of an international system in transition.

The potentially destabilizing role of criminal and terrorist organizations is obvious. Not so obvious may be their role as a catalyst to force, and even to dramatize, the evolution of trends toward a new system of conflict resolution. (See Chapter 4 for a detailed analysis of terrorism as a problem for American security policy in 1977.)

FIGURE 1.1

Total Number of Conflicts, 1946-70

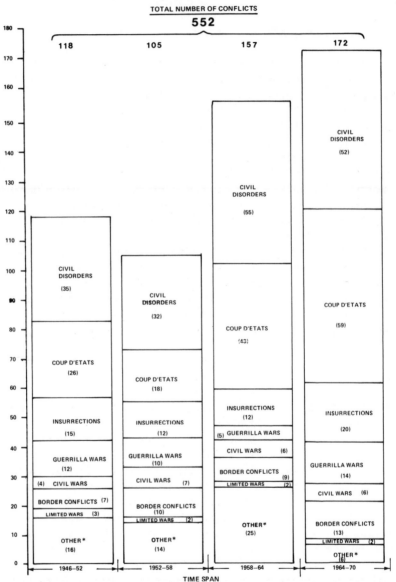

*"Others" includes blockades, shows of force, covert invasions, military revolts.

Source: Taken from Donald Blackburn et al., Restricted Engagement Options (REO) (v), 2 vols. (Vienna, Va.: BDM Corporation, November 30, 1973).

Of greater interest because of its economic and incipient political power, the multinational corporation (MNC) promises to play
the role principally of a substitute for the superpower, not only during the transition to a new security environment but probably as a
major stabilizing influence in that environment. (See Chapter 3 for
a discussion of the MNC as an instrument of security policy.) The
MNC role as a supplier of weapons, technology, and management
systems, often financed by other MNCs (especially international
banks), will force it increasingly to seek compromises among existing and potential clients. Thus, in the name of financial survival,
the MNC may play the role of a buffer, often capable of compensating
for outworn Cold War procedures and attitudes and muting both East-
West and North-South confrontations. Depending upon how the superpowers handle the problem of limiting or directing MNC flexibility,
the propensity of the MNC to trade with any state that can pay the
price may well establish the origins, incentives, and institutional
procedures for an era of economic wars--a noteworthy shift away
from the political-ideological focus of the Cold War.

To summarize this long discussion of the emerging international
security environment, trends in major and minor power roles and
value-goals suggest the potential emergence of a highly volatile political structure, no longer constrained, especially at the local and regional levels, by Cold War rigidities in loyalties, opportunities, and
means. In such a world, a focal problem for American and Soviet
leaders will be the balanced assessment of issues, their potential
impact on the trends discussed above, and the degree to which superpower resources may be or should be applied in conformance with
new principles of superpower collusion, detente, and competition.

PERCEPTION OF KEY ISSUES

For all of its costs in boredom with false causes, blindness to
real causes, and doubts about leadership that could not distinguish
the difference and too often took refuge in overreaction, the Cold War
at least sustained the illusion among American leaders, the American people, and their allies that "security" was calculable. The importance of an issue could be measured against the "threat of international Communism." Anything that gave the Communists an edge
was, by definition, bad.

If that criterion is removed from the calculation of issue priorities, what should become the substitute? The question is critical because the new leaders of the Executive and Legislative branches in
1977 must select and deploy military power, "packaged" in such a way
as to influence the outcome of critical issues. How to calculate

advantages and disadvantages, not only at bilateral negotiations with
Soviet leaders but especially in separate or joint efforts to contain
local conflict?

Certainly, before 1977--and even during the first four years of
the new administration, contending weapons technologies are unlikely
to generate a new family of revolutionary weapons, a breakthrough
in strategic or tactical military capabilities to shoot, move, and com-
municate. Yet, during 1977 the new administration must make budgetary decisions in research and development that could have profound impact on such capabilities available to the administration taking office in 1981. (See Chapter 21 for an analysis of the issue of
American research and development strategy.) Indeed, if we could
believe that the primary role of superpower military power after 1977
would be the containment of regional conflict, it would be reasonable
to pour substantially greater resources into the U.S. Navy's capacity
to maintain an effective blockade for extended periods of time (presumably to preclude other states and MNCs from shipping "excessive"
arms into the theater of operations).

By 1975, three broad categories of issues confronted national
leaders everywhere, especially in the United States:
- A new political equilibrium and conflict-resolution system
to replace the Cold War system
- An improved economic system capable of a more equitable
distribution of the world's goods and services
- Planetary problems, transcending national boundaries,
challenging the continued viability of "spaceship earth."

Because warfare could be fought over access to limited resources and could generate radioactivity profoundly damaging to the
earth's inhabitants, all three categories of problems are mutually
related. Yet, security policy issues deemed significant for superpower leaders in 1977 would probably fall primarily into the first
two categories. Nevertheless, civil and military leaders must recognize that warfare before the end of the twentieth century may result
from one state's threat to pollute the air, water, or soil of another
by practices that were never intended to be deliberately provocative
or damaging.

Since the issues selected for discussion in this book are considered in greater detail later, it would appear most useful to outline the criteria by which those issues were selected and by which
alternative approaches to their resolution might be judged. Our criteria for the critical security policy issues for 1977 relate exclusively to the first two categories of problems. Because a sense of security and the perception of security relate most directly to uncertainty
and change, we may assume that any issue may be judged "critical"
by American planners (and probably Soviet planners as well) if it

- Promises a superpower military confrontation
- Significantly alters prevailing superpower roles in a region
- Changes the intraregional balance of power (regardless of impact on superpower roles)
- Promises to spread conflict outside the region of the crisis
- Clearly outrages a significant number of American voters whose expectations cannot be ignored by the administration.

A host of critical security issues, confronting the Ford administration in 1975 and likely to challenge the next administration in 1977, remained unresolved in terms of policy direction in the spring of 1976. Many of these had to do with American goals; a substantial number concerned means for achieving those goals.

Part II will outline those issues that are global in origin and implications, and already are largely beyond the control of any single power, including the superpowers: how to handle the aspirations of the Third and Fourth Worlds without encouraging either rampant local conflict or superpower and major power adventurism; how to use the multinational corporation to enhance security without thwarting its many positive contributions to a stable security environment; and how to deal with the phenomenon of terrorism (and international crime).

Part III will address specific regional issues that American leaders must discuss as they search for a consensus about America's global and regional goals. European security and stability is the single most important focus for security policy decisions in the next administration. Closely related and potentially damaging to European stability is the question of peace in the Middle East--the regional conflict situation most requiring "quarantine." The sequence of chapters thereafter is not meant to suggest the priority of American interests. However, they underscore several common themes that challenge American political leaders, who must be explicit about the instruments of security policy.

It is to such instruments that Part IV is devoted. American economic strength is the foundation for all other issues of security policy instruments. The crucial problem of intelligence demands an early decision from new leaders in Congress and the Executive branch after January 1977. Chapters follow on various aspects of the worldwide proliferation of armaments, and Part IV ends with an examination of issues surrounding a new strategy for research and development.

Part V, the final chapter, explores alternative philosophies whereby American power may be applied to resolution of the issues outlined in this book. In a certain sense, this exploration may suggest the new "noun" of international security for the final quarter of the twentieth century. To anticipate for the busy reader, and to suggest a "noun" that has general significance, most particularly for

Americans, the policy of "quarantine" of war and its spreading consequences may be the ultimate criterion for measuring the utility and success of a new generation of American security policy decisions and instruments, the "adjectives" of peace.

NOTES

1. Note, for example, the Senate vote (54 to 22) on December 19, 1975, blocking further covert CIA funds to U.S.-supported factions in Angola; and the Washington Post comment on December 21, 1975, p. 1, that Kissinger's critics in Congress believe that he is "years out of touch with what is politically or morally tolerable in the United States."

2. For a penetrating analysis of these Chinese views, see Jack Harris and Peter Sargent, Chinese Assessments of the Superpower Relationship, 1972-74 (Vienna, Va.: BDM Corp., 1975).

3. See, for example, Chiao Kuan-hua's speech at the United Nations, September 26, 1975 (New York Times, September 27, 1975).

PART

II

U.S. GOALS:
MAJOR GLOBAL ISSUES

As suggested in Part I, the nation-state system, at least as American security policy planners have understood it since 1945, is being subjected to massive pressures from a host of global issues and new transnational actors. While the superpowers were devising means for mutually defining the ground rules of the East-West competition, other forces were redefining the issue of survival in terms of a North-South axis of conflict. Reflecting that trend in political orientation, transnational actors increasingly question the utility of the existing system for resolving conflict over the world's goods and services.

Part II addresses these dimensions of the emerging global security environment. It argues simply from the premise that the fate of food supply to the Third and Fourth Worlds will probably become the focus for superpower and regional power security policy decisions. As that focus sharpens, urgent American government decisions will be required about the permissible flexibility of both terrorist and multinational corporate power.

In sum, in attempting to ameliorate the threat of widespread food shortages, can the security of the average American's values, savings, and hopes survive in a bureaucratic context of increasing government controls aimed at disciplining multinational corporate, as well as terrorist, "free enterprise"?

RELATIONS WITH THE THIRD AND FOURTH WORLDS: THE PROBLEM OF GLOBAL STARVATION

Charles P. Shirkey

THE ISSUE

An issue of increasing importance for the United States is what it should do toward alleviating the world food problem, a very complex issue with very high stakes for the United States. It is also an integral part of a much bigger issue--how to close the gap between the rich, industrialized nations of the North and the poor nations of the South. In fact, the two issues are so interrelated that it is impossible to consider solutions to the world food issue without considering relations between the developed and developing nations.

The objective for solving the world food problem per se is deceptively simple--to get everyone in the world fed, in order to avoid malnutrition and starvation. But food, population, and income are not distributed evenly over the globe: Some countries produce more food than they need; others have a shortage. Some countries can readily pay for imported food; others cannot. Some countries have rising per capita incomes; others have falling per capita incomes, with many of their people already at the level of subsistence. Trends and projections for food, population, and income indicate that the disparities are increasing at a rapid pace and will continue to do so for the foreseeable future. Hence the near-term problem is essentially the maldistribution of food and income.

The long-term problem, however, is somewhat different. Many forecasts point to a spiraling world population in the twenty-first century that will outstrip projections of available food supply at some point after the turn of the century. To alter the food/people equation in the twenty-first century, a relatively greater effort must be put on stabilizing population, because of the long time lags in seeing results. Therefore, the long-term problem is focused more on population growth and agricultural development.

The questions raised by the uneven distribution of food, population, and income are very much at the core of what has been labeled
the "new cold war." On one side are the rich industrialized nations
of the First World (North America, Western Europe, and Japan); on
the other side, a very diverse group of developing nations (Asia,
Africa, and Latin America). Frequently referred to as the Third
World, it includes nations that can generate wealth by exporting resources or goods and those that cannot generate such wealth but still
have to import food and fuel. The latter group is now being called
the Fourth World.

Increasingly over the past few years, the United States and
other industrialized nations have been confronted by Third and Fourth
World demands for radical changes in the international economic system. They want a "new international economic order"--which, translated, appears to mean "share the wealth." The list of demands is
long and far-reaching--from terms of trade and the international
monetary system to the legal status of multinational corporations.
It has been described by some as a "global class war." As P. E.
Steiger notes: ". . . some analysts believe [it] may be the most
serious diplomatic challenge the nation faces over the next decade--
more difficult than relations with the Soviet Union and China, potentially more dangerous than even the Arab-Israeli conflict."[1]

Any workable way of coping with the world food problem should
take the following factors into account:

● Food security concerns the market problem of supply, varying between extremes of surplus and shortage, and the attendant problems of volatile price fluctuations, inequitable distribution, dysfunc-
tional incentives, malnutrition, and even pockets of starvation.

● Meeting nutritional needs is mostly an ongoing problem in
poor developing countries, but is not limited to them. It becomes a
matter of world concern when regions and national populations lack
access to balanced and adequate diets. Emergencies may arise for
economic reasons, as well as from natural causes and armed hostilities.

● Food production development pertains to the necessity,
over time, of the food supply to meet or exceed anticipated world
demand while making more countries self-sufficient.

● Population stabilization involves the many efforts designed
to bring population growth within the projected limits of available
resources, in this case food.

How the United States will address these factors in seeking to
deal with the world food problem will depend to a great extent on how
it responds to the challenge of the Third and Fourth Worlds. At this
juncture two alternative perspectives are discernible:

• On the one hand, the demands of the Third and Fourth
Worlds may be viewed as valid (if not reasonable); redistribution of
existing and potential wealth is necessary; accommodation is deemed
appropriate; and concessions and sacrifices are serious options.
This is what we might call an accommodation strategy.

• Alternatively, their demands may be perceived as unreasonable (if not ungrateful); economic betterment is best achieved through
growth and an ever-increasing pie; isolation and autarky are worthwhile goals; and opposition and resistance are serious options. By
way of contrast, we can call this an opposition strategy.

BACKGROUND

Politically, the scope of the issue confronting American policy-
makers today is largely a product of coincidence. Food would not
loom as a major world issue in the mid-1970s were it not for a series
of unrelated events taking place concurrently during 1972-74. Similarly, the developing countries would not have become a force to be
reckoned with in international politics had it not been for events in
the Middle East and the strange chemistry of oil politics. Some observers cautioned about the possibility of such developments years
ago, but few could predict their timing and political significance.

Concern about the world food system and prospects for the
food/people equation was, in recent years, limited to the experts and
special interest groups. During 1972-74, however, that changed dramatically. Suddenly, the world was confronted with the worst food
crisis in history. Deaths rose sharply, particularly through malnutrition. World grain reserves went from record levels to almost
nothing, and most of the world's idle cropland was recultivated.
Meanwhile, shortages developed in fertilizer, cereals, and major protein sources. The greatest price increase in modern times occurred
as the price of food doubled, while the prices for fuel and fertilizer in
some countries as much as quadrupled. The foreign-exchange position of many food-importing nations was further eroded by declining
prices for their export commodities. The net effect of the diverse
markets involved in the production and sale of food was inefficiency
(for instance, fertilizer not allocated to the most productive areas in
the world) and, depending upon where you "sat," inequities.

Such events as these, however, were not predictable in 1971.
Moreover, no one could foresee the full ramifications of the major
factors that brought on the crisis. In 1972, the world's food supply
dropped--for the first time in twenty years. Major grain producers
independently cut back grain production in order to maintain prices.
At the same time, adverse weather resulted in poor harvests in much

of Asia and Africa. This immediate drop in production was compounded by diminishing gains of the "green revolution" in many developing countries, inadequate incentives to expand fertilizer production capacity and increase the amount of land under cultivation,
and an unexpected drop and then leveling off in the world fish catch.

While supply decreased, demand increased unexpectedly. Detente encouraged the Soviets to enter the world market at a record
level (rather than tighten their belts) and close the highly publicized
wheat deal with the United States. A major factor was affluence,
particularly in the United States, Europe, and Japan; and the associated rise in demand for meat, poultry, and eggs in turn created
a greater demand for grain.

During this crisis, official attention was directed to the problem at the World Population Conference convened in Bucharest by
the United Nations in early 1974, and particularly at the World Food
Conference in Rome later the same year. Among other things, these
conferences helped focus knowledgeable opinion on the food and population problems and stimulated the emergence of an official U.S.
position.

The Third and Fourth Worlds became a political force in 1974
in the aftermath of the Arab oil embargo. The success of the
thirteen-member Organization of Petroleum Exporting Countries
(OPEC) in raising the price of crude oil has been interpreted as the
first time a non-European power has been successful against the
West since Japan defeated Russia at the turn of the century. Although
the effects of OPEC's policies on many developing countries are relatively far more severe than on the United States and other industrialized nations, OPEC has the solid backing of most developing nations.
They all share the experience of long periods of domination by the
West. Many of them hope to follow OPEC's example with other commodities. In mounting their counterattack, differences are suppressed, even at very high costs to themselves.

In recent years, this bloc of nonaligned nations of the Third
and Fourth Worlds has become a force to be reckoned with. At the
U.N. Conference on the Human Environment held at Stockholm in
1972, the developing world viewed American efforts to curb pollution as an attempt to keep them suppressed by hampering their economic development. In 1974, the United Nations held a Special Session on Raw Materials and Development, at which two resolutions
were passed calling for a "new international economic order." A
similar resolution was passed later in 1974 by the U.N. General
Assembly, titled "Charter of Economic Rights and Duties of States."
Basically, the Third and Fourth World want the following: full sovereignty of states over all their resources and economic activities;
better terms of trade, such as OPEC has achieved for petroleum;

and greater financial aid from the industrialized nations. At subsequent meetings in Dakar and Lima in early 1975, these demands became more vocal. In the process, the positions of the governments involved became less flexible. This spirit of confrontation changed dramatically at the U.N. Special Session on Development and International Economic Cooperation held in New York in September 1975. Apparently in response to an American initiative, representatives of the developing nations changed the tone of their remarks and sought cooperation rather than confrontation with the industrialized nations.

The style may have changed; but the underlying conflicting interests remain between rich and poor, North and South, white and nonwhite. As reflected in the complex of issues surrounding the world food problem, what's in the interest of one is not necessarily in the interest of all. Moreover, the stakes are high for all concerned.

For the United States, the full force of this issue comes at an awkward time. In varying degrees the Western industrialized nations are in economic trouble. (See Chapter 14 for an independent analysis of American economic strategy.) Inflation and balance of payments were problems for many before the oil embargo; the rapid increase in the price of fuel only made things worse. Likewise, inflation countermeasures invoked to cut consumption and strengthen currency positions did not always work as intended, and created a problem of their own: recession. Politically, the West is very weak. There is a noticeable lack of strong leaders and strong governments. Moreover, foreign aid is not popular and, after Vietnam, internationalism has a limited appeal.

How the United States handles these difficulties and responds to the allied problems of food, population, and incomes will depend on tugging and hauling among 1977 leadership over many issues involved in the U.S. government. Decision-making on the world food issue is characterized by the involvement of many different U.S. governmental actors--more than on most other issues of foreign policy and national security. These actors represent a wide range of power bases with very different perspectives, priorities, and concerns. Specifically, it involves bureaucratic politics on a broad scale, domestic politics in a way unusual in foreign affairs, and Congressional politics.

Most of the technical issues involved in devising specific policies or reacting to the proposals of other countries must be worked out in the bureaucracy, and getting decisions out of the bureaucracy is hard enough on any issue. In writing on the politics of food aid, Leslie Gelb and Anthony Lake suggest it is more difficult than usual on the world food issue.

In traditional political-military decisions,
State, the NSC staff, and Defense are the
major participants, with an additional speak-
ing role for the CIA. In food aid politics,
State, AID, Agriculture, Treasury, OMB
(Office of Management and Budget), CIEP
(Council for International Economic Planning)
and the CEA (Council of Economic Advisors)
are all important. The effect of doubling the
number of agencies is enormous--in coordination of cables and memos, in possible foul-ups
and delays, in the number of senior officials
involved, and in the staggering range of interests that must be accommodated. To compound the problem, these officials are not
used to working with one another, and are un-
familiar with each other's agency politics. [2]

Whatever decisions are made on food stockpiles or food assistance, American farm prices are affected. There is an immediate
and direct impact on both family budgets and the incomes of farmers
and agrobusinesses. Consequently, domestic political considerations are very important and must be taken into account in the administration as well as on Capitol Hill.

Meanwhile, in Congress, policies and programs bearing on
the world food problem are addressed in piecemeal fashion. Most of
the substantive legislation directly related to the world food issue is
divided between the Agriculture Committees and the Senate Foreign
Relations and House International Affairs Committees. Other committees become involved on matters pertaining to trade and international monetary affairs. The Appropriations Committees pass on
the funds available annually, but the tradeoffs that directly address
how much the United States is prepared to contribute to the allevia-
tion of the world food problem are likely to be made in the new
Budget Committees.

URGENCY OF THE ISSUE

Immediate pressure for American decisions in 1977 probably
will come from the initiative taken by Secretary of State Henry
Kissinger in his Labor Day (1975) address to the U.N. Special Session on Development and International Economic Cooperation. In a
concerted effort to move from rhetoric and confrontation to problem-

solving and cooperation, it proposes a substantial shift in U.S. policy
on world food matters and on economic relations in general with the
Third and Fourth Worlds. The initial reaction of the representatives
of the developing countries was favorable. For this reaction to continue, however, complex international agreements must be negotiated
and major changes enacted in U.S. policies and programs.

One of the major reasons cited in support of American action
now is the widening "food gap." In the near term, between now and
the mid-1980s, population is simply a given. Currently, the world's
population is 3.9 billion and growing at a predictable rate. Over the
next ten years there is no morally acceptable way to change that fact.
In any event, most experts indicate there is a high probability that
the world's food system can produce sufficient supply. But that is
aggregate supply.

The problem remaining is one of distribution between the rich,
surplus nations and the poor nations with food deficits. Under current policies, food deficits in the developing countries are projected
to double by 1985. At the same time, their ability to earn foreign
exchange is expected to deteriorate further, so long as international
trading and financial relationships remain unchanged. Thus, many
of the food transfers would have to take place on concessional terms.
Yet both rich and poor nations view that prospect as neither desirable
nor likely. Unless this trend is altered, then, rich and poor nations
alike will seek bargaining power or some way to offset the reaction
of others. (It is in this context that the discussion of terrorism in
Chapter 4 translates the food problem into a national security problem for the United States.)

Whatever the international community does to alter that trend
will depend heavily on the choices and actions of U.S. government.
Because of its position, the United States has a unique responsibility.
First, it has considerable influence as the world's dominant agricultural power--what one observer has called "the Arabia of food." It
has the capacity to provide a hedge against poor grain harvests and,
at the same time, to stabilize grain prices in world markets. The
United States also has the technology and the food production and
processing base that many nations need to tap in order to modernize
their agricultural sectors as rapidly as possible. At the same time,
it has the kind of broad and diverse research and development base
to pursue much-needed research into many aspects of the world food
problem.

The United States is also in a position to influence how others
address the world food problem in the ongoing dialogue between rich
and poor nations. Despite recession, it has one of the strongest
economies of the industrialized nations. Moreover, the American
economy is less affected by OPEC's actions than Europe or Japan,

and the dollar has returned to a strong (albeit still vulnerable) position in international money markets. As the world's major trader, the United States has a major voice in tariff negotiations and any future commodity arrangements. It is one of the leading nations in technical and economic development assistance. Furthermore, the United States has the single most dominant voice in international institutions, such as the World Bank and the International Monetary Fund (IMF), which are increasingly important to the economic development and financial stability of the developing world.

To benefit from the position of influence it has, America must make decisions without delay. If little or nothing is done in 1977, the United States will lose valuable momentum for dealing with the many problems involved in a practical, nonideological way. The world food problem will not go away, and the United States may find it very difficult to regain, at a later date, the initiative it would lose.

In response to Secretary Kissinger's Labor Day address, there will be pressure to obtain American decisions on the following in 1977:

● Kissinger proposes a grain reserve of about sixty million tons. It would provide a cushion against crop failures, and only those countries participating in the program would have access. This proposal is consistent with what Senator Hubert Humphrey has advocated for many years. Secretary of Agriculture Earl Butz, however, favors a free market to regulate domestic farm prices and has pushed hard for a further expansion of agricultural exports.

● Kissinger promises six million tons of food aid in 1976. This represents a significant increase in food aid, so much of the attention will be on the dollar level. Other decisions concern the terms for extending such assistance and, particularly, any strings that might be attached in order to provide some constructive leverage. An important question is how best to extend food aid to the needy without creating disincentives in the recipient country to expand its own food production capacity.

● Secretary Kissinger endorses a proposal made in 1974 at the World Food Conference by Arab nations for a new International Fund for Agricultural Development.

● He promises U.S. assistance in integrated delivery of basic health services at the community level--combining medical treatment, family planning, and nutritional information--as the best means of dealing with the overwhelming problem of population.

● He offers the poorest countries access to financial aid and emergency balance-of-payments support. For this purpose, he promises increased U.S. contributions to the World Bank, if the OPEC nations will also contribute. But the United States is already two years behind in contributions to the World Bank and the Inter-American Bank.

● The Secretary proposes a new "development security facility." It would be managed by the IMF and would provide up to $10 billion in loans or make grants to cushion fluctuations in export earnings by developing countries. In addition, changes in IMF voting arrangements are designed to give the Third and Fourth World nations a larger voice.

● He proposes trade preferences for less-developed countries, with a lifting of restraints on exports in return. Moreover, he declares the American intention to commence lower tariffs and a reduction of nontariff barriers in January 1976. Trade concessions, however, are subject to Congressional veto.

● Secretary Kissinger proposes establishment of consumer-product forums for each key commodity, in order to promote growth and stability of their markets, as well as liberalization of IMF financing of buffer stocks.

Another issue may arise over the size of development assistance. At the end of the Special Session, the United States approved the general resolution calling for rich nations to contribute 0.7 percent of gross national product, although it did voice a reservation to the specific clause. If it is to abide by the guideline, foreign aid would have to more than double from the current level of about $3 billion to nearly $7 billion.

ALTERNATIVES

With so many questions raised and so many decision-makers involved, a clear course of action for the United States will not be established with one official act. Most likely, it will become noticeable as the accumulation of a number of important decisions begins to take effect and a momentum is established. Consequently, the alternative courses of action which are now discernible are primarily symbolic. They resemble political persuasions and broad strategies and doctrines rather than specific, action-oriented policies and plans. Perhaps most important, these strategies are based on values--not on facts that can be confirmed, denied, or computed. The food issue raises the ultimate issue in political economy--"Who gets what, when, how?" Another way to phrase the issue is "Who benefits and who pays?"

Most of the arguments heard to date fall into one of two categories. For discussion purposes, they have been labeled an accommodation strategy and an opposition strategy. These strategies are broad and encompass a diversity of reasoning. But within each there are some fundamental unquestioned value judgments shared by all.

Accommodation Strategy

The fundamental argument of this strategy's proponents is that there are new realities in the world, and the United States must accept them. Frequent reference is made to the fact that the American economy consumes about 40 percent of the world's resources, yet it accounts for only 6 percent of the world's population. Such a disparity cannot be sustained. Consequently, some form of redistribution of the world's wealth is prudent and necessary. Listeners are reminded of the relative indifference of the United States in recent years: a substantial decline in foreign aid, and infringement of national rights and sensibilities, usually by multinational corporations and the CIA. (See Chapter 3 for a discussion of multinational corporations as a major factor in U.S. security policy for the late 1970s.)

The basic point made by proponents of the accommodation strategy is that the Third and Fourth Worlds have valid demands. Being confronted with those demands, the United States (if not the entire developed world) has more to lose in ignoring or resisting them than in meeting those demands. Several lines of reasoning are used in arriving at that conclusion.

One line of argument places heavy emphasis on moral factors and notes the principles for which the United States has stood, especially the dignity of man. With rare exceptions, such principles are indivisible. Consequently, the United States cannot expect to turn its back on countless millions of undernourished and starving people abroad without losing its principles at home. If a man is worth nothing in Calcutta, a man can be worth no more in New York.

Some advocates conclude by wanting the United States to assume the blame for the problems confronting the Third and Fourth Worlds. The content of this approach usually is heavy on rhetoric and short on practical solutions. Still others point to the need for Americans to begin making sacrifices now, for our own good as much as for the benefit of prospective recipients. For example, calls have been made for meatless days, and bans on the use of fertilizers on golf courses and home gardens. The most frequently heard reason for extending assistance, however, is to alleviate suffering as an end in itself. The spokesmen most often associated with this latter view are Senators Hubert Humphrey and George McGovern.

Others, however, maintain that assistance should be granted on more than humanitarian grounds, usually citing the explosive security potential in the developing world. Unless trends are arrested and reversed, Robert Heilbroner and others see an increasing possibility of atomic and terrorist blackmail by hungry nations. It is argued that they would be willing to risk a holocaust for a larger share. Morality in this sense is not charity, but simply common sense. Such reasoning is also compatible with the notion that there are inherent limits of growth for the world system, ecologically as well as politically and economically. In their well-publicized report on the subject for the Club of Rome in 1972, a group of scientists concluded that the survival of civilization, and of man himself, required an early abandonment of the growth ethic. It is in this moral sense that Norman Cousins takes the position that the food problem is ". . . rapidly becoming the most important issue before contemporary civilization. The attitudes of the rich toward the poor and the poor toward the rich are setting the stage for what could become the costliest showdown in history."[3]

Another more pragmatic argument contends that some, but not all, of the developing world's demands are legitimate. Consequently, U.S. policy should be responsive to the legitimate demands and resist those that seem excessive or unjustified. The dominant concern is with the threat the developing world already poses to vital U.S. interests and to world peace. This position is stated well in a series of articles in Foreign Policy by C. Fred Bergsten, a senior fellow at the Brookings Institution. The case is made that the power of the Third World and the poverty (cum desperation) of the Fourth World already pose such a threat. They can wield oil cartel power, form other commodity cartels, harness multinational corporations, penetrate our markets, block urgently needed economic reform, exploit nuclear weapons potential, and exert terrorist and conventional force against neighboring states.

In formulating a U.S. response, some maintain that this "tilt" of the Third (and Fourth) World is largely of our own making. Tariff preferences for goods of developing countries were never implemented. Foreign aid was cut back drastically, at our convenience. All recent agreements with major commodity exporters to establish price floors have been opposed. Likewise, the United States has opposed linking creation of international monetary reserves (called special drawing rights, or SDRs) to development assistance. Moreover, the United States took these positions virtually alone among the other industrialized nations.

To reverse these positions to the benefit of the developing nations is to create a new framework for international economic cooperation. It would not, however, go as far as conceding to a "new international economic order" such as the developing world has demanded in recent years. What is advocated is conciliatory, not an indulgent giving-in to any and all demands. It also is not ideological, but seeks to develop policies that provide practical answers to very real problems. Hence the United States has to take diplomatic initiatives toward establishing such a framework. In addition, it must

take decisive national actions to increase leverage in international
forums and to show good faith in meeting the developing nations
halfway.

Opposition Strategy

Those who advocate this strategy begin by noting that the
United States cannot help other nations or itself by weakening its
economic and political base. As in domestic politics, the distinction drawn is between an ever-expanding economic pie with bigger
shares for everyone and trying to share a constant-size pie among
more and more people. It is the politics of growth versus the politics of redistribution.

At one extreme, the arguments are a reaction to what has happened with American involvement in the developing world over the
past thirty years. For many it is difficult to see how much American
assistance has accomplished over that period. Much of the economic
development of the 1950s and 1960s was overtaken by growing populations. More recently, higher oil prices cost the developing nations
an extra $11.5 billion in foreign exchange in 1974. That equals the
total aid disbursed by the industrial nations to the developing world
in 1975. There is also a tendency for many to be bitter when confronted with ingratitude from Third and Fourth World politicians.
From such beginnings, it is not hard to conclude that their problems
are insoluble, largely of their own making, and of little concern to
us. These views were frequently expressed in the Nixon administration. (It has even been alleged that Secretary Kissinger shared
this attitude.)

One proposal compatible with this line of reasoning is that the
United States take the lead in establishing a triage system for dealing
with the poor developing nations. The idea was first advocated in
1974 by a biology professor, Garrett Hardin, from the University of
California at Santa Barbara, and has attracted little support. Based
on the medical evacuation system the French developed in World
War I, it would differentiate among countries that can manage without help, those that can manage with help, and those that cannot
manage regardless of how much help is extended. The argument is
that the United States should not "waste" valuable resources on the
first and last groups of countries, but should concentrate its efforts
on the second group. Supposedly, more people would be saved this
way. An analogy is made with a lifeboat that is not large enough to
carry all of the survivors. If an effort is made to get everyone into
the lifeboat, it is swamped and sinks, and no one is saved.

Perhaps the most frequently heard arguments for the opposition strategy concern the Free World economic system and the future of free enterprise in this country. The most vocal spokesmen of this viewpoint are Agriculture Secretary Earl Butz and Treasury Secretary William Simon. Underlying their view is an abiding faith in the efficiency and even equitability of free markets and, by extension, of free trade. The Free World's postwar economic system has evolved into a vast complex of rules and procedures that govern foreign economic relations. Even when it could not be implemented in fact, the principle of free markets and free trade has been held as the ideal.

Some view the rhetoric of many Third and Fourth World politicians as a direct attack on the system in which their gains are our losses and vice versa. Others, however, maintain that their gains would be temporary and we would both lose in the end. The reasoning here focuses on production incentives, in both rich and poor countries, and the formation and direction of investment capital. For example, many developing countries have long maintained a policy of inexpensive food, in deference to their growing and politically sensitive urban populations. The prices are not high enough to provide an incentive for farmers to increase agricultural production capacity. At the same time, development policies do not direct enough capital to the food system in many countries--not only farming and fishing but also the transit, storage, processing (if any), and marketing of food.

On the whole, this opposition strategy advises caution and a considerable amount of stubbornness. The developing world's demands are viewed with skepticism, and some are inclined to point out to all concerned when such demands are considered unreasonable. Much of the "reality" confronting the United States, and other industrialized nations, is a state of mind that will change over time. U.S. Ambassador to the United Nations, Daniel Moynihan, attributes Third and Fourth World attitudes to the postwar influence of British socialism in the many former British colonies that now comprise the majority of the developing world. Their emerging attitudes are against growth and profits, and in favor of a redistribution of existing wealth; they are anti-American; they favor the right of nations to economic as well as political independence; and they support parliamentary procedure. Their views are reinforced by the common heritage of exploitation and discrimination (often racial) at the hands of the West, leaving many scores to settle both internationally and internally.

The proposals that flow from this reasoning differ from the others discussed in both tone and content. The United States should take a firm, businesslike stance in any and all deliberations with the developing nations. For example, in general or special sessions of the United Nations, U.S. representatives should not hesitate to go on

record in opposition to an overriding majority of nations. The failure of the United States to "get tough" with developing nations in the
past is cited as a factor contributing to the current situation.

In addition, the United States should not hesitate to use all of
the power and influence it has available. Wherever possible, it
should insist on reciprocal performance by the beneficiaries. Developing nations should not expect something for nothing. Moreover,
the United States should not abandon the strong position that it has in
such institutions as the IMF and the World Bank.

CONCLUSION

Both of the strategies outlined in this chapter have their weaknesses, particularly if extreme positions are taken. First, it is
possible within both strategies to overreact to events and, in the
process, to adopt very unrealistic positions. Rushing to accept
without question all of the demands of the Third and Fourth Worlds
would be committing the United States to more than it can accomplish,
even with the best of intentions. Like the Alliance for Progress in
the 1960s, such action would create expectations we cannot meet.
At the same time, it is unrealistic to think that a nation as powerful
as the United States can safely ignore two-thirds of mankind. As
some observers have noted, the appropriate analogy for the world's
current situation is not a lifeboat but a spaceship: it is not possible
for some nations to survive while others do not. Rich and poor nations need one another, and must cooperate if any are to survive.

Second, many arguments will be needed at home and abroad.
In the process of such political debate, it is easy to fall into an
ideological mold and resort to rhetoric alone. What is accomplished
in the process contributes nothing toward solving the problem--the
conflict of interests merely becomes more inflamed. Some may find
it tempting to echo the militant demands of Third and Fourth World
politicians, but the language they use often is very bitterly anti-
American and grossly overstates the case. Right or wrong, it is
likely to alienate a large segment of American public opinion. Arguments equally uncompromising in defense of the free market system
could run a similar risk. Regardless of the merits of the arguments,
the doctrinaire insistence on market-derived prices for food may
sound to many like a twentieth-century version of that regrettable
quip, "If they don't have bread, let them buy cake."

Third, either of these strategies could result in ineffective or
even counterproductive policies and programs. For example, extending food aid on humanitarian terms alone runs the risk of a still
larger population sharing in current levels of misery. In the words

of one observer of what has happened recently in Sahelian Africa,
"It will serve only to maintain the problem and, in a quantitative
sense, to make it worse." On the other hand, any attempts to pursue autarky and truly insulate ourselves as a nation from the power
and influence of others, such as OPEC, can result in large costs and
no lessening of interdependence.

The wide-ranging set of proposals and promises presented by
Secretary Kissinger in his Labor Day speech to the U.N. special
session is not a pure strategy. Rather, it is a mixed strategy--a
very adroit compromise between what we have called an accommodation strategy and an opposition strategy. It tends to be a compromise
of moderate positions within both strategies. It is not an even compromise, however, for most of the reasoning and economic proposals
are drawn from the accommodation strategy. Yet elements of the
opposition strategy can be seen in the insistence on reciprocity and
an emphasis on incentives in recipient countries.

Although compromises are involved, Secretary Kissinger has
launched a very bold initiative. In fact, it is the biggest U.S. initiative in foreign economic policy since the Alliance for Progress. It
is bold not only in size but also in content. If implemented, the
many proposals and promises will represent a very major shift in
American foreign policy. Nevertheless, it is far from a total submission to the demands of the Third and Fourth Worlds. The proposals do not add up to the "new international economic order" they
have clamored for. Still, it calls for some fundamental changes in
foreign economic relations at the political expense of all the industrialized nations (including the United States), as well as the newly
rich oil-producing nations of OPEC.

Despite the imagination and common sense that this initiative
represents, there are some hazards worth noting. First, it has a
very rough road ahead in American domestic politics. Rapidly, it
will be parceled out among the many bureaus and Congressional committees concerned. In such circumstances it will be very difficult
for an administration to keep the forest in mind while keeping tabs
on all the trees. The new budgeting system will force the issue of
what gets cut in new or ongoing programs to fund the American contribution to the programs the Secretary has proposed. Finally, these
proposals are being thrown into the American political hopper during
an election year. If this issue is allowed to become a political foot-
ball in 1976, concerted Presidential and Congressional action are
unlikely; and any administration--Republican or Democrat--will find
its options in 1977 very limited.

Second, some difficulties abroad are very likely. Most of the
proposals would be financed by the industrialized countries as a
group, plus the members of OPEC. Therefore, a great deal of the

package of proposals can be put into effect only by negotiation of complex international agreements. One potential stumbling block may be the effort to create a split between OPEC and the other members of the developing world. On commodity agreements, many developing countries may not be content with the objectives of stabilizing prices and supply. After all, many desire to emulate OPEC and boost prices to what the market will bear. Hence chances are as good for conflict as for cooperation.

Finally, even if a coherent package is implemented by the United States and by the other nations involved, it has to begin to make a difference on the world food problem. Specifically, it has to increase food supply worldwide, reduce the dependence of food-importing nations, assure the availability of food at reasonable prices, reduce malnutrition, and reduce birth rates. Much will depend on the ability of experts to work with insufficient funds laden with constraints, and on the determination of recipient governments and cultures to make an effort.

Regardless of what we do, there will be risks. But the greatest risk is in doing nothing or in starting too late.

NOTES

1. P. E. Steiger, "What Do Poor Nations Want from Us?," Providence Sunday Journal, September 7, 1975, p. F9.

2. Leslie H. Gelb and Anthony Lake, "Washington Dateline: Less Food, More Politics," Foreign Policy 17 (Winter 1974/75): 176-89.

3. N. Cousins, "Of Life and Lifeboats," Saturday Review, March 8, 1975, p. 4.

3

THE ROLE OF THE
MULTINATIONAL CORPORATION:
THE PROBLEM OF
GLOBAL TECHNOLOGY TRANSFER
Marc James Hersh

THE ISSUE

The fundamental issue is the degree of control that the U.S. government can and should impose on multinational corporations (MNCs). More specifically, what is the national security impact of technology transfer on the United States? Currently, there is a relatively free flow of technology from the United States. Existing restrictions are under the Office of Export Control, which prohibits the dissemination of technologies that would have a negative impact on security interests, such as weapon hardware. However, little consideration has been given to the national security consequences of the impact of technology transfer on the U.S. commercial sector-- the comparative and competitive advantages that currently exist. If these advantages are irreparably lost, the consequences could be as follows: The United States loses its competitive position in the world marketplace; the nation's balance of international payments is negatively affected; the dollar exchange rate depreciates, increasing the cost of imports and inflation; the United States becomes increasingly dependent on foreign technologies and places more reliance on foreign sources for basic natural resources; the nation's strategic military position is eroded by the loss of research and development funds for natural resources; the nation's strategic military position is eroded by the loss of research and development funds for new tactical weapon systems; there are inadequate resources to allow for the maintenance of a meaningful military presence in strategic foreign areas; and so on.

BACKGROUND OF THE ISSUE

Technology transfer is the transfer of knowledge generated and developed in one place to another, where it is used to achieve some practical end. There are numerous avenues by which technology can be transferred:
- Technical publications
- Licensing agreements/patent sales
- Forums, such as technical conferences and trade fairs
- Product sales of components or end products, with maintenance manuals and blueprints
- Aid programs
- Joint ventures
- Nationalization of foreign corporations with technical expertise
- Immigration/emigration (for instance, Dr. H. S. Tsien, who was trained in the United States and then returned to China, where he has been responsible for much of his country's tactical nuclear capability)
- Company purchases (mergers, acquisitions)
- Intracompany personnel transfers
- Industrial espionage
- MNC operations.

The focus of this chapter is on the role of the MNC in technology transfer. There are several reasons for this emphasis:

1. The MNC has come under increasing public scrutiny in the last few years. This is partly a result of a number of dramatic revelations about MNC activities:
   a. Paying bribes to foreign officials to influence the awarding of sales and service contracts, and favorable tax treatment
   b. Making illegal gifts to the campaign funds of domestic political candidates in order to influence government scrutiny of the company
   c. Interfering with the political structure of host governments in countries such as Chile
   d. Becoming the instrumentalities of foreign states--for instance, the oil MNCs during the Arab oil embargo in 1973. (In the view of some analysts, these MNCs actively participated in the withholding or diverting of oil supplies at the behest of the Arabs.)

2. Another reason for the increased interest in the MNC is concern about the current world recession and income redistribution, and its role in this crisis.

3. There are two types of technology flow to and from the
United States that are readily quantifiable and that therefore give us
some "handle" on this subject. These are intracompany (between
an MNC's affiliates) and among firms that are not related. In the
former case, between 1964 and 1970, U.S. parent companies received $2.5 billion in royalty and licensing fees. During this same
period, U.S. affiliates of foreign companies paid out $442 million.
In the latter case, U.S. companies received $523 million and paid
out $120 million.[1]

On balance, it might appear that these transfers have been
favorable to the United States, at least in the balance-of-payments
sense. However, this may not be so from both the economic and
the strategic military standpoints. A number of economists believe
that there is a correlation between technological change, productivity gains, and economic competitiveness. If this is correct, the
transfer of technology may have a substantial negative impact on the
ability of the United States to remain competitive in world markets. [2]
The countries that have been the greatest recipients of our technology
are now our chief competitors. They have achieved this advantage,
in part, by importing technology that would upgrade their industry
and by relying on their lower labor costs, an advantage that in some
cases is fast disappearing. The impact, assuming that technological
lead time--and thus competitive advantage--cannot be reestablished
by the United States, is the loss of the economic advantage that allows this country to maintain its dominant international military,
political, and economic status.
    Aside from the impact on the national economy and its strategic
consequences, the individual business enterprise does not want to
lose its competitive advantage and, ultimately, sales and profits. In
order to minimize this problem, some MNCs establish internal restrictions. These include restrictions on selling or licensing abroad
products or processes embodying the latest technology, even at the
risk of adverse criticism about selling "second-line only"; construct-
ing "antique" plants in less-developed countries; developing technologies that can be applied only in certain countries because of resource limitations, such as availability of certain types of raw material and manpower; and concentrating research and development
work in the United States in order to avoid or limit the risk of losing
key research people to foreign competitors.
    Nevertheless, the MNCs face a major dilemma. In the ab-
stract, there might appear to be a simple trade-off: the sacrifice of
major short- and/or medium-term profits for more modest long-
term profits guaranteed by technical advantage. But, in fact, the
trade-off is more complex because the United States has no monopoly

in many high-technology areas. Thus, if there is a competitive foreign technology available, the U.S. company is deprived of the choice of an immediate sale or maintaining a long-term advantage. A recent case in point is the sale of a major nuclear system, complete with fuel-processing equipment, by Germany's Seimens Company. Westinghouse, Bechtel, and others, which for various reasons were unable to transfer the technology, saw a comparable product sale made by a competitor. In addition, it cannot be assumed that an existing technical advantage can be held because no further technical advances with market significance are likely.

Further, technology transfer has been necessitated by the following considerations: inability to gain entry to a particular market because of tariff barriers; protectionist and nationalistic buying practices forcing a company to set up a local operation if it wishes to sell a market; maintenance of a market share; realization of faster market growth than is possible domestically; maintaining competitive position by avoiding excessively restrictive financial conditions or labor problems; availability of raw materials.

The magnitude of the transfers taking place and the possible implications are best illustrated by some recent examples of large foreign contracts (Table 3.1). These follow different patterns, but all have components of planned technology transfer.

As mentioned above, corporations develop their own system of controls to prevent uncontrolled technology transfers. Because there are so many avenues of transfer, this may not be especially effective. In addition, controlled transfers may take place only in the more sophisticated and/or larger corporations. The small firm, anxious to establish a market or realize a profit, may willingly license or sell its technology overseas, ignoring the possibility of compromise by either the company or the country.

Government regulations also may be an effective barrier to technology transfer. Export controls may limit foreign sales to certain customers to second-line technology equipment. In addition, antitrust laws, when applied to overseas operations, may work to deter the export of technology in cases where there may be an impact on U.S. markets.

From both the national security and individual corporate standpoints, a key issue in this debate is the availability of alternative sources of technology. As Edward M. Graham of MIT has pointed out, in technology transfer we may be accelerating our own undoing, or we may be capitalizing on the last vestiges of an already shrinking technical lead. While there may be no direct impact on our military status in an immediate sense because of the economics of technology transfer, there may be a compromise of our strategic hardware advantage in a more immediate sense. Such a compromise depends on

the recipient country's political/military orientation, and its technological and socioeconomic environment. An additional factor is the
quality of the technology transferred.

In order to relate the issue of technology transfer more directly to possible military weapon systems, it is necessary to note the
three basic types of technology transfer that take place: direct--
technology developed in one country is used in another for the same
purpose; new application--old technology is utilized for new purposes; new problem--existing technology is used to deal with an entirely different problem, such as the use of lasers to polish silver
metal surfaces to reduce oxidation.[3]

The degree of technical innovation increases dramatically as
one goes from direct to new problem transfer. The political/
military orientation of the recipient is one of the motivating forces
in stimulating a particular type of innovation. But this comes into
play in a complex environment, and is not an effective motivating
force without the requisite technological foundation, economic development, and social system. Thus, technology transfer without the
necessary socioeconomic conditions in the recipient society is not a
threat in economic or military terms.

Returning to the commercial sector for the moment, technology
introduced into a society capable of using it may never find practical
application unless the requisite market expectations, at least as perceived by the marketing executive, exist. Thus, the Japanese perceived demand for transistor and semiconductor consumer products
in the mid-1950s, when U.S. manufacturers had all but turned their
backs on the technology. The application of that technology to the
sector was successful. Undoubtedly, similar markets exist in the
military hardware area.

Similarly, a key question that must be asked with regard to the
strategic impact of technology transfer is "What kind of profile does
the recipient have?" In the case of the Soviet Union, and perhaps
China, we believe that these countries can produce anything they want
to. But the methods employed are excessively costly in cases where
their technology lags behind that of the United States, and the end
product is likely to be less sophisticated--for instance, by machine-
shop fabrication of individual models instead of more automated,
serial production. The technology transfer profile of these societies
is such that while the United States, even in cooperation with our
Cocom (Consultative Committee) partners, may not be able to deny
anything to these countries, it can impose delays and increased research and development costs.

It is difficult to prevent another country from acquiring a technology, especially if it is commercially available. As was discussed
earlier in this chapter, there are numerous avenues by which a

TABLE 3.1

Large Foreign Contracts Involving Technology Transfer

Corporation	Country	Amount	Comment
GTE-Sylvania	Algeria	$240 million	Turnkey plant for manufacturing consumer electronic products. Integrated facility handling raw materials through finished product. Includes $25 million contract for training Algerian technicians to manage plant and handle future R&D.
Control Data Corp.	Poland, Rumania	n.a.	Computer technology. Barter of technology on manufacturing, paid for by export of components to CDC in Western Europe for final main-frame assembly. CDC gains reduced component costs, no capital investment, expanded sales opportunity in Eastern Europe.
M. W. Kellogg Division of Pullman	People's Republic of China	n.a.	Fertilizer plants. 8 urea-ammonia plants. Equipment/technology via Pullman, Chinese technicians trained to develop and engineer future projects independently. Construction by Chinese.
Ford Motor Co.	Brazil	$200 million	Automotive engines: 400,000 units per year, 75% for export.
General Electric	France	n.a.	Jet engines. Joint venture, with 50% sharing of component supply and ownership.

Company	Country	Amount	Description
General Electric	Japan, Iran	n.a.	Housing. Joint venture and licensing, respectively. Technology/capital investment for production of prefabricated housing.
Anaconda	Iran	n.a.	Copper. Development of mines on management fee basis. Training of technical personnel and transfer of technology. Vehicle for company to maintain large management team recently displaced from Chile. No fixed investment.
Kennecott Copper	Poland	n.a.	Copper. Development of mines/processing. Management fee, limited technology transfer (no sale). Company indicates it will not participate in transaction involving turnkey plant.
MIT	Iran	n.a.	Nuclear science program. Major expansion of program to allow 25 Iranian students/year in M.S. program. Major concern on part of university over implications in terms of proliferation of nuclear capability.
TRW	U.S.S.R.	$20 million	Petroleum production equipment, submersible pumping units.
IBM	U.S.S.R.	$10 million	Computers. Direct sale.

n.a. = not available.

Source: Compiled by the author.

39

technology can be transferred. Even if we are able to control access
through the various channels, a transfer may be effected through theft
or espionage. One celebrated case of espionage to circumvent export
controls was the subversion of IBM executives and technicians in Germany to steal technological secrets for the Soviets.

Interestingly, the IBM case is referred to by some executives
in the computer industry as an example of why the United States
should be less restrictive in its export control policies. One industry spokesman states that the Soviets lack the technical-innovation
orientation that would enable them to develop the systems we are producing. While they may have the same basic technology available,
they are incapable, at least in this area, of applying it to use in
either a direct or new problem transfer. This executive argues that
since the Soviets would opt for a direct transfer, resorting to espionage if they were unable to buy commercially--and probably obtaining the technology--it makes more sense to sell the product
directly and "hook a customer." A problem with accepting this position is that we know little about the dynamics of technological innovation, especially in a closed society such as the Soviet Union. It may
be that the USSR represents a type of society to which we can
sell the most advanced technologies for direct use without worrying
about new application or new problem uses.

Some industry spokesmen claim that there is virtually no
cross-fertilization taking place between the military and commercial sectors in the computer field in the USSR.   Thus, although
the military may possess systems as sophisticated as those in the
United States in certain cases, there is no application of this technology to the commercial sector. Therefore, the Soviet interest in
our commercial units does not necessarily mean a direct transfer to
military uses. One computer industry spokesman told this author
that there is reason to believe that there is little or no transfer from
the commercial to the military. But this may be a self-serving view.
It is to the advantage of the public company to maximize sales and
profits so that the stockholders can maximize their return on investment. If this becomes the main priority, it may color the company's
perception of the sensitivity of technology transfer. In any case, the
technology transfer profile of a country should include the above considerations.

We do not know at what point the Soviets, Chinese, or our chief
economic competitors will be able to start making these connections,
assuming they cannot now do so. In addition, it may be that selling
these countries ready-packaged technology will free them from making the huge research and development investments that we make.
This may allow them to concentrate their assets in areas that may be
detrimental to our interests. It is argued in some government circles

that providing basic foodstuffs to the Soviet Union, China, and Eastern Europe ultimately compromises our position by allowing resource
allocations in these countries that are unfavorable to us.

For the policy-maker, serious questions must be raised as to
this country's present stance vis-a-vis technology transfer. What is
being done in the name of detente or in order to promote a greater
sharing of the world's resources may ultimately undercut our nation's economic viability. Clearly, greater understanding of this
complex area is necessary. It may be that export control standards
should be developed to deal not only with the obvious military-
strategic application but also with the economic security impact of
a transfer on this country. The economic dimensions of U.S. strategic interests are often overlooked as the process of deciding what
is exportable takes place in the private sector. In the public sector,
this is a consideration that may be debated but that rarely is implemented in government policies, such as tax disincentives or export
controls.

ALTERNATIVE STRATEGIES

Along a continuum from no control to absolute control of MNCs,
there is a diversity of choices available to the decision-maker in
dealing with the issue of MNC technology transfer, if it is indeed determined to be a problem. Initially it is apparent that control is difficult, given our current social structure and the large number of
transfer avenues. Nevertheless, if the technologies most important
to our society are transferred through a limited number of channels
such as the MNC, they will potentially be subject to greater control
than currently exists.

Once it is determined that control is possible, the key question
is what restriction should or should not be imposed. It may be that
the market should be left to determine what transfers, into and out
of the United States, take place. However, a market determination
may not be optimal vis-a-vis our social goals. Thus, it is apparent
that some of the more significant high-technology MNCs have a
modus operandi developed independently of the needs, goals, and
welfare of the host state. In addition, if a market determination is
acceptable, it will have to be as close to a free market as possible--
if this is achievable. Thus, if it were shown that the research, development, and engineering manpower and information pool available
to this country has a correlation to the value of the dollar, major
exchange-rate fluctuations could interfere with the U.S. technical
basis. Such changes in exchange rates might be manipulated by countries with interests opposite to ours.

If government is to have a more active role in this area than it does through current export control standards, how may the policy maker define this role? It might take various forms, such as establishing strict regulations with guidelines on what is exportable. But there may be an immediate reaction to this by other countries' imposing similar sanctions, thus depriving the United States of important technological inputs. Further, it is hard to imagine controls sophisticated enough to deal with this area without substantially interfering in the creative processes that are involved. It is not axiomatic that availability of technology means applicability utilization.

Further, in the MNC and other institutions of technological innovation, development is often piecemeal. Processes, information, and development from various sources complement one another. Assuming that alternative technologies are not available, technological isolation may be destructive to product innovation, development, and commerce.

Since government is not in commerce, it is inadvisable to establish broad, per se restrictions and usurp the corporate technology transfer prerogative. Yet controls, based on well-designed guidelines, might be constructed on several models:

- Graduated tax imposed on classes of technology transfers, scheduled according to the likely negative impact on U.S. security interests (economic, military, and political)
- Government restrictions on the foreign cross-licensing of technologies developed on U.S. government contracts and let out to the private sector
- Insurance: the exporting corporation would be required to provide indemnification payments to correct dislocations caused by the technology transfer activities. (In certain respects, the company might face the dual liability of indemnification plus loss of market or competitive advantage.)

CONCLUSIONS

Ultimately, the problem of controlling technology transfer requires the cooperation of all those involved in the transfer channels. As with many issues facing America today, there is a need for established policies and guidelines. Any basic desire in the business community to cooperate with government in order to preserve the nation's economic integrity may be negated by the absence of adequate and consistent guidelines. Under the circumstances, the corporation opts for maximizing the short-term commercial advantage, which in the broader national perspective may be detrimental to our medium- and long-term interests.

NOTES

1. Office of Business Economics, Survey of Current Business 1965-70, April 1971; June 1971.

2. E. Ginzberg, Technology and Social Change (New York: Columbia University Press, 1964).

3. Factors Affecting the International Transfer of Technology Among Developed Countries, report of the Panel on International Transfer of Technology to the Commerce Technology Advisory Board (Washington, D.C.: U.S. Department of Commerce, 1970).

4

THE ROLE OF
TERRORIST ORGANIZATIONS:
THE PROBLEM OF
GOVERNMENT RESPONSE
Edward W. Gude

THE ISSUE

Although not a new problem, domestic and international terrorism has been increasing. In both a real and a psychological sense, terrorism is a concern. The fundamental issue is to devise a strategy to counter both domestic and international terrorism that will maximize American individual Constitutional rights to liberty and collective Constitutional rights to domestic tranquillity. The problem is to achieve a proper balance between these sometimes conflicting values.

Background of the Issue

Violence and terrorism have been issues for political societies over the millennia. In fact the definition of the state involves a claim to the sole legitimate use of violence. Legitimate state use of force can spill over into repression just as legitimate protest can spill over into violence and terrorism. These transformations form the core of the problem.

In almost all periods of history, terrorism has been a persistent and irritating phenomenon but rarely a central concern of governments. Such is the case today. As a cause of death, injury, and destruction, terrorism does not rank very high in the United States. Regardless of its objective level, the fear engendered and the values threatened raise the issue to greater prominence than it is otherwise entitled. If, for example, we compare annual American deaths from automobile accidents with deaths from terrorism, the terrorist issue might seem insignificant for the next administration.

The impact of terrorism derives from the fear spread by seemingly senseless attacks and random target selection. This fear multiplies the political implications far beyond the act itself. In addition, terrorism attacks strongly held symbols and values of a society, thus leading to forceful political response. Attack on these symbols appears to both governmental authorities and the general public to be more important than the actual damage, death, or injury resulting from the act itself.

The sources of terrorism vary, depending on the particular political grievance of the moment. Sometimes it occurs as an adjunct to regular warfare, sometimes as part of a nationalist war, sometimes as an outgrowth of ethnic or religious conflict, sometimes as part of a revolutionary movement, and sometimes as a fringe of a largely nonviolent protest movement.

An example of the use of terror during wartime was the movement led by Marshall Tito in Yugoslavia during World War II; as part of a nationalist war, in Palestine by the Stern Gang supporting the Israelis in the 1940s and by the Palestine Liberation Organization supporting the Arabs in the 1970s; as an outgrowth of ethnic or religious conflict, Cyprus and Northern Ireland; as part of a revolutionary movement, the use of terror by the Vietcong; and as a fringe to a largely nonviolent movement, the Symbionese Liberation Army. There are sometimes free-floating movements, such as the Japanese Red Army.

In each of these cases the terror was (or is) used by the perpetrators as a political instrument to achieve a specific goal. Terror is an instrument of the weak who lack either the political or the military means of achieving their objectives directly. Fear augments the means, and the possibility of overresponse by authorities can multiply the impact. The response to terrorism thus becomes as important as the act itself.

Before developing the dynamics of terrorist acts and government response more fully, it will be worthwhile to digress and look at some of the background factors affecting the role of terror.

In open, democratic societies, particularly in the United States, there are various avenues through which political dissent may be manifested, including an implicit threat of violence. This tolerance of anti-establishment or anti-status quo behavior insures the democratic society of the opportunity to "hear" strongly felt but unrepresented grievances. Totalitarian systems, in repressing all dissent, often do not "hear" such grievances until they reach the stage of open revolution.

It has been stated that unemployment in a free-enterprise system provides a signal of economic dislocation that becomes readily apparent to government authorities. The opportunity for dissent provides strong incentives to correct the problem. In a socialist system underemployment is more difficult to spot, and thus makes response more difficult and less timely. The resort to violence can provide the same type of signal to a democratic society regarding a political grievance. Again totalitarian systems are denied this early warning.

This notion is predicated on the fact that individuals do not lightly resort to violence or terror. Whether an act is perceived as "irrational" by authorities or an objective observer does not disturb the mental set of the terrorist. He or she believes in the political purpose of the act. The terrorist act is meant to project that belief to the body politic as a whole. Today's media gladly assist in that purpose.

Typically, terrorist leadership is recruited from a disaffected middle class that senses that the values espoused are different from those acted upon. It is in this sense that revolutionary terrorism involves a turning back to more "pure, simple, and original" values. Terrorist rank and file are normally in their late teens or early twenties, without family or career ties, who are also driven by value discrepancies.

One of the universal issues in terrorist ideology revolves around the question of freedom. Unfortunately, freedom is not a simple, unidimensional value. One type of freedom is contained in the notion of "freedom from"--freedom from governmental restraint. This is more typically referred to as liberty. A second type of freedom is contained in the notion of "freedom to"--freedom to achieve personal ends. This is more typically referred to as opportunity or equality. The unfortunate aspect of the value of freedom is that it is not possible simultaneously to maximize both liberty and equality. Every society must decide where the balance will be, and that decision will represent a situational definition of justice for that particular system. If there is not a strong consensus on that balance, there is a serious possibility for violent conflict.

During the eighteenth and nineteenth centuries the dominant thrust for social change concerned the question of liberty. While this change ended many forms of despotism, it spawned the drive for equality that has led the movement for social change in the twentieth century. The libertarian character of dissent in the Soviet Union, as exemplified by Aleksandr Solzhenitsyn, may indicate a shift away from equality. These strongly held value positions, when translated into specific grievances, have provided a powerful engine for terrorist activities.

When there is a weak consensus on the balance between liberty and equality, many specific grievances can surface and become the rallying cry for extreme political movements. It is important to note that such grievances normally have a base well beyond a specific terrorist group, and a government must be careful not to exacerbate broader dissent by overresponse to specific terrorist acts.

The dynamics of terrorist acts and government response involves complicated political perceptions. The acts themselves are rarely serious military threats to a state, but represent a symbolic attack that cries out for response. A very important objective of a terrorist is to trigger an overreaction by the government that will be perceived as illegitimate by a sizable portion of the population. A government, struggling under the handicap of not being able to clearly identify the attacking group, has great difficulty in responding discriminately. The terrorist objective is to commit an act they know will be perceived as illegitimate, in order to force the government to commit an act that will be perceived as even more illegitimate, thus gaining a certain credibility for the terrorists. Terrorists attack government symbols and hope that the response will include uninvolved members of the general public.

Terrorists become a serious threat when they generate perceptions of the illegitimacy of governmental response. In this sense they rarely succeed without the missteps of governments. By definition being weak in comparison with governments, terrorists twit sensitive nerves and achieve notoriety beyond their importance. Governments must summon all their political skill and savvy in responding.

The United States has been spared any serious outbreak of terrorism; but the response to a few cases, both real and imagined, suggests that the pattern of decision and nondecision in this area is in serious need of review. The Nixon administration, with Presidential Counsellor Charles Colson prepared to walk over any opposition and young lawyer Thomas Houston preparing unconstitutional plans for the use of police, military, and intelligence agencies against "enemies," laid the ground work for a totally inappropriate response to possible terrorism. In fact, it can be argued that such transparent illegality and unconstitutionality was a cause for the demise of the Nixon regime. Whether the post-Watergate mood will lead to the development of proper responses to threats is unclear, in the absence of much concern on the part of authorities.

Public authorities are right in assigning a low priority to the problem of terrorism as a military tactical issue, because it has not been, and is unlikely to be, a serious problem. Nevertheless, there must be better understanding of the political strategic problem and a more responsive machinery to deal with any future acts. Missteps by governments in the early phases of terrorism can have long-lasting and important implications. The shootout between police and the Symbionese Liberation Army in Los Angeles suggests

that the government is better able to cope with the military aspects
of terrorism than with the political. The political may well prove to
be the more important.

So far the discussion has been limited to what might be called
conventional terrorism. Unfortunately, the advances of science that
have led to the development of mass-destruction weapons have also
opened the possibility of mass-destruction terrorism. There has
been much talk about the possibilities of diverting nuclear material,
but little about the possibilities of diverting chemical and biological
agents that are more readily available if not quite so destructive.
The question of nuclear terrorism has become more salient because
of the rapid proliferation of nuclear capability, including in the en-
richment process. The question of chemical and biological terrorism has been made more salient by revelations concerning the CIA
in these areas.

The whole area of terrorism and government response, on
both the domestic and the international levels, has been made more
urgent because of the potential for mass-destruction terrorism.

URGENCY OF THE ISSUE

The United States has been fortunate in being spared the levels
of terrorism that exist in other parts of the world. It has even been
spared a spillover from the violence of the Middle East and Northern
Ireland that has occurred in Europe. While the potential for domestic
terrorism appears to be minimal for the foreseeable future, an expansion of violence by the Palestine Liberation Organization or the
Irish Republican Army is not out of the question. In addition the
small base of terrorists in this country, with more destructive
weapons, could greatly increase the urgency of the issue. As governments plan for natural disasters in the hope that they will never
occur, so governments have to be prepared to deal with large-scale
terrorism. Recent patterns of federal, state, and local government
responses at both the physical and rhetorical levels suggest that the
U.S. government is not adequately prepared.

AMERICAN POLICY ALTERNATIVES

The basic approach of the United States has been to stress the
criminal nature of terrorist acts, relying on police and military
means of response while downgrading political importance, and thus
the political implications.

While on the international level there has been some progress in the area of air piracy on the multinational and bilateral levels, the intensely political nature of this form of conflict has made substantial progress impossible. It was largely in response to international terrorism, particularly the Munich incident, that President Nixon established the Cabinet Committee on Terrorism. The international focus of this group is reflected in its being chaired by the Secretary of State.

The committee has developed policy for the international arena that dictates that the United States will not negotiate with terrorists, nor will it consider meeting ransom or other demands. This policy led to the rebuke of the American Ambassador to Tanzania because he was reported to have facilitated negotiations between officials of Stanford University and guerrillas from the Popular Revolutionary Party of Zaire who had kidnapped two Stanford students. Ironically, the ransom money was reportedly sent from London to Dar es Salaam in a diplomatic pouch.

The inflexible policy of the United States in international terrorism has yet to be tested in a difficult situation. In fact, total inflexibility gives a terrorist great power by being able to determine U.S. policy and actions in a particular situation. It is the position of the U.S. government that not to give in to a terrorist demand, no matter how difficult and painful a given situation, will deter future actions. At the cost of a few lives in the present, it is believed, many more lives can be saved in the future. This policy has not been put to the test, and almost invites terrorists to kidnap a person of such importance or prestige that it would be politically impossible to refuse to negotiate.

Statements by officials of the Cabinet Committee and the Department of Justice before Congressional committees and in other public forums, as well as actions such as in the Stanford student case, suggest that there has not been careful planning for the difficult cases that might occur in the future. Even the air piracy conventions might break down if several prominent U.S. citizens were aboard a hijacked aircraft. While one would not expect public disclosure of contingency plans for terrorist attacks, there is no indication that they exist at the present time.

Domestically, most of the planning for terrorism has been carried out on the state and local levels, with the major focus on police work in the context of criminal statutes. The federal government has opposed efforts of Congressional leaders, such as Richard Ichord, to establish regional teams of experts to assist local authorities in the event of a terrorist act. It is the position of the Department of Justice and the Cabinet Committee that sufficient expertise exists at the local level to handle an act without further involvement

at the federal level. Of course, the Federal Bureau of Investigation
would become involved if a federal law were violated. The nature of
terrorism is such that most acts would involve federal law.

The question of political sensitivity of the police and military
to violence and terrorism has been debated extensively since the
ghetto rioting of the 1960s and the disburbances at the 1968 Democratic National Convention. There has been extensive documentation
of the use of excessive force and political insensitivity that raises
serious questions about the command and control of police and national guard units faced with political violence and terrorism. Although some increase in training has taken place, it has been primarily on the tactical level, and not on the political implication of
the use of force. The question is not over the enforcement of the
law, but over doing it in such a way that the political ramifications
will be minimized.

The question of the conflict between individual and collective
rights came to the forefront in the controversy over the role of the
Army intelligence-gathering in 1971 and in the abuses committed by
the FBI and CIA in 1975. To many, these activities seemed clumsy,
excessive, and, most important, ineffective in preventing violence.
The balance of judgment from the Rockefeller report of the Ford administration was that individual civil rights had been violated in an
attempt to promote domestic tranquillity. This conclusion does not
address the problem of developing proper planning to ensure both individual rights and collective security. In an ironic twist, the Secret
Service was roundly criticized for not arresting certain individuals
and not maintaining files on two women who apparently became serious threats to the life of President Ford in September 1975.

In an analogue to the notion of quarantine of local conflicts in
the international environment (see Chapter 1), it is possible to conceive of "quarantining" acts of terrorism so as to minimize the death
and damage done and to minimize the political implication without
seeking to eliminate terrorism entirely. To attempt to do the latter
is to flirt with a degree of repression that would further the very
terrorism one is attempting to eliminate.

Collective security does not necessitate eliminating all danger,
but bringing the danger within acceptable bounds. For instance, in
automobile safety, the objective is to design cars, highways, and appropriate traffic laws to reduce accidents to a reasonable level. If
automobiles were eliminated, traffic deaths would be reduced; but
other dangers might well be introduced with increased use of bicycles
and motorcycles. The policy problem is one of defining balance.

Quarantining terrorism would take a considerable revision of
the current approach. First, it would involve a lower-keyed public
posture that would deny the terrorist the satisfaction of seeing the

massive outpouring of reaction that escalates his importance and increases the advantage of the terrorist, not the state. Second, it would involve a degree of training and command and control that is lacking at the present time. Just as "Mission Impossible" was an improper popularization of proper intelligence activities, so the television show "SWAT" is an improper dramatization of proper police work. Third, there is a need for a different political response. Paranoia has no place in a sophisticated effort to minimize the dangers from and effects of terrorism. Effective police work, under proper political control, is needed to achieve the twin goals of respecting individual civil rights and maintaining collective security.

It may be necessary to provide some form of federal help to local and state police forces, since they are already stretched so thin with their criminal problems that they have little time to devote to preparing for the remote events of terrorism. It is unreasonable to expect that every local, county, or state police force has the resources to divert to a problem that may arise and away from those that are present in almost overwhelming magnitude. Yet jurisdictional prerogatives and even jealousies make effective federal help difficult to achieve. Incentives are available, and the mechanism of the Law Enforcement Assistance Administration could be utilized to obtain a response from local authorities.

The above discussion assumes that the issue is conventional terrorism. In conventional terrorism the threat may possibly involve hundreds of victims. In the case of nuclear, biological, or chemical terrorism, the casualties could be in the thousands or more. In such a case it would seem that the responsibility would have to be national in scope and that the technical expertise would not exist at the local level. Because of the potential magnitude of the disaster, the most careful planning is necessary to possibly eliminate the threat, certainly limit damage, and coordinate rescue, rehabilitation, and reconstruction if such a threat were carried out.

Mass-destruction terrorism does not make sense for terrorists, in that it is hard to conceive of an act that would further their goals. Nevertheless, the potential costs are such that it is necessary to have detailed procedures, in the very remote case that such an act might occur. The federal government has spent considerable resources to deal with the highly remote possibility of a peacetime nuclear accident, yet there has been relatively little planning or even thinking about the problem of the damage that could be wrought by a purposeful or demented individual or group. The technology exists; and access to agents can be acquired, albeit with considerable difficulty. The urgency of this issue cannot be doubted.

CONCLUSION

As stated at the beginning of this chapter, the fundamental question is to balance individual Constitutional rights to liberty and the collective rights to domestic tranquillity. The right of liberty is the essence of the right of freedom from undue interference by government. This leaves unresolved the dilemma of the right of "freedom to"--the notion of equality and opportunity. Fundamentally the right of "freedom to" does not include the right to use violence to redress grievances without the sanction of the law. It does include the right to be judged by the law--fairly or unfairly, justly or unjustly, from the perspective of the perpetrator. For better or worse, there is no birthright to justice from the perspective of the individual--only from the perspective of the social consensus. This is the struggle to reconcile the intellectual solution to the problem of fairness and justice with action by an individual or group, who from their particular perspective undertake action to achieve their notion of the proper balance between liberty and equality. This wellspring of violence and terrorism, though rarely utilized, puts the criminal nature of the acts in a political perspective.

The United States has had a remarkable record in achieving social change with minimum violence. Many other systems have failed. The fact that the problem of terrorism has been largely remote and the prognosis is for more of the same, does not mean complaisance, but vigilance to the proper response that will not augment the legitimacy of the perpetrators.

A strategy of quarantine provides a useful framework for training, indoctrination, and command and control, which should minimize the probability of overreaction. The purpose is not to repress all dissent that might turn to violent means, but to be responsive to grievances. Responsiveness does not necessarily mean acceptance of demands, but primarily a fair hearing. By quarantining, the perpetrators will be prevented from gaining the legitimacy necessary for their success. In fact, a minimum response to low-level violence and terrorism may be the best defense against its escalation.

This doctrine of quarantine applies primarily to domestic perpetrators who have the potential of establishing a base of support within the country. It is not applicable to foreign terrorists attempting to spread conflict to our shores. In that case the calculus of individual American rights versus collective rights of domestic tranquillity moves toward the latter. In addition, the risks of overresponse are greatly reduced. Without a domestic political base, foreign terrorists pose little threat to the U.S. government.

The events of the last decade indicate that the police and other instruments of the state are at best poorly prepared to deal with new forms of violence and terrorism. It seems inconceivable that the Democratic National Convention in 1968 and the reactions to the invasion of Cambodia could have led to the reactions of the Nixon White House. Repression does not work in a society in which civil liberties have a long tradition. In such a society, excessive appeals to national security and collective security have a way of backfiring.

American politics has been able to ride with, absorb, and, if necessary, throw out what were ultimately perceived as illegitimate threats and demands. The early labor movement had its share of violence and terror, but so did the Pinkertons. In the end, however, the position of labor came to be viewed as the legitimate one. In that sense the Symbionese Liberation Army cannot, and never will, be a threat to the American system.

Terrorism must be handled at the appropriate level, and domestic tranquillity must be maintained; but not at the substantial sacrifice of individual Constitutional rights. Neither domestic terrorism nor foreign terrorism on American soil is, or will be, a basic threat to the American political system unless governmental authorities make it so.

III

U.S. GOALS:
MAJOR REGIONAL ISSUES

Despite the emphasis in Part II on the global issues of Third and Fourth World development, the role of the multinational corporation, and the potential destabilizing power of terrorism, political succession in the late 1970s will be inspired by neonationalism and will be haunted by shortages of raw materials and barely controlled inflation. As suggested in Chapter 1, these forces must inevitably direct the attention of new leaders to immediate political problems of internal stability, crime and unemployment, equitable distribution of power and income, and "ways of life" under siege. We may expect a turning inward of political energies everywhere.

In Part III, probable manifestations of this trend in the principal regions of the world will be addressed. "Eurocentrism," discussed in Chapter 5, demonstrates the point that wealth and industrial power have not immunized "developed" countries from these trends. Chapters on the Middle East and Africa provide the prototypical scenarios confronting the new American leadership: whether and how to become involved without directly confronting the USSR in a military contest. Other chapters, in no order of priority, lead the reader from Europe and Africa eastward across the Indian Ocean and the Pacific, each region being addressed in terms of the focal security policy issue likely to confront America's elected leaders in 1977.

5

EUROPE: THE PROBLEM OF CONSENSUS
Herbert Schandler

THE ISSUE

The next few years will bring to the fore serious questions of the future of the NATO alliance. The questions of U.S. force levels; the extension of special relationships within NATO, such as those enjoyed by France and Greece; and the cohesion of the alliance itself will be high on the agenda of discussions between the United States and her European partners. The basic issue is how to maintain a credible European deterrent in the face of changing relationships within the NATO structure?

BACKGROUND OF THE ISSUE

In the words of General George S. Brown, Chairman of the Joint Chiefs of Staff, "Western Europe's strategic importance to U.S. national security interests is second only to that of the territorial United States itself. . . ."[1] The case for American involvement in Europe has been based traditionally on our common cultural heritage and deeply shared values, including aspirations for a peaceful and stable world order. Beyond these strong historic and cultural ties lie equally important economic realities. Europe is the world's second largest economic power, supporting a greater combined population than either the United States or the Soviet Union, and with a combined gross national product almost double that estimated for the Soviet Union.

A peaceful and stable world order was a European-imposed fact throughout much of the nineteenth and the first half of the twentieth centuries. During that period, the nations of Northern and

Western Europe dominated history. The Western democracies gave the world its major treasures of art, literature, and music. The history of the world was in large part the history of "Western civilization" and the spread of this civilization, through commerce and colonial conquest, to the nonindustrial, non-Western nations of the world. Although they possessed great populations and resources, the United States, China, and Russia looked inward to their own political and economic development throughout this period, and played only a peripheral role in international politics.

The nations of Western Europe, in this process of development, commerce, and colonial conquest, each developed a strong sense of national identity. Rivalries in trade, colonial acquisition, and national ambitions inevitably grew. The nations of Western Europe sought their own security in a series of shifting alliances in order to maintain a balance of power and prevent any one nation from becoming dominant. A series of major wars among the Western powers occurred during the period 1870-1945, in order to maintain this balance.

The end of World War II, however, saw major changes in the Western European order that presaged a change in the traditional balance-of-power relationships of the previous century. The war saw the elimination of one great power--Germany--and the serious weakening of two others--France and Great Britain. On the other hand, two of the peripheral powers--the Soviet Union and the United States--emerged from the war with greatly enhanced military power and seemed destined to play a new, important, and unaccustomed role in world power politics.

The Western democracies, led and urged by the United States, based their view of the postwar structure of international relations on the assumption of agreement among the major powers. The United Nations Charter, which was to be the basic regulatory instrument of the new international order, depended for its effectiveness on agreement among the five permanent members of the Security Council: the United States, the Soviet Union, Great Britain, China, and France. True to their wartime pledges and bowing to popular demand, the Western democracies demobilized the bulk of their armed forces. The Soviet Union, on the other hand, continued to keep its forces on a wartime footing and quickly moved to fill the power vacuum in Eastern Europe by imposing Communist-controlled governments there.

Backed by their occupation troops, and employing threats, deceit, and internal subversion as the occasion demanded, the Russians had imposed Communist rule on Poland and Rumania by the end of 1945. A Peoples' Republic was proclaimed in Bulgaria in 1946, although that country was under effective Communist rule the preceding year. Anti-Communists were gradually eliminated from the Hungarian government, and the Communists were substantially in control by 1947. In Czechoslovakia the Communists seized power outright in 1948, dropping all pretense at peaceful cooperation with non-Communist parties. Indigenous Communists had gained control of Albania in the wake of the German withdrawal in 1944. Thus Communist power was consolidated over Eastern Europe.

Communist support of rebellions in northwest Iran and in Greece, and of domestic Communist parties in war-weakened Western Europe aroused fears that the Soviet Union would extend its expansionist drive to the shores of the Mediterranean and the Atlantic. The subversion of free institutions by domestic Communism became a real possibility, especially in France and Italy. It became vital to American security that a policy be implemented to block the spread of Communism, and hence the establishment of Soviet power, in Western Europe while concurrently making the countries of Western Europe effective partners in their own military and economic well-being.

Thus, the policy of "containment" was elaborated by George F. Kennan in 1947, the Truman Doctrine and the Marshall Plan were established in 1947-48, and the North Atlantic Treaty Organization (NATO) came into being in 1949, with West Germany being included in 1955 (Greece and Turkey were added in 1952). The United States also strongly supported the cause of European integration, at first in the interest of recovery and later in the interest of European political unity and economic strength. The European Coal and Steel Community was established in 1951, and the 1958 Treaty of Rome established the European Economic Community (EEC).

It had become clear, however, that the Western democracies, the predominant actors on the world scene before World War II, had become pawns in the Cold War between the two superpowers, incapable of providing their own military security and dependent upon American economic strength and the American nuclear umbrella for their protection from Russian military expansion and subversion. NATO was established as a means for its European members, each militarily incapable of providing a credible defense on its own, to ally themselves with the United States. The United States, for its part, was able to stop the threat of Soviet expansion into Western Europe and thus increase its own security by insuring the security of the population, territory, and industrial resources of Western Europe.

Essentially the North Atlantic Treaty provided the framework for wide cooperation among its signatories, not only in the military area but also in the economic, social, and political fields. Article 5 contains the treaty's most important security provisions: "The

Parties agree that an armed attack against one or more of them in Europe or North America shall be considered an attack against them all." Signatories are required, individually and in concert, in the event of armed attack to take such action, including the use of armed force, as each deems necessary.

The evolution of the Atlantic Alliance has been characterized by successive phases, the cumulative effect of which has been to change vastly the original basis. The immediate task following the treaty's signing in 1949 was the construction of an effective system of collective defense; the first five years of the Alliance were concentrated on implementing coordinated defense plans. The invasion of South Korea by Communist forces in 1950 gave impetus to this defensive buildup and shook Alliance's confidence in the assumption that American nuclear power alone could deter Communist forces from overt aggression. Thus, the Korean War served as the catalyst for the first serious attempt to create ground forces sufficient to withstand a massive Soviet conventional attack upon Western Europe.

This defensive buildup resulted in the appointment of an American (General Eisenhower) as Supreme Allied Commander Europe (SACEUR) in April 1951, and the dispatching of four additional American divisions to Europe late in 1951. The European allies also increased their defense forces, periods of military service, and military expenditures. Although this buildup culminated in the accession of the Federal Republic of Germany to NATO in May 1955, and the initiation of the Warsaw Pact that same month, it seemed increasingly unlikely that NATO conventional force goals would be met. Trends in European countries to reduce force levels and defense expenditures, and increasing pressures on the U.S. dollar, pointed toward the probability of a chronic and perhaps widening gap between NATO's conventional force goals and the actual troop contributions of its members.

Ironically, during this same period the United States was moving away from the tenets of "massive retaliation" that had been advanced in the mid-1950s and toward strategic views in which strong conventional forces assumed renewed importance. The strengthening of conventional forces continued to receive high priority in U.S. defense planning in the 1960s, and led to the adoption of the strategy of "flexible response." In essence, this strategy called for a wide range of conventional and nuclear capabilities, in order to yield options between the extremes of humiliation and all-out nuclear action in responding to varying levels of hostile pressure or aggression.

By 1969, NATO had entered a new phase. From that time, with British entrance into the EEC and with U.S. preoccupation with its commitment in Vietnam, the common interests that had contributed

to the unity of NATO during its first twenty years began to diverge
and to be viewed differently by the members of the alliance. Once
viewed as axiomatic, the assumption of an identity of interests between the United States and Europe began to be questioned. The
growing economic integration and strength of the EEC, the resulting
economic competition between the United States and Western Europe,
the deterioration of the U.S. trade position, and the crisis of the
dollar in the international monetary system led the European nations
to emphasize their separate economic, political, and military interests that seemed to be different from those of the United States.

On a political level, the U.S.-European divergence stemmed,
in the U.S. view, from an increasing introversion of the European
outlook. Withdrawing from overseas territories, the nations of
Western Europe had become Eurocentric to an extent unparalleled
in their modern history. They were accused by the United States of
having only a regional outlook, while the United States must devote
itself to the defense of freedom throughout the world. Divergent U.S.
and European positions vis-a-vis the Middle East in 1973 emphasized
this difference in outlook, and may have done great damage to the
unity of the alliance.

Unwilling to assume major burdens outside Europe, the NATO
nations also appeared to the United States to be unprepared to play a
role in their own security that would permit the lessening of the
American commitment and the withdrawal of substantial U.S. forces
from the continent. The alleged effects of the U.S. troop presence
on the balance of payments, the general desire of Americans to reduce overseas commitments, and a concern that Western Europe,
with its great prosperity, should bear a more equitable portion of
its own defense encouraged opposition in the United States to the continued presence of U.S. forces at existing levels. Unfortunately,
the diminished willingness of Americans to maintain large armies
has not been accompanied by a growth in European defense prepared-
ness. Instead, parallel political and economic trends on both sides
of the Atlantic have placed constraints on defense.

While U.S. spokesmen have frequently called for increased
European contributions to Western defense, Europeans have been
fearful that a major commitment by European countries would lead
the United States to withdraw even larger numbers of troops. In
addition, they have shown dissatisfaction with the manner in which
the United States has sought to allocate the burdens of Western defense. The Europeans have been reluctant to provide large conventional armies equipped with arms purchased from the United States,
leaving exclusive control of the strategic deterrent force in U.S.
hands. This reluctance of European leaders to upgrade their own
forces so as to lessen the U.S. burden reinforces the position of

Americans who argue for force reductions. As a result, preservation of the existing Western force posture becomes increasingly difficult, even as the United States argues that a credible conventional capability is within NATO's grasp with the expenditure of limited additional funds.

Similarly, in the field of nonmilitary cooperation, the grandiose goals of European political and economic unity appear even more elusive today than in the past. The EEC, divided by differences of opinion concerning floating currencies, has become deadlocked on basic issues ranging from energy policies and internal tariffs to relations and consultations with the United States. This attitude was reinforced by the Middle East oil embargo of 1973, when each of the European nations, faced with its own oil shortage, showed little regard for a common European policy. Each nation, indeed, sought to make its own advantageous arrangements with the OPEC nations, even at the expense of its European allies. The growing scarcity of other raw materials and the spectacular increase in their prices, with the resultant strains on supply, full employment, financial stability, and balance of payments, will almost surely accelerate this damaging economic noncooperation in the future. There is growing concern that the EEC has lost momentum toward economic and political unity, and may shrink to little more than a customs union, if it does not actually fall apart.

Curiously, Europeans feel more secure today than at almost any other time in the twentieth century. Paradoxically, this sense of security prevails at a time of increasing Soviet military capabilities. It has reinforced a psychological climate in Europe that may be detrimental to the strengthening and modernization of NATO forces and the creation of a security framework adequate to keep pace with Soviet capabilities during a period of U.S. reassessment of overseas commitments.

In addition, U.S. interest in exploiting the opportunities afforded by great-power detente diplomacy has, whatever its intrinsic merits, created problems for NATO unity.

The simple fact is that NATO has remained an international, not a supranational, organization. It is composed of sovereign nations that have relinquished none of their independence in carrying out their own foreign policy. Recent events have raised the question of whether such an alliance has outlived its usefulness or whether it has a greater permanence and a more lasting function to perform.

On the basis of the diverging interests of Western Europe and the United States and the perceived lessening of the threat that brought the North Atlantic Alliance into being, the major trends in Western Europe, unless corrected by decisive leadership directed toward increased unity, would seem to converge in a decline of military, political, and economic power.

URGENCY OF THE ISSUE

Thus, the most critical issue facing U.S. interests in Western Europe in the next few years concerns the cohesive unity of NATO. The resolution of this policy problem must be the concern of American decision-makers in the immediate future.

In his speech to the North Atlantic Council in May 1975, President Ford warned that "partial membership or special arrangements" in carrying the burden of allied defense would seriously undermine NATO's ability to defend Western Europe in the future.[2] But NATO seems to be rapidly evolving toward such a situation, and a series of special relationships within an altered alliance organization may be more the norm than the exception in the future. France was the instigator of this movement toward a "special relationship" within NATO, removing its forces from NATO military commands in 1966 while retaining all other advantages of NATO membership. Greece followed suit over the Cyprus crisis of 1975. The form of the Greek relationship to the alliance is currently being negotiated. Turkey has threatened to reassess its relationship with NATO because of the U.S. cutoff of military aid. The change of regime in Portugal has led to a degree of political turmoil whose ultimate outcome may call into question the continued membership or effectiveness of Portugal in NATO.

Increased pragmatism in the international field in a NATO no longer dominated by military security problems, however, would seem to be the primary factor in the possible future decline of European unity. The nations of Europe, each having its own view of its vital international interests, will increasingly tend to see these interests as clashing with American global interests. Condemned to impotence in world affairs by their lack of unity, the nations of Europe seem unwilling to concede to the EEC the power to coordinate economic and foreign policies. On the other hand, they appear to be losing their confidence in the ability and willingness of the United States to represent their special interests, especially if such representation imposes high costs.

Thus, the problem facing U.S. decision-makers in the future concerns the form that the various special relationships with the European members of NATO will take, rather than the elimination of such special relationships and the preservation of NATO as it is currently structured.

ALTERNATIVE STRATEGIES

A reorganized European-American security structure could take many possible forms. Some of the more likely may be the following:

- Reorganization of NATO to emphasize European participation
- Multilateral regional agreements
- Bilateral agreements
- Unilateral security.

Reorganization of NATO to Emphasize European Participation

Although the United States has always seen itself as, and indeed has been, the leader of the Atlantic Alliance, many of the European members of NATO have come to feel that the United States dominates NATO and involves, or attempts to involve, it in matters of concern to the United States but not vital to Europe. In addition, the American Congress has long felt that the European nations have not done enough in their own behalf and that the United States has borne an inordinate share of the defense burden for Europe. Also, in the interests of European strength and political cohesion, the United States has consciously accepted the commercially discriminatory implications of European integration. Thus both the Americans and many Europeans might find attractive a reorganization of NATO that would reduce U.S. dominance while maintaining the ultimate American military commitment to the defense of Europe.

Various types of reorganization have been suggested in the past. All have in common the lessening of American influence on and direction of Western European security matters. They suggest a type of European security arrangement inside a loose Atlantic community with the United States and Canada. Within this subdivision, NATO might be organized with a summit, or Atlantic level, in Washington exercising supreme civil/military direction and command and control, and a European level with key military commands assigned to Europeans. An American deputy might be retained to insure U.S. nuclear support and would be available to command U.S. troops in time of war. Various national levels would constitute the wartime operational commands, with the commanders, for the most part, being nationals of the country for which they are assigned responsibility.

Such an organization, of course, would give Europeans a much larger voice in their own defense policy and strategy, making the primary initiative theirs for organizing Europe's defense. This would present the possibility and, perhaps, the necessity of greater European military cooperation.

To the extent that the European nations could link in some form of defensive grouping, paralleling in the military sphere what has been accomplished in the economic, a West European nonnuclear defense might be feasible. France could be brought back into an integrated European defense without losing face. Italian and French manpower could be made available on the Central Front. A European combined command could make more coherent force planning among the European nations. Such a European force, of course, would be deficient in nationally controlled nuclear weapons.

The United States, therefore, would retain supreme overall political command in order to insure the retention of NATO's nuclear capability. Military commitments would remain very much the same as under the present arrangement and indeed, under a European command, might become more tightly knit. U.S. balance-of-payments problems, to the extent that they still exist, would be eased, since some or most U.S. troops would be removed from Europe.

The removal of large numbers of American forces, however, would make Western Europe's defense capability less credible, particularly in view of the time required to reintroduce American forces. Without U.S. leadership, it is doubtful that the divergent interests of Great Britain, France, and West Germany could be submerged to the extent necessary for a stable military coalition among them. Without American participation, it is also doubtful that the Western European nations would provide the resources required to build a credible European conventional deterrent. Indeed, U.S. troop withdrawals would probably lead not to compensatory increases in European forces but to imitative cuts. In either case, European defense would be required to contemplate a much lower nuclear threshold, making it more dependent upon the U.S. strategic nuclear capability. An American commitment to defend a Western Europe free of American forces would itself lack credibility. Confidence both in the credibility of NATO's power to contain a major Russian attack and in the nuclear deterrent would diminish. Doubt that the United States would honor its nuclear guarantees would grow in the minds of both American and European leaders.

Thus, at some point, the creation of a European nuclear force would be called for. But the creation of such a force, and its ultimate control, would pose many political problems and is hard to envisage for the near future. Control of this nuclear force would require a political authority with wide discretion in planning for and utilizing the force in order to make it credible. The Germans would have to participate in developing and controlling the force, a prospect not easily acceptable to the British and French. In any case, the Germans would insist upon a right to veto the use of nuclear weapons on their soil. None of these conditions, especially the degree of supranational political control that might make such a European deterrent credible, is foreseeable in the near future.

With the United States committed to provide the nuclear weapons
for the defense of Europe, but with U.S. forces removed from the
Continent and U.S. officers removed from NATO commands, the
United States would find itself in the situation of being committed
militarily, even to the extent of using nuclear weapons, without a
major voice in the political and military actions leading to such a
decision. If NATO's nuclear defense ultimately depends exclusively
on the United States, then any responsible American government
must continue to have a major say in NATO's military arrangements.
To continue the commitment but lose all control over local events
would be a policy that would be almost impossible for responsible
American leadership to support.

Multilateral Regional Agreements

The North Atlantic Treaty could be replaced with a series of
multilateral regional treaties that would cover the present NATO
countries, plus others if desired. For example, a Central Region
treaty with France, Great Britain, West Germany, and the Benelux
countries could be negotiated; separate treaties and defense organizations would cover the northern and southern regions. In some respects this system of defense treaties might be stronger and more
advantageous than the present European defense system. Common
national interests are to some extent a product of geography; and it
is possible that each regional organization would, in some respects,
be stronger than the current organization because of the elimination
of issues that may be peripheral to a particular region. Thus, the
Central Region might be stronger because of possible French participation and Spanish adherence to a more limited treaty. The same
might be true of the nations of the southern flank, which could concentrate on their regional defense problems rather than on problems
perhaps more remote from their immediate interests. In this way,
the credibility of each of these alliances would be enhanced, in that
each would be expected to respond only to threats in its own region
that directly affected its own, or regional, security. Since each
member nation would see a threat to its region as a direct threat to
itself, members might be willing to increase defense expenditures
in the interest of national security. Problems of internal coordination and command and control would be lessened because there would
be fewer nations involved in each regional organization. It would appear to be easier to reach consensus on regional political and defense
problems in an atmosphere of common cultural traditions, which is
not presently emphasized throughout NATO.

On the other hand, under this arrangement the United States would have to deal with at least three regional organizations of sovereign states rather than with one. Problems almost surely would arise concerning the employment of any U.S. forces committed to one region in order to meet a threat in another. As the one common member of all of these regional alliances, the United States would be caught up in rivalries and political disputes within and between regions. Priorities among the regions for U.S. defense efforts almost certainly would have to be established, thus adding to political frictions and jealousies. The homogeneity of deterrence, wherein a threat in one area is considered a threat to all, would be destroyed. The overall credibility of the alliances would be reduced, for each group would not be expected to respond to a threat or to an attack in another region. Individually and collectively, the regional alliances would necessarily be less strong than the present alliance. There would be a lessened degree of coordination along regional boundaries, notwithstanding an increased requirement for coordination; and in certain vital areas, such as the Baltic approaches and the Mediterranean, defense planning would suffer. The military interdependence and inseparability of the regions would be destroyed. For example, the defense of the northern approaches is, of course, vital to the defense of the Central Region, as are the freedom of the Mediterranean and the security of oil supplies from the Middle East.

Bilateral Agreements

The United States could enter into a series of bilateral treaties with the European nations to insure that its security interests are maintained. Indeed, it is highly likely that, in case of a major reorganization or weakening of NATO, the nations of Europe would look first of all to their direct relationship with the United States for the protection of their security interests. This is especially true for West Germany, which sets much store on its direct links with Washington and on the American troops on German soil. A bilateral defense treaty with Germany probably would continue to form the basis for the maintenance of U.S. troops in Germany. Similar treaties with Great Britain, France, Spain, and other countries could insure U.S. access to and use of air and naval bases and logistical support facilities in those countries, as well as provide for mutual action against a threat from the Soviet Union.

This type of security arrangement would continue the U.S. commitment to the security of Europe and would allow the continued maintenance of U.S. forces there. Dealing with each individual nation on issues of interest to it could perhaps be easier than dealing with

fifteen nations on all issues in an international forum that requires
unanimity for decision.

Such a system of bilateral arrangements, on the other hand,
would present a great number of problems. The credibility of conventional deterrence in Central Europe would be diminished, thus
lowering the threshold of nuclear war. The very rationale for NATO--
the binding together of many West European nations and their alliance
with the United States to form a credible deterrent--would be undermined. U.S. forces remaining in Germany, then, would serve only
as a tripwire. The nations of Europe, unwilling to face the possibility of a nuclear holocaust, might seek accommodation with the USSR
rather than alliance with the United States. The European countries
would be subjected to "Finlandization," and the Germans most probably would seek to develop a national nuclear capability. National
rivalries would develop concerning the extent of the U.S. commitment to each country. The United States would have to reconcile and
compromise issues unilaterally with many nations, each with different outlooks, interests, and objectives. The stability of Europe
could be undermined, and the potential for the achievement of Soviet
objectives by nonmilitary means would be enhanced. There would be
little or no integrated defense planning, and a conventional defense
of Europe would not be practical.

Unilateral Security

The ultimate, although unlikely, reaction of the United States
to a NATO characterized by "special relationships" and varying degrees of commitment from its member nations would be to abandon
the NATO concept and to plan for and take actions necessary to protect its own vital interests. Such a unilateral defense posture could
take one of several forms:

• The United States could seek bases, base rights, and logistical facilities around the world in order to deploy forces as required to meet threats to its vital interests and to those of its
allies.

• The United States could withdraw its forward deployed forces
and maintain the minimum forces necessary to defend the United
States, leaving to diplomacy the protection of U.S. interests elsewhere in the world.

• The defense of U.S. interests worldwide would become the
subject of bipolar diplomacy, crisis management, and arms-
control negotiations.

Such actions, of course, would destroy the concept of Western
collective security so laboriously nurtured and implemented during

the twenty-five years of the Cold War. A conventional defense of Western Europe would become highly unlikely, even if the European nations were to band together to provide for their own collective security. Even an integrated European Defense Community would require U.S. forces to provide any sort of credible conventional defense, and it would also require a European nuclear force to provide a nuclear deterrent independent of that of the United States. In the absence of these forces, the sole course of action open to the United States to counter a Soviet attack in Europe (if, indeed, it would elect to confront the Soviet Union over Western European security) would be a nuclear response. Each European nation would, within its capability, seek to develop its own nuclear capability while also seeking its own accommodation with the Soviets.

As President Ford pointed out, any form of special relationships within NATO tends to weaken the ability of the alliance to defend Western Europe. Such a series of special relationships would call into question the credibility of NATO's conventional defense and would increase Soviet opportunities in Western Europe's economic, political, and military spheres. Any weakening of U.S.-NATO ties might well embolden the Soviet Union to seek its own bilateral ties with the individual nations of Western Europe. The European nations, on the other hand, might see advantages in entering into balance-of-power relationships with the Soviet Union and the nations of Eastern Europe. Such relationships might be seen as enhancing the leverage in world politics of the individual nations of Europe that still yearn for their great-power status of the past. European nations, on the other hand, might be encouraged to retreat into neutralism, attempting to reach their own accommodation with the East. Or they could pursue their separate military policies. This could include Germany's development of a national nuclear capability, with resultant strains on the European political system. One can then envision the gradual disappearance of NATO into a web of special relationships. The alliance could contain several categories of members acting together, depending on particular interests in the activity involved. One can foresee diminishing participation by, or individual withdrawal of, some of NATO's peripheral members: Canada, Iceland, Turkey, Greece, Portugal, Norway, Denmark, and perhaps even France.

Any decrease in the perceived ability of the Western European nations, in conjunction with the United States, to provide for their own security through the NATO Alliance would politically destabilize Europe. Any form of "special relationships" in defense commitments (as outlined above) would be a defeat for the twenty-five-year effort to enhance Western European unity and security. In the final analysis, however, the nations of Western Europe, individually or

in concert, will probably continue to look to the United States as
their shield and protector in the face of a threat of external aggression.

Thus, it is in the interest of the United States and the other
nations of NATO to develop, in the immediate future, a new conception of partnership to overcome the issues dividing them and to engender true political consultation and cooperation. There is, however dimly perceived, a Free World with indivisible interests on
many issues in many parts of the world. A confident, increasingly
united, and self-reliant Western Europe, playing a larger role in its
own security and joining with the United States in protecting the common interests of the Free World wherever it is threatened, is likely
to remain the central goal of American diplomacy in the years ahead.

THE MILITARY POWER OF THE WESTERN ALLIANCE

Regardless of the form that the NATO alliance may take in the
near future, whether it be increased unity or an arrangement based
on "special relationships" within the alliance, a major issue that will
face member nations will be the preservation of the military power
of the alliance.

The costs of manpower and major weapons systems are likely
to increase in the immediate future more rapidly than gross national
product (GNP). Consequently, even if nations devote the same proportion of their GNP to defense, conventional forces and weapons
capabilities within the alliance cannot be maintained at existing levels
without a higher degree of integration and efficiency. And there is
increasing pressure in every member nation of the alliance to devote
a lesser percentage of GNP to defense purposes. In addition, Congressional pressures for force reductions in American forces based
in Europe can be expected to increase. Since the maintenance of
troop levels in Europe has no domestic constituency in the United
States, these efforts at reduction may, in the not too distant future,
succeed. Thus, a major problem facing NATO in the next few years
will be the maintenance of a credible conventional capability in the
face of rising manpower costs, national inclinations to reduce defense
budgets, and the need to modernize with increasingly complex and
expensive weapons systems.

Unilateral reduction of U.S. forces in Europe (and other overseas localities) has been proposed in Congress annually since 1966.
These efforts at reduction are based, inter alia, on a concern over
the cost of these forces, particularly balance-of-payment costs; an
idea that the NATO nations are not carrying a fair share of the defense burden; a presumption that reducing deployed forces would

reduce the chance of being involved in a foreign war without Congressional sanction; and a skepticism concerning the old Cold War arguments, in the midst of detente, for maintaining a high troop strength abroad.

Any reduction of U.S. forces in Europe can be planned and based upon qualitative improvements in organization, armament, and mobilization capabilities, or they can be unplanned, unilateral, and destabilizing. Under the latter circumstances, it will become necessary to develop a deterrent posture at lower levels of manpower. The strategic doctrine of flexible response, as now constituted, would diminish in credibility. The nuclear threshold would be raised.

Thus, national leaders in the coming years must find alternatives to unilateral reduction of U.S. (and other national) forces that would avoid both the military consequences and the serious political risks associated with a significant decline in the ability of NATO to mount a credible defense of Western Europe. Among the proposals designed to accomplish this end are the following:

- U.S. withdrawals based upon force reorganization
- NATO-Soviet negotiated force reductions
- Increased NATO specialization and rationalization of military forces.

U.S. Withdrawals Based upon Force Reorganization

Although NATO strategy continues to maintain that there is a requirement for a strong and successful initial forward defense based primarily on forces capable of winning a short conventional war, U.S. ground forces are not organized according to that concept. They are organized in a small number of large divisions designed to be indefinitely sustainable in extended combat, either in Europe or in contingency situations that might arise elsewhere. This provides a much higher ratio of organic and nonorganic support for U.S. forces than their Warsaw Pact counterparts and helps explain why the U.S. Army generates only four and one-third large divisions out of almost 200,000 men in Europe, while the Russians, whose forces are configured for an overwhelming armored and air thrust across NATO's center region, manage to have twenty divisions, with much higher aggregate shock and fire power, out of only 300,000 Red Army personnel in East Germany.

Our NATO allies, analysts indicate, do not plan to mobilize large numbers of reserve forces in order to fight a long war in NATO Europe. In fact, they have very few reserve divisions, although they do plan to mobilize substantial personnel to flesh out support for

existing active units. These allies seem to be posturing for a conventional war of limited duration before a nuclear response would
be required.

The United States, on the other hand, maintains numerous reinforcement divisions and support forces, both active and reserve,
that it contemplates deploying to Europe gradually over a ninety-day
period to sustain extended conventional conflict. The United States
is also posturing for an extended campaign to keep open the Atlantic
sea-lanes against a conventional submarine threat, in order to support our deployed forces by sealift over a considerable time period,
and for an air war of interdiction whose effects might well be felt too
late to break the momentum of an enemy assault.

This contrast between the American and allied postures, and
between American strategy and organization, is difficult to justify.
Critics charge that the United States seems to be planning for a re-
play of World War II, while our allies shrink from that possibility.
Controversial as it may be, the restructuring of U.S. ground forces
in Europe to utilize expensive active personnel more efficiently offers a viable way of fielding a more credible conventional posture at
the same or lower cost while bringing NATO's posture and organization into conformance with its strategy. Estimates as to how much
troop strength could be saved by this restructuring while retaining
equivalent combat strength range from 29,000 to almost 60,000 of
total U.S. Army strength in Europe.[3]

NATO-Soviet Negotiated Force Reductions

Negotiations between NATO and Warsaw Pact nations on force
reductions began on October 30, 1973. The aim of these talks is "to
enhance security and stability in Central Europe by achieving a more
stable balance at lower levels of forces with undiminished security
for all participants." Although these negotiations have made little or
no progress, it might be useful and advantageous for the NATO allies
to make necessary concessions to reach some agreement on force
reductions in the near future. Such an agreement would dampen
Congressional pressure for more immediate and greater U.S. unilateral force reductions. The fact that these negotiations have been
in progress has had such a temporary effect, but this will not continue to be persuasive if there is lack of progress over a considerable period of time. Similarly, such an agreement might arrest
tendencies toward large force reductions in other NATO countries.
Such an agreement would test Russian intentions and allow the United
States and Western Europeans to make qualitative improvements in
their forces.

Increased NATO Specialization and
Rationalization of Military Forces

Given the likely constraints on the resources that the nations
of the Atlantic Alliance will devote to their defense forces in the
future, greater efficiency in the use of those resources through increased standardization will be a prime means of maintaining and
perhaps enhancing the overall military effectiveness of the alliance.
Over the past twenty-five years, the NATO nations have failed to
achieve standardization of weapons and communications equipment,
tactical doctrine, and complementary research and development
projects. Because of this, NATO has not been able to provide the
maximum defense possible for the resources expended and the military forces maintained.

Thus, forces of the various NATO allies are unable to support
one another logistically, and their equipment is often not compatible
or interoperable. This reduces tactical flexibility (for example,
forces of one nation cannot be shifted to support forces of another
nation without moving the entire logistics "tail"). These factors result in a waste of defense resources estimated at some $10 billion
annually (approximately the sum of the entire British defense budget).
While NATO's population, GNP, military budgets, and military manpower levels are greater than those of the Warsaw Pact, the Pact
nevertheless enjoys superiority in conventional forces.

Alliance military officials have estimated that increased standardization and rationalization* could improve NATO's military effectiveness from 25 percent for some ground units to as much as 300
percent for tactical air units.

The problem of different and incompatible armaments has
arisen because the responsibility for equipping and maintaining forces
earmarked for NATO remains a national responsibility, as does the
logistical support of those forces. Some degree of standardization
was achieved in the early years of the alliance by the provision of
extensive military equipment from the United States. However, as
each member nation developed and sought to protect its own armament industry and production base, the inclination was to supply its

---

*Rationalization is the term that has been adopted within NATO
to describe any action that makes a more efficient use of the defense
resources of the NATO nations, including greater cooperation, consolidation, and reassignment of national defense resources to higher
priority NATO needs without changing total planned defense funding
of the member states. In its simplest form, rationalization is any
action which makes more efficient or effective use of the resources
devoted by the alliance to defense. One element of rationalization
is standardization.

own troops with its own native-made equipment, and thus to be less dependent upon purchases from the United States. For its part, the United States has been unenthusiastic in making standardization a two-way street by purchasing European-developed and -manufactured equipment for its own forces.

Thus, if the posture of NATO conventional forces is to be improved without significantly increased expenditures, a cooperative effort in weapons development and procurement offers the opportunity for significant progress. This has now been recognized at the highest levels within the alliance, and initial steps have been taken to begin to address this problem. The U.S. Congress has also recognized the efficiencies attainable in NATO's defense posture by increased standardization. The Culver-Nunn Amendment adopted as Section 814 of the fiscal year 1976 Defense Authorization Bill states:

> It is the sense of the Congress that equipment, procedures, ammunition, fuel and other military impedimenta for land, air and naval forces of the United States stationed in Europe under the terms of the North Atlantic Treaty should be standardized or made interoperable with that of other members of the North Atlantic Treaty Organization to the maximum extent feasible. In carrying out such policy the Secretary of Defense shall, to the maximum feasible extent, initiate and carry out procurement procedures that provide for the acquisition of equipment which is standardized or interoperable with equipment of other members of the North Atlantic Treaty Organization whenever such equipment is designed primarily to be used by personnel of the Armed Forces of the United States stationed in Europe under the terms of the North Atlantic Treaty.

The amendment also requires the Secretary of Defense to report the initiation of procurement action on any new major system that is not in compliance with the policy set forth above. In addition, the Secretary of Defense is required to report annually to the Congress the results achieved with NATO allies in standardization.

The Culver-Nunn Amendment appears to be the first statute enacted by the legislature of any NATO country that specifically establishes standardization of weapons, procedures, ammunition, fuel, and other military equipment as a stated policy.

Other considerations, such as "buy American" legislation, balance-of-payments concerns, transfers of technology, and employment problems will militate against progress in this area, as they have in the past. The implementation of this "sense of Congress" will, therefore, be a challenge to decision-makers in the immediate future and will, to a great extent, determine the ability of the North Atlantic Alliance to present a credible conventional deterrent in Central Europe in the face of static or declining defense budgets.

CONCLUSIONS

The maintenance of the relative military power of the NATO alliance whether through a negotiated reduction of U.S. and Soviet forces, or through reorganization of NATO and standardization of weapons and support facilities, will remain an additional goal of American diplomacy in the coming years.

U.S. military forces committed to NATO and present in Europe, beyond their clear military purpose, serve as a political symbol of the continuing U.S. commitment to Europe. The U.S. presence in Europe as part of the NATO alliance is at this time, in a very real sense, the foundation that makes NATO possible, and the fact that it stays together is perhaps the principal stabilizing factor in Western Europe. Since it is a voluntarily determined position taken by an otherwise unlikely group of allies, it has a credibility that no alternative security system could duplicate. The current NATO strategy of flexible response, and the organization and means to carry it out, provide the United States and its North Atlantic and European allies with a feasible, effective, and realistic approach to collective security. To supplement this military element of collective security, the United States must pursue two additional objectives: a genuine detente with the Soviet Union that will provide suitable guarantees for the security of U.S. allies; and a Europe moving toward greater economic and political unity, and thus capable of playing a major independent role in the international struggle to maintain and foster those institutions cherished by free men. Success in this second objective will encourage success in the first.

NOTES

1. General George S. Brown, "United States Military Posture for FY 1976," statement by the Chairman, Joint Chiefs of Staff, before the Senate Armed Services Committee, February 5, 1975, p. 122.

2. Washington Post, May 30, 1975, p. 1.

3. R. W. Komer, "Treating NATO's Self-Inflicted Wound," Foreign Policy no. 13 (Winter 1973-74): 39.

6

**THE MIDDLE EAST:
THE PROBLEM OF
QUARANTINE**
John W. Amos II

THE ISSUE

How to avoid or contain war is the critical question facing U.S. policy in the Middle East. There are basic differences over the extent of U.S. commitment, over the nature of U.S. interests in the area, and over the degree to which the United States can affect events. There are disagreements over means to achieve peace, but little disagreement over the ends sought.

BACKGROUND OF THE ISSUE

Any discussion of issues facing U.S. policy-makers concerned with the Middle East might usefully begin with a rough outline of specific goals/interests in the area. These goals/interests have been expressed at different times by different U.S. officials, with some variations. However, they can be usefully summarized as follows--not necessarily in order of importance, for that order varies with the particular contingency facing the United States:
- Avoidance of a superpower confrontation over the Middle East
- Securing strategic access to the Mediterranean
- Preservation of access to the area's oil resources
- Preservation of the stability of the area
- Prevention of outside influence from penetrating the area, especially Soviet and, secondarily, Chinese influence
- Defending the integrity of Israel and those Arab states that are pro-Western in outlook and policy. [1]
This statement of goals highlights and puts into perspective the issues facing U.S. policy-makers. In terms of both its location and its oil

reserves, the Middle East is of strategic importance. Control over the land mass means control over a major communications bridge between Africa, Asia, and Europe. As such, trade routes can be disrupted by land-based forces at a series of "choke points," wherein the terrain narrows either land or sea passages. Control over oil-fields alone confers the power to unhinge European and Asian economies, to deny NATO forces fuel, and thus sharply to reduce NATO's ability to conduct operations. Control over the Mediterranean, like control over the center of a chessboard, permits the application of naval power to littoral countries. [2] These goals, therefore, tend to range themselves into two categories: goals having to do with protection of strategic access to the region as a whole, and goals having to do with the maintenance of stability--and therefore defense against outside encroachment--within the Middle East.

Thus, the primary strategic issues facing U.S. policy-makers hinge on preservation of the Middle East/Mediterranean as an area in which U.S. power can be effectively employed. Since the area is so sensitive from a strategic point of view, it is only natural that other powers attempt to move into it. Hence, the continuing possibility of a U.S./USSR confrontation, a possibility that has materialized three times: 1956, 1967, and 1973--and each time with ominously greater intensity. Therefore, the politics of the Middle East are, from time to time, directly linked with threats to U.S. national security. In this sense, perhaps no other area of the world has posed such a continuous threat.

Secondary are those issues revolving around the international stability of the area: the support of Israel and other friendly governments and the reduction of conflicts within the area. Added to this, or rather part and parcel of this, is the requirement to control or contain those conflicts that provide targets of opportunity for USSR, China, or other hostile powers to move into the area, either directly in terms of emplacement of troops and warships, or indirectly as armorers to the parties concerned.

In this context, the three major problems confronting U.S. policy-makers (the Arab/Israeli and the Greek/Turkish conflicts, and the oil issue) have remained relatively unchanged in terms of their basic parameters. Of these, the Arab/Israeli confrontation is the most explosive and seemingly least susceptible to solution.

At its core, this is a three-sided conflict involving maintenance of the security of Israel; settlement of Palestinian populations displaced as a consequence of the 1948 and 1967 wars; and territorial adjustments among Israel, Egypt, Jordan, and Syria of land occupied by Israel during the 1967 war. There are thus three categories of actors directly involved, each with specific demands: Israelis demanding a secure existence; Palestinians demanding a return to

their lands; and surrounding Arab states demanding a return of their
territories.

The problem here is that these demands have become intertwined at the core, and then projected onto the politics of outlying
populations of Arabs and Jews. For the Israelis, any disposition of
Arab territories that involves a reduction in their parameters is
tantamount to a military defeat. Any settlement of large numbers of
Palestinians within Israel is seen as the creation of an Arab fifth
column, the importation of an enormous and hostile Arab population.
For the Palestinians, any solution less than maximum demands for
a return to Palestine/Israel is perceived as the equivalent of the destruction of the Palestinian people. For Egypt, Jordan, and Syria,
continued Israeli occupation of their territory is likewise viewed as
a threat to their continued existence.

This would be intractable enough even if no other groups were
involved. However, much larger numbers of Arabs and Jews have
become involved over time: Jewish communities in Europe and
America see Israel as a last haven for a persecuted people. Therefore, anything that affects Israel's security affects the survival of
the Jewish people as a whole. Arab populations territorially far removed from the scene of the conflict have likewise become emotion-
ally involved in its outcome. Decades of Arab political rhetoric have
made an anti-Israeli stance the cornerstone of every Arab regime's
legitimacy. Moreover, Arab leaders have attempted to legitimize
themselves by outbidding each other in expressions of their commitment to the Arab cause. Therefore, even if Israeli and Arab leaders
on the spot wished to compromise (and could convince their immediate audiences of the wisdom of such a policy), they would still face
attacks from the spokesmen of these outlying groups.[3]

These territorial/population issues are made even more complex by the fact that Jerusalem contains religious shrines holy to both
Muslims and Jews, shrines that are in close physical proximity to
one another. Therefore, larger populations of Muslims and Jews
have an interest in the territorial settlement. The late King Faisal,
for example, considered himself the protector of Islamic holy places
in Jerusalem; and part of the motivation of Saudi oil policy was a desire to use the "oil weapon" to recover the holy places.

In fact, a solution to the problem of Jerusalem may be the
most difficult of any of the issues dividing Arabs and Israelis. Jews
refuse to consider giving up control of the city; Muslims insist that
it must be returned to Arab/Muslim hands. Indeed, in this respect,
the dialogue over the fate of Jerusalem and its relationship to the
Arab/Israeli conflict in general has taken on theological overtones.
Or, as one observer put it: "The prospects for settlement would be
dim enough were God thought to be a partisan of either protagonist;
but alas, he has emerged as the ally of both. . . ."[4]

Second in intractibility to the Arab/Israeli dispute is the Cyprus issue. Like its counterpart, this is a multisided conflict involving Greek and Turkish Cypriot populations, on the one hand, and larger populations in Greece and Turkey, on the other. The central issue here, as in the Arab/Israeli matter, is that of incompatible territorial demands. Greek Cypriots--encouraged by Greek homeland elements--demand enosis, or union with Greece; Turkish Cypriots, likewise supported by Turkish governments, demand separation, taksim. The mutual hostility of Greeks and Turks is of long standing, originating in Christian/Muslim fighting in the nineteenth century and continuing unabated into the present. Much like the Arab/Israeli conflict, this has taken on religious overtones. The Greeks consider themselves heirs to Byzantium; the Turks, as the legatees of Ottoman glory. [5]

Here, too, the issue is complicated by other factors. Both Greek and Turkish governments have viewed policies toward Cyprus as a test of their own fitness to rule. The Greek sponsorship of the anti-Makarios coup appears to have been, at least in part, an attempt to legitimize itself at home. The Turkish invasion equally seems to have reflected governmental fears that inaction would worsen an already deteriorating domestic situation.

If this were not enough, there is yet another point of contention: claims over an area of the Aegean adjacent to the Turkish coast. The dispute here is twofold: on one hand, it involves a dispute about the relationship of Greek-populated islands just off Turkey to the Athens government. The Turks claim that these islands are threats to Turkish national security; the Greeks fear another Turkish invasion. On the other hand, it takes the form of competing claims to Aegean waters--or, more precisely, claims to oil exploration rights in these waters. [6] The Aegean confrontation surfaced with a vengeance in the spring of 1974: Greek and Turkish naval units engaged in mutually provocative maneuvers in the disputed waters. These added to already escalating tensions and reinforced the Greek government's determination to do something to halt what appeared to be a Makarios-sponsored drift to the extreme left in Cyprus.

Unlike the two previous situations, in which definable constellations of opposing forces are at work, the oil issue is much more diffuse. At bottom it rests on a simple equation: Western countries have expanded their reliance on oil as the principal energy source; with this expansion has come increased concern that access to oil--in increasing amounts--be maintained at a relatively stable price. Conversely, the producers are faced with the twofold problem of conserving a dwindling natural resource so as to maximize its income over the longest possible time while somehow linking its price to the increasingly inflated prices of Western products.

However, economic differences are not the sole point of contention. Underlying a whole range of oil producers' policies, some of which seem contrary to economic logic, is a set of attitudes stemming from the historical nexus of Arab relations with the West. In this context, oil-exporting arrangements are seen apart from the economic and social benefits they confer. Therefore, there has always been the urge for oil producers somehow to reverse this arrangement, to regain control of their own resources, and to make amends for years of one-sided (in their view) exploitation. Given such attitudes on the part of Arab oil states, a collision was inevitable, even where there was a recognition of the value of stable economic relations with the West.

The sudden and well-publicized Western realization that the gap between Western energy consumption and its production was dramatically increasing set the stage for this collision. It was foreshadowed by the Libyan strategy, started in 1970, of cutting production in order to increase reserves; and by a series of participation agreements concluded in 1972, by means of which oil companies were forced to relinquish ever greater shares of profits. [7]

Given the premise that none of the foregoing conflicts had much real hope of solution, U.S. policy options before October 1973 seemed both unattractive and of limited utility. Insofar as maintenance of the oil flow was concerned, it seemed preferable to maintain a low profile, and let oil companies deal with the producers. The arguments for this posture were persuasive. On the one hand, the oil producers were extremely conservative in their politics and, therefore, at loggerheads with those Arab extremists who were most vocally anti-Israeli. This fundamental split between the so-called radical and conservative camps polarized and intensified as each side progressively supported one faction in the Yemen civil war during the early 1960s. [8] Therefore, the likelihood of a coalition of oil and Arab radicalism seemed extremely unlikely.

On the other hand, experience with past oil stoppages, by Iran in 1950/51 and the Arabs in 1956 and 1967, seemed to have shown that a sustained embargo was equally unlikely. In every instance, the economic self-interest of each of the several producers had led them to break the embargo; in some cases they even raised output to garner a greater share of the market at the expense of their followers. [9]

Even when concern over the energy gap began to surface, it was articulated in terms either of holding fast to existing arrangements, or, as an abrupt alternative, of seizing the oilfields themselves. The possibility of a successful oil embargo still seemed too remote to be seriously considered. [10]

Similarly, Cyprus appeared manageable. Both Greek and Turkish governments appeared to be overwhelmed by domestic problems: inflation, agricultural dislocations, and political unrest. Neither looked strong enough to mount a determined effort to intervene in Cyprus. And the situation on the island, while tense, seemed tolerable enough, even with flare-ups of fighting in 1963 and 1967. Except for President Johnson's dramatic intervention in late 1967 to forestall a Turkish invasion of the island, U.S. policy was geared to settling the conflict via either NATO or U.N. auspices, thus avoiding probable adverse consequences of direct action: the loss of base rights in either Greece or Turkey. But here, too, the seeming success of U.S. efforts to prevent full-scale hostilities in late 1967 led to an acceptance of the status quo as being at least tolerable.

While the Cyprus and oil issues were discussed, it was the Arab/Israeli conflict and what to do about it that produced the most prolonged debate. The arguments of the two sides went something like this: Those advocating U.S. support for Israel held to the thesis that Israel was really the only dependable ally in the Middle East; that it was the only democracy in the area; that it was a key force for stability in the area and a key defense against Soviet intrusion; and that, in the final analysis, Israel was "objectively" more important to the United States than any conceivable set of interests in the Arab world. Moreover, Israel or not, U.S. relations with Arab regimes would be uncertain and touchy at best. Therefore, U.S. policy should aim at supporting a known factor for stability in the region.[11]

Those who took the opposing view maintained that U.S. interests in the Arab world were very real; that these interests could be protected only by policies aimed at creating ties with Arab countries; and that, in the absence of such policies, the USSR was polarizing the area against the United States and the West, and slowly taking the area into its sphere of influence. Therefore, U.S. policy should be concerned to reverse an anti-U.S./Western drift in the region.[12]

The 1967 war marked a watershed insofar as these arguments are concerned, since it seemed to demonstrate the validity of the first contention: Israel was clearly the dominant power in the area. And if the Middle East was conceived as a comprehensive system, then Israel was clearly the critical element in holding the balance of power in favor of the West. Moreover, the magnitude of the military defeat inflicted on Soviet clients seemed to bode well for a policy of status quo post bellum. Let the Soviets lean on their clients to come to terms with the war's victor. Why should the United States intervene to aid regimes that had not only broken off relations, but seemed oblivious to any rational diplomatic approaches? The United States would intervene only to prevent unreasonable escalation, such as the Suez Canal cease-fire brokered by Secretary of State Rogers in 1970.[13]

Events outran all of these theories. The strains that had built up since 1967 detonated in a roar of Arab artillery; Arab leaders, acting independently, launched a war. U.S. intervention on the side of the Israelis provided the spark that triggered the oil embargo.[14] In an aftershock, Cyprus exploded in July 1974. The Greeks, perhaps sensing U.S. preoccupation with the Arabs and Israelis, moved to solve their problems by supporting a pre-enosis coup on Cyprus.[15] The Turks, likewise sensing this U.S. preoccupation, which appeared to mean de facto U.S. support for the Greek moves, took matters into their own hands and invaded. And U.S. Middle Eastern/Mediterranean policy appeared on the verge of collapse.[16]

In short, by the end of the war, the United States found itself confronted with a new set of realities in the Middle East:

1. An Arab World more or less unified as a consequence of an Egyptian/Saudi alliance, an alliance in which Egyptian military power and Saudi Arabia's oil joined forces; an alliance of heretofore opposing powers. The previous ability of U.S. policy-makers, therefore, to count on a separation of the Arab/Israeli dispute, on one hand, and U.S. oil interests in the Arabian Peninsula, on the other, was nullified.[17]

2. The premise that Israeli military strength was sufficiently superior to that of Arab forces to make U.S. intervention unnecessary was also sharply challenged:[18] The United States was forced to deplete its own arms inventories to make up Israeli losses.

3. The assumption that preservation of a status quo in which Israel continued to occupy Arab territories would sooner or later force Arab leaders to come to reasonable terms was also disproved. Arguments that time was on the side of prevailing U.S. policies, and that time would erode Arab intransigence, proved invalid.

By demonstrating their ability to destabilize the military balance, Arab leaders gained the initiative in terms of time. And, if Arab public utterances are to be taken seriously, Arab leaders seem to have come to the conclusions that:

● A successful military confrontation with Israel is possible, and that such a confrontation can, therefore, be usefully resorted to as a policy option.

● Both the United States and Western Europe are sufficiently dependent on Arab oil and that another embargo would have a devastating effect.

● As a result of the foregoing, the initiative in dealing with the Arab/Israeli situation has gone over to the Arab side.

For these reasons, Arab willingness to tolerate a situation of protracted negotiations can be presumed to be limited at best. President Sadat of Egypt expressed this new-found Arab determination thus:

> Brothers and sisters, we are persevering but
> there is no return at all to a situation of "no
> peace, no war" that existed prior to October
> 1973. It is regrettable that many forces
> throughout the world misunderstood that
> patience. Perhaps the October lesson will be
> useful and nobody will misunderstand our
> patience again.[19]

However, if the war produced some unpleasant surprises for
the United States, it was equally disastrous for the Soviet Union. Its
Arab clients precipitated a major escalation of Middle East fighting,
and did so either without consulting the Soviets or in spite of Soviet
opposition.[20] The Soviets were then forced by the logic of their past
commitments to these Arab regimes not only to resupply them, but
also to directly confront the United States. Even so, these efforts
did not prevent the defection of Egypt, the geographical lynchpin of
the Soviet position. The Egyptians have announced their intention,
not only to develop extensive economic relations with the West but
also to replace Soviet arms with Western ones wherever possible.
In this, they have been supported by Saudi Arabia, easily the most
anti-Communist country in the region. Therefore, if the United
States found that many of its previous policy assumptions had been
invalidated, the USSR found its Middle Eastern posture on the verge
of collapse.

OCTOBER REASSESSED

In retrospect, both arguments concerning U.S. policy toward
the Arab/Israeli issue were aimed at the same concern: how to
stabilize the area. The argument for supporting Israel rested on the
thesis that this could best be accomplished via the stick, using Israel
as a deterrent to forestall untoward Arab/Soviet behavior. The argument for increasing U.S. ties with Arab states advocated the carrot, U.S. policy accommodations that would engender Arab recipro-
cations.

Neither was really correct. Utilizing Israel as the chief protector of U.S. interests placed it in a role exceeding its capabilities.
Israel is a small power, beset by its own concerns, possessed of
finite resources, with its own grave security problems. To require
it to subordinate these considerations to U.S. interests was asking
too much. Likewise, to assume that any U.S. move toward the Arabs
would be met by an Arab countermove was to ignore the forces of
Arab nationalism, pride, and self-interest. All of these would

operate to limit any movement toward the United States. In addition, inter-Arab politics has its own dynamic, which would complicate any situation.

The problem that both attempted to solve could not, in fact, be solved on either terms: the absence of any Arab leadership able or willing to deal rationally with the issues at hand prevented any consistent Arab response to such strategies. Part of the reason for this lay in the complexities of Arab politics. But part also had to do with Arab identity problems. At the risk of overstating the case, the Arabs as a people are quite conscious that they are the heirs to a glorious and powerful heritage. The contrast between this former greatness and the present condition was intolerable. Arab frustration with a situation in which the Arabs always seemed to be defeated and the psychology of constant humiliation effectively thwarted any meaningful dialogue.

The upshot of this was that the United States and Israel did not really have any option to negotiate with the Arabs. Therefore, reliance on territorial acquisition, either as a security measure or as a technique to force concessions, became policy by default; Israeli dialogue with Arab neighbors was reduced to across-the-border violence; and in such an environment it is small wonder that immediate security concerns overrode the luxury of alternative diplomatic options.

The war reversed this state of affairs for the Israelis; the shock of the Arab attack demonstrated that the military gap between Arab and Israeli forces was closing. The enormous cost of the war altered their options. The policy of military deterrence had failed, and had proved intolerably expensive. For the Arabs, the war had even greater impact. It reversed their negative self-image, and the argument that they had regained their lost honor runs through Arab assessments of the war: "We have changed the image the whole world had of us. It used to think of us as a lifeless corpse, but now it has seen that we are capable of movement, capable of fighting, capable of victory. And it is not only the image of Egypt that has been changed, but the image of the whole Arab nation. . . ."[21]

In addition to the psychological impact on the Arabs, the war was politically crucial because it was planned and coordinated by a relatively moderate Egyptian leadership, aided by a pro-Western Saudi regime. During the months of negotiations that preceded the war, these leaders succeeded in impressing their strategic vision on other Arabs: the vision of a controlled crisis that would trigger negotiations.[22]

This is in sharp contrast with earlier conflicts, in which radical Arab leaders were involved. Moreover, these moderates were, and are, operating under the assumptions that only the United States

had sufficient power to make a diplomatic solution possible and that
the Soviet contribution was limited to arms. An Arab editor summed
up this feeling: "The defeat of Soviet arms brings the Arabs closer
to the U.S.S.R., while victory of Soviet arms brings the Arabs
closer to the U.S.A. The Arabs make war with Russian armaments
and peace through American diplomacy."[23]

Therefore, a few new possibilities have opened up that did not
previously exist. The Israelis need an alternative to continued war.
The Arabs now can negotiate. As long as these Arab moderates remain in power, and as long as their strategy of diplomatic bargaining
appears to bring results, negotiation is possible. The United States
will be able to deal with both Arabs and Israelis on a rational basis.
The missing side, the Arab side, of the negotiating equation now appears to be a reality.

On the Arab side, the Egyptians are the critical political factor.
Sadat has committed himself not only to the principle of negotiation
but also to the thesis that Israel is a fact of life in the Middle East.
Moreover, there would seem to be a natural trade-off of interests
between the United States and Egypt. The Egyptians want an alternative to the USSR in terms of economic and military aid. The United
States can supply that aid. In turn, the United States needs Egyptian
prestige and political clout in the Arab world. The Egyptians have
leverage with the oil producers, leverage that could be usefully employed to facilitate negotiations between the West and the oil producers.

In terms of the oil question, Saudi Arabia and Kuwait are the
keys. Of all the members of OPEC, only the Saudis and Kuwaitis
have sufficient cash reserves to be able to alter their production
levels for political reasons. Other OPEC countries are constrained
in their oil policies by the need to keep oil revenues as high as possible in order to meet domestic economic requirements. Saudi
Arabia and Kuwait, therefore, are the "swing" countries through
their ability to make or break OPEC pricing and production policies.

As with the Egyptians, there is a natural trade-off of interests.
The Saudis and Kuwaitis are concerned to maintain working relations
with the United States for a number of reasons: as a source of political support against radical elements in the Arabian Peninsula, and
potentially against the Iranians; as a source of military and technological aid; and as a counterweight to Soviet influence in the region.

In turn, the United States could utilize Saudi influence to promote moderate Arab behavior. The Saudis have considerable leverage with the Palestine Liberation Organization, the Jordanians, and
the Syrians. If any "give" is to be negotiated on the territorial disposition of the Golan Heights or the fate of the Palestinians, Saudi
leverage is going to be necessary.

TIME AND URGENCY: THE POLITICAL-
MILITARY EQUATION

It is a truism of Middle Eastern politics that after each war, there is a period when conflicts are sufficiently fluid to permit successful attempts at solving them. Much of the agony and bitterness of the Palestinian part of the Arab/Israeli equation could have been prevented had aggressive measures been undertaken to alleviate the issue immediately following the 1948 war. After 1956 a more modest chance of altering the situation presented itself. Following the 1967 war, the near collapse of the radical camp, combined with de facto Israeli control of lands containing the bulk of the Palestinian population, seemed to offer a spectacular chance to end the stalemate. Immediately following the war, no Arab state was in a position to resist an imposed settlement. But by August 1967, Arab leaders meeting in Khartoum had sufficiently regrouped to adopt a rigid stance: no peace, no negotiations, no recognition of Israel.

In the aftermath of October 1973, another such state of flux has arisen; but its duration will be limited, if previous historical patterns repeat themselves. The available time is defined in the general sense by Arab expectations of a United States-imposed settlement. Statements by American spokesmen have, intentionally or not, raised Arab hopes in that regard to a fever pitch. If or when these hopes are dashed, if these expectations turn to disillusionment, Arab moderates will lose whatever control over events they now possess. The older pattern of Arab politics, the efforts by Arab leaders to protect themselves from accusations that they contributed to a United States-sponsored "sellout," will reassert itself with a vengeance. Any U.S. gains from the current situation will be wiped out; the Arab world will move even further from the West, toward the Soviets.

In a more specific sense, negotiating time is delineated by the political situation facing Sadat. In opting for a go-it-alone policy of accepting the U.S. negotiating framework, he has risked everything. At present he is under sustained and increasing attack, both within and without Egypt for identifying himself too closely with the Americans. He badly needs, at the very least, to have the Syrians, Jordanians, or Palestinians brought into the negotiations to demonstrate that he is not alone in seeking a settlement.

If these expectations are shattered, if Sadat is either overthrown or forced to radically reverse himself, war becomes almost inevitable. If there is any overriding military lesson to be learned from 1973 and past wars, it is that the attacking forces have an overwhelming initial advantage. Therefore, surprise becomes the critical military factor; and defense against surprise or preemption becomes the corollary consideration. The critical importance of a

successful first strike has resulted in the institutionalization of uncertainty: a situation where neither side can afford to be caught off
guard; a situation in which a policy of preemption becomes infinitely
preferable to a policy of caution.

In Cyprus, too, time is short, but it is not nearly so critical.
In the long run, however, it is, paradoxically, only a matter of time
before extremists in the Greek Cypriot community organize an anti-
Turkish insurgency. The cycle of violence and counterviolence on
Cyprus will escalate again; the uneasy dialogue now going on between
Greek and Turk will cease. And with this escalation, the chances
for a negotiated settlement will diminish.

ALTERNATIVE STRATEGIES

U.S. policy choices with respect to the Middle East/Mediter-
ranean may not be undertaken in vacuo; they must be fitted into a
global framework of preferences, a global pattern of resource allocation. In this respect the twin issues of the strategic importance
of the area, in relation to other areas in which the United States has
national interests, and the character of Soviet intentions toward the
area become crucial in defining Middle Eastern policy options.

The strategic importance of the Middle East for the United
States has been, and will remain, the subject of considerable debate.
One side argues that the Middle East is not important to the United
States: its oil resources are not crucial to the U.S. economy; and
its military value, in terms of base sites, has diminished with the
development of longer-range weapons systems. [24] Alternatively, it
is averred that the Middle East is critical to U.S. security for precisely the converse reasons: access to oil is essential to NATO;
NATO is the key to European security; European security is vital to
U.S. security; therefore Middle Eastern oil is critical to the United
States. In addition, the Middle East is still geographically important,
if not in the positive sense of an actual U.S. presence, then in the
negative sense that an expanded Soviet presence would constitute a
threat to NATO's southern flank and to maritime traffic in and through
the Mediterranean. [25] In part, the foregoing arguments depend on
assessments of Soviet policy toward the area, assessments that are
based on considerations outside the scope of this chapter. In this
connection, there are three general arguments as to Soviet intentions
and objectives: maximalist, minimalist, and targets of opportunity.

The maximalist view holds that the Soviets are out to dominate
the area, to exclude the United States entirely, and to utilize the
Middle East as a lever to alter the global balance of power against
the West. [26] In this scenario, the Soviets are using Middle Eastern

conflicts, especially the Arab-Israeli issue, to polarize the Arabs against the West. As long as the West continues to back Israel, the Soviets will continue to expand into the area.

The minimalist view is the converse. The Soviets are in the Middle East unwillingly, being forced to move into it in response to U.S. moves. Having once projected their power into the region, the Soviets have found themselves saddled with unreliable Arab allies and faced with a potential confrontation with the United States over issues not directly related to Soviet security. Therefore, the Soviets are reluctant to expand their position, and would prefer to retrench, if possible. The Arab/Israeli conflict, in particular, presents the Soviets with problems, not opportunities, because of its escalatory potential and because of the demands of its Arab clients that it act in their behalf. This being the case, the Soviet position in the Middle East is extremely unstable, its clients liable to defect--as the Egyptians did in 1972--if their exaggerated demands on the Soviets are not met. [27]

The targets-of-opportunity argument falls between these polar extremes. The gist here is that Soviet strategy in the Middle East cannot be (and is not, in fact) divorced from general considerations affecting Soviet policy, considerations of detente with the United States, problems of containing Chinese power, domestic demands for economic development, and so forth. In this situation, Soviet leadership finds itself constrained on a number of counts: to the east, by the Chinese; to the west by NATO and the United States. The only avenue open to a successful forward policy is to the south, to the Middle East. And this area has any number of attractive features insofar as the Soviets are concerned. With relatively little effort, they can destabilize the area, polarize its several conflicts to the detriment of the United States, possibly unhinge NATO, or adversely affect European economies backing Arab economic extremism. Therefore, by judiciously promoting controlled conflict, the Soviets can play the superpower game with small risk. [28]

Assuming, then, that the 1973 explosion of violence cleared the air enough to permit negotiations, what approaches are open to the United States? Three broad alternatives have been presented: the Geneva Conference framework, providing for a comprehensive settlement of all outstanding issues between Arabs and Israelis (or Greeks and Turks, or oil producers and consumers) in the course of simultaneous negotiations among all parties; or shuttle diplomacy, a sequential approach in which issues would be compartmentalized and settled on a step-by-step basis, the approach currently pursued by Secretary Kissinger; or collegial diplomacy, a combined effort by both the United States and its major allies.

The attractiveness of the first approach lies in its simplicity. Get all the parties together, get them talking, and then broker a solution acceptable to all. This has the additional advantage of being immediate rather than protracted, a sudden burst of crisis diplomacy which would then avert war.

In fact, this has been tried on a number of occasions, and it has not worked. The differences have been too great, the interests too complex, and the timing too delicate. Secretary Kissinger summed up U.S. disillusionment with this approach: ". . . the intractibility of the issues would only be compounded by their being combined. Bringing all the parties, including the most irreconcilable, together in one dramatic public negotiation was an invitation to a deepened stalemate. . . ."[29]

Alternatively, the step-by-step approach could be tried. This might avoid the problem of interlacing issues by breaking them down into components. The component easiest to negotiate would then be dealt with. If a successful compromise was reached, the next component would be tackled, and so on. By so doing, it has been argued, the parties concerned would develop a stake in the negotiating process, mutual confidence would be built up, and momentum created that would facilitate further agreements.[30]

There are pitfalls here also. Such negotiations would of necessity be protracted, giving ample time for any party interested in preventing a settlement to intervene. For example, radicals such as the Palestinian "Rejection Front" could take advantage of the situation and torpedo the talks by some act of terror. Moreover, there are problems of momentum. If the talks reach deadlock, as they did in March 1974, there is no alternative diplomatic substitute immediately available. Tensions immediately escalate; military alerts are called; a new crisis is created. Therefore, this approach tends to succeed or fail according to the virtuosity of the principal negotiator--in this case Secretary Kissinger, and to inject problems of personality into an already complex situation.

The third approach has been suggested as a variant to shuttle diplomacy. The argument here is that the United States surround itself with a coalition of European allies committed to the same negotiating stance. This coalition would then attempt to move the parties concerned toward a settlement. Such a tactic, it is averred, would substantially reduce the risks posed by shuttle diplomacy. The United States and its allies would be in agreement from the outset; the rancorous breach in NATO that occurred as a consequence of differences over the October crisis might be avoided. The United States would not be diplomatically overextended, in the sense that unreasonable expectations would be placed on them. The responsibility for upholding any settlement would be shared among several major powers.[31]

In any event, negotiations on the Arab/Israeli issue had become critical by 1976. They could be the key to re-creating
Mediterranean/Middle East stability. A settlement of, or even a
movement on, this issue could positively affect not only Arab/
Israeli relations, but also the Cyprus and energy questions. In the
Arab area, movement on this question could release forces of nationalism and Soviet clients, notably Syria and Iraq. In these countries, as in Egypt, nationalism is a driving force for national autonomy. This force has been held in check by the overriding military
dependence on Soviet arms. If the level of tensions between Arabs
and Israelis were reduced or Western sources of arms became available as a consequence of nonbelligerence agreements, then dependence on the USSR might radically diminish. The Arab drive for independence would be directed more equally at the Soviets, instead of
entirely at the West. Arab movement away from the Soviets, already
apparent in the case of Egypt, would be expanded to other Arab countries.

In terms of energy and Cyprus, a settlement would have equally
positive benefits. Arab oil producers' actions would no longer be
constrained by the exigencies of Arab/Israeli relations; economic interests could then be given full play. And the major markets for
Arab oil, and therefore Arab economic interests, are in the Free
World. As for Cyprus, it should be remembered that one of the reasons for bringing Greece and Turkey into NATO was to block Russian
expansion into the Mediterranean. The extension of this arrangement
via CENTO was designed to further block Russian movement into the
Arab world. It failed because the Soviets were able to leapfrog these
arrangements, and develop positions in the Arab world itself. If,
however, the Arab Middle East is stabilized from within, and there
is Arab nationalist pressure on Soviet facilities, then the urgency
for holding the line at Greece and Turkey lessens. This, in turn,
may give time and, with time, flexibility in dealing with the Cyprus
problem. Negotiations might no longer be conducted under the threat
of immediate Soviet exploitation of the gap in eastern NATO.

NOTES

1. See George Lenczowski, ed., United States Interests in the
Middle East (Washington, D.C.: American Enterprise Institute,
1968); Alan Dowty, "Does the United States Have a 'Real' Interest in
Supporting Israel," in Great Issues of International Politics, ed.
Morton A. Kaplan (Chicago: Aldine Publishing Company, 1970), pp.
312-20; Harry N. Howard, "U.S. Interest in the Middle East," Military Review 50, no. 1 (January 1970): 64-76; William M. Carpenter

and Stephen P. Gilbert, Great Power Interests and Conflicting Objectives in the Mediterranean-Middle East-Persian Gulf Region (Arlington, Va.: Stanford Research Institute, 1974), for various lists of U.S. interests.

2. Admiral T. H. Moorer, "The Strategic Importance of the Middle East," Commanders Digest 15, no. 22 (May 30, 1974).

3. See C. O. Huntley, "Arab Versus Jew: The Evolution of Two National Strategies," Naval War College Review 22, no. 3 (November 1969): 69-91.

4. Malcolm Kerr, "The Arabs and Israelis: Perceptual Dimensions to their Dilemma," in The Middle East: Quest for an American Policy, ed. Wilard A. Beling (Albany: The State University of New York, 1973), pp. 3-31.

5. See Dankwart A. Rustow, The Cyprus Crises and United States Security Interests (Santa Monica: RAND, 1967), for an overview.

6. Steven V. Roberts, "Dispute Goes on Over Aegean Sea," New York Times, February 16, 1975.

7. Strategic Survey 1975 (London: The International Institute for Strategic Studies, 1974), pp. 30-36.

8. Malcolm Kerr, Regional Arab Politics and the Conflict with Israel (Santa Monica: RAND, 1969); George Lenczowski, "The Objects and Methods of Nasserism," in Modernization of the Arab World, ed. J. H. Thompson and R. D. Reischauer (Princeton, N.J.: D. Van Nostrand Company, Inc., 1966), pp. 197-211.

9. Fuad Itayim, "Strengths and Weaknesses of the Oil Weapon," in The Middle East and the International System. II: Security and the Energy Crisis, Adelphi Papers, no. 115 (London: The International Institute for Strategic Studies, 1975), pp. 1-7.

10. James Akins, "The Oil Crisis: This Time the Wolf Is Here," Foreign Affairs 51, no. 3 (April 1973): 462-90, was one of the few that took Arab threats to impose an embargo seriously.

11. Dowty, op. cit., provides a concise statement of this viewpoint; and Bernard Lewis, "The Great Powers, the Arabs and the Israelis," Foreign Affairs 47, no. 4 (July 1969): 642-52.

12. See Georgiana Stevens, ed., The United States and the Middle East (Englewood Cliffs, N.J.: Prentice-Hall, Inc., 1964).

13. Nadav Safran, From War to War: The Arab-Israeli Confrontation 1948-1967 (New York: Pegasus, 1969), contains the most persuasive statement of this argument.

14. Robert E. Hunter, The Energy "Crisis" and the U.S. Foreign Policy, Headline Series no. 16 (Washington, D.C.: Foreign Policy Association, 1973), predicted the conditions under which an oil embargo would be imposed.

15. J. Bowyer Bell, "Violence at a Distance: Greece and the Cyprus Crisis," Orbis 18, no. 3 (Fall 1974): 791-808.

16. John C. Campbell, "The Mediterranean Crisis," Foreign Affairs 53, no. 4 (July 1975): 605-24, for an analysis of Middle Eastern/Mediterranean politics in these terms.

17. Richard L. Crump, "The October War: A Postwar Assessment," Military Review 54, no. 8 (August 1974): 12-26, as well as the other accounts of the war cited in the bibliography.

18. John C. Campbell, "The Arab-Israeli Conflict: An American Policy," Foreign Affairs 49, no. 1 (October 1970): 51-69, for an articulation of the thesis that Israeli military preponderance would be maintained for some time into the future.

19. Anwar al-Sadat quoted in FBIS, October 1, 1974.

20. There is considerable debate over the Soviet role in planning and carrying out the Arab attack. For contrasting arguments see Alvin Z. Rubinstein, "Moscow and Cairo: Currents of Influence," Problems of Communism 23, no. 4 (July-August 1974).

21. Field Marshall Ahmad Ismail Ali, interview in al-Ahram, November 18, 1973.

22. Anwar al-Sadat interview in Ruz al-Yusuf, translated in FBIS, September 23, 1974. Liberation was the objective of the battle and reactivation was one of the means that we used to shock the enemy, those behind him and the entire world to make them understand our cause and compel the enemy to retreat. We understand and realize the dimensions of the international balance as well as the sensitivity and importance of the Middle East to the West and the East. Thus, the October War was a limited war which was intended to strike the Israeli theory of security at its core.

23. Ghassan Tueni, "After October: Military Conflict and Political Change in the Middle East," Journal of Palestine Studies 3, no. 4 (Summer 1974): 114-30.

24. Dowty, op. cit., provides a concise statement of this viewpoint. See also Lewis, op. cit.

25. Lenczowski, United States Interests in the Middle East, op. cit., contains this thesis.

26. George Lenczowski, Soviet Advances in the Middle East (Washington, D.C.: American Enterprise Institute, 1971); Tom Little, "The New Arab Extremists: A View from the Arab World," Conflict Studies, no. 4 (May 1970).

27. A. S. Becker and A. L. Horelick, Soviet Policy in the Middle East (Santa Monica: RAND, 1970), provides an authoritative analysis of the options facing Soviet decision-makers dealing with Middle Eastern politics; Robert Hunter, The Soviet Dilemma in the Middle East: Problems of Commitment, Adelphi Paper no. 59 (London: The Institute for Strategic Studies, 1969).

28. Campbell, op. cit.

29. Secretary Henry A. Kissinger, "Global Peace, the Middle East, and the United States," The Secretary of State (Washington, D.C.: Bureau of Public Affairs, September 16, 1975).

30. Ibid.

31. Campbell, op. cit.

7

AFRICA:
THE PROBLEM OF
NATIONALISM
E. Philip Morgan

THE ISSUE

In many respects, Africa poses the same challenge to American leadership in the 1980s that was posed by Southeast Asia in the 1950s: adolescent nationalism. In contrast with the Middle East security environment, where intraregional war threatens vital petroleum sources, the security environment of Africa promises a succession of subnational civil wars and violence attending the early growth of new nations, still searching for self-identity. Such violence will threaten vital resources (and the investments of American transnational corporations) at the least, and existing or potential base rights for the new deployment of American military power at the most.

For new Congressional and Executive leaders of 1977, the critical issue is one of policy perspective. What should be the American role in the political and economic development of the African states? Should the United States take a position in the 1980s similar to its paternalistic approach to Southeast Asia in the 1950s? If not, what should be the alternative? Perceived incorrectly, this issue could consume billions of dollars and thousands of American lives in futile causes. Perceived properly, the American role may help direct the enormous energy of African nationalism into constructive channels.

BACKGROUND OF THE ISSUE

Prior to World War II, U.S. behavior would suggest that America had no policy toward the bulk of Africa separate from that of its European allies. The territories of Africa were regarded as as extensions of their respective metropolitan colonial powers, and their peoples played a role in the security interests of the Allies by way of the national directives of the respective European power concerned. (The possible exception here was the Union of South Africa, which, in aiding the Allied cause, was more independent and selective in evaluating Anglo-American interests against her own.) The United States did not perceive its security interests in Africa apart from those of its European allies until after World War II.

As the political map of the continent began to change in the late 1950s, America was presented with a host of new states, seventeen in 1960 alone. The heady years of the early 1960s were characterized by large doses of bilateral economic and technical assistance. An American aid program was quickly devised for virtually every country soon after it became independent.[1] Great enthusiasm and optimism were generated through the rhetoric of "nation-building" and democracy. The Congo experience, however, would suggest that the U.S. response could have a strategic as well as an altruistic dimension.* African claims to nonalignment reflected a desire to remain free from Cold War entanglements. America supported such impulses to the extent it meant discouraging Soviet probes on the continent.

The behavior of the United States during the Kennedy-Johnson years suggests there was essentially one broad dimension to American policy for tropical Africa--the needs of the new states of Africa represented the opportunity--nay, the duty--of America, once a colony herself, to assist with "nation-building" and the installation of democracy. Having been an advocate of human rights, the United States could now make good on its claims by conveying its confidence and know-how to Africa, so that the new countries could liberate and consolidate themselves much as the United States had. A corollary to this posture, however, was that Africa could become yet another theater for Cold War competition and adventure. Therefore it was

---

*The U.N. force in the Congo in 1960, backed by the United States, was ostensibly there to remove the Belgian soldiers who were supporting the Katanga secession. Premier Patrice Lumumba lost patience with the United Nations for taking upon itself the role of guarantor of the peace instead of actively moving the Belgians out. When Lumumba requested military aid from the USSR in order to expel the Belgians and secure Katanga himself, the United States, through its U.N. officials, chose sides in what was essentially a local dispute between President Joseph Kasavubu and Lumumba. The United States thus became deeply involved in the internal affairs of the Congo. See Melvin Gurtow, The U.S. Against the Third World (New York: Praeger, 1974), Ch. 3.

in the general strategic interest of the United States to assist African states with stable, enlightened governments.

Ali Mazrui once characterized U.S. policy toward Africa during the Kennedy-Johnson years as a combination of "missionary" and "Boy Scout" impulses.[2] The missionary dimension was the zeal with which democracy, nation-building, and the containment of radicalism were purveyed; and the Boy Scout aspect was the innocence, optimism, and naivete of the American outlook, which missed the irony of the self-fulfilling character of America, a great power, getting involved in African affairs. Since American policy in tropical Africa at that time was vague, one has to conclude that the security dimension was implicit: African success in nation-building would bring stability, and that would discourage the Soviets or Chinese from "fishing in troubled waters." Stability would require the development of local resources; thus U.S. aid and private investment would also be instrumental.

The above paragraphs apply essentially to the independent African states north of the Zambezi River. In contrast, U.S. security interests in southern Africa have been slightly more explicit. It is a fact, dating back to World War II, that the Republic of South Africa has been perceived to be of special strategic significance to the United States. This is no doubt because of its location, industrial economy (read military capability), and explicitly anti-Communist ideology. In purely military terms, a friendly South Africa has been perceived to be important to the United States for many years. America had a military aid program for South Africa until the 1963 U.N. arms embargo.[3] (The United States has honored the U.N. arms embargo with regard to weaponry and equipment for the South African military or police.) Most South African military officers attended courses at U.S. military staff colleges, such as Ft. Leavenworth, until 1965.

By the mid-1960s, however, a genuine debate was engaged on what the posture of the United States toward South Africa ought to be. The State Department had to express its disdain for apartheid. Not only did U.S. relations with the rest of Africa depend on it, but the South African system stands against America's basic national myths. The period was also the high point of the black reform movement in the United States. A multifaceted and informed lobby against normal relations with South Africa was growing in size and voice, including a more critical Congressional subcommittee. By the later years of the decade the compromise was that the United States was not supplying the military in South Africa, but it was not discouraging the nearly $1 billion of U.S. private investment from expanding.

Another feature of the Southern Africa region that had a security dimension for U.S. policy-makers were the Portuguese territories of Angola and Mozambique. The persistence of the Portuguese in defending the territories in Africa as logical extensions of mainland Portugal made a categorical response by the United States difficult. * Portugal is a member of NATO. Even though the United States might have sympathized with the liberation movements, America could not openly undermine an ally. Not only did the United States need continued access to bases in the Azores; but over thirty U.S. companies had invested in Angola by 1970, involving $200 million. So the United States stipulated that no NATO weapons were to be used by Portugal in the war being waged to retain her empire. The extent to which this stipulation was honored was to plague the United States intermittently in her relations with Africa and the Third World until 1974.

As the end of the decade drew near, Africa in general took a back seat to other concerns of President Nixon and Henry Kissinger, the President's Security Advisor. America was preoccupied with Southeast Asia and the Middle East, on the one tension-ridden hand, and with great-power detente on the other (the opening to China and improved political relations with the USSR). The Nixon-Kissinger security strategy remained essentially Eurocentric, or at least great-power "centric," meaning that a new but stable relationship was being sought with the main centers of industrial-military power in the world: Europe, the USSR, the People's Republic of China, and Japan. Africa, including South Africa, was not a major area of security concern in the late 1960s relative to other points on the globe. The only notable American responses to African affairs in the late 1960s were that William Rogers, the Secretary of State during Nixon's first term, officially disengaged the United States from a maverick white Rhodesia, and that the United States stayed materially, if not morally, uninvolved in the Nigerian war.

Perhaps a few other observations help account for the lack of a clearer focus of American policy, security or otherwise, on Africa in the early 1970s. The great development decade in Africa simply had not happened.

---

*Just after the Angolan rebellion began in 1961, the United States supported a U.N. resolution against Portuguese colonial possessions. The United States also banned the commercial sale of arms to Portugal and reduced military assistance from $25 million to $3 million that same year. See Melvin Gurtow, The U.S. Against the Third World (New York: Praeger, 1974), p. 73. But this firm posture did not last. Various crises led the United States to retreat on its criticism because it needed access to the Azores base. The total military assistance program for Portugal in fiscal years 1950-70 has been reported as $319.7 million, of which $310.2 million was delivered before FY 1964. Ibid., p. 75.

The democracy not only has failed to take hold, but the African landscape came to be plagued with almost cyclical coups. Bilateral technical assistance was so mixed in its outcome that it had to be rather fundamentally rethought by both recipients and donors. American aid to Africa declined absolutely throughout the 1960s: from $326 million in 1962 to $155 million by 1970.[4] Deliberation insurgencies in Mozambique and Angola were stalled, faction ridden, and morale was low; so it appeared there would be no basic changes there. In South Africa, all organized internal resistance had been crushed since the mid-1960s.

As we approach the pivotal year 1974, the previous six years having been a case of "benign neglect" by the Kissinger foreign policy perspective, there is essentially one broad security interest in Africa which one can identify as important to the United States: the concern that localized political conflicts in Africa not convert great power political competition into great power intervention and confrontation.

CHANGING CONDITIONS

With the coup d'etat in Portugal in April 1974, everything has changed in Southern Africa. That seeming hyperbole is warranted by just looking at the map: independent status for Mozambique and Angola removed the buffers around Rhodesia and South Africa. Perhaps more importantly, the capitulation of Portugal effectively removes the psychological underpinning for the whites about the effectiveness of African guerrilla insurgencies. No longer can white Rhodesians and South Africans be sure that a guerrilla insurgency could be contained. That prospect has caused major reconsiderations in Pretoria, and Rhodesia cannot now be assured of South African military assistance. (South Africa has withdrawn the units of South African police that had been assisting the Smith regime in containing the nationalist insurgency.)

The Southern Africa region, after April 1974, changed so rapidly--and is still changing--that it is hard to characterize the alterations to date in a way that might be good for a year's worth of working assumptions. The following are the main interacting political elements for the immediate future:

● Mozambique, now independent, has announced its intention to pursue a revolutionary transformation policy.

● The constitutional situation in Rhodesia is stalemated, aggravated by pressure on both parties to the negotiations by elements of their respective constituencies to take a tougher line (at the time of writing it appears that a renewed shooting war could break out almost any time, certainly by 1976).

● A fragmented, bloody civil war in Angola, about which Portugal can do little, with outside interests becoming more involved, drags on.

● South Africa indicates that it will give up its claim to
Namibia, but on terms embodied in some pluralistic experiment
to be worked out by the peoples of the territory, not by the United
Nations.

● A newly aggressive diplomatic effort has been mounted by
the Vorster government to Persuade Ian Smith to settle with his
majority in Rhodesia, to persuade other African states that South
Africa is an "African" state, and to persuade the Western defense
alliance that South Africa is crucial to its viability in the face of
the move to the left in Southern Europe and the increased Soviet
presence in the Indian Ocean.

The meaning of these events for the security interests of the
United States will be examined in the next section. Before we do that,
we must note another arena of major change on the continent with
which the above events converge.

Once of strategic interest to the major powers of the nineteenth
century, the Horn of Africa has again become a focus of increasing
international interest. The Horn normally includes Somalia, Djibouti,
Ethiopia, and Sudan, although countries contiguous with these are relevant to our discussion. Some salient political changes in the Horn in
recent years include the following:

● The Soviet Union has been giving military assistance to,
and now has a facility in, the Somali Republic. *

---

*Aid to Somalia and Ethiopia, 1954-73
(millions of U.S. dollars)

	Somalia	Ethiopia
Economic		
United States	79	249
USSR	90	18
China	110[a]	84[b]
Military		
United States	--[c]	200
USSR	55	--[c]
China	n. a.	n. a.

---

a = offered, 1971.
b = offered, 1972.
c = negligible.
n. a. = not available.

Source: Helen Desfosses, "Naval Strategy and Aid Policy: A
Study of Soviet-Somali Relations," in Chinese and Soviet Aid to Africa,
ed. Warren Weinstein (New York: Praeger, 1975), p. 194.

- The USSR has substantially increased its presence in the Red Sea and Indian Ocean sea-lanes (see Chapter 8).[5]
- Aid from the People's Republic of China is now quite visible in the region (Tanzania, Somalia).[6]
- The United States has given military assistance to Ethiopia since 1953, which is now being reviewed because of the virtual civil war.[7]
- The Eritrean secessionist movement is being supported by Arab countries.
- The Suez Canal has been reopened.

A third important context of change in Africa is not geospecific-- it is the generic, even endemic, tendency toward economic malaise in most of the poor, and relatively poor, countries of Africa. Inflation, deficit trade balances, shortages of foreign exchange, and other fall-out from the world economy combine with high birth rates and all the other problems of social integration to make nation-building a very problematic venture in the 1980s. The point of raising this contextual issue here is that there are likely to be breakdowns in presently unpredictable places in Africa that, though traceable to the economic crisis, will have security relevance.

What do the changes in southern Africa and the area of the Horn mean for U.S. security interests? What are the problematic situations raised? A genuine overriding reality for the United States is that Africa has indeed become an arena of great-power competition. Whether or not such political competition becomes a security issue at any given time or place depends upon many things, one of which is the degree of rivalry between the powers. Are two powers willing to coexist in the same area, competing for political influence and good-will with primary regard for the well-being of the people and environment of that area?

The answer to this is important because of the buildup of Soviet and Chinese aid in the Horn and East Africa. There is conspicuous Chinese assistance in the TanZam Railway project.[8] More significantly, continuing Soviet military assistance to the Somali Republic is facing competition from the Chinese. Among other things, the Chinese are building a 600-mile north-south road.[9]

A clue as to how important it is to the USSR that the Chinese presence in the area be contained is the military assistance the Soviets have been giving Idi Amin in Uganda. Given Amin's threats to his neighbors, the willingness of the Soviets to provide the mercurial and unpredictable general with missiles suggests that the Soviets might be more concerned with countering the Chinese presence than with building stability in the area. Certainly this has caused considerable anxiety in Kenya, since two of her immediate neighbors now have military strength far exceeding her own. If this interpretation is correct, then the presence of the two Eastern powers could be a conflict-provoking combination anywhere--and that creates a security issue for the United States. How should we respond? One trend in superpower detente is that the United States and the Soviet Union may reach mutual agreement that stability characterized by political competition is better for both parties than instability and political conflict, at least in most areas of the world. But the Soviets have no such detente with the Chinese--and that creates conflicts.

Ethiopia is no longer a stabilizing force in the area because of civil strife there. The Eritrean secessionist movement, with its headquarters in Damascus, has lately been every bit the match of the Ethiopian army. The new Ethiopian military regime is encountering civilian unrest on a number of fronts after having summarily executed over sixty former government officials in November 1974, and embarking immediately upon a land nationalization policy. The Ethiopian government has requested more U.S. military assistance, but because of the instability in the area the United States is reluctant to add more weapons to the conflict and is reviewing its military commitments to Ethiopia. A dimension of any debate on what the U.S. response here should be will be whether the "new" Ethiopia or its location on the Red Sea is all that crucial any more. (The U.S. communications station near Asmara will be phased out in any case.)[10]

A number of local political problems could create the potential for local interstate conflict. The unresolved Somali irredentism in Ethiopia and Kenya could destabilize the situation quickly if the Somalis made a move to take advantage of a vulnerable Ethiopia and weaker Kenya by asserting claims on the Somali-inhabited provinces of the two countries and threatened to use force to acquire them as part of a greater Somali Republic. Arab support for the Eritrean Liberation Front through the supply of Soviet weaponry could close off Ethiopia's access to the Red Sea, except for the railway through Djibouti (FTAI), which might tempt Ethiopia. The increasingly fluid political situation in Kenya could create a vacuum, not just in the event of President Jomu Kenyatta's death, but perhaps even before that as Kenya's internal politics boils amid the revelations of large-scale elite corruption. None of these local accelerators to violence may occur in the next year, but any one of them could.

Further south, newly independent Mozambique will attract both Soviet and Chinese assistance to support its dramatic plans for radical transformation. Should Mozambique decide to aid militarily a guerrilla war in Rhodesia, or less likely in South Africa, the Machel government would no doubt call upon one or both of the Eastern powers to provide assistance.

The ongoing civil strife in Angola, which is likely to be protracted, affords yet another opportunity for great-power involvement. The three contending groups in Angola are divided along ethnic, ideological, and leadership lines. In addition, a valuable appendage of Angola, the enclave of Cabinda, is separated from the country by the Zaire River. Apart from the outside interests now focusing on that tiny spot, there are contending forces within Cabinda itself whose goals range from alignment with a particular group in Angola to independence for the enclave. Zaire is perhaps more critical to the outcome in Angola than any of the major powers, although the United States and USSR have been identified with the FNLA and MPLA, respectively, for some time. So the possibility for Angola becoming an international issue is growing.[11]

Before we can examine the possible responses the United States might make to this complex environment, one has to inject a major change in great-power presence to the east of Africa: that of the Soviet navy in the Indian Ocean. The meaning of this has been a subject for debate for a number of years, with the Pentagon calling for more ships and developing a base at Diego Garcia to accommodate large ships and transport aircraft. The argument appears to focus on whether this is indeed a changed strategic situation for the United States or whether military technology as it exists could compensate for this situation should a crisis occur. The military takes the position that this development represents a change that could at best embarrass the United States from time to time, or at worst inhibit the movement of the U.S. fleet to a crisis point in the East, or impede access to oil markets. The State Department seems to view this development as essentially a political rather than a military exercise by the Soviets.[12] South Africa, of course, plays up her own potential strategic significance, given the buildup in the Indian Ocean, and wants the West at least to acknowledge her importance to the sea-lanes in the Indian Ocean with friendly agreements regarding U.S. and Western use of the expanded naval facilities at Simonstown on the Cape of Good Hope.

Thus we can identify a number of problematic situations, or issues, that interact to complicate the search for an appropriate U.S. response:

• Local inter- or intrastate political conflict, exacerbated by great-power competition--this includes the countries of the Horn, Rhodesia, and Angola for the present

• Increased Soviet naval activity in the Indian Ocean, Red Sea, and Persian Gulf

• Consequences in all these areas, or around their peripheries, to U.S. private investments or potential investments that are of longer-term strategic significance.

ALTERNATIVE RESPONSES

Given these broad issue areas and the patchwork pattern of
U.S. responses in the past, U.S. action in the near future will no
doubt continue to be piecemeal. We can get some clues as to how
these responses are likely to go by looking at responses in the months
and weeks prior to the time of writing. We can then evaluate some
alternatives.

The United States has already taken short-term steps in the
potentially destabilized area of the Horn. It has agreed to $5 million
in military aid to Kenya, to help her bring her defense forces more
into line with those of her neighbors to the east and west (Somalia
and Uganda).[13] The United States has refrained from committing itself to more military aid to Ethiopia, except for what was already in
the pipeline, since the coup of September 1974. The Congress has
agreed to allocate $13.8 million for the upgrading of the base on
Diego Garcia in the Indian Ocean.[14] All of these measures presumably are meant to convey a message that the United States wants to
contribute to stability in the region, in the face of the increased
rivalry of the Soviets and Chinese.

Other steps the United States might take include assisting the
military regime in Ethiopia in overcoming the Eritrean secessionist
movement. Along with the U.S. aid to Kenya, this might balance
the Soviet military aid to Somalia and Uganda to some extent. However, the United States was greatly shocked by the way the Dergue
dispensed with Haile Selassie's government, and has not yet responded
to the request for $55 million more in military assistance. Also,
American military aid to the Addis Ababa government, used to wage
war against the Eritreans, might provoke the Arabs and, perhaps in
turn, the Soviets. This could threaten access to Israel's port of
Elath in the Gulf of Aqaba. The Arabs now have their own ways of
applying pressure on the United States that must be taken into account.

The United States also could build up a strong presence in the
Indian Ocean itself. When Defense Secretary Schlesinger originally
asked for funds to upgrade the base on Diego Garcia, there were
many in Congress who saw the reference to the Soviet buildup as a
scare tactic to get more funds. The debate really turns on an assessment of Soviet motives in the area. Is the USSR really attempting to
flex its military muscle, or more straightforwardly assert greater
political influence? The State Department tends toward the latter
view, the Pentagon the former.[15] Although $13.8 million was allo-
cated, the Pentagon would like more. This is likely to be difficult,
in view of the recent revelations regarding the way in which the
Diego Garcia inhabitants were removed from the island.[16] (There
may be hearings on the matter of who is responsible for the Garcians,

now living in Mauritius, who perhaps were forcibly removed from
the island by either the British, from whom Diego Garcia was leased,
or the United States). Whatever happens regarding an increased U.S.
military presence in the Indian Ocean, it will unfold rather slowly,
as it has done over the past several years, largely because the next
Congress will probably be in no mood for greater military expenditures or military encounters.

Moving down into Southern Africa, one would expect the United
States to attempt to establish good relations with the new government
of Mozambique, both as a matter of course with new states and as a
strategic necessity in view of Soviet/Chinese involvement in the area
and likely involvement in Mozambique. America was not invited to
the independence celebrations on June 25, 1975, ostensibly because
she did not assist FRELIMO in the struggle against the Portuguese,
so it is problematic whether Mozambique will welcome U.S. interest.
To date there have been no dramatic changes in Mozambique's relations in the region, especially with respect to South Africa. President Machel has not altered the open communication with South Africa,
nor curtailed the migration of Mozambique laborers to the mines.
In fact, he has intimated that Mozambique will likely sell electric
power to South Africa when the Cabora Bossa dam is operational. [17]

What the United States might do in Angola is difficult to assess.
On the one hand, it has been backing the FNLA (National Front for
the Liberation of Angola), off and on, for many years. Lately the
United States has made great efforts to work out friendly terms with
President Mobutu Sese Seko of Zaire, who also supports the FNLA.
But so do the Chinese. The Soviets support the MPLA (Popular
Movement for the Liberation of Angola), which is presently in control
of Luanda and its environs. In this complex situation a number of alternatives are possible: The United States could hedge in order to
prolong its access to the minerals of Cabinda and Zaire. If Zaire
has her eye on annexing Cabinda, the United States might stand by
and let that happen, or support Cabindan independence, if the MPLA
gets the upper hand in Angola. On the other hand, if the FNLA appears to be winning in Angola, the United States might be predisposed
to Cabinda's remaining a part of Angola. The United States has officially warned Zaire not to use its military assistance to influence the
outcome in Angola. But the United States might provide covert money
to the FNLA through Zaire, as has already been suggested in recent
reports. [18] In the short run it matters more to the United States what
happens in Portugal proper than in its colonies. A Communist Portugal could change the picture in Europe, and perhaps the strategic
significance of South Africa. At the time of writing, the social democratic forces seem to have the upper hand in Portugal.

A final arena for examining possible U.S. responses to change is vis-a-vis South Africa. For the past five to eight years, the official position on U.S./South Africa relations could best be described as a hedge--a posture with its own costs. The United States officially "abhors" the apartheid system as fundamentally wrong. Therefore it does not encourage American investments in South Africa. However, it does not actively discourage them, except in Namibia. U.S. private investment in South Africa now approximates $1.5 billion. This helps discourage U.S. politicians and policy-makers from identifying with any radical nationalist solution to the problem of the distribution of power. The United States encourages American companies to pay equal wages for equal work across the color lines, but insists it cannot force companies to do so. There is leverage there, however, if the American government chose to use it. Official restrictions on commercial dealings with adversaries have been imposed at other moments in history, as with Cuba.

At the same time, there is a lobby in the Pentagon, actively supported by South Africa, that perceives the latter as of strategic importance to U.S. security. South Africa plays up the notion of its critical sea-lanes to Europe, its vast industrial and mineral resources, and its Western ideological orientation. In this vein, the revelation in 1974 of a "tilt" of U.S. policy toward white South Africa between 1970 and 1973 reflects a continued policy of fence-straddling.[19] The option put forward in a memorandum that reached the press, especially the South Africa press, argued that the whites would determine political change in the region; therefore the United States should ease its pressure on white South Africa. The alternative measures included relaxation of the arms embargo. It has been reported that ten C-130 transport aircraft were sold to SAFAIR, a South African charter firm, between 1970 and 1974.[20] The State Department insists that this alleged tilt is not policy.[21] Naturally South Africa wishes it were, since it has continued to expand its facilities at Simonstown to accommodate ships in far greater numbers than its own navy would justify.[22] Also, South Africa has an electronic intelligence warning system at Silvermine on the Cape that reputedly can identify all ships in the South Atlantic and western Indian Ocean. South African officials are hoping the Western powers will take advantage of these facilities, but so far official U.S. policy has not. Whether the United States has some informal arrangement with South Africa that such facilities would be available to the United States in a crisis cannot, of course, be known. In any case, the uproar over the so-called "tar baby" memorandum suggests that Kissinger's State Department is still straddling.

The political costs of the ambivalent policy of the United States to South Africa are beginning to necessitate a rather fundamental

assessment of this posture. The dramatic political changes in
southern Africa present the near-term prospect that South Africa
will be the only white-minority regime left. If the United States continues to hedge, it will create important credibility problems for itself in the rest of Africa. Africa's resources are now more important to the United States than they used to be (Nigeria is America's
second largest foreign supplier of oil). The United States has now
placed over three-fourths of its private investment in Africa in
African-governed independent states. Collectively, the rest of
Africa can confound the United States at the United Nations. The
sensitivity to fundamental matters of racial equality being stronger
than ever, the U.S. veto of the African efforts to get South Africa
expelled from the United Nations caused great suspicion. In sum,
the United States has to decide whether South Africa is indeed of
strategic value to U.S. security.

So far, as is common in the general literature, we have not
questioned that South Africa is vital to the security of the Cape sea
routes. America apparently does not rely on that assumption in
practice. If it is true in principle, what is the evidence? This has
not been examined in the Indian Ocean debate, but merely asserted.
On inspection, the hedging might actually be based on ideological or
commercial grounds. If so, a reassessment is all the more important, in view of the changing configuration of those parameters, as
noted above. The costs of continuing this policy might jeopardize the
future peace in that country. Does not the absence of a firm, arms-
length posture tend to convince the Vorster government that internal
changes can be minimized? This is so far the upshot of South
Africa's overt policy. Despite the milestone speeches, nothing important has changed within the country.

Since there is obviously no consensus on the answers to these
questions within the U.S. government, perhaps a new compromise is
in order. For example, even if building up Diego Garcia into a major
naval-air base is not justified strategically, it might be a trade-off
with those who believe that the United States should shed the albatross
of South Africa. In other words, the military South African lobby
could be assuaged with an upgraded facility in the Indian Ocean that
would allow the United States to disengage from South Africa. This
would solve the moral dilemma and improve U.S. relations with
Africa in general. Such alternatives need to be explored and new
solutions found that do not require major dislocations or entering the
policy corridors of other great powers.

CONCLUSION

The largely ad hoc, incremental responses of the United States to potential and actual crises in Africa and environs suggest that security policy is ill-defined. Perhaps this is because Africa has not been of any great strategic importance to the United States in the past. Now that its importance is growing and collective action by Third World countries has been shown to be effective in confronting the industrial world, Africa might receive more cogent attention from policy-makers.

Perhaps more important for the United States in the longer run than anything that has been discussed specifically is the danger that many African states will face severe economic and financial crises in the coming years. The recent speeches of the President of the World Bank, the U.S. Secretary of State to the U.N. General Assembly, and the Shah of Iran to his OPEC colleagues suggest some awareness that stability, security, and economic well-being go together and that the present structure of the world economy is inimical to those goals.[23] It is precisely because the structure of trade and the international monetary system do not impact as negatively on the United States as they do on so many other countries that this is perhaps not appreciated for its security fallout over time. More flash points mean more ad hoc responses, uncertainty, and danger. There is a greater need now than ever to look at preventive institutional parameters for future security.

NOTES

1. The United States assisted forty countries in Africa between 1946 and 1971. See William Cotter, "American Aid to Africa," Africa Report 17, no. 7 (September-October 1972): 18.

2. "American Policy Toward Africa: The Kennedy-Johnson Years," paper presented at the Program of Eastern African Studies Seminar, Syracuse University, 1966.

3. Although the information is buried, one can get some ideas from U.S. Overseas Loans and Grants, July 1, 1945-June 30, 1973; AID Statistics, May 1974, p. 169.

4. Cotter, op. cit., p. 19.

5. There are good analyses on this development in the essays in Pt. V of Alvin J. Cottrell and R. M. Burrell, eds., The Indian Ocean: Its Political, Economic and Military Importance (New York: Praeger, 1972).

6. See the essays by George T. Yu and Warren Weinstein in Chinese and Soviet Aid to Africa, ed. Warren Weinstein (New York: Praeger, 1975).

7. J. Bowyer Bell, The Horn of Africa (New York: Crane, Russak and Co., 1973), p. 39. Also see U.S. Overseas Loans and Grants, May 1975, p. 92.

8. See George T. Yu, China's African Policy: A Study of Tanzania (New York: Praeger, 1975), for an excellent case study.

9. See Bruce D. Larkin, "Chinese Aid in Political Context, 1971-73," in Weinstein, op. cit., p. 15.

10. See interview with former Assistant Secretary of State for African Affairs, Donald Easum, in Africa Report 20, no. 1 (January-February, 1975): 2-7.

11. Kenneth L. Adelman, "Report from Angola," Foreign Affairs 53, no. 3 (April 1975): 558-74.

12. See David Johnson, "Troubled Waters for the US Navy," Africa Report 20, no. 1 (January-February 1975): 8-10. For greater depth of analysis, see Helen Desfosses in Weinstein, op. cit.

13. "U.S. to Sell Kenya $5 million in Arms," Baltimore Sun, August 20, 1975, p. 1.

14. "Diego Garcia Funds Get Final Approval," Washington Post, September 30, 1975, p. A4.

15. See Johnson, op. cit.

16. David B. Ottaway, "Diego Garcia's Ragged Residue," Washington Post, September 9, 1975.

17. "Mozambique Hydroelectric Project Passes Test," Christian Science Monitor, July 25, 1975.

18. Leslie Gelb, "East and West Said to Give Millions to Portugal and Angola," New York Times, September 25, 1975, p. 1.

19. Bruce Oudes, "South Africa Policy Watershed," Africa Report 19, no. 6 (November-December 1974): 46-50.

20. Ibid., p. 48.

21. Edward Mulcahy, "U.S. Foreign Policy Towards South Africa," African Studies Program Occasional Paper (Bloomington: Indiana University, December 1974), p. 12.

22. Neil Ulman, "Fishing for Alliances," Wall Street Journal, July 31, 1975, p. 26.

23. Hobart Rowen, "Outlook for World Poor Grim," Washington Post, September 2, 1975, p. A5; "Kissinger U.N. Speech Well Received,"ibid., p. A12; Clyde H. Farnsworth, "Countries of OPEC Agree to 10% Rise in the Price of Oil," New York Times, September 28, 1975, p. 1.

8

SOUTH ASIA:
THE PROBLEM OF
SECURE LINES OF
COMMUNICATION
Donald Charles Daniel

THE ISSUE

As part of its fiscal year 1975 budget submission to the Congress, the Department of Defense sought to obtain $32 million to convert the U.S. naval communication facility on Diego Garcia, an island in the Indian Ocean, into a logistical resupply center for U.S. naval forces operating in that ocean. The request was minuscule in light of the overall Defense Department minimum forces budget of over $83 billion, yet it served as the catalyst for a widespread and well-publicized debate that continues to this day. At issue is not only what support infrastructure the United States should maintain for naval forces in the Indian Ocean. There is another, more primary, question, and it constitutes the central issue of this chapter: What surface-ship naval presence should the United States maintain there? This question became widely discussed because of the concern of many that upgrading Diego Garcia would allow the Navy to operate more frequently in a distant ocean at a time when the wisdom of such activity was considered questionable.

The central issue has seen the formation of at least three analytically distinguishable schools of thought as to its answer. The first is made up of individuals who present and justify the official U.S. position. Prominent spokesmen here are high-ranking civilian and military officials of the Departments of State, Defense, Commerce, and Navy as well as the Arms Control and Disarmament

Dr. Daniel is an assistant professor of political science at the Naval Postgraduate School, Monterey, California. The views expressed herein are his own and do not necessarily reflect those of any branch or agency of the U.S. government.

Agency. A second school encompasses those whose views "go beyond" official U.S. policy. They tend toward that end of the opinion spectrum calling for the maximum in naval presence and will, for convenience, be called the "maximalists." Among the outspoken members of this group are academicians or commentators on national security affairs such as Alvin Cottrell, R. M. Burrell, Lawrence Griswold, and Anthony Harrigan. A third school is that of "minimalists," who fear U.S. policies "go too far" and who tend toward that end of the spectrum desiring the minimum as far as buildup of U.S. naval forces there is concerned. Outspoken minimalists include Senators Claiborne Pell and Mike Mansfield, Representative Lee Hamilton, and members of the attentive public, such as retired Rear Admiral Gene La Rocque and his staff at the Center for Defense Information.

There is no immediate urgency to resolve the debate among these groups. Indeed, from the viewpoint of policy implementation, the President can, and does, "settle" the issue when he approves or vetoes naval operating plans for the Indian Ocean. Yet it seems safe to assume that, for the next few years, there will always be policy advocates who use occasions such as a Diego Garcia request or a Presidential campaign to keep the issue alive and press for their preferred alternative. In this light, this chapter hopes to contribute constructively to the debate by presenting--albeit in composite and cursory fashion--U.S., maximalist, and minimalist alternatives together with related rationale, * and by appraising the alternatives from the viewpoint of inquiry into some of the subissues raised in the arguments associated with each school.

BACKGROUND OF THE ISSUE

Ever since 1948 the U.S. Navy has maintained a flagship and two destroyers or escorts in the Indian Ocean. These ships constitute the Middle East Force (MEF), and they perform essentially politico-diplomatic functions, such as showing the flag, demonstrating U.S. interest in that part of the world, and enhancing U.S. friendship with littoral states through an extensive schedule of port visits by individual units.

---

*The aim here is not so much to present the views of specific individuals as it is to present contrasting alternatives and arguments useful for bringing out the many ramifications of the central issue. Hence each alternative and rationale presented does not necessarily reflect all of the views of each individual associated with a particular school.

Over the years this force has occasionally been augmented for short periods of time by additional naval units. The Navy planned in 1965 to have these augmentations take place on a regular basis, but was unable to do so until 1971 because of the heavy requirements of the Vietnam War. In April 1971 the carrier Ticonderoga exercised in the Indian Ocean, followed in July by the cruiser Truxton and in September by the carrier Enterprise. Enterprise returned with her task force in December as part of the American response to the Indo-Pakistan War. That she remained for maneuvers after the crisis had subsided was explained as delayed implementation of the 1965 plans.

The Secretaries of State and Defense have since reaffirmed the policy of periodic augmentation, and the Navy has continued to implement it. For example, between October 1973--when the Navy increased its presence in response to the Yom Kippur War--to March 1975, five carriers and two cruisers have operated in the Indian Ocean. The Chief of Naval Operations provided more specific information on the policy's content when he said in January 1975 that the Navy intends to send carrier task forces there about once a quarter. The MEF remains at three ships, with no indication that any change is contemplated in its size or general makeup.

POLICY AND RATIONALE

In short, U.S. policy concerning surface-ship naval presence is to maintain the MEF and occasionally augment it (about once a quarter and during crises) with carrier task force ships or other major units. The rationale for this policy builds upon the proposition that the Indian Ocean area is important to U.S. interests and is becoming more so. Consequently, say American spokesmen, the United States must exhibit determination to protect and further its interests. They see a surface-ship naval presence serving that purpose by being one of the "diplomatic levers" available to insure that American interests are "factored into the regional political equation."[1] The MEF is described as providing tangible evidence of U.S. concern for the region, with its augmentation highlighting the region's growing importance. The fact that augmentation is periodic is viewed as a "middle option" between doing nothing beyond having the MEF and maintaining a permanently augmented force.[2]

Eight American interests worthy of protection and furtherance are specified in elaboration of the above views. Three are economic in nature, with the first summarized by one word: oil. The argument here is that the United States, a net exporter in the 1950s, now imports about one-third of its consumption, with approximately one-third of the imports coming from the Indian Ocean area. American dependence on this oil is predicted to rise to as high as 50 percent by 1980 if internal measures are not taken to restrict consumption. The fact that Western European and Japanese reliance is already higher--about 65 and 75 percent, respectively--is viewed with concern, since the United States is so closely intertwined with them economically. Any severe disruptions of their economies would have repercussions for the United States extending beyond economic well-being, since, the argument goes, the very position of the whole Western bloc in a worldwide balance of power is to a large extent a function of economic and industrial capabilities.

Though not of the same strategic importance, a second identified interest is the potential of the Indian Ocean region as a market for American goods. The United States, it is said, engaged in substantial trade with India, Pakistan, the African littoral, and the oil-producing states. This last group is singled out as most important. Prior to the OPEC boycott, they represented a $1.5 billion yearly market for U.S. goods and $500 million balance-of-payments surplus. Since the boycott, oil prices have increased fourfold, significantly increasing both the revenues available for foreign purchases and the pressure on the United States for foreign sales in order to maintain a healthy payments balance.

A third interest is that the Indian Ocean area is a focal point for American investments. The example invariably offered in this regard is that of the American oil industry, whose assets in the area are calculated to be worth over $3.5 billion.

Two specified interests are maritime in nature. Both relate to freedom of movement in and through the Indian Ocean. The first concerns merchant ship traffic. It is emphasized that, as a nation heavily dependent on the unhampered flow of international trade, the United States must stand ready to deter any activities that might threaten that flow. Special attention is given in this argument to the need to secure the safety of oil tanker traffic from the Persian Gulf, in view of Western reliance on oil from the area.

The other maritime interest relates to naval ship activities. U.S. spokesmen link American concern for the freedom of movement of naval ships with a 1971 U.N. General Assembly resolution designating the Indian Ocean as a "zone of peace." This resolution specifically called upon the great powers to halt further expansion and escalation of their military presence in the Indian Ocean. It originally passed with sixty-one nations voting for it, none against, and fifty-five, including the United States, abstaining. It was overwhelmingly reaffirmed, again with U.S. abstention, in 1972 (95-0-33), 1973 (95-0-35), and 1974 (103-0-26). The official American attitude is that, while sympathetic with the motives of some of the resolution's

sponsors, the United States must "take unswervingly the position that
the high seas are not to be limited by any group of nations, particularly . . . those who happen to be on a particular ocean."[3] Because
the Indian Ocean has been designated a zone of peace, a periodically
augmented presence there is useful, it is argued, to reinforce the
point that the United States does not intend to be restricted by such
designations.

Finally, American arguments suggest that the United States has
three closely connected political interests in the Indian Ocean area.
One is to exhibit support for regional friends and allies. Another is
to insure the stability and security of the region. More specifically,
say American officials, the United States must act both to deter potential threats to stability and to meet actual threats as they arise.
Threats involve the destabilizing activities of outside powers (such as
the Soviet Union) and the destabilizing consequences of intraregional
conflicts or rivalries. Using the Yom Kippur War as an example,
U.S. spokesmen contend that visible U.S. naval power during the war
"demonstrated the importance we attach to our diplomatic objective
of bringing the parties together to seek a peaceful resolution of the
issues that . . . produced so much discord and strife. . . ." While
it is not the American desire, they add, to play the role of a policeman, the United States must act to make it "clear that conditions of
stability" constitute "the right way to settle intraregional problems."[4]

A third political interest is an alleged need for the United States
to respond to the Soviet naval presence in the Indian Ocean. The Soviets, it is pointed out, rarely operated there prior to 1968, yet in
that one year they nearly matched the United States in total number
of ship-days (defined as one ship operating for one day) in that ocean.
(See Table 8.1.) By the end of 1973 their forces had 5.5 times the
number of ship-days. While the permanent American presence remains the three-ship MEF, the permanent Soviet presence in 1974-75
grew to about twenty naval and naval-associated ships.

Most simply put, the government argument is that these forces
further Soviet interests, often at the expense of American interests.
For instance, during times of crises they are built up to support
Soviet allies and to neutralize corresponding U.S. buildups. Their
capability, furthermore, to cut oil lines of communication automatically gives them political leverage vis-a-vis oil consumers and oil
producers alike. Their port visits, to cite a third example, serve
to win and cement friendships with states such as Somalia, which,
at one time, had been pro-West but is now definitely pro-Soviet.

In view of such activities, American spokesmen believe it imperative that the United States augment its naval presence. While
they do not believe it necessary to match the Soviets ship for ship,
they are concerned to prove to all--including the Soviets--that the

TABLE 8.1

U.S. and Soviet Navy Presence in Indian Ocean
(in ship days)

	1968 US	1968 USSR	1969 US	1969 USSR	1970 US	1970 USSR	1971 US	1971 USSR	1972 US	1972 USSR	1973 US	1973 USSR
Carriers	6	0	0	0	5	0	6	0	23	0	80	0
Surface combatants[a]	1,380	405	1,010	640	870	790	670	1,030	940	2,380	1,310	2,840
Amphibious	0	0	0	110	0	300	185	290	25	275	20	265
Auxiliaries	210	445	280	875	220	1,080	340	1,245	425	2,780	670	4,350
MSC auxiliaries/ USSR Naval Assoc.												
Merships	190	b	30	b	155	b	145	400	25	780	70	455
AGS/AGOR	0	815	0	640	0	415	0	100	0	490	0	115
AGI	0	100	0	10	0	20	0	10	0	30	0	0
Subtotal	1,786	1,765	1,320	2,275	1,250	2,605	1,346	3,075	1,438	6,735	1,550	8,025
SESS/SVRS[c]	0	b	0	1,391	0	972	0	772	0	1,268	0	519
Total	1,786	1,765	1,320	3,666	1,250	3,577	1,346	3,847	1,438	8,003	1,550	8,544

[a]Cruisers, destroyers, destroyer escorts, and minesweepers.
[b]No record.
[c]Space event support ships/space vehicle recovery ships.

Source: Drawn from statement by Rear Admiral Charles D. Grojean, Director, Politico-Military Policy Division, Office of the Chief of Naval Operations, July 11, 1974 as found in Military Construction Authorization Fiscal Year 1975: Hearings before the Subcommittee on Military Construction, Committee on Armed Services, U.S. Senate, 93rd Cong., 2nd Sess., p. 144.

United States will act to protect its interests against any Soviet
threat, to prevent undisputed Soviet naval preponderance in the area,
and to guard against being squeezed out of the area. This last concern reflects the fear that the substantial Soviet naval presence
might "come to be regarded as an acceptable part of the political
landscape while any augmentation of [U.S.] forces from their present
levels might be regarded as unacceptable if not provocative." Should
that occur, the argument goes, the United States might then find itself
"being squeezed out . . . while Soviet influence would grow. . . ."[5]

Periodic augmentation is presented as not only serving these
American needs but also as corresponding to the desires of some
Indian Ocean leaders for a balancing of Soviet naval power. On this
point, U.S. spokesmen acknowledge that augmentation runs counter
to the publicly expressed views of a great many of the Indian Ocean
states and peoples. They indicate, however, that some leaders from
the area have communicated privately that they are "not nearly as
upset by the notion of our presence" as might be concluded from public statements and, indeed, would be "more upset by continued imbalance of the Soviet presence. . . ."[6] They cannot make their desires public, it is said, because the topic of the U.S. presence is
politically too sensitive with their people.

ALTERNATIVE STRATEGIES

The alternative generally desired (with some variations) by
maximalists "goes beyond" U.S. policy in two ways. It calls upon
the United States to permanently augment its naval presence and to
initiate a coordinated effort with allies aimed at permanently balancing Soviet naval power in the Indian Ocean.

The maximalists accept most of the arguments underlying U.S.
government policy. They differ in giving more exclusive attention to
what they view as concerted Soviet efforts to subvert or control the
states of the area--especially oil-producers and countries strategically located for dominating trade routes. They contend that Indian
Ocean states cannot be expected to maintain their friendship with the
West or to publicly welcome a permanently augmented U.S. presence
in the absence of steadfast U.S. resolve to provide such a presence.

Being skeptical that Congress would approve the expenditures
necessary to allow the United States to neutralize the Soviet threat
alone, the maximalists recommend that the United States put pressure, if necessary, on Western European and Indian Ocean allies to
provide both naval forces and bases in a common effort to balance
the Soviets. In this regard, they believe that no state should be ignored, including strategically located South Africa, a "natural ally"
regardless of its "household management."[7]

Generally accepted minimalist policy is that the United States should not--except on relatively rare occasions--augment its Indian Ocean naval forces beyond the low visibility presence associated with the MEF. In support of this policy, there are some minimalists who question just how important the Indian Ocean area really is to U.S. interests. Their view is that the "U.S. has no vital interests at stake in the region and . . . U.S. security interests there are comparatively limited."[8] In elaboration they quote from official U.S. policy statements to that effect made in the early 1970s and before. They also contend--in response to arguments that the region has recently taken on added importance because of oil--that the United States demonstrated during the OPEC boycott that "it can survive for a long period without Mideast oil."[9]   Prior to the boycott, these minimalists point out, the Mideast accounted for only 9 percent of U.S. oil consumption and an even smaller share (about 2 percent) of total U.S. energy sources consumed.

Regardless of the importance of the area, all minimalists agree that U.S. interests can best be furthered by means other than the use or presence of augmented naval forces. Indeed, reliance on an augmented force as a diplomatic lever is viewed as positively detrimental for at least five reasons:

1. It would contribute to an Indian Ocean arms race with the Soviets, who can be expected to match any U.S. increase.

2. It could heighten the prospects for a Soviet-American military confrontation.

3. It could decrease the prospects for Indian Ocean naval arms limitation, a goal strongly advocated by most minimalists.

4. With an augmented force the United States may, in effect, assume the role of policeman in charge of maintaining stability, and thereby ignore the lessons of the Vietnam War.

5. It runs contrary to the desires of the majority of the littoral and hinterland states as revealed in "zone-of-peace" voting and public statements.

Should the United States instead push for naval arms limitation talks, the argument goes, it would earn the goodwill of these states.

All minimalists seem to be especially skeptical of U.S. and maximal arguments when these seek to justify an augmented American presence by reference to the Soviet presence. They view such arguments as ignoring or glossing over what they (the minimalists) accept as relevant facts:

• The Soviets have a legitimate right to operate in the Indian Ocean.

• Over half the Soviet Navy ships normally maintained there are noncombatant support ships.

● U.S. ship-day arguments ignore the combat qualities of the ships involved--for instance, U.S. aircraft carrier ship-days are equated with Soviet minesweeper ship-days.

● When necessary, U.S. forces in the Indian Ocean can be augmented fairly quickly from the Mediterranean or Western Pacific.

● Port visits are among the most politically significant of naval presence activities, and the United States has always held the lead in this category.

● In the absence of an all-out war, it is unrealistic to believe the Soviets would ever take the risks associated with threatening U.S. sea or oil lines of communication.

Finally, some minimalists recommend that if the United States should ever have to augment, it should do so in conjunction with allies. However, any reluctance on the part of allies to participate, they caution, should cause the United States to reconsider whether augmentation is really necessary or the best solution for the problem at hand.

From the arguments presented above, one can see that U.S., maximalist, and minimalist positions on the central issue reflect their respective positions on each of its many subissues. While it is impossible here to deal with each subissue, it is both possible and appropriate to deal with some of the more important ones.

What should American policy be on naval presence when one considers the feelings of the Indian Ocean states and peoples toward it? The significance of this subissue is obvious if one accepts that it is in the U.S. interest to earn the good will of others while avoiding what will alienate them.

Looking first at the three-ship MEF, this writer found no evidence that the Indian Ocean states or peoples object to its presence. Even the minimalists in the United States seem willing to accept it. It remains what it presumably has been for over twenty-seven years: a modest force whose primary role seems to be that of increasing goodwill toward the United States in the course of port visits. It is difficult in an a priori sense to judge whether the "amount" of goodwill earned is worth the cost of maintaining it; but in the absence of any evidence to the contrary, it probably should be retained at the present level.

The more significant question is whether it should be augmented. From the viewpoint of the feelings of the Indian Ocean states and peoples, it is impossible to give a definitive answer; but a basis for a negative response certainly does exist. As emphasized by minimalists and acknowledged by U.S. and maximalist proponents, much of the publicly expressed governmental and popular opinion does not favor augmentation. These feelings are reflected not only in public statements but also in active U.N. lobbying. It is the

Indian Ocean states themselves, led by India and Sri Lanka, that have provided the initiative in having the United Nations adopt the "zone-of-peace" resolutions specifically calling upon the great powers not to increase their presences. Of the thirty or so Indian Ocean states, only two (Oman and South Africa) have abstained in "zone-of-peace" votes since 1972.

The governmental picture, however, is not entirely one-sided. Some states publicly favor augmentation or seem willing to tolerate it. With varying degrees of confidence, one can place at least nine states in this category: Singapore, Iran, South Africa, Oman, Pakistan, and probably Yemen, Abu Dhabi, Malawi, and Ethiopia.[10] No doubt there are others whose privately communicated views would justify adding them to the list. Yet it must be remembered that their populations seem so strongly against augmentation that the governmental leaders cannot make these privately favorable views public.

This writer's personal preference is to accept public views as controlling. If Indian Ocean leaders sincerely desire augmentation, then let them say so publicly and educate their peoples accordingly. Otherwise the United States leaves itself open to criticism--even by leaders privately wanting augmentation--that it ignores the wishes of the states and peoples of the area.

It cannot be expected, of course, that all Indian Ocean states and peoples would ever be of one mind on the U.S. naval presence. One can recommend that if publicly expressed opinion is overwhelmingly in favor, then augmentation should definitely be considered. If opinion is overwhelmingly opposed, then augmentation should be avoided except when absolutely necessary to protect vital interests. For situations in between these two extremes, little guidance can be given except to suggest that priority should be given to the views of the oil states--especially those friendly to the West. These states are absolutely vital to the smooth running of the Western economies during the foreseeable future. Some minimalists discount their importance by pointing out that, prior to the OPEC boycott, they provided only 9 percent of total U.S. oil consumption and 2 percent of total U.S. energy sources consumed. Granting those facts, one still cannot get away from the considerations set forth in U.S. and maximalist arguments: that U.S. dependence is projected to increase and (more important for the present) Japanese and Western European reliance is absolutely vital to their economies. As such it is derivatively vital to the U.S. economy, which is so closely integrated with their.

These considerations seem fairly well established, and to ignore them is to place one's head in the sand. Consequently, it seems wise to assume that until alternative sources of energy are developed, the standard of living and power position of all Western states--to the extent that they depend on industrial output--will be tied to the area's

oil. In this writer's opinion, this reliance makes the oil producers--
especially those friendly to the West--important enough to justify
giving greater weight to their views than to those of the other states
of the area. That these states may be important markets for U.S.
goods serves only to reinforce this conclusion.

U.S. and maximalist proponents would have the United States
maintain permanently or periodically augmented forces in the Indian
Ocean area in order to deter threats to American interests, such as
the integrity of merchant lines of communication. Minimalist advocates see little utility in maintaining such forces for this purpose.

This writer leans toward the minimalist point of view. The
very existence of mobile U.S. naval and military power is, most
probably, deterrent enough as far as the Indian Ocean area is concerned. I see no need for maintaining augmented naval forces to
"remind" any state or group that the United States has the power to
react when appropriate. Even if it is out of sight, it should not be
out of mind to anyone who contemplates threatening vital U.S. interests.

Admittedly, waiting until a threat is imminent or present runs
the risk that by the time additional forces arrive, it may be too late
to prevent serious harm to valued interests. Such a situation could
occur, however, even if forces were permanently augmented. Naval
units cannot be at all places at all times, especially in such a vast
area as the Indian Ocean. To some extent this problem can be
averted or minimized if intelligence information is adequate and if
events occur in such a way that the crisis or other triggering event
is predictable. If necessary, air power, including troop transports,
could be immediately brought to bear if the need to use force is immediate.

Applying the above argument to the question of merchant lines
of communication, this writer sees no need to augment U.S. forces
unless interdiction attempts have already taken place or are predicted to occur with better-than-minimal probability.

Should the United States augment in order to stabilize and secure
the Indian Ocean area? The United States and maximalists say "yes";
minimalists say "no." This writer straddles both positions, perceiving the views of the former two groups as too broad and the
views of the latter group as too narrow. I would suggest that all
groups emphasize certain conditioning factors. One is whether a
direct, actual threat to vital U.S. interests is involved. Another is
whether augmentation has been requested by the Indian Ocean states,
including the oil powers, even if no actual threat to U.S. interests
has arisen.

This writer's position is based partly on agreement with a
minimalist argument: that the official American position lends itself

too easily to the interpretation that the United States actually does
intend to play a policeman's role. Official U.S. disclaimers do not
dispel this conclusion. A State Department spokesman addressed
himself to this point in Congressional testimony, saying:

> If [the U.S. position] leaves that impression, that
> it is one of the policemen of the world, then the
> fault is in the language rather than the intent.
>
> . . . . . .
>
> What . . . we were trying to get across . . .
> was that we unfortunately still live in a world
> which is a competitive one. . . . We would like
> to have a world arranged very neatly where
> people find it possible always to settle their dif-
> ferences amicably. We obviously are not in that
> situation. Naval power has in the past contrib-
> uted--and we think it will in the future contrib-
> ute in a deterrent sense, not in an active involve-
> ment sense--to making it clear that conditions
> of stability is [sic] the right way to settle prob-
> lems. Now, that is the general theme that I in-
> tended to get across. . . .[11]

Is the problem really only one of language after all? Granting that
the United States does not intend to get involved actively but only in
a "deterrent sense," is it still not committing itself to the role of a
cop on the beat trying to prevent "crime"--that is, destabilizing activities? To this writer, the answer is clearly in the affirmative.
I have no objections to such an answer where vital U.S. interests
are involved and directly threatened, or when such involvement is
requested by the area's states, including oil powers. In the absence
of these conditions, it seems unwise to become involved. The political costs, especially in terms of accusations of being "neocolonialist"
or "imperialist," seem too great.

U.S. and maximalist spokesmen desire augmentation in order
to reaffirm that the United States will not allow "zone-of-peace"
resolutions to restrict its ships' freedom of movement on the high
seas. The minimalists do not view the question in these terms.
They prefer to argue for Indian Ocean naval-arms limitation.

This writer believes that there are times when the United
States may have to take advantage of its naval power to establish a
temporarily augmented presence in the Indian Ocean and possibly use
force, if necessary. Naval units in most circumstances probably
constitute the most efficient military instrument the United States
can utilize there. They are mobile, flexible as to tasks performed,

and possessed of excellent staying power in high seas areas now legally open to use by any state. Hence, the United States must do all it can to prevent others from restricting the freedom of its naval ship activities.

U.S. practice in the Black Sea may provide a useful analogy applicable to the Indian Ocean in this regard. In order to counter Soviet claims that the Black Sea is a closed sea controlled by the littoral states, the United States has for over twenty years sent warships into the Black Sea for a few days about twice a year, simply to make the point that U.S. warships have the right to transit there. Permanently maintaining the Middle East Force--and possibly augmenting it for a few days once or twice a year--could serve to make the same point in the Indian Ocean.

How the United States should react to the Soviet naval buildup in the Indian Ocean is a complex subissue involving a number of different questions.

One is the alleged need for augmentation to prove that the United States will not cede undisputed naval preponderance in the area to the Soviets. This writer accepts that the United States must maintain a capability to balance, if not surpass, Soviet naval power in any area of the world should the need arise. As previously argued, however, it does not seem necessary to maintain this capability in the Indian Ocean in the absence of any triggering event. What is necessary is maintenance of adequate and ready forces in the Mediterranean or Western Pacific for use when appropriate. This is exactly the capability that the United States exhibited during the Indo-Pakistan and Yom Kippur Wars. A longer-term necessity is engaging in shipbuilding, repair, and modernization programs to insure that requisite hardware is available. It may also be useful to have facilities in the Indian Ocean (such as an upgraded Diego Garcia) for more efficient resupply of forces.

A second question is that of Soviet threats to Western interests in noncrisis periods. Does the Soviet naval presence pose any potential threat to Western interests such that the United States should augment its Indian Ocean naval contingent?

One threat singled out by U.S. and maximalist advocates is that to Western sealines of communication resulting from Soviet naval power per se and Soviet attempts to control states strategically located for dominating Indian Ocean trade routes. On this point this writer is in total agreement with the minimalists, who find it inconceivable that the Soviets would actually engage in or threaten interdiction in the absence of a general war. Merchant lines in general, and oil lines in particular, are vital to all the Western economies. The Soviets would have to assume that the United States would respond. If at all prudent, they must view the prospects of a Soviet-

American military confrontation as high. This writer cannot envision a "safe" sea control-sea denial type of war in the Indian Ocean--a war where each opponent can be assured that the other would not resort to nuclear threats or worse. Even if nuclear threats did not take place, the Soviets could be severely hurt if the United States chose to limit its response to attacking Soviet merchant and fishing vessels through the world. The Soviet Merchant Marine ranks first in number of ships and approximately seventh in dead-weight tonnage. The Soviets also have the world's second most productive fishing fleet. Fish products provide one-third of the animal protein in the Soviet diet and one-fifth of all protein. The assets are too extensive and important to be risked lightly.

As far as strategically located states are concerned, since the writer believes the prospects for a sea control-sea denial war to be slim, it seems more relevant to view Soviet attempts in that respect as the next threat to be considered.

U.S. and maximalist proponents are very concerned about the Soviet Navy's role in increasing Soviet influence and obtaining client states at the expense of the West. Reference to the testimony of CIA Director William Colby is relevant to judging the validity of their concerns. It was the judgment of his organization that the "roles of military, particularly naval, forces have been secondary to diplomatic efforts and aid programs in promoting Soviet interests in the Indian Ocean."[12] If the United States is seriously concerned with countering Soviet influence activities, then it may be best for it to do what the Soviets are doing: concentrating first on nonnaval political-diplomatic and economic efforts. Augmented naval efforts beyond the modest Middle East Force may, in fact, not be in the best interest of the United States. The controlling factor here should probably be the attitudes of the Indian Ocean states, especially the pro-West oil producers.

A more amorphous question relates to U.S. and maximalist fears that the United States will be "squeezed out" of the Indian Ocean area by the Soviets. This writer is uncertain but skeptical about the extent to which this question constitutes a real problem. If the Indian Ocean states, especially the friendly oil powers, do not desire augmentation, then it may be best to respect their wishes as much as possible in noncrisis periods. If a crisis does occur where U.S. vital interests are at stake, then these states must be made to realize that the United States will do what it must--including use of naval power--and that nothing less can realistically be expected.

U.S. and maximalist fears may be somewhat unwarranted if it is true that the Indian Ocean states do not desire to see the Soviets operate there relatively unfettered. The same advocates who are afraid of being squeezed out tell us that a number of states do welcome (privately if not publicly) a balancing U.S. presence. Newspaper reports indicate that the Prime Minister of Singapore has already publicly proposed that the United States, Japan, Australia, other Asian--and, ultimately, Western European--states form a joint naval-air task force in the Indian Ocean to balance Soviet naval power. The Shah of Iran, while expressing his preference that the United States and USSR both vacate the Indian Ocean, also asserted his acquiescence to the U.S. presence as long as the Soviets were there. Reportedly, the Australian Labor government of Gough Whitlam was considering backing away from its support for "zone-of-peace" proposals also out of concern for Soviet naval activities. Even Prime Minister Sirimauo Bandaranaike of Sri Lanka, a leader behind the "zone-of-peace" effort, was reported to have muted criticism of the U.S. naval presence for the same reason.[13]

In short, the situation may not so much be one where the United States is "squeezed out" of the Indian Ocean area by the Soviets as one where the Soviets may, through their presence, make the Indian Ocean states desirous of a reciprocal U.S. presence.

How valid are minimalist predictions if the United States should augment for the above purpose? Would augmentation significantly increase the prospects of a Soviet-U.S. naval confrontation, as suggested in minimalist arguments? This writer thinks not. The times when such confrontations might occur would most probably be periods of crisis in the Indian Ocean--periods when the United States can be expected to have its ships there anyway.

Would augmentation hinder the prospects for Soviet-American naval-arms limitation centering on the Indian Ocean? Again, this writer thinks not. The United States cannot expect the Soviets to withdraw without having comparable U.S. forces that can be withdrawn from the area. It may be enough for the United States to tell the Soviets it will augment its forces in the absence of an agreement, in the hope that this warning will prod the Soviets to agreement. Should this tactic fail, however, the only realistic alternative might be to go ahead and augment, in the hope of a favorable reaction if naval-arms limitation is really desired.

Finally, would augmentation serve to fuel an Indian Ocean naval-arms race with the Soviets by forcing them to increase their forces accordingly? It is difficult to say. The official CIA estimate seems as valid as any. According to Director Colby, the Soviet presence will increase by one or two combatants a year no matter what the United States does. The Soviets will, furthermore, act gradually to match any substantial additions to the U.S. presence. To do so, however, will require "reordering their priorities and shifting naval forces from other areas."[14]

Both maximalists and minimalists recommend that the United States work with allies in any augmentation. The maximalists are very insistent that we use "stern diplomacy," if necessary, to encourage allies to cooperate, and that no potential ally (including South Africa) be ignored.

That the United States should seek to work with allies seems very sensible in these days of declining U.S. Navy ship resources. The active U.S. naval fleet is now the smallest it has been since 1939 (slightly under 500 ships), and the Navy has recently experienced difficulties in maintaining its normal number of carriers on station. Both France and Britain already maintain naval forces in the Indian Ocean, and Britain and the Netherlands have worked out an agreement to conduct joint patrols there. The United States should seek to work with them and other Western forces. If a U.S. naval presence is requested by the littoral states, the United States should also seek to have them do their share. Iran already seems to be well on its way to making itself a preeminent local naval power. The Saudis are buying American patrol craft and sending sailors for training in the United States.

Whether the United States should use "stern diplomacy" to secure cooperation is a delicate question that would seem to depend on the extent of the threat to be handled by the naval forces and the political costs involved in forcing others to act. This writer leans toward the minimalist argument that the greater the reluctance of allies to act, the more the United States should reconsider the need or appropriateness of naval action.

No matter how willing South Africa might be, however, it may be best to avoid working with her until the apartheid problem is resolved. The political costs vis-a-vis the black African states are viewed by this writer as being too high.

CONCLUSIONS

There are seven general conclusions to be made:

1. Maintain the three-ship MEF. It constitutes a modest and nonthreatening presence. It plays essentially a political–diplomatic role of trying to earn goodwill for the United States. Its political utility seems worth the costs of maintaining it.

2. The MEF should be augmented for the duration of a crisis if that crisis involves vital U.S. interests.

3. The MEF should be augmented for a few days once or twice a year to reaffirm the U.S. right to augment forces and to operate them in the Indian Ocean.

4. The United States should seriously consider augmentation, either permanent or periodic, if it is desired by the Indian Ocean states, including oil powers.

5. Permanent or periodic augmentation should be considered if naval-arms limitation talks are sincerely desired.

6. Other reasons reviewed herein for augmenting the MEF do not seem adequate at this time.

7. The United States should work with allies in any augmentation, assuming that their interests are also involved. Reluctance on the part of allies to participate should give the United States pause about the need for naval action.

NOTES

1. Statement of Seymour Weiss, Director, Bureau of Politico-Military Affairs, Department of State, March 6, 1974, as found in Proposed Expansion of U.S. Military Facilities in the Indian Ocean: Hearings Before the Subcommittee on the Near East and South Asia. Committee on Foreign Affairs, House of Representatives, 93rd Congress, 2nd Sess., p. 25; and statement of Rear Admiral Charles D. Grojean, Director, Politico-Military Policy Division, Office of the Chief of Naval Operations, July 11, 1974, as found in Military Construction Authorization, Fiscal Year 1975: Hearings Before the Subcommittee on Military Construction, Committee on Armed Services, United States Senate, 93rd Congress, 2nd Sess., p. 138.

2. Statement of James Noyes, Deputy Assistant Secretary of Defense for International Security Affairs, March 12, 1974, as found in Proposed Expansion . . ., p. 78.

3. Statement of J. Owen Zurhellen, Deputy Director, U.S. Arms Control and Disarmament Agency, February 21, 1974, as found in Proposed Expansion . . ., p. 8.

4. Weiss, op. cit., pp. 24, 40.

5. Statement of Admiral Elmo Zumwalt, Chief of Naval Operations, April 11, 1974, as found in Briefings on Diego Garcia and Patrol Frigate: Hearings Before the Committee on Foreign Relations, United States Senate, 93rd Congress, 2nd Sess., p. 7.

6. Weiss, op. cit., p. 29.

7. Lawrence Griswold, "From Simonstown to Singapore," United States Naval Institute Proceedings, November 1971, p. 29.

8. "The Indian Ocean: A New Naval Arms Race," Defense Monitor, April 1974, p. 2.

9. Ibid., p. 9.

10. Trying to determine who is for and against is a complicated question, especially since some views are privately expressed. See Weiss, op. cit., pp. 37, 44-45; Zumwalt, op. cit., p. 16.

11. Weiss, op. cit., p. 44.

12. As found in Military Construction Authorization, Fiscal Year 1975 . . ., p. 166.

13. See New York Times, May 12, 1973, p. 2, and September 29, 1974, p. 5; Christian Science Monitor, February 6, 1975, p. 3A; New York Times, March 5, 1972, p. 10.

14. Military Construction Authorization . . ., pp. 165-66, 171-72.

9

SOUTHEAST ASIA:
THE PROBLEM OF
AMERICAN CREDIBILITY
George Osborn

THE ISSUE

The key issue for the United States with respect to Southeast Asia in the late 1970s in some ways is subsumed in a larger issue: Will the United States remain an Asian and Pacific power, or will it become primarily a Pacific power? Another way of putting the question might be whether the United States will be an active, constructive participant in the evolutionary movement of Southeast Asian states toward some new, relatively stable balance of power, or a passive observer of revolutionary change that could, but might not, spill over into adjacent subregions in Asia and Oceania. It is unlikely that these questions will be answered definitively before 1977, although major trends may appear. At the same time, 1977 will present a favorable opportunity to look at the issues and their components. A new administration will be in office in Washington-- either a new Republican administration, with a popular mandate for the first time since 1974, or a Democratic one--and it will be appropriate to lay down the policy guidelines for the ensuing four or eight years.

It may turn out, of course, that Southeast Asia will have such a low priority among the multiple security issues facing a new administration that no comprehensive review of where we are and whither we are tending will be made. Certainly a low priority is justified, at least in the short term, for the immediate and direct impact of Southeast Asian events on U.S. security likely must pale

---

The opinions expressed here are those of the author and are not necessarily those of the United States government.

in significance alongside such other regions as Northeast Asia or
Central Europe, as well as such issues as SALT or nuclear proliferation. Yet failure to address the issues raised at the outset of
this chapter in some comprehensive and integrated fashion could result in a policy drift, in which ad hoc decisions on specific issues--
say, U.S. base rights in the Philippines--collectively commit the
United States to a course that ultimately will have an unfavorable impact on the regional balance as well as on U.S. security. In such
cases no decision--the lack of coordinated policy--constitutes a decision to drift. The United States then becomes the prisoner of
events, always reacting to others' policies and decisions.

BACKGROUND OF THE ISSUE

At mid-decade, U.S. policy with respect to Southeast Asia was
in limbo, without much prospect of immediate change in that status.
The declaratory policy remained essentially that of the so-called
Nixon Doctrine:

> If we are going to have peace in the world, poten-
> tially the greatest threat to that peace would be
> in the Pacific. For that reason the United States
> should continue to play a significant role. We,
> of course, will keep the treaty commitments that
> we have. I believe that the time has come when
> the United States, in our relations with all of our
> Asian friends, are quite emphatic on two points:
> One, that we will keep our treaty commitments,
> our treaty commitments, for example, with
> Thailand under SEATO; and that, two, that as
> far as the problems of internal security are
> concerned, as far as the problems of military
> defense, except for the threat of a major power
> involving nuclear weapons, that the United States
> is going to encourage, and has a right to expect,
> that this problem will be increasingly handled by
> and the responsibility for it taken by the Asian
> nations themselves.[1]

In the aftermath of the sudden collapse of the Saigon regime and the
U.S. response, in the face of the triumph of the Khmer Rouge in
Cambodia, in view of the increasing control of the Pathet Lao in
Laos, and noting the evacuation of U.S. air power from Thailand,
one might begin to question U.S. intentions to carry out even the
somewhat limited propositions contained in the Nixon Doctrine.

The reasons for this state of affairs are not difficult to discern, but they do deserve some explication. First, despite our increasing preoccupation with Southeast Asia in general, and the Indo-China peninsula in particular, during the 1950s and 1960s, the region and its component states simply do not play a central role in the vital security interests of the United States or, if one concedes that they did from 1950 to 1975, they no longer play such a role. Such security interests as the United States may have in Southeast Asia appear to be secondary--the naval complex at Subic Bay in the Philippines and free access to and through the South China Sea--or derivative-- Japan's access to markets and resources. Such secondary and derivative interests still may be important; but they lack the salience, in the minds of policy-makers and their publics, of other, truly vital, interests.

Second, turning away from Southeast Asia and downgrading the importance of events there, at least in a policy sense, may represent an attempt to resolve the cognitive dissonance associated with the U.S. experience in Vietnam. Corollary to this is the oft-heard phrase "No more Vietnams," meaning, one infers, that almost any involvement abroad may lead to a repetition of the Vietnam experience of the United States, presumably accompanied by the same costs, trauma, and outcome.* The more subtle manifestations of these attitudes lead many to create psychological distance from the source of unease and uncertainty. In this connection it may be instructive to recall what one Secretary of State pointed out: ". . . one lesson we must learn from this experience [Vietnam] is that we must be very careful in the commitments we make, but that we should scrupulously honor those commitments that we make."[2] One can join a Malaysian observer in saying: ". . . It is important to international order that the fall of American dominoes does not so shake American confidence that its present strategic retreat in Indochina should turn into strategic rout worldwide. The fall of American military dominoes need not presage the fall of political dominoes."[3]

Third, the depth and bitterness of the Sino-Soviet dispute, the increased recognition of polycentric tendencies in the Communist movement, and the detente appearing in the early 1970s between the United States, on the one hand, and the USSR and the People's Republic of China (PRC), on the other, have melded with other events and circumstances to erode the official and public conceptions of international politics that fit all actions and policies into the framework

---

*The perceptive individual of course will appreciate that there are no more Vietnams, in the sense of the geographic, ethnic, and historical experience of the Vietnamese; neither are the circumstances surrounding the U.S. involvement likely to be replicated.

of dyadic relationships between two hostile, armed camps. Indeed,
one hears, from time to time, the suggestion that had the United
States somehow pursued other policies, at one time or another, Ho
Chi Minh would have become an Asian Tito or the Democratic Republic of Vietnam (DRVN) a Southeast Asian Yugoslavia, whatever
one might infer from those metaphors. In addition, it should be
noted that both the future of the Sino-Soviet dispute and of detente
well could be in doubt. The former has much to do with personalities who could pass from the scene, leaving open the possibility of
future Sino-Soviet rapprochement. Detente is by no means a permanent or guaranteed status, and could be replaced by exacerbation of
tensions for various reasons. Further, those who confuse detente
with either rapprochement or entente do both themselves and others
a disservice. Finally, despite the fissiparous tendencies historically apparent in Communist movements, polycentrism may be at the
mercy of determined applications of the Brezhnev doctrine--at least
in states within easy reach of USSR bayonets and tanks.

In Southeast Asia it should be obvious that both endogenous and
exogenous powers have a collective interest in seeing that no single
state dominates the region. Such a collective interest, in time,
could provide the framework for the evolution of a relatively stable
balance. However, failure to recognize the collective interest and
to follow policies designed to reinforce it could influence one or another state to attempt to establish hegemony, thus destabilizing the
entire region. The implications of this for the United States, one of
the major exogenous powers, should be apparent. Unfortunately,
for some, they are not.

For the endogenous states of Southeast Asia, the departure of
the United States from Vietnam constitutes a reversion to the pre-
colonial era of political relations. That is, these states now must
work out their relationships among themselves without the overt intervention of one or more of the great powers. Given the long-
standing historical differences between various peoples, it is not
surprising that there is a certain amount of tension in the postcolonial
period. Further, the four great powers--Japan, PRC, United States,
and USSR--loom large on the horizon. Hence, while there has been a
degree of devolution of power to the regimes holding sway in the endogenous capitals, decisions in Moscow, Peking, Tokyo, and Washington may have profound impact on the states of the region. These
decisions may introduce additional tension, as the regional states
seek to balance their own interests within the framework of great-
power interests.

Obviously, with the military departure of the United States
the greatest source of tension within the region remains Vietnam.
Militarily, the DRVN is the strongest single endogenous state; and

the intentions of its leadership with respect to the other Indochina states, Cambodia and Laos, are in doubt, as are intentions toward the remaining peninsular states--Thailand, Burma, West Malaysia, and Singapore. The Lao Dong Party, successor to the Indochina Communist Party (ICP), has not renounced the ICP claims to all of Indochina. The internal weaknesses of the DRVN, principally economic, and the requirement to perfect relationships between the two Vietnams are ambiguous factors. One could argue that such weaknesses will require a long period of turning inward and concentration on nation-building, but the same weaknesses could be factors in stimulating aggressive expansionist policies in Hanoi. The historic Vietnamese interest in the Tran Minh Plateau (Plain of Jars) in Laos and the historical movement of ethnic Vietnamese south and west along the rice-bearing lowlands add to uncertainty and ambiguity.

Five of the non-Communist states in the region--Indonesia, Malaysia, Philippines, Singapore, and Thailand--have joined together to form the Association of South-East Asian Nations (ASEAN). Progress in building ASEAN has been slow--indeed imperceptible at times--but much has been accomplished. It remains to be seen, however, whether ASEAN can work out a common policy of accommodation with the three Indochinese states, especially the DRVN. The possibility exists of a split in ASEAN if the two insular states-- Indonesia and the Philippines--decide that they have less to fear from the DRVN, and perhaps more to gain from a different kind of accommodation.

Thailand occupies a critical geographic position. It has a long frontier with Cambodia and Laos, and there are large Khmer and Lao ethnic minorities in present-day Thailand. The Mekong River, forming much of the Thai-Lao border, is more a highway than a barrier, and there always is considerable movement of people and goods in both directions across the river. In the north, the land frontier between Thailand and Laos is in inhospitable and remote mountains, traditionally the home of ethnic minority groups whose members move back and forth with little respect for international boundaries and no knowledge of the niceties of passports, visas, and immigration regulations. The Thai-Cambodia border, too, seems to be porous. In Northeast Thailand, there is a large ethnic Vietnamese minority, composed chiefly of refugees from the first Indochina war and their descendants. *

---

*There is an ethnic Vietnamese minority in the Bangkok-Thonbury region, but most are descendants of Vietnamese who settled there in the late eighteenth and nineteenth centuries. They have not been as susceptible to DRVN control as those Vietnamese in the northeast.

Thailand also has a serious internal security problem, with at least five geographically separate insurgencies under the control of the Communist Party of Thailand. While these insurgencies present no clear and present danger to Bangkok, their persistence and capacity for growth do constitute major obstacles to continued Thai political and economic development. In the far south, in the Thai provinces adjoining the border with peninsular Malaysia, the Malayan Communist Party (MCP) maintains extensive base areas and underground networks. Still targeted against Malaysia, rather than Thailand, the MCP nevertheless recruits extensively among the ethnic Chinese Malay (Thai-Muslim) populations of the area.

The close association of Thailand with the United States, dating from the Free Thai Movement during World War II and the identification of Thailand with U.S. policy in Indochina, is a poisonous legacy to contaminate Thai relations with the Indochinese states, especially the DRVN. The use of Thailand as an unsinkable aircraft carrier to support the various U.S. aerial campaigns in and over Indochina makes normalization of relations between Thailand and her neighbors both more difficult and more tenuous.

Burma has faced serious internal security problems almost from the moment of independence. More recently, it has experienced a long period of economic stagnation. However, the majority of Burmese generally have remained loyal, and the government has managed to maintain control of the central core along the Irrawaddy River. Burma shares a common border with Laos, along the Mekong River, between Thailand and China. Relations with Hanoi long have been established, and there appear to be no major obstacles to friendly contact between Rangoon and Hanoi. Burma has remained out of ASEAN, despite indications that the members would welcome its participation. Relations with Thailand generally have been good, despite occasional charges of Thai collusion with various insurgent groups and despite Burmese suspicion that the Thais continue to harbor designs on Kengtung state in northeastern Burma.

The state of emergency in Malaysia ended in 1960, following the retreat of most of the guerrilla forces of the MCP north of the Thai frontier. However, the ability of the MCP to sustain itself and grow, as well as its occasional forays into Malaysia, constantly serve to remind the government of its potential for mischief. Indeed, the MCP's success in recruiting Muslims from the southern Thai provinces may bode ill for the future when, and if, the MCP decides to launch a major effort in Malaysia.* Further, ethnic peace in

---

*The MCP had only a small Muslim (Malay) membership at the outset of the emergency, and it soon was dropped, so that the whole

peninsular Malaysia is precarious at best, and the government has
made little headway in its attempts to foster a Malaysian nationalism
overriding ethnic loyalties. Malaysia is split further by geography,
and East (insular) Malaysia, including the states of Sabah and Sarawak,
also has its share of ethnic and religious differences. Malaysia mild-
ly supported U.S. efforts in Vietnam to include a modest level of
training in jungle warfare, but never was closely identified with U.S.
policy.

The largest of the Southeast Asian states in population, territory, and natural resources is Indonesia. Its potential and claims
by its leaders of a position of regional leadership tend to make its
neighbors somewhat wary. Nevertheless, since Sukarno, Indonesia
has participated in efforts aimed at greater regional cooperation,
and Indonesian statesmen have demonstrated awareness of the need
to bring the Indochinese states out of their isolation. However, it is
likely that this will take place only over an extended period of time.

Meanwhile, much of Indonesia's potential is yet to be realized,
and development is hampered by lack of capital and the serious over-
population of Java. Indonesia did survive one attempt at a Communist
takeover--the so-called Gestapu Affair of September 1965--and the
Communist Party of Indonesia (PKI) virtually was eliminated in the
aftermath. However, the conditions that abetted PKI growth in the
1950s and 1960s, especially in central and eastern Java, remain.
This, plus the lack of any permanent government presence at the vil-
lage level, may permit the resurgence of a reorganized PKI. For
the interim, the armed forces appear in firm control.

In the Philippines, one Southeast Asian experiment with Western-
style democracy ended in the early 1970s with the proclamation of
martial law. Although overt political activity virtually ceased, serious internal security problems remain to be resolved. The Philippine
Communist Party continues its efforts to mount a successful insurgency in the north. In the south, the demands of the Moro (Muslim)
population for autonomy and independence, encouraged and aided from
Sabah and some Muslim states, run counter to the desires of Christian Filipinos, who constitute a majority of the population of the largest southern island, Mindanao.

The Philippines has been closely associated with the United
States and identified with U.S. foreign policy. Like Thailand, the
Philippines served as a major staging area for the U.S. effort in
Vietnam. Unlike the Thai, however, the Filipinos have had difficulty

---

affair took on ethnic overtones--disastrous in the long run for the
MCP. Now one of the three regiments under MCP control in Thailand
is made up of ethnic Malay Muslims.

in establishing their independent identity, both in their own eyes and in those of others. The long period of U.S. tutelage and the close ties with the United States following independence have contributed much to impressions, both at home and abroad, that the Philippines was with, but not of, Asia. This has created considerable frustration for many Filipinos. Nevertheless, with territorial claims and counterclaims between the Philippines and Malaysia momentarily in abeyance, the Philippines has participated in the slow evolutionary development of ASEAN. But, like Thailand, the Philippines remains involved with the United States in the Southeast Asia Collective Defense Treaty and in the organization established under the aegis of that treaty.

Singapore, virtually a city-state, has become the economic miracle of Southeast Asia. Politically, it has managed to resolve its differences with both Malaysia, with which it temporarily was united, and with Indonesia. There remains a potential conflict involving the three, however, over the status of the Straits of Malacca, where Indonesia and Malaysia sometimes make territorial claims. Generally, Singapore attempts to pursue friendly relations with all its neighbors, and has been an effective participant in ASEAN.

PRC interests in policies in Southeast Asia have been both obscured and complicated by a number of factors. First, there is the existence of a rival regime on Taiwan. Second is the presence in many Southeast Asian states of a sizable ethnic Chinese minority--many of whom have not sought local citizenship or have been barred from citizenship by suspicious regimes. (Singapore has an ethnic Chinese majority, but fear of the influence of the PRC on local Chinese is not less because of this fact.) Third, Chinese support of local insurgencies in Burma, Malaysia, and Thailand, rumored support of insurgencies elsewhere (Philippines, Kalimantan), and Chinese involvement with the PKI in Indonesia contribute to fear of PRC intentions because the Chinese distinctions among state-to-state, party-to-party, and people-to-people relations, apparently clear to the PRC leadership and to some analysts, are not always clear in some Southeast Asian capitals.

Nevertheless, it seems clear that the PRC has an interest, at least in the short and medium term, in a modicum of regional political stability in Southeast Asia. Peking's moves to limit the potential expansion of Vietnamese power in Indochina may be the clearest indication that this is the case. The Chinese presence in northwestern Laos serves as a buffer between the DRVN and Burma, and also keeps open, under Chinese control, infiltration routes from the PRC to Thailand. (The inclusion of this area in Laos was a French action, splitting an area known as the sip song pan no ["twelve thousand fields"], which had a long tributary relationship with China.) Chinese support of the Khmer Rouge in Cambodia also may be seen as an attempt to limit Vietnamese influence there.

The PRC also fears the possibility of increased Soviet influence in Southeast Asia in the wake of U.S. withdrawal. The willingness of the PRC to enter into state-to-state relations with Malaysia, the Philippines, and Thailand so quickly and to normalize strained relations with Burma appears to be directed primarily against the USSR. (Obviously there are other ingredients, including the long-standing diplomatic competition with Taiwan and the loyalties of overseas Chinese. However, one should note that PRC fears of encirclement, expressed at least since 1962, are real.) Further, PRC support of a continued U.S. presence in the region implies Chinese sensitivity to the possibilities of a power vacuum.

In contrast with the PRC political interests in Southeast Asia, Japan's chief interests are economic. Indeed, one might infer that the growth of Japan's economic ties in the region is a partial attempt to attain the World War II goal of a Greater East Asia Co-Prosperity Sphere without the earlier military and political overtones. Periodic outbursts of anti-Japanese sentiment in some Southeast Asian states, as well as less violent but significant expressions in the media, provide some clues to the depth of residual fear of Japanese imperialism left over from World War II and new fear of ultimate loss of independence as a result of Japanese economic penetration. The Japanese government has shown increased sensitivity to Southeast Asian criticism.

While the total trade between Japan and Southeast Asia ranks far behind U.S.-Japanese trade in value, it is likely that the economic importance of Southeast Asia to Japan will increase. The threat to Japan's comparative advantage in international trade, caused in part by the aging of Japan's labor force and increased competition for land and labor at home, indicates that overseas investment by Japanese industry should rise. The growing internal markets in Southeast Asia, along with the relative access to many resources--including labor-- will make that region attractive. However, for trade to flourish and investment to succeed, a certain degree of political stability is required, both within the various states and among them. Hence, Japan's important political interest in Southeast Asia. Short-term factors may be misleading, however. Japan's reduced reliance on Indonesian oil in the mid-1970s, because of the availability of cheaper Chinese oil, is one example. The future rise in Japan's energy requirements, as well as those of the PRC as economic development proceeds in the latter, may counter the short-term trend. Further, at some point Japan may prefer to avoid too great reliance on the Chinese source.

The USSR appears to have both state-to-state and party-to-party interests in Southeast Asia, but in anything but the longest term the former predominate. Soviet access to Southeast Asian Communist parties has been limited, especially in recent years, except in the DRVN and, to a lesser extent, in Laos. Soviet influence in Indonesia was eclipsed with the deposal of Sukarno, and the modest USSR involvement in Burma produced no significant political results. Nevertheless, the USSR does maintain large missions in several capitals; and trade, while not large by comparison with U.S. or Japanese levels, plays a modest role in several states.

In the case of the Indochinese states, particularly the DRVN, Sino-Soviet rivalry is clear and fairly intense. Despite the geographic propinquity of the PRC, there are certain things for which the DRVN must turn to the USSR, such as access to advanced technology. The reluctance of the DRVN to turn to the non-Communist world for technology, which may erode over time, forces it to look to the USSR and East European states. Further, the fear of PRC domination, born of centuries of Vietnamese experience with the Chinese, also encourages the DRVN to maintain an opening to Moscow. *

The USSR also has an interest in maintaining access to and through the South China Sea, both for commercial shipping and for its navy. Despite the increasing use of Arctic routes from European USSR ports to the Soviet Far East, routes from Black Sea ports and the Indian Ocean remain important. Fleet deployments also are easier using the Straits of Malacca for access to and egress from the Indian Ocean. Should the United States deploy Trident missile submarines from the Pacific to stations in the Indian Ocean, Soviet interest in port access in the region--already evident in Singapore--may rise. (The Russian fleet deploying to Asia during the Russo-Japanese War used Camranh Bay, on the Vietnam coast, for coaling.)

ALTERNATIVE STRATEGIES

Returning to U.S. security, one might ask this question posed by Ferdinand Foch: "De quoi s'agit-il?" If, to paraphrase the late Dean Acheson, the object of U.S. national security policy is to make

---

*Having cordial relationships with a neighbor once removed, especially for minor powers, is sound diplomacy. The example of Albania is instructive. Geographically close to Yugoslavia, Albania sided with the USSR in the 1948 split between Yugoslavia and the Cominform. Subsequently it sided with the PRC in the Sino-Soviet split. Result: the Albanians have all of the benefits of alliance with a great power but few of the disadvantages.

it possible for us to pursue our experiment with democracy, what sorts of decisions with respect to national security and Southeast Asia must be made in 1977? The answer clearly, but superficially, is very few, if any. In the near term, U.S. interests there, including economic interests, are of relatively low priority and do not, in any event, appear to be seriously threatened.

At the same time, it should be reasonably clear that after more than thirty-five years of warfare and over a century of colonial domination (much more in the Philippines and Indonesia), the states of Southeast Asia badly need time to work out their own relationships with each other, and with the exogenous great powers, peacefully. Such time could be bought, at relatively low cost, by a positive U.S. policy of encouraging stability and negotiation. The opportunity may be lost if the United States takes a negative attitude or simply turns its back and walks away.

Such a modest policy might include continued economic and military assistance to Thailand; greater understanding of and sympathy with the Philippines' search for its national identity; support of commodity agreements on tin, rubber, and perhaps oil; encouraging U.S. private investment in the region; some support of ASEAN; encouraging resumption of work on the Mekong Development Plan under the auspices of the Economic Commission for Asia and the Far East; and willingness at least to talk to the three governments of Indochina. In the case of Thailand and the Philippines, where the United States has formal treaty commitments, we should avoid actions that would lead to further doubts about our will to carry out those agreements and seek opportunities to reinforce their credibility. In short, a modest policy for a modest part of the world in which the United States has modest interests.

NOTES

1. United States Security Agreements and Commitments Abroad: Kingdom of Thailand (Washington, D.C.: U.S. Government Printing Office, 1970), p. 700. The official gloss on President Nixon's remarks follows:

> Simply stated, the Nixon doctrine contains three basic propositions:
> 1. The United States will keep its treaty commitments;
> 2. We will provide a shield if a nuclear power threatens the freedom of a nation allied to us or of a nation whose survival we consider

vital to our security or to the security of the
region as a whole; and

    3. In cases involving other types of aggres-
sion, the United States will furnish aid and economic assistance when requested and appropriate. But we shall look to the nation directly
threatened to assume the primary responsibility of providing the manpower for its defense.

See "Address by Marshall Green, Assistant Secretary for East Asian
and Pacific Affairs on the Nixon Doctrine," Department of State
Bulletin, February 8, 1971, pp. 161-65.

    2. As quoted in Survival, July/August 1975, p. 185.

    3. Tan Sri M. Ghazali Shafie, Malaysia's Minister of Home
Affairs, May 6, 1975.

10

NORTHEAST ASIA:
THE PROBLEM OF
BALANCING POWER
Jack H. Harris

THE ISSUE

Major decision points regarding America's Northeast Asian
security structure will be passed in 1976 and 1977. Whether that
structure will be restored to something resembling the 1955-69
model, or whether an entirely new structure will emerge, or whether
it will remain on ice--as it has for the past three years--depends
upon the way in which American policy-makers confront the critical
decisions of 1976 and 1977.

BACKGROUND OF THE ISSUE

The United States has twice attempted in the twentieth century
to radically alter the Northeast Asian security structure. The second attempt was President Nixon's in 1971 (discussed at length below).
The first was President Roosevelt's, undertaken during World War II;
its failure led to many of the issues at stake in the current dilemma
facing U.S. decision-makers.

Roosevelt believed that U.S. security would be best served by
a strong, unified, independent China; he frequently voiced his intention to see China emerge as one of the "great powers" at the end of
the war. Toward this end, he supported (albeit occasionally half-
heartedly) Chiang Kai-shek and the Nationalist forces against the
Japanese, who occupied the Chinese heartland throughout the war,
and the Chinese Communists, who challenged Nationalist control
from the Chinese hinterlands.

Stalin wished for quite another kind of China to emerge after
the war: a weak, decentralized nation that might serve as a harmless

buffer along the Soviet Union's soft Asian underbelly. In pursuit of this goal, Stalin supported both the Nationalists and the Communists at various times during the war.

At Yalta, Roosevelt and Stalin apparently compromised upon a mutually acceptable (or, perhaps, mutually unacceptable) model for postwar China. To the extent that this model can be reconstructed on the basis of the postwar policies of Moscow and Washington toward the Chinese civil war, it can be said that it called for a north-south division of China, with Communist forces controlling the northern regions--the territory bordering on the Soviet Union--and the Nationalists controlling areas to the south. A coalition government was to rule, thereby guaranteeing that this emerging "great power" would be fully occupied with its internal problems and that it would neither play a constructive role in maintaining the stability of Northeast Asia nor pose a threat to the vulnerable, adjacent Soviet Union.

Obviously, the Yalta agreement was not adhered to by either the United States or the Soviet Union. Stalin's "compromise" had been offered at a time when the likelihood of a Chinese Communist victory over the Nationalists seemed very low. Ideological considerations had outweighed practical ones in Stalin's calculations, and the Chinese Communists had been written off as a potential vehicle for control of the entire Chinese nation. However, after the Japanese surrender, the tide turned in the Chinese civil war--in part because of the acquisition of Japanese arms by the Communists, and in part because of American restraint of the militarily superior Nationalists, who threatened to overrun the Communists and blemish the American image of adherence to agreements. Turning with the tide, Stalin abandoned the agreement. By the time the United States reacted, the civil war was unalterably headed for the Communist victory that was marked on October 1, 1949.

America's delayed realization of what had happened in China, dramatically manifested in the "who lost China?" investigations, contributed substantially to the development of the Cold War. So, too, did the Korean War, a second case in which American expectations in no way corresponded to actual behavior on the part of the Soviets and the Chinese Communists. The Korean War gave rise not only to a "twice burned, thrice shy" cynicism in U.S. dealings with Communist states, but also to the alteration of U.S. policies toward Japan. Japan would now become what China was supposed to have become: the regional force of "good" in Northeast Asia. The bipolarity of the 1950s found Northeast Asia divided into two mirror-image camps: the powerful Soviet Union, less powerful China, and client state North Korea on the one side, and the United States, Japan, and South Korea on the other.

Until 1957, the solidarity of the two camps was virtually unshaken, with the most interesting event in this competition being the pitting of developing China against reconstructing Japan. From the U.S. side, the objective was to frustrate the development of China while stimulating the resurgence of Japan. The Soviet side pursued the opposite goals. The either/or perception of developments in the region persisted, even into the 1960s. Interestingly, this perception seems to have been shared by all parties except the Chinese and Japanese. The constructive development of the Sino-Japanese relationship far outpaced the development of any other intercamp relationship.

By the late 1950s, the Sino-Soviet partnership had fallen on hard times. Since the consolidation of Communist power in China in the late 1940s, the primary goal of the Peking regime had necessarily been the reconstruction of the badly disintegrated Chinese nation. Political and social reconstruction, largely do-it-yourself projects, were both making satisfactory progress from Peking's point of view. But economic development--nation-building--was another matter; it could not be accomplished at an acceptable rate without the import of vast amounts of capital equipment and technology. And the sources of the required equipment and technology were limited in the early 1950s. Japan and Europe had their own reconstruction problems, and the United States could see no self-interest served by contributing to the economic development of "Red" China.

Whatever Peking's objective preferences might have been in the early 1950s, Moscow was the only resort; and, throughout the decade, the Soviet Union was deeply involved in the task of Chinese nation-building. The cost of Soviet assistance was exorbitant in terms of both money and political independence--but Moscow ran the only game in town. By the late 1950s, China's external situation had changed--or so it appeared to the Peking leadership. The United States and U.S.-controlled sources of nation-building wherewithal apparently came to be viewed as viable alternatives to the Soviet Union. The decision was made in 1958 to cease exclusive dependence on Moscow and to continue the task of nation-building either with Western assistance or, if necessary, alone--but, in any case, without the political costs of permitting an external power to manipulate the Chinese leadership and build a China in its own image for its own ends.

Peking obviously miscalculated. It took the United States years to recognize the Sino-Soviet split for what it was. In the meantime, the United States did all that it could to deny the Chinese access to what they needed. The Japanese sources that had been so carefully cultivated by Peking were forthcoming, but not to the extent hoped for when the 1958 decision was made. Similarly, otherwise willing

European sources found themselves severely constrained by an effective U.S. veto of Western technology transfers to China. The years from 1958 through the mid-1960s were grim ones for China and for those Chinese leaders who had taken a chance on the possibility of forming limited partnerships outside the Sino-Soviet bloc.

Those same years were grim ones for U.S. relations with Asian Communists. In December 1960 the Soviet Union initiated the Hanoi-Vientiane airlift in an attempt to, among other things, draw the U.S. military into operations on China's southern flank, thereby creating a security crisis for Peking and forcing a restoration of the Sino-Soviet alliance. Perhaps Moscow's strategy worked too well: the United States was indeed drawn into a military campaign in Southeast Asia, but events moved so quickly that Moscow lost control of the situation. Peking was fully aware of the game being played at her expense. However, rather than acting according to Soviet expectations, the Chinese elected to pour assistance into the region, in an effort to secure a Communist victory before the United States could deploy forces in sufficient measure to check the Pathet Lao and North Vietnamese. Had this counterstrategy worked, the region would have been pacified on Chinese terms, Peking would have emerged as the champion of the "revolution," and--most important-- a confrontation with the United States would have been averted and hope would have been kept alive for Chinese acquisition of Western assistance in their task of nation-building.

Peking miscalculated, however, just as Moscow had done. The rapid rise in the level of Southeast Asian violence spurred, rather than deterred, U.S. deployments to Vietnam. China's ability to supply the battlefield was totally inadequate to the task of matching the U.S. buildup in Southeast Asia. Almost everything had gone wrong: without committing combat troops to the conflict, a move that would under no imaginable circumstances have been undertaken by the Chinese leadership, there was really no way that the region could be pacified on Chinese terms; neither could Peking hope to emerge as the champion of the "revolution"; and, worst of all, the United States had concluded from its observation of Chinese support that it was fighting a war against "Chinese expansionism." The prospects for Sino-American reconciliation had returned to zero, at least for the balance of the Johnson administration.

The only aspect of China's larger Vietnam strategy that "worked" was that manifested in Peking's denial to Khrushchev of rail access across China to North Vietnam. Peking apparently believed that it could turn the table on Moscow and stage a Soviet-American confrontation in Southeast Asia. There were only three high-volume logistic routes into the combat zone: the rail route across China into North Vietnam, and the ports of Haiphong (in North Vietnam) and Sihanoukville (in Cambodia). The Soviets had no alternative to supplying the ally that they had urged into action; and, by denying Moscow the luxury of Chinese sanctuary for logistic shipments, the Chinese hoped to force the Soviets to run the gauntlet of the U.S. Seventh Fleet in order to supply the battlefield. Having no alternative, the Soviets did precisely that; but, until President Nixon ordered the destruction of supply routes across Cambodia and the mining of Haiphong harbor, the United States showed no inclination to confront the Soviet Union over the Southeast Asian issue. As it happened, the Chinese themselves were unable to withstand pressures to reopen the rail line; the policy had not led to any benefit (in the form of a Johnson-Brezhnev showdown), and Peking was in danger of losing the support of its few allies in the Socialist camp. By the time that Nixon took office, the rail line was again wide open; and one must judge from the events of 1971-72 that it took some hard bargaining and generous promises on the part of the United States to persuade the Chinese to participate in the Nixon "secret plan" for ending the conflict by constricting the flow of military equipment to Vietnam.

The period 1945-70 saw a number of dramatic transformations in America's Northeast Asian security structure. It began with the United States and the Soviet Union, the only two actors in the region to emerge from World War II with enough power to control events, dividing the region into two camps. Bipolarity became even more a way of life for the region with the Communist victory in the Chinese civil war and the subsequent Sino-Soviet alliance; the Korean War, initiated and supported by the Soviet Union, and fought largely by the Chinese; and the rise of Japan as a major regional power, an unswerving U.S. ally, and the anchor of America's Asian security structure. The solidarity of the two camps was maintained for nearly a decade, until the Chinese decision in 1958 to terminate its junior partnership with the Soviet Union. The American camp did not experience such a fissure until a decade later, when Washington decided that Japan had been a junior partner for too long. By 1970, the Northeast Asian structure was on the brink of another major transformation. Much had happened since 1945, and much more was about to happen.

Nixon's first major task was to end the Vietnam war--or at least to terminate U.S. involvement. Had his goal been simply to extricate U.S. combat forces from the battlefield, he might have done so with great speed, following the plans advanced by either of his 1968 and 1972 election opponents. He chose instead to follow a course more consistent with his broader goals of restructuring America's Asian (and global) security arrangements. China, Japan, and the USSR were slated for important new roles in the post-Vietnam security structure envisioned by Nixon; China and, to a lesser extent, the Soviet Union were introduced to these new roles as Nixon's "secret plan" (read: "Chinese connection") for ending the Vietnam conflict unfolded.

Only a handfull of Americans have been privy to complete knowledge of the discussions and agreements between the Nixon administration and the Chinese; and, if one had to render a judgment on the basis of the recently revealed incongruities between what the administration told the Thieu regime and what it said it told the Thieu regime, then one would have to suspect that there is little correspondence between open accounts of the Washington-Peking negotiations and the actual discussions that occurred. One is well advised to deduce the content of those discussions on the basis of the subsequent behavior of the parties involved.

Nixon's Southeast Asia strategy obviously called for the logistic isolation of the battlefield. When accomplished, this would lead to a substantial reduction in North Vietnamese offensive capabilities, making it possible for the Americans to turn over the defense of South Vietnam to the South Vietnamese. In other words, scaling down the war would guarantee the success of "Vietnamization." As noted earlier, the battlefield could be isolated by choking off three supply arteries: the rail line, Haiphong, and Sihanoukville. The Sihanoukville artery could be severed by destroying the overland logistics line from the port to the battlefield, as was done during the Cambodian "incursion." The harbor at Haiphong could be blockaded or mined; Nixon elected to do the latter. But the rail line posed quite a different kind of problem. The flow of weapons and supplies by rail had to be cut off in China, before it reached the dispersal point at the border. Nixon had to choose between attacking Chinese territory and inducing the Chinese themselves to cut off the flow of goods by rail. He chose the latter course.

In making this choice, Nixon gave the Chinese what they had been looking for since 1958: an opportunity to bargain with the United States. The short-term quid pro quo appears to have called for the Chinese to substantially reduce the flow of military goods across the border and to employ their good offices to facilitate the extrication of U.S. forces. In return, the United States delivered Peking's membership in the United Nations, a Presidential visit to Peking, and a relaxation of the embargo on "strategic trade" with China. What Nixon presumably hoped to achieve in the longer run was the drawing of China into a constructive partnership with the United States in Asia and, of course, reelection in 1972 (by which time all American forces should have been evacuated and the North Vietnamese should not yet have regained sufficient strength to overrun the South). Both these goals were shared by the majority of the Chinese leadership; and both governments were enthusiastic, if not euphoric, during the early months of this new joint venture.

Unfortunately, this incipient partnership was established at the expense of Japan--or, more precisely, the Sato government. Nixon, like many others, probably believed that a useful Sino-American relationship could not be built within the context of the existing U.S.-Japan relationship. The operative strategy, then, was based upon two principles: untether Japan and permit Tokyo to assume a more balanced position between Washington and Peking; but don't let Japan get too far ahead of the United States in establishing a new relationship with China.

The Sato government could not have been more pro-American, but the real America had changed while Sato's America remained the same. He had repeatedly jeopardized his political career by resisting domestic pressures to formalize Japanese relations with Peking. His resistance was based upon his commitment to Japanese-American relations and his belief that the normalization of Sino-Japanese relations would do irreparable damage to the U.S.-Japanese relationship. He undoubtedly believed correctly; had he stepped out ahead of Washington, he would have severely upset Nixon's plans for restructuring the Northeast Asian security environment. But he was totally unprepared for the "shock" of July 1971, when President Nixon announced that Secretary of State Kissinger had just returned from Peking, where he had arranged a Presidential visit in the near future. Sato and his government were devastated, and Japan was abruptly cast free to seek its own relationship with the Chinese. When the Tanaka government assumed power, it was only a matter of days before the Prime Minister journeyed to Peking to negotiate a new relationship.

The Sato government was not the only victim of the dramatic change in Sino-American relations. Lin Piao, who in 1969 had been officially designated as Mao Tse-Tung's successor, did not remain on the scene even as long as Sato. Although outside observers have yet to untangle all the conflicting accounts of Lin's ouster and death in September 1971, it is clear that his downfall was largely the consequence of his opposition to the new Sino-American relationship. And, during the initial months of Sino-American enthusiasm, the Chinese who had engineered the new relationship wielded considerable domestic political power.

Perhaps the greatest pain of all was that felt by Moscow. American and Chinese public assertions to the contrary notwithstanding, the new Sino-American relationship was (and is) decidedly anti-Soviet. All other Sino-American mutual interests combined do not compare in importance with the common goal of undermining and limiting Soviet power; without that common goal, there would hardly

be a basis for a serious Sino-American relationship. A decade of
Soviet actions in Southeast Asia, on the Sino-Soviet border, and
elsewhere had been calculated to pressure China back into Moscow's
preferred Asian security structure. The events of 1971-72 capped a
decade of failure.

Superpower "detente" has become a catchword for many things.
One of them is polycentrism--or multipolarity. Under such a structure, which appears to have been desired more by the United States
than by the USSR, the superpowers would "preside" over a world in
which regional powers or regional alliances would exercise primary
control over events. However, the manner in which the United
States sought to implement this principle in Northeast Asia did not
conform to Moscow's idea of fair play. Judging from the events of
1971-72, Northeast Asia was going to be controlled by a Sino-
Japanese-American consortium, with no role for the Soviet Union--
save perhaps the role of spoiler, which role Moscow has adequately
filled since 1972. In short, what Moscow learned in Northeast Asia
was that the price of detente was going to be very high in terms of
compromised security interests and loss of dominance in key geographical regions.

By the end of 1972, when the Nixon administration was forced
to abandon its concern with remaking the world and turn its attention
instead to the power struggle in Washington, only the first phase of
the grand restructuring plan had been completed: the old structure
had been dismantled. Japan had been cast adrift politically and, to
a lesser extent, economically. The new Sino-American relationship
was developing at a surprisingly rapid pace. The Soviet Union had
been confronted in Haiphong and, in a sense, in Northeast Asia,
given the anti-Soviet flavor of the new Sino-American accords. Most
U.S. combat troops were out of Vietnam, though the war still raged
at a level higher than had been anticipated by Nixon in 1970. Moscow
had been excluded from an effective role in Northeast Asia, a slight
that probably had some bearing on Moscow's decision to encourage
the 1973 Middle East War. And, not incidentally, both Japan and the
United States had significantly, but not completely, reduced their
commitments to Taiwan.

What has happened lately in U.S.-Soviet detente? in Sino-
American relations? in U.S.-Japanese relations? in Sino-Soviet
relations? in Sino-Japanese relations? In each case, the answer
is the same: not much. Progress continues in Strategic Arms Limitation Talks (SALT), with the promise that the next round will bring
actual reductions, rather than just limits on selected categories of
growth. But in most other areas, detente has been just a word. Developments in the Middle East in 1973, which culminated in the U.S.

worldwide military alert, provide the best example. While the alert was not taken very seriously in the United States, apparently because of the propensity of observers to relate it to domestic events rather than view it in the global context in which it took place, it was understood by other nations (undoubtedly including the Soviet Union) as an expression of the very essence of the U.S.-Soviet relationship. The Chinese, for example, were forced virtually to abandon the belief that the superpower relationship was one of "collusion," even though "collusion" is what "detente" is all about. Most Chinese now argue that SALT is simply an exception within a superpower relationship that is conducted primarily at dagger point.

The four-year-old Sino-American relationship has avoided major crises, but also has made little progress. It may be that the quid pro quo of the early 1970s was the beginning and end of the relationship; that relationship appears now to be something that Foreign Service officers do, for its development no longer commands a high priority in either capital. From the Chinese point of view, the next political step should be progress in the resolution of the Taiwan issue, which implies American recognition of Peking as the only legitimate government of China. From the U.S. point of view, the Chinese have little to offer in exchange for such a major concession. Perhaps there can be no basis for exchange except where Peking "misbehaves" and the United States bargains for the cessation of misbehavior. Should the Chinese resume the active development of ICBMs capable of reaching the United States, or give the appearance of entering into an alliance with the Japanese that excludes the United States from its traditional influence in Asia, there might be an incentive for new bargains.

Relations between Washington and Tokyo have improved since 1971-72, but they will never be the same. The new relationship that is now developing will necessarily be a product not only of the firm Cold War alliance, but also of the Nixon "shocks." This implies greater independence for the Japanese and an end to the extraordinary deference once paid by Tokyo to Washington's preferences. To the extent that Japan and America are competitors, as in the economic arena, the new relationship may be less satisfactory (for the United States), although one might argue that the Japanese have rarely conceded anything in the economic arena out of deference to the United States. In the international political arena, however, this new independence on the part of Japan may work either good or ill for the United States. Japanese self-interests don't uniformly coincide with American interests, although there are few instances of diametric opposition.

Northeast Asia is a case in point. There is little incentive in the current international climate for the Japanese to play a strong

independent role in the maintenance of Northeast Asian security. Yet
this is precisely the kind of Japanese role that would best suit U.S.
interests--at least to the extent that Japan might relieve the United
States of the burden of maintaining Japanese security, as we have
done by deterring war in Korea and by guaranteeing the security of
oil supply routes in the Pacific. In a word, the danger is that Japan,
rather than becoming the guarantor of its own security, will see
greater security in a partnership with China or, perhaps, the Soviet
Union.

The substance of Sino-Soviet relations has remained virtually
unchanged for fifteen years. American understanding of that relationship has had its high points and low during the period, but little
has happened to drive the two Communist powers either closer together or farther apart than they were in 1960. In fact, Soviet pressure upon Peking--applied first in Southeast Asia and then on the
Sino-Soviet border--has served effectively to galvanize the Chinese
leadership and, in a sense, to stabilize the unhappy relationship.
Continuing political campaigns in China against "pro-Soviet elements"
suggest that there may be some residual pro-Soviet elements in the
leadership; but beyond this, there is little reason to expect an imminent dramatic change in Sino-Soviet relations, save a possible deterioration in the wake of a Soviet military campaign against the
Chinese.

Of all the bilateral relationships in Northeast Asia, the only
one that appears to be making real progress is the Sino-Japanese relationship. The Japanese have successfully preserved their commercial interests on Taiwan while normalizing political relations
with Peking. More important, though, is the fact that both the Chinese and the Japanese have come to realize the extent of their common security interests in the region. Neither power is capable of
dominating the region, but together they are fully able to control the
events and destiny of Northeast Asia. Neither power seems to view
the other as a significant security threat. In fact, one of Japan's
primary security interests, the maintenance of a continuous flow of
petroleum to the islands, has been provided for by the Chinese, who
have agreed to supply Japan with quantities of petroleum that exceed
what was once thought to be China's total annual production.

This same pattern of interest integration can be seen in the
complementarity of the Japanese and North Chinese economies. Long
a matter of fact, it has only recently become a matter of importance.
Japan is rapidly becoming a competitor of South China as a buyer and
seller to North China. Chances are that much of the opposition in
Peking to the furtherance of Sino-Japanese relations resides in what
is essentially a South China lobby.

Of more immediate interest than economic integration is the incipient integration of the two nations' military capabilities. Like economic integration, this is probably unintentional. Nonetheless, it does appear to be developing; and the odds for its continuing to do so are quite high.

There has not been much progress in the "right direction during 1973-75. An American observer in Peking suggested that we think of this stagnation as "crossing a plateau." Although he was referring specifically to Sino-American relations, he might have been discussing all the bilateral and multilateral relationships in the region. Only the Sino-Japanese relationship seems to be growing stronger, and it is not at all clear that this is desirable for any of the other powers in the region.

URGENCY OF THE ISSUE

A number of developments may take place in Northeast Asia during 1976-77--some of them very probable, others only remotely possible, but all of them bearing upon critical U.S. security interests and therefore worthy of consideration today.

Without doubt, there will be a leadership succession in China. Thus far, everyone who has predicted the deaths of Mao Tse-tung and Chou En-lai has been wrong; this China watcher has learned to steer clear of such predictions. This, however, does not bar one from predicting a leadership succession. Over the past several years, in the case of Mao, and over the past two years, in the case of Chou, these men have given an increasing proportion of responsibility to the next generation of leaders. Routine authority is exercised by a reasonably stable second echelon. However, the stability of this leadership layer is largely the consequence of Mao's and Chou's ability to preside over the resolution of major issues and personnel changes. This ability is fading, though; and when it is no longer effective, as a consequence either of death or of political feebleness, this second echelon will sort itself out according to rules other than those imposed by Mao and Chou. It is this succession that is most critical--not the succession to the titles now held by Mao and Chou but succession to the decision-making power that is now collegial.

No other plausible development in Northeast Asia is as certain as the redistribution of decision-making authority in China. Sino-Soviet war remains a very real possibility, with its likelihood dependent to a significant degree upon Soviet expectations regarding American response. The continuation of Sino-Japanese political, economic, and military accommodation is fairly certain; but it is impossible to predict how formal or rigid this integration will be--whether the two powers will operate on the basis of a treaty of friendship or whether they will enter into a formal alliance. Japan has been forced to choose between the Soviet Union and China; neither neighbor has been willing to "share" Japanese friendship with the other. In fact, Chinese offers to sell petroleum to Japan were initiated primarily in response to the announcement of Soviet-Japanese plans for joint exploitation of energy resources in Siberia. Naturally, the cessation of this plan was a condition for the purchase of Chinese oil. Thus, the odds of major improvement in the Soviet-Japanese relationship will diminish with continued improvement in Sino-Japanese ties.

U.S. objectives must be taken into account in order to weigh the advisability of tampering with current trends--all of which, it should be noted, are continuing in the absence of any active U.S. involvement in the region. Our objectives are both limited and achievable: to limit and reduce Soviet influence over the region, to prevent the outbreak of war in the region, to retain our relatively free access to markets in the region, to carry less of the burden for the security of the region than we carried in the 1950s and 1960s, and to retain a measure of positive control over developments in the region. Most of these objectives, though achievable through positive action on the part of the United States, may be directly threatened by developments in the region. Power in China could easily devolve to a group much less inclined than the present one to support American achievement of these objectives. Also, a Sino-Japanese partnership that excluded the United States from a position of influence in the region might deny us several of our objectives. War will remain a possibility regardless of U.S. policy, but its likelihood might be considerably reduced by an active U.S. regional role. Unfortunately, this means that the likelihood of war will be diminished by our increasing (through active participation in the region) the odds of our involvement in such a war, should it occur. However, U.S. influence over events in Northeast Asia will necessarily be proportional to the depth of its involvement in the region. The question that the policy-maker must ask is whether the gains expected from involvement are worth the cost, or whether the consequences of developments that take place in the absence of U.S. involvement are sufficiently serious to warrant a change in our current laissez-faire policy.

ALTERNATIVE STRATEGIES

As implied in the preceding discussion, American policy-makers have four general alternatives in Northeast Asia, the first three of which will be discussed in this section: a continuation of laissez-faire, a rebuilding of the U.S.-Japanese alliance, and the development of an operative Sino-American relationship.

President Ford's Northeast Asian policy has essentially been one of laissez-faire--at least at the time of this writing, which predates the President's visit to Peking in December 1975. Such a policy is certainly consistent with the overall policy of primary attention to Europe and the Middle East that has characterized the current administration. And, as the 1976 elections draw near, there is much to be said for treading lightly in a region unlikely to erupt or in any other way create a crisis during the next few months.

Indeed, none of the four policy alternatives has a higher short-run payoff than laissez-faire: its short-term costs and risks are very low. But it likely has no long-term payoffs, except those left to chance; and it carries considerable long-term costs and risks, measured in terms of lost opportunities and influence over events that impact upon U.S. security interests. To adhere to the current policy is, in effect, to write off China and Japan as potential U.S. partners in Northeast Asia, and to encourage them to develop their own partnership without U.S. participation.

The second alternative is to rebuild the U.S.-Japanese alliance and once again rely upon Japan as the anchor of America's Northeast Asian security structure. This alternative has much to recommend it. Over a twenty-year period, Japan proved itself to be the most reliable of American overseas allies. To the extent that that reliability was predicated upon faith in American consideration of Japanese interests, it cannot be regained in the near future. But the alliance was built upon more than faith; there is a considerable commonality of interests between the two powers that would be the best guarantee of endurance in an alliance, providing a contrast to those partnerships predicated upon short-term expedience and hostage to a continuous accounting of quid pro quo.

A new U.S.-Japan alliance would undoubtedly require some important modification of the old relationship, which proved unsatisfactory to the United States. Japan would be expected to bear a greater share of the burden of maintaining the security of Northeast Asia, which would, in turn, entail greater costs to Japan and probably the development of a Japanese military force adequate to the task of maintaining regional security. Whether the Japanese are willing to incur these costs in return for a new, improved alliance with the United States is questionable.

The third alternative--the development of an operative Sino-American relationship--is not entirely separable from the fourth-- the cultivation of a Sino-Japanese-American partnership. It might be thought of as a first step toward the fourth, although the latter need not follow. This third alternative, like the second, has much to recommend it. In general terms, there is something to be said for initiating a partnership with the one power (except the Soviet Union) most able and most likely to disrupt the security of the region. One must assume that such a partnership would act as a restraint upon each partner's inclination to act against the interests of the other. More specifically, such a partnership would be likely to influence the current succession contest in Peking in a relatively pro-American direction, deter the Soviet Union from initiating hostilities against China, drastically reduce the likelihood of Sino-Soviet reconciliation, improve the prospects for pacification of the Korean Peninsula, and open markets that have heretofore been closed to Americans.

On the other side of the ledger, the costs of such a policy would probably be high--both in dollars and in politics. U.S. participation in Chinese nation-building, which is an unavoidable adjunct to this policy, implies substantial long-term credits and the transfer of considerable quantities of foodstuffs, capital equipment, and technology. The political costs will be paid both at home and abroad. Much that is proposed under this third alternative would be unattractive to major segments of the American political system, and it could also be expected to damage Soviet-American relations.

A fourth alternative, the one preferred by this writer, is the cultivation of a Sino-Japanese-American partnership. Under any circumstances, such a partnership would have the appearance and substance of an alliance and, as such, probably ought to be developed as one. The most important common goal of the three powers is the limiting of Soviet influence in the region. What is proposed here is essentially a scaled-down version of NATO, which might be referred to as NEATO (Northeast Asian Treaty Organization). In the process of pursuing this primary goal, a number of secondary goals would be served.

There is no doubt that NEATO could guarantee the security of Northeast Asia. Except for the Soviet Union, none of the other Asian nations would be in a position even to think of challenging the alliance; and the Soviets would be most unlikely to act against three of their four principal adversaries (Western Europe being counted as the fourth). A long list of hypothetical advantages of NEATO might be generated, but most of them are obvious.

What, then, are the disadvantages? What are the costs? What is proposed is that the United States incur an obligation unmatched since we pledged ourselves to defend South Vietnam against its northern attackers. Such obligations are not incurred easily, especially as we survey the losses we have suffered on the international scene since the 1960s. Dollar costs, like these psychological costs, would be high. The United States would necessarily serve as the armorer to such an alliance. Chinese military equipment is largely obsolete, as is Chinese military technology. Both would require substantial updating.

The most important question to be answered is whether the Chinese and Japanese would participate in such an alliance. The answer is a qualified "yes." Much of the groundwork for the partnership has already been laid. As noted earlier, there is already a complementarity in Sino-Japanese military capabilities. What the Japanese lack--infantry, armor, attack aircraft, bombers, and nuclear weapons--the Chinese have. And Japanese naval and air defense capabilities would fill critical gaps in the Chinese military.

There has developed a similar "fit" between Chinese and American military forces. There is nothing the Chinese have that the United States lacks, save a three-million-man army. The United States, on the other hand, possesses the long-range strategic delivery systems and high-technology precision weapons that the Chinese have not yet developed. In addition, the United States has highly sophisticated intelligence-collection, warning, and communication systems not otherwise available to either the Chinese or the Japanese.

The Chinese have made clear their interest in establishing military ties with the United States. There is no public indication that they have suggested a relationship resembling NEATO; but such a relationship, if styled correctly, could be very appealing to Peking. To suit Peking, NEATO would probably have to be a tacit, rather than explicit, alliance. This probably would also be the case with the Japanese, for neither nation is likely to see any benefit in brazen antagonism of the Soviet Union.

For Peking, NEATO probably would have to hold the promise of developing Chinese military self-sufficiency. But, within limits, this would suit the interests of the other two parties. For Tokyo, NEATO would have to guarantee that densely populated and rabidly nonnuclear Japan would not be the locus of key counterforce targets and nuclear arsenals. This has long been an issue in U.S.-Japanese military relations and would be likely to plague NEATO as well.

Beyond these costs and barriers, however, NEATO (in one form or another) is probably workable. The costs, however, are "up front"; the payoff is very long-term. But the payoff is very high, and well worth the serious consideration of the U.S. policy-maker whose eye is on long-term security.

KOREA:
THE PROBLEM OF
SUPERPOWER WITHDRAWAL
William V. Kennedy

THE ISSUE

The central question for U.S. involvement in Korea remains the issue of military presence: force levels, positioning, and doctrine. The next five years will be critical in augmenting South Korean forces to allow U.S. withdrawal. The issues in debate revolve around the means to achieve that withdrawal.

BACKGROUND OF THE ISSUE

At the conclusion of President Ford's visit to South Korea in November 1974, he and President Park Chung Hee issued a joint communique stating, ". . . President Ford assured President Park that the United States has no plan to reduce the present level of United States Forces in Korea."

The principal element of the U.S. forces in Korea is the Second Infantry Division, which is stationed north of Seoul, the Republic of Korea's capital. The division has been withdrawn from the front line of South Korean defense, but it continues to occupy a reserve position athwart the principal invasion route to Seoul.

From the time of its participation in the Korean War, 1950-54, the Second Division has contained a sizable contingent of Korean soldiers. They have served to fill the chronically understrengthened American units to something approaching wartime authorizations; but their presence has made it difficult, if not impossible, to use the Second Division for any purpose except defense of Korea.

On March 19, 1975, the newspaper <u>Army Times</u> reported that "Defense officials . . . confirmed a March 12 . . . <u>Times</u> report on

adding more troops to the 2d Infantry Division in Korea. The . . .
division is programmed for a manpower increase during FY 76 thus
placing it in a better posture for deployment outside Korea. . . .
Times also reported that South Koreans serving with the . . . division would be replaced by the additional troops."[1]

An increase in the American strength of the division need not
mean an increase in the overall level of about 38,000 Americans now
serving in Korea. The additional strength could be provided by transferring additional logistical functions to the South Koreans and assigning the saving in U.S. manpower to the Second Division.

The Ford-Park communique and the reported decision to increase the Second Division were made against a background of substantial Congressional opposition to the U.S. presence in Korea, at
least of the present size.

In July 1974, the House Appropriations Committee published a
report by two staff members, Derek J. Vander Schaaf and Donald J.
Alderson, based on a fifteen-day trip to Hawaii, Japan, and Korea.
Vander Schaaf and Alderson concluded, "Prompt and decisive action
is needed to reduce the risks of automatic combat involvement [in
Korea]. The goals should be to gain freedom of political and military
action while continuing to honor international commitments, and to
lower the cost of the US presence while preserving its value for deterrence and defense."[2] To accomplish this, Vander Schaaf and
Alderson recommended withdrawal of the Second Infantry Division to
a location south of Seoul and conversion of the division to a theater
rather than a localized mission. Portions of the Vander Schaaf-
Alderson report were printed in the report of the House Appropriations Committee on the fiscal year 1976 Department of Defense appropriations request. These excerpts were treated as advisories,
however, and did not carry the force of law.

The withdrawal of Koreans from the Second Division and the
increase in American strength reported by Army Times indicate an
acceptance of at least that part of the Appropriations Committee
recommendations pertaining to availability of the division for use
outside Korea.

The Vietnam debacle had a profound effect on further consideration of the Appropriations Committee recommendations. Vander
Schaaf and Alderson had discounted U.S. military and diplomatic expressions of concern over the effect of U.S. troop withdrawals from
Korea on our relations with Japan. Immediately following the fall of
Saigon, however, the New York Times reported a statement by a
Japanese "Foreign Ministry official" that "Japan . . . must rectify
her position of having relied excessively on the United States."[3] In
a later dispatch the Times reported: "The speed with which a consensus on Korea and its dangers [to Japan] seems to have evolved

has been striking. The Japanese, in their innate caution and groping for agreement usually take plenty of time. In this instance, proximity and history appear to have dictated a swift reaction."[4]

The significance of Korea to Japan and of Japan to the United States is discussed by Ralph Clough of the Brookings Institution in his book East Asia and US Security:

> The Japanese have traditionally been concerned about who controlled [the Korean] peninsula--this "dagger pointed at the heart of Japan." The forcible seizure of South Korea in 1950 by North Korean Communists, backed by the Russians, would have dismayed the Japanese and might have caused a political evolution within Japan highly unfavorable to US interests.[5]

Clough, a retired Foreign Service officer with extensive experience in East Asia, sees a primary U.S. interest in enabling Japan to continue as "a lightly armed, nonnuclear power." Vander Schaaf and Alderson had reached a contrary conclusion: that "the most prudent course may be to recognize the inevitability of substantial Japanese rearmament in the relatively near future and to attempt to guide the process along lines consistent with American goals in the Far East."[6]

Clough and Dr. William H. Overholt of the Hudson Institute see a diminishing chance of the United States guiding Japan anywhere once she decides to rearm as a major power. Overholt, in a paper delivered at an Army War College symposium in March 1975, expressed the belief that major Japanese rearmament, if it does occur, will almost certainly come about in an anti-American context. Clough also warns that major Japanese rearmament would be likely to occur in an anti-American environment.[7] He adds that one of the choices open to a rearmed but still vulnerable Japan would be to "ally its military strength to that of the USSR or China. . . . Even a nonaligned Japan, relying heavily on military strength, . . . would make East Asia a less stable region."[8] Both authors see the security status of Korea and the American role therein as a key factor in Japan's decision on whether to rearm as a major power or to continue to rely on the present security relationship with the United States.

The question of future U.S. policy in Korea is further complicated by domestic South Korean politics and by the status of Taiwan. President Park Chung Hee has been in power since the military coup of 1961. He has relied on increasingly repressive measures to maintain power. The domestic and foreign reaction to these measures has steadily increased. Former U.S. Ambassador to Japan Edwin O.

Reischauer has urged that the United States demand an end to repression and a "move back toward a freer, more democratic system." To convince President Park that we mean business, Reischauer recommends "cutting down on our military aid and the number of troops we have in Korea, with a clear indication that we will be forced to continue on to complete disengagement if conditions in Korea do not improve."[9]

It seems apparent that President Ford and Secretary of State Kissinger have rejected the Reischauer formula as unworkable, particularly following the collapse of South Vietnam. Following an interview with President Ford on May 8, South Korean Ambassador Hahm Pyong Choon stated that the President had expressed a firm commitment to the defense of South Korea and an intention to maintain U.S. troop strength. Even before the fall of Vietnam, Secretary Kissinger indicated that the Reischauer formula had been considered and rejected. On July 24, 1974, Secretary Kissinger stated that the Ford administration had decided "to authorize economic and military assistance even when we would not recommend the actions of the Government of South Korea." He described South Korea as "very crucial" to Japan, a judgment that he said is "shared by the government of Japan." On April 15, 1975, Secretary of Defense James Schlesinger described the U.S. defense commitments to both Japan and South Korea as part of "the highest law of the land."

If the principal element of the issue of the level of forces in Korea is the security of Japan and Japan's future policies, then it must also be recognized that Japanese defense planners traditionally have regarded Taiwan as "only slightly less important" than Korea to the security of Japan. An identical assessment was made by the United States at the time of the North Korean attack on South Korea in 1950. At the same time that an American Army was sent to Korea, the U.S. Seventh Fleet was ordered to protect Taiwan. That commitment is still in force.

Current U.S. policy in East Asia is built on three mutual security treaties--with Japan, the Republic of Korea, and the Republic of China (Taiwan).

The treaty of mutual cooperation and security between Japan and the United States entered into force on June 23, 1960. It provides: "Each Party recognizes that an armed attack against either Party in the territories under the administration of Japan would be dangerous to its own peace and safety and declares that it would act to meet the common danger in accordance with its constitutional provisions and processes." In practical terms, the treaty has been given meaning by the positioning of American forces in a manner that would involve them directly in Japan's defense in the event of attack. Japanese confidence in the strength of the treaty, as expressed in the press and by public officials, has tended to decline in almost direct proportion to the physical presence of U.S. forces in and around Japan. Paradoxically, that decline has occurred, in part, because of Japanese public--as distinguished from governmental--pressures.

The mutual defense treaty with the Republic of Korea entered into force on November 17, 1954. It states: "Each Party recognizes that an armed attack in the Pacific area on either of the Parties in territories now under their respective administrative control . . . would be dangerous to its own peace and safety and declares that it would act to meet the common danger in accordance with its constitutional processes." The risk of "automatic" U.S. involvement in Korea stems, therefore, not from the strict language of the treaty, but from the positioning of U.S. forces in a location where they would become engaged almost immediately in the defense of the South Korean capital.

The mutual defense treaty with the Republic of China has been in force since March 3, 1955. Its purpose, as stated in the preamble, is essentially identical to that of the treaty with South Korea: to affirm "that no potential aggressor could be under the illusion that either [party to the treaty] stands alone in the West Pacific Area." The treaty pledges both signatories

> separately and jointly by self-help and mutual aid [to] maintain and develop their individual and collective capacity to resist armed attack and Communist subversive activities directed from without against their territorial integrity and political stability. . . . Each Party recognizes that an armed attack in the West Pacific Area directed against the territories of either of the Parties would be dangerous to its own peace and declares that it would act to meet the common danger in accordance with its constitutional processes . . . the terms "territorial" and "territories" shall mean . . . Taiwan and the Pescadores . . . [and] such other territories as may be determined by mutual agreement.

Thus the United States is free to include or not to include under the provisions of the treaty the China Coast islands of Quemoy and Matsu, held by the Republic of China and periodically under bombardment by the Communists.

There has been a growing public assumption since President Nixon's visit to China in 1972 that the United States is moving to abrogate the treaty with the Republic of China in the interest of better relations with Peking. This assumption is based on the communique issued at Shanghai at the conclusion of the Nixon visit, in which the United States recognized that the Chinese on Taiwan and the Chinese on the mainland regard Taiwan as part of China.

The Shanghai communique did not address the question of the native Taiwanese, who form the great majority of the island's inhabitants. Visitors to Taiwan are virtually unanimous in the belief that, given a choice, the native Taiwanese would choose independence over reunion with the mainland. The complexities and the ambiguities of this situation are reflected in the following exchange between Kaoru Nakamaru of the Japanese magazine Jiyu and Marshall Green, then U.S. Assistant Secretary of State for East Asian and Pacific Affairs, published in February 1973:

> GREEN: All that we can say [in regard to the future of Taiwan] is that we think that the situation must be settled peacefully and we can only hope that the situation will be settled by the people living on either side of the Taiwan Strait. We cannot sway them in any way.
>
> NAKAMARU: In other words, the [Nationalist] Government's and the Chinese Government's settling it. . . .
>
> GREEN: That is not what I said, you know. I am certainly trying to be extremely careful in my choice of words. I do not want it rephrased carelessly.

During a press conference on May 7, 1975, President Ford stated that the United States intends "to reaffirm our commitments to Taiwan."

A factor that must be considered in assessing the relationship of Taiwan to the overall political situation in Northeast Asia is the concern expressed from time to time in the Japanese press that a Taiwan cut off from American support might turn to the Soviet Union. Access by Soviet air and naval power to Taiwan would be an explosive issue in both China and Japan, and potentially in the United States as well.

Senator Mike Mansfield of Montana has long been a leader of Congressional forces seeking a reduction in the U.S. forces deployed overseas. In a speech at Georgetown University and in an interview on Public Broadcasting Television, both on May 25, 1975, Senator Mansfield made his first formal statement on the subject since the U.S. defeat in Vietnam. There was a notable departure from the tone of previous statements. In regard to withdrawals of U.S. forces

from Europe and Korea, he stated that such withdrawals should be
made over a period of time and in the context of an improved system
of international stability.

The long-established position of the United States, reemphasized in recent months by President Ford, Secretary Kissinger, and
Secretary of Defense Schlesinger, is that neither a Communist Korea
nor a divided Korea can provide the buffer needed to neutralize the
conflicting interests of China, the Soviet Union, and Japan--all of
which converge in Korea. Chinese intervention in 1951 and the decision of the United States not to pursue a forced reunification of Korea
have been followed by a U.S. policy of seeking peaceful reunification
of the peninsula under a government acceptable to the population of
both North and South Korea. However remote achievement of such
an objective may be, it seems certain that only a viable, unified, and
genuinely independent Korea can provide some reasonable assurance
that the country will not become a springboard for aggrandizement by
one of the major Asian powers.

URGENCY OF THE ISSUE

Resolution of what future U.S. policy is to be in Northeast Asia
has acquired an increasing urgency in regard to both future Japanese
policy and the Sino-Soviet dispute. All concerned now clearly recognize that U.S. commitments are only as good as the extent to which
Congress will support them. Japanese and Korean domestic politics
are in a state of flux. Taiwan is doubtful about U.S. intentions. The
future leadership of the People's Republic of China and the future relations of China with the USSR are in doubt. Continuing uncertainty
about the future U.S. policy toward Northeast Asia is bound to increase the instability and the danger of this situation. The longer
this uncertainty continues, the greater the possibility that Japan or
Taiwan, or both, might seek an alternative international relationship
to the present security ties with the United States. There would be
a strong temptation in both cases to increase bargaining power by
acquiring nuclear weapons. Some clear consensus must be achieved,
therefore, within and between the legislative and executive branches
of the U.S. government on the question of whether the United States
is to continue as a full participant in the Northeast Asian political and
military equation, or to leave Asia to its own devices come what may.

ALTERNATIVE STRATEGIES

In general, there appear to be four courses of action open to
the United States.

Alternative I

The United States can retain and make more credible its present commitment in Northeast Asia. Some of the actions that might be taken to this purpose are the following:
- Maintain the Second Infantry Division in place and increase its readiness by reallocating manpower and resources within the existing overall Northeast Asian U.S. force level.
- Reaffirm U.S. intentions to preclude change in the status of Taiwan by external aggression.
- Improve command and control by substituting a Joint Northeast Asia Command for the present somewhat fragmented U.S. command structure in the area.

This represents essentially a continuation of the policy the United States has followed in Northeast Asia for the past twenty-five years, with some adjustments to resolve doubts created by the Indochina situation. The principal argument for continuance of such a policy is that while it has been operative, there has been no large-scale military clash anywhere in the region. Its major disadvantage is the risk of "automatic involvement" of U.S. forces in any new North Korean aggression against South Korea. In the opinion of some senior U.S. and Japanese military and diplomatic officials, it is precisely the "automatic involvement" of U.S. forces that has kept the peace.

Alternative II

The United States can reduce its mainland Asia (Korea) presence to a token force but retain other East Asia deployments (air and naval, Marines on Okinawa).

The desirability of this alternative comes down to a question of how large a U.S. force is needed in Korea to maintain the U.S.-Japanese security relationship and to deter military action by other powers, notably North Korea against South Korea and the USSR against China.

Senior Japanese defense officials already have made pointed references to the number of U.S. divisions committed to the defense of Europe, compared with the number available for early employment in Northeast Asia. It seems apparent from these private comments, and from the public expression of concern by the Japanese Foreign Ministry cited earlier, that adoption of this alternative would involve a risk of further weakening Japan's confidence in its security relationship with the United States.

Alternative III

The United States can withdraw from the Asian mainland and attempt to retain a residual presence based in Japan. All of the evidence currently available indicates that the ending of U.S. land combat capability in Korea would produce a fundamental reassessment by Japan of its security posture and international relationships. Maintenance of U.S. bases and forces in Japan under these circumstances is doubtful.

The failure of U.S. policy in Indochina appears to have set in motion an initiative by North Korea to secure China's support for more aggressive action against South Korea. China has publicly discouraged military initiatives. Whether it could dissuade North Korea from such action in the absence of "automatic involvement" by U.S. forces is questionable.

For the Soviet Union and China the question of the continued existence of a significant U.S. land combat force on the flank of Manchuria--a key area of conflict between the two giants--complicates consideration of military operations in either direction. Withdrawal of the force would remove this factor and, to some degree, lessen the constraints felt by a potential attacker.

Alternative IV

The United States can withdraw to mid-Pacific or Alaskan bases, except for air and naval forces based in the Philippines; abrogate the treaty with Taiwan; force Japan to take a more active role as guarantor of the peace in East Asia; and maintain its nuclear commitment to Japan.

Following the fall of Vietnam, President Marcos of the Philippines expressed a need to "reassess" the U.S.-Philippine relationship, in particular with reference to the U.S. bases in his nation. Since this alternative includes a return by Japan to a fully armed and possibly nuclear status, it is possible that Philippine fear of Japan would bring about a further reassessment of the U.S. presence, in the direction of keeping the present base arrangements. The response of the USSR and China to Japan's new role must also be considered, however, This alternative implies a military role for Japan in Korea. Since substitution of Japanese for U.S. troops would be unacceptable to the Koreans, the only means available to Japan for protection of this vital avenue of approach would be acquisition of a nuclear-armed missile force based in Japan and expansion of the Japanese navy to the full range of naval weaponry, including missile-armed submarines and aircraft carriers. Mindful of the fact that the

original Sino-Soviet treaty of friendship and alliance (1950) was
aimed at Japan, many observers see full-scale Japanese rearmament, particularly with nuclear weapons, as one force that could
bring about a rapprochement between Peking and Moscow.

In an interview with US News and World Report, published on
March 25, 1974, Admiral Noel Gayler, U.S. Commander-in-Chief,
Pacific, stated: "I have looked quite hard, but I have never found
any credible cost studies which would tell me what extra costs, if
any, there are in keeping an Army division in Korea compared to
keeping it, say, in Hawaii or on the mainland."

The U.S. forces in Korea are, at present, largely a net charge
against the U.S. balance-of-payments account. However, if the same
forces were to be retained on U.S. territory for the same theater
mission, it would be necessary to provide substantial additional airlift and sealift. Withdrawal of the U.S. force in Korea to mid-Pacific
bases would involve new costs for cantonment, training areas, and
substitution of the industrial support now provided by the Korean and
Japanese economies. The principal cost, however, would be in the
dismantling of the intricately balanced international system built by
the United States in Northeast Asia since World War II. What would
take the place of this system is anyone's guess. Nor is there any
guarantee that the United States would be able to accept whatever did
emerge. There is at least the germ of a possibility in this that the
political consequences could result in an even greater U.S. commitment than is now the case. That was the consequence of the last attempt by the United States, in 1950, to declare itself a nonparticipant
in Asian power politics.

CONCLUSIONS

It can be concluded that the question of the future of U.S. forces
in Korea cannot be resolved without considering future U.S. policy
toward Japan and the future role of Japan in the Northeast Asian political equation. Nor can either of these questions be considered
apart from the future status of Taiwan. Reduction of U.S. forces,
particularly the land forces in Korea, is almost certain to lead to a
reorientation of Japanese defense policy. It could also lead to a
change in the domestic political context in which Japan has been gov-
erned since World War II. Such changes would have significant implications for great-power relationships in Asia and throughout the
world.

During the latter part of the Vietnam War, there was an obvious split between the Executive and Legislative branches of the U.S.

government concerning future U.S. policy in Asia. Announced Presidential policy was for a continued strong U.S. presence. Congressional opinion appeared to be headed in an opposite direction. The dimensions and the suddenness of the debacle in Indochina and the immediate public questioning of U.S. reliability throughout much of the world produced even stronger Presidential statements and a decided hesitancy in opposing Congressional opinion. As stated earlier, the resulting uncertainty abroad about the future direction of U.S. policy could have far worse consequences than a clear-cut decision to stay or to get out.

To government leaders and to large groups of their countrymen in countries such as Taiwan and South Korea, changes in the politics of the region involve much more than the loss or retention of office. For many of these people it is a matter of personal freedom and even of life. Under that sort of pressure there can be no waiting for U.S. policy to evolve over a long period of debate and adjustment. Having chosen to take a direct hand in the conduct of U.S. foreign policy, there is now a clear need for Congress either to affirm or disavow a continuing principal role for the United States in Northeast Asia.

Lack of Congressional action on this issue will convey an attitude of indifference. This would convince many Asians that, because of its predominant cultural and racial background, the United States is unable to recognize the scope and importance of its interests in Asia, that the United States is thereby unable to act in a timely manner, and that its friends in Asia had better act on their own behalf-- whatever the consequences to the United States. The Philippines and Thailand already are a considerable distance down this path.

The procedural and structural obstacles that stand in the way of a timely solution of this quandary suggest that Congress may be more deeply involved in the operation of U.S. foreign policy than it really wishes to be and that some more satisfactory arrangement must be found for assertion of Congressional influence.

NOTES

1. Gene Famiglietti, "2 Brigades, 10 Battalions Slated for FY 76 Activation," Army Times, March 19, 1975, p. 6.
2. Derek J. Vander Schaaf and Donald J. Alderson, Report of Staff Visit to U.S. Military Commands in Hawaii, Japan, and Korea, U.S. Congress, House, Committee on Appropriations (Washington, D.C.: U.S. Government Printing Office, July 1974), p. 1.
3. Joseph Lelyveld, New York Times, May 2, 1975, p. 16.

4. Richard Halloran, "Japanese Fearful of Conflict in Korea," New York Times, May 14, 1975, p. 17.

5. Ralph Clough, East Asia and US Security (Washington, D.C.: Brookings Institution, 1975), p. 34.

6. Vander Schaaf and Alderson, op. cit., p. S-6.

7. Clough, op. cit., p. 51.

8. Ibid., p. 32.

9. Edwin O. Reischauer, "The Korean Connection," New York Times Magazine, September 22, 1974, p. 69.

12

JAPAN:
THE PROBLEM OF
SHARED RESPONSIBILITY
James H. Buck

THE ISSUE

The issue is whether the United States ought to restructure its security relationship with Japan as formalized in the U.S.-Japan mutual security treaty (MST).

BACKGROUND OF THE ISSUE

Since the 1950s Japan has been essentially isolated from global politics, consciously pursuing a low-risk and low-posture foreign policy, unburdened by external political commitments, concentrating on economic development, and depending on the United States for its external security.

The MST has contributed importantly to this posture; and Japan has become a world economic power while nurturing a strong, free, open, and democratic society. The United States has made the MST the cornerstone of its search for international peace and stability in the Western Pacific.

The 1960 revision of the MST entered into force for a period of ten years, following which either party could terminate on one year's notice. The treaty has been renewed automatically since 1970. The signatories affirmed their adherence to the principles of the United Nations Charter; agreed to "maintain and develop, subject to their constitutional processes, their capacities to resist armed attack"; and agreed to consult, at the request of either party, "whenever the security of Japan or international peace and security in the Far East is threatened." For this purpose Japan granted the United States the use "by its land, air and naval forces of facilities and

areas in Japan. " An armed attack against either party in the territories "under the administration of Japan" [emphasis added] would
be dangerous to its own peace and safety, and each party declared
it would act to meet the common danger "in accordance with its constitutional provision and processes. "

Two essentials differentiate the U.S.-Japanese MST from U.S.
security arrangements with non-Asian states: the U.S. "guarantee"
to Japan is unilateral, in that no reciprocal "guarantee" is accepted
by Japan; and military action under the agreement is not automatic,
but subject to the "constitutional provisions and processes" of each
party.

Provisions are also made for "joint consultation" regarding
the use of U.S. forces in Japan. U.S. ground combat forces have
not been stationed in Japan (except Okinawa) since 1957. Nuclear
weapons are not, as a matter of Japanese government policy, permitted on Japanese territory.

Recent remarkable changes in interstate relations have had
their impact on U.S.-Japanese relations, which are now in a state
of transition qualitatively distinct from the normal evolution experienced in the past few decades. It stems in part from the more
or less common experiences of these two great industrial democ-
racies--experiences that promise to alter the basic character of
social, political, and economic organization in each country in ways
not clearly understood, but dealt with conceptually in terms of the
"postindustrial age" or the "technetronic age." Japan's dominant
experience has been economic growth and peace, while that of the
United States has been economic growth and war. Both now suffer
from economic dislocations, and the problems of inflation and access to energy and other resources.

The MST has, so far, served the interests of both countries
well; but the need and desire to restructure it are becoming apparent,
particularly on the Japanese side.

In his Report to the Congress of February 18, 1970, President
Nixon reported that the United States "seeks for Asia . . . a community of free nations able to go their own way and seek their own
destiny with whatever cooperation we can provide. . . ." He summarized the policy he had announced at Guam--that the United States
will keep all its treaty commitments, will "provide a shield if a
nuclear power threatens the freedom of nations allied with us, or of
a nation whose survival we consider vital," and will provide military
and economic assistance, if asked, but will look to the threatened
nation to "assume the primary responsibility of providing the manpower for its defense." He said a sound relationship with Japan "is
crucial in our common effort to secure peace, security and a rising
living standard in the Pacific area. "

As an "economic superpower and competitor," Japan was accorded much more attention in the President's <u>Report</u> of May 3, 1973. In the mid-1950s Japan began to move out independently in her foreign economic policy, staking out a role in bridging the gap between East and West with economic ties, while the United States held back. Japan had accelerated and broadened her political involvement particularly in Asia, but also globally. In the security field, Japan relied on the MST to free resources and energies that would otherwise have been used for defense. This U.S. military protection, Nixon noted, "no longer suffices as the principal rationale for close partnership and cooperation." The gross national product of Japan and the United States together was 40 percent of the total world gross national product, Nixon stated, and Japan could no longer act as a junior partner to the United States, nor afford "an almost exclusive concentration on her economic advancement." The unilateral economic initiatives taken by the United States a few years ago were an abandonment of "our paternalistic style of alliance leadership" and meant primarily that Japan was now a full partner. Japan has interests of its own, and Japan is the ultimate judge of those interests. Japan now has, Nixon added, "the obligations of a major power--restraint, reciprocity, reliability and sensitivity to her overriding interest in a stable pattern of global relationships."

Secretary Kissinger said in a speech at St. Louis on May 12, 1975, that U.S. leaders today see the MST as a "cornerstone of world stability and progress." Nevertheless, some Americans, in contrast with Japanese perceptions of the MST, tend to see Japan as the major beneficiary of the agreement, reaping the rewards of economic development while the United States paid for the nuclear umbrella that guaranteed Japan's security, "stabilized" Asian politics, and protected Japan's interests. In short, the Japanese have enjoyed a "free ride." Japan has not been properly appreciative of the sacrifices Americans have made in Korea and Southeast Asia. The Japanese media, intellectuals, and many politicians too frequently criticize U.S. actions. Japan is accused of disregarding the "mutuality" of the MST by refusing to increase the size of its defense forces. It simply has not held its part of the bargain.

A contrary view is that Japan's defense capacities are indeed appropriate to the domestic situation, considering the Constitutional prohibition on armed forces imposed by the U.S. Occupation. Furthermore, the low military posture has benefited both U.S. and Japanese interests domestically and internationally, strengthening our alliance by contributing to Japan's economic development and by relieving other Asian countries of anxieties that would necessarily accompany a significantly stronger Japanese military posture.

While emphasizing the need for the MST, U.S. officials have
not publicly addressed the question of its revision, partly because
of an acute awareness of Japan's sensitivities about defense policy,
or perhaps because of public lack of interest. In any event, there
have been no specific public U.S. policy statements calling for revision of the MST. Some commentators have, however, interpreted
the Nixon Doctrine as a call to Japan to increase its military forces
and "to pick up its share of the burden" in Asia. If so, the call has
generally fallen on deaf ears.

The main value of the MST to Japan has been to provide a symbol of shared values and interests, and to deter nuclear attack or external aggression against Japan by conventional means. Japanese
leaders no longer see any likelihood of a conventional attack against
their nation, and even less probability of a nuclear attack, although
all of her Asian neighbors have a greater capability for such action
than at any time previously in the life of the MST. In domestic politics, the MST has justified the relatively low level of Japanese defense expenditures in per capita, if not in absolute, terms. As
former Premier Tanaka once inadvertently stated during a Diet in-
terpellation: "If there were no Japan-U.S. Security Treaty, Japan
would naturally expand its defense forces drastically beyond the
present strength."

Many Japanese do not consider the terms of the MST to be
"mutual," and consider the United States to be the main beneficiary
of the arrangement. U.S. military bases in Japan, they argue, have
been there mainly to support U.S. policies in other parts of Asia;
they have not approved of some of these policies; and they do not
subscribe to the opinion that U.S. bases in Japan are meant mainly
to defend Japan. These bases are seen by some as an invitation to
attack Japan in case of future U.S. military involvement in Asia, as
a visible infringement of Japanese sovereignty, as the cause of un-
wanted social problems near base areas, and as symbolic of a deterioration in morality. The psychological price paid by Japan for
such bases is indeed high; the political price paid by some Liberal
Democratic Party (LDP) leaders to support certain U.S. policies
has been damaging to individual political careers. The overall result of the MST has been a continuing and nagging sense of Japanese
subservience to U.S. interests and derogation of "autonomy" in
Japan's foreign and defense policies. These sacrifices, some Japanese aver, are overlooked in America.

Japanese views of the MST have shifted in response to American recognition of a changing world power distribution, symbolized
by the Nixon Doctrine, by Nixon's Kansas City speech of July 1971
(suggesting a balance of power in the next few years consisting of
the United States, Europe, the Soviet Union, China, and Japan), and

the "Nixon shocks" of that summer--the announcement of his plans
to visit China, of a series of new economic policies (including the
suspension of dollar convertibility to gold), and problems associated
with textile imports. Other important U.S. actions contributing to
this changed perception include the disengagement from Southeast
Asia, the reduction of U.S. forces in Korea, and active pursuit of
"detente" with the Soviet Union.

Judgments derived from these actions have led some Japanese, such as Kunio Muraoka, to express strong doubt whether any
American President would dare risk American lives in a crisis involving Japan because the United States has lost nuclear superiority
over the Soviet Union, and because American policy has lost that
moralistic commitment to contain Communist expansion anywhere
in the world at any cost.

While Japanese opinion leaders express reservations about the
U.S. security guarantee, Premier Miki repeats that the U.S.-
Japanese relationship is "vital for stability in the Asia-Pacific region," and President Ford repeated (April 10, 1975) the policy of
his predecessors: "We will stand by our friends, we will honor our
commitments, and we will uphold our country's principles." Nevertheless, the extent and firmness of the U.S. commitment is increasingly open to doubt in the minds of many Japanese. The rapid and
effective U.S. response to the Cambodian seizure of the Mayaguez
is not a sure guide to future U.S. reactions to challenges from other,
more powerful states.

Although the MST is generally acceptable to the Japanese public, it is not now enthusiastically supported by Japanese opinion,
and never has been. It served Japanese interests admirably when
Japan was weak economically and publicly identified her interests
almost totally with those of the United States. Neither condition exists today.

Equality and reciprocity are said to characterize the current
relationship, but these attributes are subject to wide disparities of
perception on both sides. Definitional problems are complicated by
the relative decline in America's international influence, conceived
mainly in terms of decreased credibility of American military guarantees, and further by the enormous relative increase in Japan's
economic power.

A desire to restructure the MST has been stated publicly by
prominent Japanese leaders. In the summer of 1969, then Director-
General of the Japan Defense Agency Yasuhiro Nakasone said it was
"necessary to make rearrangements regarding the American military bases in the Pacific-belt zone," that Japan should coordinate
efforts with the United States concerning its nuclear deterrent and
the Seventh Fleet, and that all other facilities maintained in Japan

should be under Japanese control. Later that year, Nakasone, who is now Minister of International Trade and Industry, stated, somewhat ambiguously, that the MST should be replaced with a "new friendship treaty" by 1975 because Japan is "too big a power to rely blindly" on that agreement.

Muraoka has suggested that a "no change" policy could be costly to the United States, particularly if a serious deterioration in economic relations were to be accompanied by a rise in nationalism in Japan that could lead to electoral losses by the governing LDP, the emergence of a coalition government, and eventually to disenchantment with parliamentary government, perhaps followed by extremist control.

Although Japanese leaders and defense intellectuals proclaim the need to adjust U.S.-Japanese security relations, there are few specific recommendations. Ideas range from Nakasone's broad suggestion of a "friendship treaty" to the demand of some leftist elements for unconditional abrogation of the MST. The Japan Socialist Party (JSP), the major opposition party, rigidly embraces the idea that the MST must be abrogated, with the precondition that Japan adopt a stance of unarmed neutrality.

Muraoka has suggested that the MST be altered to an "emergency deployment formula." This concept, essentially what former Premier Yoshida envisoned in the late 1940s, calls for the United States to withdraw from bases in Japan, but for Japan to maintain these bases for U.S. use in case of emergency. This formula, it is argued, would remove the base issue as a factor in "anti-American" feeling in Japan, make the MST less provocative to China and the Soviet Union, weaken the leftist extremist elements in Japan, assist the incumbent LDP, and still provide for nuclear protection of Japan by the United States--which, in any event, does not have nuclear capability inside Japan anyway.

Another specific recommendation (which lies outside the realm of U.S. policy initiatives) has been advanced by Shinkichi Eto. His suggestion is that the MST be "reinsured" by complementary agreements, such as a nonaggression pact with China and possibly one with the Soviet Union. Muraoka echoes this idea. Kiichi Saeki has suggested that a Soviet nuclear umbrella might more actively deter a Chinese nuclear threat than a U.S. guarantee, arguing that as the Chinese nuclear capacity grows, the Soviet Union will be the state most interested in deterring it.

U.S. nuclear power is the heart of the military deterrence aspect of the MST. As an initiator of the Nuclear Nonproliferation Treaty (NPT), the United States is committed to a policy that opposes the dissemination of nuclear weapons technology, the sharing of nuclear weapons with other states, and the acquisition of an independent nuclear capability by any other nation.

Japan's policy on nuclear weapons is equally clear: to develop atomic energy solely for peaceful purposes; to promote nuclear disarmament around the world; to refrain from possessing, producing, or bringing nuclear weapons into Japan; and to rely on the U.S. nuclear umbrella for deterrence against all forms of nuclear attack. Although fifty-six nations signed the NPT immediately after its completion, Japan waited eighteen months, until February 3, 1970, to sign, and has not yet ratified the treaty.

The Diet is scheduled to consider ratification of the NPT during the summer of 1975. David Okimoto recommends caution in drawing any neat conclusion from Japan's action, whether it be failure to act or ratification. The failure to act so far may be attributed to a complex of factors, including "fears of commercial disadvantage, misgivings about superpower hegemony, technical problems of safeguards and domestic political circumstances," and should not be taken to mean that Japan intends to go the way of China or France. Ratification, on the other hand, should not be interpreted as a perpetual foreswearing of nuclear weapons. Nor should one conclude that ratification means increased dependency on the U.S. nuclear umbrella. Influential Japanese defense analysts tend to be skeptical of the "umbrella" and to doubt that the United States would support Japan if the consequence were probable retaliation against U.S. territory, a clear capability of the Soviet Union and a likely future capability of China. The importance of the umbrella is not the certainty of U.S. guarantees but the symbolism of the more vital economic, diplomatic, political, and psychological ties.

Japan's military security rests on the U.S. deterrent. With its own resources, Japan has only a very modest capability for ground combat, coastal defense, or air defense. The Self-Defense Forces (SDF) have no offensive, out-of-country mission or capability, although Japan ranks sixth or seventh in the world in total defense expenditures. Japan has no defense, active or passive, against nuclear missile attack. An initial minimum nuclear strike of four weapons could achieve "assured destruction" criteria because of Japan's long, narrow conformation and its highly concentrated population, industrial, communications, and government centers. In an interview in March 1975 with US News and World Report, Osamu Kaihara, former Secretary of the National Defense Council, said the quarter-million-man SDF would be totally ineffectual against a conventional attack by an adversary like the USSR. He said the ground forces could fight as an army for only three or four days and that the air force could be destroyed in ten minutes, and he gave the Sea of Japan a new name—the Sea of Russia. But, Kaihara continued, "As long as U.S. military forces are stationed in Japan, no country would dare attack us."

The provisions for joint U.S.-Japanese military planning and cooperation do not exist even in the most rudimentary sense. U.S.-Japanese military cooperation has not been close because of differing political situations, and because Japan's leaders feel secure from a conventional attack and the threat of a nuclear attack is mostly theoretical, if not felt to be "unreal."

MST provisions for consultation in case of an area threat are, at best, suspect. In any event, even if the domestic situation in Japan were to alter fundamentally to favor military cooperation outside Japan with the United States or under U.N. auspices, Japan could not add any significant military increment to other participating forces.

If these assertions are correct, U.S.-Japanese resistance to any conventional attack is likely to be short-lived and ineffective. One may argue cogently that if the two countries were allied mainly because of a shared perception of threat, then both would be better prepared to meet the threat jointly. The converse is the case. Neither genuinely perceives a military attack against Japan to be more than remotely possible.

The primary rationale for the MST is found in shared concern for peace and stability in the Korean Peninsula. (See Chapter 11.) Historically, Korea has been a focus of interstate competition--for Japan and China reaching back fifteen centuries. Since the 1880s it has been a locus of Sino-Japanese military competition (1895), of Russo-Japanese competition (1904-05), and of U.S.-Soviet-Chinese competition (late 1940s and 1950s). Its future is of major concern to China, the Soviet Union, Japan, and the United States, not to mention the governments of North Korea and the Republic of Korea (ROK). During the Korean War, Japan was a vital base for the U.S./U.N. forces and contributed importantly to the U.N. conduct of that war. Japan has diplomatic ties with the ROK and is the major foreign investor in that nation. At the same time Japan pursues improved relations with North Korea.

In the Sato-Nixon communique of 1969, for the first time a postwar Japanese Premier stated that the security of the ROK was vital to the security of Japan. Early in 1975 Premier Miki stated that he favored the continued presence of U.N. troops in South Korea because real peace and stability have yet to be restored to the Korean Peninsula. Miki said, in June 1975, "Stability in the Korean Peninsula has close bearing with peace in Japan." These statements do not mean that Japan intends to take any concrete military steps to contribute in any way to ROK security. Nor could one conclude that Japan would necessarily be ready to repeat its role of 1950-52, for at that time Japan was still subject to Occupation controls. Japan's reaction to renewed fighting in Korea would necessarily depend on

many factors; but it can not be assumed that the United States would
automatically be permitted to use Japanese bases for direct participation in hostilities in Korea, a point also made by Miki, nor that
Japan would again contribute logistic support.

URGENCY OF THE ISSUE

There has been a striking change of mood among Japan's leadership as a result of Communist victories in Southeast Asia, and it
is clear that Japan's defense policies are being rethought for the
first time since 1952.

Japan's concern over defense matters is made more urgent by
both domestic and international events. Domestically, the opposition
Japan Socialist Party (JSP) created (May 1975) the Military Problems
Research Society, consisting of JSP defense experts, "progressive"
university professors, and military critics. It is pushing hard to
gain a national consensus for its advocacy of unarmed neutrality for
Japan and peaceful abrogation of the MST. The JSP demand for withdrawal of U.S. military forces from the ROK (and all other areas of
Asia) dovetails with international activity seeking dissolution of the
U.N. Command in Korea. A General Assembly resolution to do just
that barely failed on a tie vote in 1974 and certainly will be reintro-
duced.

North Korean President Kim Il-sung's visit to Peking and other
capitals, his warnings that "war may break out at any moment," and
constant reference to unification of Korea have served only to heighten
a sense of urgency in Japan.

For its part, the government of Japan established for the first
time, in April 1975, a special advisory organ charged to submit to
Japan Defense Agency Director-General Michita Sakata recommendations for formulation of Japan's Fifth Five-Year Defense Plan (1977-
81). Premier Miki has authorized contingency planning to deal with
problems of U.S.-Japanese military cooperation, and at least one
official has said that joint operations under the MST might extend
beyond Japan's territorial seas and skies. Sakata visited the United
States in November 1975 to discuss Japan's role under the MST.

Japan is ready to take the initiative to restructure the MST.
This move supports the U.S. policy of increased defense strength
and self-reliance for its allies and is, in fact, pursuant to that portion of the MST under which both parties agree, by effective self-
help and mutual aid, to "maintain and develop . . . their capacities
to resist armed attack."

Revitalization and restructuring of the MST are necessary to
reassure Japan about the U.S. commitment to the ROK and to Japan;

it is necessary to discourage Japan from seeking alternatives to the MST; and it is vital as a symbol of common determination to maintain peace and stability in East Asia and the Pacific area.

ALTERNATIVE STRATEGIES

Two assumptions underlie this discussion. The first is that Japan will not acquire nuclear weapons by 1977 for three general reasons:

1. The acquisition of nuclear weapons as an independent national capability or on a sharing basis with the United States is perhaps the most emotional and divisive issue that could be raised in Japanese politics.
2. The technical capability probably is not there for the short run.
3. There is no cogent "ends-means" rationale for the acquisition, although it has been suggested that a sea-based second-strike capability makes strategic sense in lieu of a land-based first strike (which it probably is impossible to make credible) or a land-based second-strike force.

It is possible that by 1977 Japan may decide to acquire nuclear weapons, but the United States should not encourage this development, nor should it try to foreclose such an option by urging Japan to ratify the NPT.

The second assumption is that neither the situation in the Korean Peninsula nor U.S.-ROK relations will change significantly.

Simply stated, American policy alternatives are to terminate the MST, allow things to drift, or to react positively to Japanese initiatives for modification. In essence, the future of the MST lies importantly in Japan's hands, so American policy alternatives are considered here in terms of Japan's alternatives and the probable U.S. reaction to each. U.S. pressure on Japan to pursue policies not derived from Japanese consideration of Japan's interest would be no more than what has been perceived, in the past, as unwarranted American domination of Japan's foreign and defense policies. American policy must be construed in such a manner as to accord with a cooperative relationship between equals.

A goodly number of Japanese alternatives could be postulated, but theoretically they fall under four broad headings: a disarmed neutral/nonaligned Japan; several varieties of bilateral/multilateral arrangements; an autonomous, militarily stronger Japan; and continuation of the MST with modifications.

A disarmed neutral/nonaligned Japan is rejected within Japan by all but a vociferous minority led by the JSP. This formulation is vague in concept and divorced from reality. Its pursuit would detract from Japan's security (political, economic, and military), encourage highly competitive Soviet and Chinese interference in Japan's affairs, and cause great harm to relations with the United States, its most important foreign partner. Even Chou En-lai has warned JSP visitors from Japan to expect no support in their advocacy of abrogation of the MST, and has openly supported the U.S.-Japanese military arrangement. U.S. support of this option would entirely discredit public policy directed toward the maintenance of stability and peace in Asia, would be interpreted as complete disinterest in Asian affairs, would probably require U.S. withdrawal from the Western Pacific, and would nullify U.S. commitments to the ROK and other states in Asia.

Some suggestions for bilateral arrangements supplementary to the MST were briefly noted above. Essentially they derive from a concept of Japan operating in some sort of "equidistant polycentrism" and are rooted in the belief that Japan can have relations of equal significance with a number of states varying importantly in strategic importance, institutional characteristics and ideology, economic strength, and international goals. Given Japan's global economic interests, its shared values with the United States and Western Europe, its dependence (both for raw materials and for markets) on the advanced industrial countries for its economic prosperity, and the strained competitive relations between its two powerful Asian neighbors--the USSR and China--it seems unlikely that Japan could enter additional alliances without incurring significant risks. Neither China nor the USSR is willing to see the other develop closer ties with Japan to its own relative exclusion, although both will attempt to do just that. Japan will try to avoid being used by either power against the other, although she will probably continue cautious negotiations with both. Bilateral arrangements by Japan with China and the USSR could contribute to East Asian stability, but only if all three parties and the United States benefit equally. Any Japanese moves to secure military guarantees from the USSR and/or China against external aggression would be a complete repudiation of policy over the past twenty-five years and could be construed by the United States as a rejection of the MST.

A third alternative--the development of an autonomous, strong, and potentially aggressive Japan with significantly increased military power--is anathema to all Asian states and would re-create a spectre from the past of a Japan seeking to consolidate, protect, and expand its economic power with a threatening military backup. Some Asian leaders have, in fact, imputed this course to Japan, which is

acutely aware of its lingering image of militaristic nationalism and
consciously avoids any actions that could cause Asian states to be
anxious on this matter. Japan's leaders know that to "go it alone"
militarily means that Japan will lose its hard-won international
prestige and its image of a peaceful state contributing to economic
development throughout the world. Such a course would get no support outside Japan; it would be discouraged by all nations with any
stake in Asia; it would threaten Japan's political and economic well-
being; and it assuredly would lessen its military security. This alternative has no support except among a small minority of rightist
elements.

     The fourth major Japanese option is to continue to rely on the
MST, with modifications to meet the interests of both parties. This
option has the important advantage, for both the United States and
Japan, of proceeding from a familiar current working relationship
and involves no abrupt policy change. It is preferable to Japan because it has more domestic support than the other broad options,
and is preferable to the United States because it promises a more
influential role than do the other options. It presents the least danger to other Asian states and avoids opening another area for Sino-
Soviet competition. Clearly, China favors continuation of the MST
as a check on Japanese rearmament and as a counterweight to Soviet
pretensions to "hegemony" in East Asia. It is the only option that
supports continuation of current U.S. policy in Korea. For both the
United States and Japan, this alternative is best suited to maintenance
of international peace and stability in the Western Pacific.

CONCLUSIONS

     Of the several alternatives discussed here, the strengthening
of the MST will cost the least in the short run and in the long run. It
will have the most immediate impact in allaying Japan's fears about
U.S. commitments in East Asia and particularly about the danger of
disruptive actions in Korea. It will do the most to reduce tensions
among the principal actors, and would be perceived as equitable by
most.

     This judgment must be accompanied by an answer to the ques-
tion posed in President Nixon's Report to the Congress of May 3,
1973: "How could we, in coordination with our Allies, strengthen
our mutual defense in a manner that retained their confidence in our
reliability, but permitted them to play a more prominent role?"

     Several actions can satisfy these criteria.

     If Japanese press reports are accurate, the first step in
strengthening the MST may come from a Japanese initiative for joint

contingency planning. In 1965 the JSP revealed the existence of the
Japan Defense Agency's secret "Three Arrows Study" (Mitsuya
Kenkyu), which reportedly provided that Japan would be an integral
part of U.S. strategy in East Asia and serve as a base for U.S. operations, that the Japanese Self-Defense Forces (SDF) would train
jointly with U.S., ROK, and Chinese Nationalist troops, and that the
SDF would fulfill a defensive assignment in case of another Korean
conflict, and contained plans for emergency mobilization. That the
Prime Minister has now called publicly for study of contingency
planning is indeed remarkable, and the United States should respond
positively and work jointly with Japan to ascertain appropriate areas
for joint planning. So far as is known publicly, joint U.S.-Japanese
military planning does not now exist.

The major problem to be dealt with on the operational level is
the U.S. use of Japanese bases in the event of threats to peace in
East Asia or in case of actual hostilities. There is great political
appeal in an "emergency deployment formula" whereby Japan controls
all bases in Japan and U.S. forces are located elsewhere until needed;
but it has little appeal to military planners concerned with quick response and flexibility. Joint planning must be carried out thoroughly
if the MST is to be workable in case of emergency, and must provide
for a range of plausible and relatively specific projected situations.
It requires coordination of many difficult aspects of joint operations:
command, communications, logistics, intelligence, training, operations, and rules of engagement. Certain of these areas must be approached with great caution by the United States to protect the sensitivity of the information involved.

Actual joint ground tactical training operations are probably out
of the question because the United States has no ground combat troops
in Japan and the SDF cannot be sent out of the country. Nevertheless,
ground tactical scenarios could be developed, and limited joint air defense and defensive naval operations are possible on a continuing
basis. The exchange of U.S. and SDF officers among service schools,
tactical units, and staffs would strengthen the MST in many intangible
ways.

The modesty of these general recommendations should not be allowed to obscure the urgent need for U.S. action. For the first time
since 1952, the U.S. declaration that the MST is the cornerstone of its
policy in East Asia coincides with a heightened Japanese concern with
its own defense policy and need for security in the midst of uncertainty
and bewildering changes in the distribution of power in the Western
Pacific. The United States needs to seize this opportunity to strength-
en mutual defense ties with Japan, retain confidence in U.S. reliability, and encourage Japan to play a more prominent role.

13

LATIN AMERICA:
THE PROBLEM OF
NEGLECT
Robert F. Delaney

THE ISSUE

The resolution of the conflict over the future of the Panama Canal will color the relations between the United States and Latin America for the rest of this century. It is looked upon by Latin Americans as the determinant of the nature of relations between North and South in this hemisphere. Latins are striving for a peer rather than a paternalistic relationship with the United States.

In the intimacy of one landmass and the uneasy shared history of close to two hundred years of independence, inter-American affairs remain as they started: troubled, potentially dangerous, and vastly misunderstood.

To North Americans, Latin America is a little-known, spoiled, complaining stepchild joined to us by the umbilical cord of Central America. To Latin Americans, the United States is an overpowering, intrusive, political and economic force devoid of cultural sensitivity and devoted to the arbitrary exploitation of the lands south of the Rio Grande.

Both stereotypes, while widely held, are basically out of date. Events of the 1970s--economic, military, political, and financial-- have rendered the traditional intercontinental misperceptions largely invalid. But the image lingers on.

The basic issue for the 1970s is far more compelling: the paced development, without outside interference or political coercion, of a viable psychological and economic entity known as Latin America. To be sure Latin America is not an homogeneous unity. It is a diverse conglomerate of twenty-six countries and dependencies multiracial in composition and varied in language and experience. This, indeed, is part of the problem. There is vast unevenness

in our Southern Hemisphere, from the urbane sophistication of
Mexico City to the barrenness of Tierra del Fuego. Yet one overriding reality stands out: Latin America, with almost two centuries
of self-rule behind it, remains an immense underdeveloped area.
This failure to progress has taken a considerable, unrecognized
psychological toll among the Latin peoples. When this sense of frustration is coupled with the historic suspicion of economic dominance
by North America, the seeds of conflict are well in place.

The essence of this problem rests somewhere in between, but
is rarely accepted. Latin America does have a justified grievance
regarding economic short-changing by the United States, but it is
neither new nor unique. By the same token, North America is not
the Marxist gargoyle so popular in Latin rhetoric. So the misperceptions persist, contributing both to the perpetuation of the myth
and to the continuance of the resentment on both sides. The issue is
addressed cyclically, as with Franklin Roosevelt's "Good Neighbor"
policy, which was cultural and political in orientation, or with
Kennedy's "Alliance for Progress," which had as its objective the
redefinition of social and economic goals for Latin America. But in
no single case was the basic problem of psychological and economic
development successfully met. Today the issue remains. Now,
however, the basic problem is compounded by the new elements of
global North-South, developed-underdeveloped rivalry. In this context U.S. policy confronts a highly dangerous and delicate situation.

BACKGROUND OF THE ISSUE

Historically, the United States has approached hemispheric
relations with a view to military security and economic advantage.
The Monroe Doctrine was as much an instrument of economic hegemony as it was an expression of U.S. political influence and self-
interested paternalism. This combination of forces successfully
drove North American policies over the past century, enabling and
encouraging U.S. business to develop its investment, mining, and
marketing interests throughout Latin America in conditions of absolute commercial advantage. Likewise, U.S. political-military interests centered on the Caribbean, and in the lifeline of the Panama
Canal protected the security of our soft underbelly. Against this history of protectionism, inter-American relations developed, sometimes prospered, and sometimes faltered. Ultimately, a rhythm
and style developed that unconsciously set the pace for the basic relationship that persists to this day. This is central to understanding
the current situation. Basically, despite the unending rhetoric, the
United States has largely taken Latin America for granted. One need

only reflect on the low priority of concern traditionally accorded the area, save for such personalities as a Castro or an Allende.

But of late a basic transformation has begun. One can arbitrarily date the process of change from the mid-1960s, when Panama began its pressure to acquire sovereignty over the Canal Zone, and ultimately over canal management. It has progressed at an accelerating rate as the political and economic landscape has changed: the slow acceptance of a Communist Cuba, the call for reorganization of the Organization of American States on Latin terms, the advance of a two hundred-mile territorial limit off Latin America's Pacific Coast, the rise and fall of a socialist Chile, the wide nationalization of United States-owned basic utilities and extractive industry, the increasing protest of Latin nations against U.S. economic policies and U.S. multinational corporations, and--flowing from the successful tactics of the oil-producing cartel (OPEC)--the dawning awareness that developing nations with sizable natural resources can organize to force better terms of trade on the industrial world.

A new situation has thus emerged, with the developing nations of the continent at last sensing their ability to assert their independence of U.S. paternalism, whatever the cost. This struggle is in its first phase; the lines are being drawn, yet the United States seems curiously unconcerned except for the traditional fear of Communism being implanted in the hemisphere. Given this fixation, American responses are generally military and short-term in a situation calling for political vision and economic change. The results are predictably negative, with our image psychologically depressed and our position in steady erosion.

In these circumstances it is not at all strange that few leaders have spoken out definitively on Latin America in recent years. There is literally nothing to say. The low posture and "benign neglect" of the Nixon years was a quiet message that Latin America was on its own economically. The primary U.S. concern was prevention of Communist subversion and take-over. The social-psychological link between the two was never made. Secretary of State Henry Kissinger, leaning heavily on his own world image, tried, first in Mexico and then in Atlanta, to set his "dialogue" in motion. It failed because of a lack of follow-through. The alpha and omega of the policy argument can be seen in four major documents, spanning the years 1968 to the present. First, on the U.S. side, there is the much-publicized and little-acted-upon 1969 Rockefeller report, "Quality of Life in the Americas," a middle-of-the-road incremental analysis, weighing heavily on fear of Communism and equally heavily on investment, economic development, and a special relationship between Latin and North America. At the other extreme, there is the 1974 report of the Commission on United States-Latin American

Relations. The privately commissioned Linowitz study contains a strongly worded plea for mature U.S. involvement in Latin America, coupled with a liberal readjustment of our economic, political, and commercial relations with the region.

On the Latin side, two fundamentally important documents shaped the growing awareness: the Catholic bishops' challenge to the status quo given at Medellin, Colombia, in 1968 emphasized the social nature of man and his explicit right to equity, justice, and a share of the earth's goods, and implied that if evolutionary change did not bring these conditions into being, then revolution might. The other document, cast in the aura of inter-Americanism, came to be known as the "Consensus of Vina del Mar" (1969) and asserted the existence of a "distinctive personality" in Latin America. It also stressed the need for better terms of trade and called for regional unity. It was candidly anti-American in tone. Subsequent inter-American meetings held in 1974 in Mexico and in Atlanta, Georgia, gave further evidence of new Latin assertiveness as the Southern Hemisphere sensed the tide of political and economic Third World events moving in its favor.

To all of this--the most fundamental change in our hemispheric relations since Latin independence--the U.S. response has been largely one of indecision and of preoccupation with other areas. A policy of nondecision couched in appropriate rhetoric has evolved that, when judged against traditional U.S. Latin policies, may seem to represent progress, but, when assessed against the rise of the Third World and the surge of Latin nationalism, spells conflict and severe readjustment. A tendency to maintain this laissez-faire perception is perforce balanced by a continuing military overview of the area that emphasizes Communism rather than restructuring trade and basic change of the environment in which U.S. corporations operate. It is in fact still easier, at this point, to rely on the past than to face the uncertainties of a changing inter-American future.

Economic and, to a degree, social resistance to change remains the basic obstacle. U.S. investment in Latin America runs second only to our investments in Western Europe. Our financial participation has been, until recently, quite independent and influential. Business interests have quite properly lobbied for their positions within Congress and have traditionally found a sympathetic hearing within the Department of State; in fact, they often provide experienced personnel to staff senior inter-American positions in the State Department and the Organization of American States. At times, as in the ITT case, the pressure clearly gets out of hand, with serious damage to our position in the area and calculable effects on the operations of our multinational corporations in Latin America. It is this consistent image of interference and influence that has so convinced Latin elites (and subversive demagogues, as well) of our alleged negative intentions.

Internationally, the situation is derivative. Multinational corporations are under almost universal suspicion. The Third World, in its urgent need for development (as expressed time and again in the meetings of the Economic Commission for Latin America and the United Nations Conference on Trade and Development), is reaching the conclusion, rightly or wrongly, that the "enemy of progress" is not Socialism so much as it is unregulated foreign capitalism. Latin America thus shares more objectives with the developing world than with its historic "protector" the United States. The special Latin America-U.S. relationship is a concept fewer and fewer Latins are prepared to accept.

Beyond this, the matters of bilateral versus multilateral aid and international development funding begin to emerge as Latin America looks for assistance without political strings. Politically, trade, not aid, is sought--as is an understanding of Latin sensitivities and political style. An Allende was more of a threat to his cause through incompetence than he was to the United States, but the conventional wisdom held otherwise. Internationally, the United States is being outflanked in Latin America by the issues and by the sterility of thought concerning our position there. Our posture is definitely defensive. Latin America has joined a world movement (the "have nots" versus the "haves") without so much as a "by your leave." This determination is proving increasingly frustrating to our policy-makers in Washington and at the United Nations, where formerly "safe" pro-U.S. votes of the Latin bloc are likely to be found elsewhere. To this degree Latin and hemispheric problems that historically have been a family matter under the Monroe Doctrine, have become part of world problems brought on by population growth, food scarcity, inflation, and allocation of scarce resources.

URGENCY OF THE ISSUE

As the United States enters another presidential election campaign, it is beset by frustration, self-doubt, indecision, and an array of formidable international problems far removed from the simplistic but direct days of the Cold War. New directions and mature appreciation of the vastly changed post-Vietnam world are needed. Failure to grasp the ultimate direction of these events will increasingly force the United States into isolation, defensiveness, and opposition and, with any such development, conflict, rivalry, and adventurism loom as possibilities. Psychologically, such a posture invites a change in the American ideal--a movement away from the wellsprings of our own beliefs and beginnings.

To stem this movement, action on a broad front is needed now. America must, as a nation, move from rhetoric to deed on trade, on food, on interdependence, on international and legal responsibility for multinational business growth and activity. In this manner, at least, the public example of a self-assured, confident America exercising positive, constructive leadership will become manifest. In its absence or in the face of American negative nationalism, the world faces economic and subversive warfare; and no more fertile ground exists for indigenous or Soviet-directed Communism. Democratic form is, after all, dependent upon a stable political balance; growing, enfranchised social classes; and a viable, developing economy. And reform is possible only when hope and motivation exist. To deny these givens in a world of increasing limitations on growth is to foreclose peaceful, pluralistic growth and invite the Marxist vision of life.

Thus, America must act by 1977. The antogonisms grow, not lessen. Latin America is quite properly moving out of our sphere of influence. The United States cannot, and should not, arrest this movement; it cannot, in any event, succeed in the long run. Rather, positive steps toward trade, price, and business regulation should be volunteered. Common market mechanisms should be reemphasized, especially in Central America. Raw material covenants must be reviewed, investment policies reexamined, and political reappraisal of our views of Latin governments and ideologies receive serious priority.

If no such decisions are made, drift will become endemic and piecemeal crisis management will become another bureaucratic reality. Military and clandestine involvement will literally be forced upon us by diplomatic and political inaction. Communism, confusion, and chaos will reign. Needless to say, there is no clear-cut answer to these problems because there is a genuine disagreement as to means and ends. Improved trade, joint investment, and pricing policies may be interpreted as anti-business, and thus opposed. Freedom for Latin America to develop as it wishes, warts and all, may be viewed as tolerance and weakness. Recognition that the United States is but part of the hemisphere, not the hemisphere, may be viewed as an affront to the pride of the "Colossus of the North"; thus legitimate disagreement and debate are to be expected. There exists in this country, however, a very influential body of opinion that claims for the United States the dominant voice in Latin America, primarily on the basis of security considerations, arguing that Latins are incapable of defending themselves. The argument here obviously is oriented to outside aggression. The problem, however, is internal. Peru, Chile, Cuba, and Guatemala reflect histories of domestic discord and rivalry based on internal inequities and subversive influences. Once again, failure to perceive the full extent of change enveloping Latin America can cause inadequate policy response: too little and too late understanding can bring about a very troublesome alienation.

ALTERNATIVE STRATEGIES

The burden of this commentary has been primarily nonmilitary, because the issue is basically nonmilitary. But volatile events can escalate into military situations, and the United States is immediately faced with one such potential crisis in Latin America: the question of the Panama Canal and its ultimate control and disposition. Complex negotiations over a dozen years have led to a draft treaty that in effect restores Panamanian sovereignty over the Canal Zone and in due course turns the Canal over to Panama's management, with safeguards for residual U.S. security interests. Should nineteenth-century American "jingoism" prevent Senate passage of the treaty, this will lead almost inevitably to violence against U.S. property in the Zone and a military response. Our relations with the entire area will be thrown into confusion. Soothing rhetoric will in no way meet the reality of the deed. The seeds of insurgency, massive propaganda, and Communist meddling will be sown, with predictable results. Yet it need not happen. If the United States believes in the sovereignty it preaches, if it accepts change in the world at large as quickly as it accepts it in the American environment, then the issue is resolvable diplomatically, not militarily. The cost of rejection would be difficult to assess in terms of lives lost, terror practiced, a continent enflamed.

The issues involved in the Canal negotiations are classic reflections of both the U.S. dilemma and Latin frustrations. Within the United States there exists a strong, vocal minority that is extremely nationalistic and dedicated to the status quo wherever U.S. international interests are concerned; for them the Canal is sacrosanct and not susceptible to change of ownership as a matter of principle. For the Latins the issue is sovereignty etched in dignity. It is a microcosm of potential inter-American confrontation across a spectrum of problems, and under this scenario U.S. response is fundamentally predictable. The Canal treaty will not be honored, which will entail a political and paramilitary threat. The reinvolvement of Cuba in hemispheric affairs will remain an American domestic political resentment (especially and understandably among Cuban expatriates). The mix of determined American and multinational business interests in Latin America, and Latin acceptance of Third World economic arguments against the United States and the industrialized

world, will force the United States into a defensive posture in the
United Nations and will yield a carping, continuous, low-level antagonism in bilateral U.S.-Latin relations. The future, and with it
the changes even now in evidence, will give way to the present and a
"no-win" frame of mind. Legitimate Latin grievances will be viewed
as "Red" efforts to erode U.S. hegemony. Even today simplistic accounts describe Latin feelings on the Panama Canal issue as solely
Communist-inspired.

Such a national frame of mind begets a hostile, garrison-type
mentality, and with it a propensity to rationalize the problem under
the catch-all of "national security." With it comes the argument for
a military solution and the public confusion that follows. This psychological trap may indeed be the dominant inter-American security
problem of the late 1970s. To maintain obsolete bases, to argue
from invalid political assumptions, to misread opinion, to ignore the
evolving world economic order, and to deny the impact of unplanned
change--and thus to forsake the future--is a strange yet serious manner of describing the precarious security balance (or perhaps emerging imbalance) in our basic inter-American relationship. Yet, these
are the underlying factors. Failure to recognize them leads to
marches on the Canal Zone by Latin leaders, commodity and tariff
wars, emotional and physical population pressures on our southern
boundary through Central America and Mexico (it is often forgotten
that North Vietnamese walked from Hanoi to Saigon; it is even easier
to walk from Panama to Texas, and while the reasons may be more
diverse, they are just as explosive).

Given this situation, maturity, sophistication, and subtlety must
prevail. Otherwise, the negative scenario portrayed above may indeed be played out even while the rhetoric proclaims the virtues of
patriotism and morality.

While the Canal issue is a prototype of inter-American conflict
as well as a pilot for solution, it dramatically illustrates how economic and political questions mesh into security problems if left unresolved. There is, of course, a sizable elite of well-informed,
imaginative North Americans in both public and private life that is
concerned with the state of our hemispheric security, broadly defined.
In Congress, there are Senator Claiborne Pell and Representative
Dante Fascell. In the State Department, William Rogers, as Assistant Secretary for Inter-American Affairs, is sympathetic and influential in Latin circles. In private life, the chief advocates for improved conditions of trade, a change in commodity pricing, and a
mature view of Latin political reality are Sol Linowitz, a Washington
attorney and former U.S. Ambassador to the Organization of American States; Kalman Silvert, an adviser to the Ford Foundation; and
Michael Blumenthal, Chairman of the Bendix Corporation. Slightly

more conservative and business-oriented are David Rockefeller and
the Council of the Americas. A notable loner in the field with es-
pecial political-military competence is Jack Vaughn, former Peace
Corps Director and former Ambassador to Panama. His arguments,
with particular reference to Panama and the Canal, are trenchant
and clearly reflect understanding of our changing Latin role from
dominance to parity. He fears our security will suffer if the United
States does not recognize the new Latin spirit of independence and
economic influence. One need only think of Venezuelan and Mexican
oil. But the total resource box score could well include--among
other Latin commodities--bauxite, copper, and coffee. In a word,
the United States, according to these advocates, is facing end-of-
century limits on growth in Latin America. Long-term prudence
dictates a new framework.

Part of this framework quite obviously must treat the issue of
Cuba and America's genuine security concerns in the Caribbean and
the Gulf of Mexico. The political drama of Cuba's expulsion from
the inter-American family edges toward resolution and reacceptance
with at least tacit U.S. consent. The security issue of Cuba, Communism, Latin subversion, Soviet naval presence in the Caribbean
(astride our oil lifeline from Trinidad, Aruba, and Venezuela) is as
complex as it is real. Yet here, too, rhetoric has at times taken
precedence over the military reality. An American military presence in Latin America is desirable and necessary to meet legitimate
U.S. hemispheric security considerations. Though our visibility
diminishes as the political reality changes, there remains a bottom-
line vested interest that friend and foe alike understand and ultimately accept. As Eastern Europe represents Russia's western flank,
so Latin America represents our southern strategic approach. The
Inter-American Defense Board, for all its deficiencies, is still based
on the premise of continental defense, as it should be. However, the
bureaucratic politics of military presence is awesome and inflexible,
ranging from unnecessary service missions to overzealous arms
sales (an intricate political-military matter in itself), to the outdated
U.S. doctrines on counterinsurgency and to the continuing inability to
differentiate properly between Latin America's deep-seated need for
reform and restructuring and the fear of an established power that
any change begets Communism, whether it is called Socialism,
Castroism, or Maoist extremism. The result is an insistence on
military presence as the sole countervailing force.

The political and social costs of this view are immense: loss
of prestige, influence, and flexibility, and a slow lowering of our
security posture as the welcome mat is progressively withdrawn,
tensions mount, and emotionalism turns into rampant nationalism
and hemispheric division. Curiously, in all of this the monetary

costs are not basically at issue. America's multibillion-dollar Latin investments are substantially in place. Development banks have been established. Multilateral modes for aid have been worked out. Infrastructure experience is a matter of Alliance for Progress record. Latin solutions have been made in both the public and private sectors. What is needed--and this is the difficult psychological factor--is U.S. acceptance of change and a new style of relationships.

CONCLUSIONS

There would appear to be a definable solution based on American and Latin self-interest that is designed to reduce tensions and enhance basic security. In fact, the trend line is apparent; and whether American policy recognizes the movement or not, or likes it or not, it seems apparent that a new, not special, inter-American relationship is unfolding.

Accommodating to Latin America's emergence as part of the Third World bloc with a unique American outlook, facing the painful reality of trade and commodity rearrangements, using our managerial and technical skill in restructuring American business involvement in the area, and reviewing military presence and modern security needs, will lead to considerable short-term costs in terms of business realignment, lessened influence, and (perhaps) lower profits. The long-term gains, however, will be immense. The United States will once again assert its democratic idealism, its pragmatic recognition of change, and its historic role as a creditable and more or less accepted defender of hemispheric security. Renewed confidence will follow. Dialogue will be reopened on a basis of equality and independence; and once again the Americas--as allies, not as parents and wards--can face the future with an emerging sense of security and not as a papered-over, fear-ridden reactive, often coercive, force. This is the ultimate test: the courage to foster independence and growth even if it is out of step with America's basic paternalism.

POLICY INSTRUMENTS:
THE QUESTION OF MEANS

What instruments will be available to the newly elected leadership taking office in January 1977? Apart from diplomacy, which is implicit in all instruments discussed in Part IV, economic and military instruments will require a substantial reassessment for both quantitative and qualitative impact. Since the 1950s the ability of American leaders to mobilize large economic surpluses and, through translating them into sophisticated weaponry, to project power onto the world stage has now been eroded by inflation, new advances in weapons technology, and, perhaps most important, the pervasive availability of weapons to America's former allies and adversaries.

In sum, the sources of global, regional, and national instability described in Parts II and III will be provided with an apparently uncontrolled and uncontrollable proliferation of weaponry. Arms control will be so important that four chapters are devoted to the subject, reinforced by a final chapter on American strategy for development of new weapons.

14

ECONOMIC STRENGTH:
THE PROBLEM OF COSTS
Robert Chenoweth

THE ISSUE

The United States is facing a serious erosion of its national power through the rapid inflation accompanied by debt expansion and high unemployment. The central question is how to recover economic strength so as to recover effective national power.

"Inflation is the characteristic disease of all societies which live under a government losing its authority. . . ."[1] "All inflation has international implications in an economically interdependent world."[2] ". . . the operations of the capitalist system can and will engineer its own demise. . . . the collapse may also end in world war or fascism."[3]

The security of our nation rests not only on military strength but also on economic and political stability, which provide the basis for an acceptable defensive system designed to meet external threats. Economic stability has seldom appeared so unobtainable, nor has the danger to the West from economic mismanagement ever appeared so grave. Recent rates of inflation, in the United States and throughout the world, create and highlight economic injustices that gradually erode faith in government policies--which, in free nations, are determined by the political process. In addition, rapid inflation, accompanied by rapid debt expansion, eventually cannot be sustained because the credit structure is weakened by an increasing number of unprofitable investments and unredeemable loans. The problem is one of managing a capitalist system through the political process in order to promote reasonable economic stability and thus retain political freedoms. There can be no political stability when economic stability is lost, resulting in economic collapse.

In the United States, the Federal Reserve Board has restrained the rate of monetary expansion; interest rates have risen; the economic boom has subsided; unemployment has increased; and inflation has moderated but persists at a disturbingly high rate. Concerned with rising unemployment and negative economic growth, Congressmen looking for ways to escape the blame for these economic troubles have increased the pressure on Arthur Burns, Chairman of the Federal Reserve Board, to produce a solution to the current economic crisis. We are in a period that is testing the ability of the political process to provide adequate economic stability.

If we fail this test and embark on a path of increased inflation, or turn the opposite way, to increased unemployment and depression, extremists of right or left who expect the failure of the democratic system will be vindicated, and increasing political instability will result. The fate of other governments, weaker than that of the United States, now attempting to walk the same moderate, ever-narrowing path between these increasingly severe economic extremes, will be affected by the course we take. Argentina, Portugal, Australia, India, Italy, and even Great Britain are finding economic problems more difficult to manage, with rates of inflation and unemployment rising with frustrating persistence. Their political systems are severely strained by attempts to formulate government policies to meet these severe problems. The United States is in a unique position to influence other nations for good or ill, and thus to contribute to world stability or instability. It is not only the ideological leader of the West; it is still the largest national economy in the world. As banker responsible for the management of the Free World's major currency and largest reserve assets, and as the largest single national market for the products of other nations, the U.S. economy counts heavily in setting the pace of world inflation or recession. In this economically interdependent world, failure to manage our economy will make it increasingly difficult for other nations to manage theirs.

Determining the proper rate of monetary expansion for the United States and for the world is crucial. The difficulties are immense. The Federal Reserve Board has exerted only partial control over the creation of dollars worldwide since the development of the Eurodollar market. In the international banking system of 1975, dollars can be created, in nearly infinite quantity, that are indistinguishable from dollars created within the domestic banking system. There is no fractional reserve requirement within the Eurodollar system, and only restraint and fear of loss prevent international bankers from expanding the worldwide quantity of dollars to excessive amounts. Within the United States, the Federal Reserve has less control over the creation of money each year, as the number and size of member banks decrease relative to the banks outside the system. In addition, electronic banking and credit cards threaten to accelerate the velocity of money transfer and thus to create an effective increase in the money supply, allowing money to speed faster and faster throughout the economy, adding to aggregate demand and contributing to the potential for inflation.

These mechanical problems aside, economists have no sure method for determining a "most desirable" rate of money-supply creation. Economics is not a science, even though in the 1960s many economists were convinced that it was. Then, some believed that complex econometric models, using data obtained from sophisticated sampling techniques and fed into large computers, could simulate economic reality and bring the marvels of science into economic planning. It might have worked if reasonable stability could have been sustained. But it did not work, because the models were unprepared to handle the devaluation of the dollar, the breakdown of the Bretton Woods system, floating exchange rates, rapid world inflation, and other unprogrammed events of the 1970s. Economics remains largely an art. Psychological and political factors are entwined with economics, and these unpredictable factors may prevent economics from ever becoming fully scientific.

Economists, like other artists, often disagree. Policy recommendations vary even when the same data are analyzed, and they seldom agree on what data are essential. Economists also may have a political bias that influences their judgment and promotes normative recommendations. Some economists have learned to disguise their political bias in economic theory by using invalid assumptions. Others are clearly identifiable as conservative or liberal.

Liberal economists generally are more concerned with unemployment, slow growth, and the problems of the poor, while conservative economists are more disturbed by inflation, profits, and the problems of the more wealthy. The current situation (mid-1975)-- negative growth, the highest unemployment since the Great Depression, the highest rate of inflation since the Civil War, declining profits, rising interest rates, increasing taxes, and a weakened credit structure--has nearly all economists deeply concerned but divided over policy recommendations. The issues are ones of social and political values and risk assessment. There are definite risks to continued economic mismanagement, leading to greater inflation or greater rates of unemployment. Arthur Burns has expressed deep concern about the impact of inflation on American social and political institutions: "I do not believe I exaggerate in saying that the ultimate consequence of inflation could well be a significant decline of economic and political freedom for the American people." Political extremists of both left and right agree that a crisis is pending, but disagree over both the cause and the outcome.

The left blames inflation on capitalism and excessive debt expansion of the private sector in its quest for unending growth and power. They argue that multinational corporations, stretching worldwide to increase their market share, have overexpanded; have extended their debt load beyond reasonable limits in the euphoria of rising profits associated with inflation; and now face declining profits and collapse of the debt structure. They point to the increasing number of private corporations turning to government for financial assistance and to several startling examples of bankruptcy as evidence that the current debt structure is very weak and unstable. They see the eventual collapse of the world economy in a horrendous depression when mobs will fill the streets and demand an end to capitalism. Socialism or Communism is the system they see rising from the disaster to restore stability.

The right blames inflation on excessive government spending, excessive expansion of fiat money supplies, and government policies that discourage investment and create shortages. Monopoly labor unions also are blamed for unreasonable wage demands. It believes the government will continue to spend in excess of tax revenues and, unable to borrow adequately in the open money markets, will monetize the debt in ever-increasing amounts, leading to an orgy of inflation and loss of faith in fiat money. They see a collapse of the system as money loses all value and people resort to barter or return to "true" money, such as gold. They blame the people for encouraging unwise government welfare programs and excessive spending. When the collapse comes, they believe the only way to restore faith in money will be to return to "real" money such as gold. They feel that a return to gold will return those who hold it to power, so that the wealthy will retain control over the government and restore sensible financial management. Even if they don't regain control of the government, gold may buy security and fiat money will be worthless. The far right believes fascism will replace democracy as the people prove unable to restrain the impulse to vote themselves more and more financial benefits until the financial system collapses.

The one thing both left and right agree upon is that inflation is an essential step leading to economic collapse. Economic historians recount example after example of inflation followed by political instability. Greece, Rome, France, Germany, and now England have all had excessive rates of inflation. In all cases faith in money and faith in the government have declined along with rising inflation. The inflation of the 1970s is worldwide and affects every government. Governments with controlled economies whose currencies are not freely convertible are partially isolated from the more rapid inflation of the West but are nevertheless affected. Before, there were always nations that maintained monetary stability, but the increased interdependence of the world and the reliance on the dollar as an international medium of exchange and store of value, coupled with the tremendous increase in dollar reserves in the early 1970s, during the collapse of the Bretton Woods fixed-exchange rate system, has resulted in worldwide inflation--a new phenomenon.

BACKGROUND OF THE ISSUE

The causes of inflation are myriad, and both international and internal to individual countries. The process by which the world monetary system, established at Bretton Woods in 1944, was destroyed is one of the major causes of worldwide inflation. From 1970 to 1974 total international reserves rose from $92 billion to $218 billion. From 1970 to 1975 foreign exchange (fiat money) reserves, which are the major component of total reserves, rose from $44 billion to $153 billion. The world export price index rose from 100 to 206 between 1970 and 1975. Why the tremendous increase in international reserves? Is the correlation with world inflation merely an accident?

The Bretton Woods system of fixed exchange rates collapsed because it was too inflexible, because the United States was unwilling to accept the restraint necessary to reduce the balance-of-payments deficit by deflating our domestic economy, and because the major surplus countries (West Germany and Japan) were unwilling to allow their currencies to appreciate (thus endangering their favorable trade balance). The United States, involved in the programs of the Great Society and the conflict in Vietnam, was unwilling to deflate the domestic economy and eventually adopted a policy of benign neglect of the balance-of-payments deficits, which increased in the late 1960s and early 1970s, in anticipation of the devaluation of the dollar. In a test of international will, West Germany and Japan absorbed huge quantities of dollars before they were forced to allow their currencies to appreciate. Thus the United States achieved its goal of a more realistic exchange rate and improvement in the terms of trade, but at the expense of huge dollar balances held by foreign governments and others. The world boom of the early 1970s and world inflation were an outgrowth of this collapse of the international monetary system. But inflation kills booms. The rapid worldwide inflation created, in 1974 and 1975, a money shortage as rising prices absorbed more and more of the excess world liquidity. In the first quarter of 1975, world trade declined in real terms for the first time since the Great Depression. The world economy, like that of the United States, was poised between continued inflation and deflation. The nations of the West looked to the United States for leadership in restoring economic stability.

In its early stages, inflation often induces euphoria. Everyone seems to be getting richer as money increases and flows more rapidly. Credit is easily obtained, and the prospects for profit appear bright. A feeling of well-being and loss of restraint leads individuals, corporations, and governments to overextend, overspend, and mismanage economic resources. The money supply grows at an excessive rate, inflation accelerates, and the money supply must continue to accelerate faster than inflation--or the bubble will burst. When inflation exceeds the rate of growth of the money supply, the collapse is not long in coming: money is suddenly tight, interest rates rise, and everyone begins to realize they have overextended. As they begin to retrench, the boom ends and recession begins. Excessive monetary tightness at this stage, excessive retrenchment, and an excessive rise in unemployment can lead to a deep recession from which recovery is very difficult. This is particularly true if the credit structure has been weakened and is exposed to high losses that can lead to a contracting of the entire credit system. This happened in the 1930s: the money supply contracted for a long period, world trade declined steadily over several years, and bankruptcy after bankruptcy led to a severe contraction of the credit structure.

There is some degree of truth in the arguments of both the liberal left and the conservative right as they attempt to fix the blame for inflation. Corporations and individuals do overextend, overinvest, and overborrow, thus weakening the credit structure. Witness the excessive office space in New York City, the unrented and unsold condominiums in Florida, and the idle supertankers around the world. With hindsight, many of these investments were unwise and contributed to the boom. Now they contribute to the recession because their presence discourages new construction and their debt, which is not self-liquidating because it is not profitable, threatens to topple the credit structure. Governments do spend in excess of tax revenues and borrow for unwise and wasteful expenditures. Witness New York City, which has spent beyond its tax revenues for current operating costs for several years. The possibility of default on the city debt is now seriously considered. This would be a contraction of the credit structure, for those holding the debt would be forced to write off the city obligations and absorb the losses. Witness also the U.S. government deficits and wasteful expenditures for the Vietnam war. Labor unions do use their monopoly power to gain large wage increases that often are in excess of productivity increases, thus contributing to cost-push inflation. Witness Great Britain, where labor unions demand and receive higher wages even though British productivity steadily declines relative to the rest of the developed world. Corporations do raise prices to gain the highest profits possible, even when price increases are unjustified. Consumers do shop unwisely and hoard

in anticipation of price increases, thereby creating shortages and
the very price increases they expected. Unusual weather conditions,
shifts in ocean currents, shifts of consumer tastes, international
cartels, and psychological expectations all contribute to inflation.
There is no single cause of inflation and no single or simple cure.

Here I digress to express personal bias. I resent the injustice
of the current inflationary taxation system of the United States. It
rewards a debtor by letting him deduct his interest payments from
his income for tax purposes. In addition, he repays the principal
with inflated dollars, thus returning less real purchasing power than
he borrowed, while the lender must not only pay tax on the interest
received but is robbed of real value by receiving inflated dollars
that have less real purchasing power. This results in a negative incentive to defer consumption and a positive incentive to borrow and
consume now. It has encouraged corporations to increase their debt-
equity ratios and stretched the credit structure to its current weakened condition. It is resulting in an unsatisfactory rate of saving
and contributing to a slower rate of investment and growth for the
United States in comparison with other developed countries. Inflation and its effect on savings is affecting the long-term pattern of
interest rates and the average length and maturity of debt.

The federal government has been forced to pay higher and higher interest rates for borrowed funds, and the gap between the interest rate on U.S. government securities and corporate bonds has nar-
rowed since 1940. (See Table 14.1.) In addition, the average length
of maturity of the federal debt has declined from nine years, one
month in 1946 to two years, eleven months in late 1974. (See Table
14.2.) The federal government must pay more to borrow money and
is finding it increasingly difficult to float long-term debt. Faith in
the future value of money has been shattered by thirty years of persistent, steady, and recently accelerating inflation. Governments
and corporations are finding it increasingly difficult to finance debt,
and must go to the money markets more often for increasingly large
quantities of money.

Over half the marketable interest-bearing public debt must be
refinanced each year. The federal government must refinance
$139,942,000,000 in 1975--up from $81,424,000,000 in 1964. The
strains on the financial community to absorb this quantity of debt,
even at higher interest rates, in the face of current inflationary
psychology are severe. Inflationary psychology (the fear of inflation
yet to come) and the shortage of money created by inflation force interest rates higher and place pressure on the Federal Reserve Board
to increase the supply of money by monetizing the debt, which often
generates the expected inflation. Once faith in money instruments is
weakened severely, as it has been since 1973, considerable time is

TABLE 14.1

Bond Yields and Interest Rates, 1929-74

(percent per annum)

Year or Month	U.S. Government Securities			Corporate Bonds (Moody's)		High-grade Municipal Bonds (Standard & Poor's)	Average Rate on Short-term Bank Loans to Business--Selected Cities	Prime Commercial Paper, 4-6 Months	Federal Reserve Bank Discount Rate	Federal Funds Rate	FHA New Home Mortgage Yields
	3-Month Treasury Bills	3-5 Year Issues	Taxable Bonds	Aaa	Baa						
1929	--	--	--	4.73	5.90	4.27	--	5.85	5.16	--	--
1933	0.515	2.66	--	4.49	7.76	4.71	--	1.73	2.56	--	--
1939	.023	.59	--	3.01	4.96	2.76	2.1	.59	1.00	--	--
1940	.014	.50	--	2.84	4.75	2.50	2.1	.56	1.00	--	--
1941	.103	.73	--	2.77	4.33	2.10	2.0	.53	1.00	--	--
1942	.326	1.46	2.46	2.83	4.28	2.30	2.2	.68	1.00	--	--
1943	.373	1.34	2.47	2.73	3.91	2.05	2.6	.69	1.00	--	--
1944	.375	1.33	2.48	2.72	3.61	1.86	2.4	.73	1.00	--	--
1945	.375	1.18	2.37	2.62	3.29	1.67	2.2	.75	1.00	--	--
1946	.375	1.16	2.19	2.53	3.05	1.64	2.1	.81	1.00	--	--
1947	.594	1.32	2.25	2.61	3.24	2.01	2.1	1.03	1.00	--	--
1948	1.040	1.62	2.44	2.82	3.47	2.40	2.5	1.44	1.34	--	--
1949	1.102	1.43	2.31	2.66	3.42	2.21	2.68	1.49	1.50	--	4.34
1950	1.218	1.50	2.32	2.62	3.24	1.98	2.69	1.45	1.59	--	4.17
1951	1.552	1.93	2.57	2.86	3.41	2.00	3.11	2.16	1.75	--	4.21

1952	1.766	2.13	2.68	2.96	3.52	2.19	3.49	2.33	1.75	--	4.29
1953	1.931	2.56	2.94	3.20	3.74	2.72	3.69	2.52	1.99	--	4.61
1954	.953	1.82	2.55	2.90	3.51	2.37	3.61	1.58	1.60	--	4.62
1955	1.753	2.50	2.84	3.05	3.53	2.53	3.70	2.18	1.89	1.78	4.64
1956	2.058	3.12	3.08	3.36	3.88	2.93	4.20	3.31	2.77	2.73	4.79
1957	3.267	3.62	3.47	3.89	4.71	3.60	4.62	3.81	3.12	3.11	5.42
1958	1.839	2.90	3.43	3.79	4.73	3.58	4.34	2.46	2.15	1.57	5.49
1959	3.405	4.33	4.07	4.38	5.05	3.95	5.00	3.97	3.36	3.30	5.71
1960	2.928	3.99	4.01	4.41	5.19	3.73	5.16	3.85	3.53	3.22	6.18
1961	2.378	3.60	3.90	4.35	5.08	3.45	4.97	2.97	3.00	1.96	5.80
1962	2.778	3.57	3.95	4.33	5.02	3.18	5.00	3.26	3.00	2.68	5.61
1963	3.157	3.72	4.00	4.26	4.86	3.23	5.01	3.55	3.23	3.18	5.47
1964	3.549	4.06	4.15	4.40	4.83	3.22	4.99	3.97	3.55	3.50	5.45
1965	3.954	4.22	4.21	4.49	4.87	3.27	5.06	4.38	4.04	4.07	5.46
1966	4.881	5.16	4.66	5.13	5.67	3.82	6.00	5.55	4.50	5.11	6.20
1967	4.321	5.07	4.85	5.51	6.23	3.98	6.00	5.10	4.19	4.22	6.55
1968	5.339	5.59	5.25	6.18	6.94	4.51	6.68	5.90	5.17	5.66	7.13
1969	6.677	6.85	6.10	7.03	7.81	5.81	8.21	7.83	5.87	8.21	8.19
1970	6.458	7.37	6.59	8.04	9.11	6.51	8.48	7.72	5.95	7.17	9.05
1971	4.348	5.77	5.74	7.39	8.56	5.70	6.32	5.11	4.88	4.67	7.78
1972	4.071	5.85	5.63	7.21	8.15	5.27	5.82	4.69	4.50	4.44	7.53
1973	7.041	6.92	6.30	7.44	8.24	5.18	8.30	8.15	6.44	8.74	8.65
1974	7.885	7.81	6.99	8.57	9.59	6.09	11.28	9.87	7.83	10.51	9.47

Source: Economic Report of the President (Washington, D.C.: U.S. Government Printing Office, February 1975), p. 317.

TABLE 14.2
Average Length and Maturity Distribution of Marketable Interest-Bearing Public Debt, 1946-74

End of Year or Month	Amount Outstanding	Maturity Class					Average Length	
		Within 1 Year	1 to 5 Years	5 to 10 Years	10 to 20 Years	20 Years and Over	Years	Months
		Millions of Dollars					Years	Months
Fiscal year:								
1946	189,806	61,974	21,763	41,807	17,451	43,599	9	1
1947	168,702	51,211	21,851	35,962	18,504	41,481	9	5
1948	160,346	48,742	21,680	32,264	16,279	41,481	9	2
1949	155,147	48,130	32,562	16,746	22,321	34,888	8	9
1950	155,310	42,338	51,292	7,792	28,035	25,853	8	2
1951	137,917	43,908	46,526	8,707	29,979	8,797	6	7
1952	140,407	46,367	47,814	13,933	25,700	6,594	5	8
1953	147,335	65,270	36,161	15,651	28,662	1,592	5	4
1954	150,354	62,734	29,866	27,515	28,634	1,608	5	6
1955	155,206	49,703	39,107	34,253	28,613	3,530	5	10
1956	154,953	58,714	34,401	28,908	23,578	4,351	5	4
1957	155,705	71,952	40,669	12,328	26,407	4,349	4	9
1958	166,675	67,782	42,557	21,476	27,652	7,203	5	3
1959	178,027	72,958	58,304	17,052	21,625	8,038	4	7
1960	183,845	70,467	72,844	20,249	12,630	7,658	4	4
1961	187,148	81,120	58,400	26,435	10,233	10,980	4	6
1962	196,072	88,442	57,041	26,049	9,319	15,221	4	11
1963	203,508	85,294	58,026	37,385	8,360	14,444	5	1
1964	206,489	81,424	65,453	34,929	8,355	16,323	5	0
1965	208,695	87,637	56,198	39,169	8,449	17,241	5	4
1966	209,127	89,136	60,933	33,596	8,499	17,023	4	11
1967	210,672	89,648	71,424	24,378	8,425	16,797	4	7
1968	226,592	106,407	64,470	30,754	8,407	16,553	4	2
1969	226,107	108,910	62,770	34,837	8,374	16,217	4	0
1970	232,599	105,580	89,615	15,882	10,524	11,048	3	8
1971	245,473	112,772	89,074	24,503	8,455	10,670	3	6
1972	257,202	121,944	89,004	26,852	9,843	10,059	3	3
1973	262,971	122,803	88,223	31,111	14,477	6,357	3	2
1974	266,575	139,942	77,199	26,957	17,403	5,074	3	0
1973: Jan.	271,121	131,454	88,572	29,142	16,271	6,652	3	1
Feb.	269,881	130,205	95,422	22,357	16,114	5,783	3	1
Mar.	269,775	139,187	95,425	22,356	16,053	5,748	3	0
Apr.	267,847	128,350	95,392	22,356	16,022	5,718	3	0
May	265,919	125,697	83,222	29,620	15,966	6,385	3	3
June	262,971	122,803	83,223	31,111	14,477	6,357	3	2
July	262,708	122,602	88,223	31,108	14,457	6,318	3	2
Aug.	262,405	129,072	80,594	31,106	15,345	6,288	3	3
Sept.	262,386	129,114	80,576	31,103	15,317	6,245	3	2
Oct.	264,047	130,940	80,585	31,102	15,289	6,291	3	1
Nov.	270,234	139,433	83,817	25,136	15,670	8,169	3	1
Dec.	270,224	141,571	81,715	25,134	15,660	6,145	3	0
1974: Jan.	270,131	141,590	81,716	25,132	15,596	6,098	3	0
Feb.	269,650	141,444	79,045	26,968	15,129	6,083	3	0
Mar.	273,599	145,453	79,045	26,965	16,092	6,049	2	11
Apr.	270,452	140,905	80,570	26,951	16,036	5,981	2	11
May	259,550	142,864	77,165	26,960	17,463	6,103	3	0
June	266,575	139,942	77,199	26,957	17,403	5,074	3	0
July	268,782	142,245	77,200	26,953	17,346	5,039	2	11
Aug.	272,111	142,900	79,366	28,997	14,952	5,897	3	0
Sept.	272,608	143,400	79,361	29,044	14,924	5,879	3	0
Oct.	273,583	144,373	79,360	29,027	14,304	5,865	2	11
Nov.	277,585	143,351	84,730	27,916	14,855	6,645	3	0
Dec.	282,891	148,122	85,273	27,889	14,832	6,765	2	11

Source: Economic Report of the President (Washington, D.C.: U.S. Government Printing Office, February 1975), p. 334.

required to attract money at lower interest rates. It is surprising
that faith has lasted as well as it has, since inflation has repeatedly
undermined the real purchasing power of money instruments. In
1973 and 1974 canned beans, sugar, and soft drinks would have been
a better investment than U.S. Treasury bills. After paying taxes on
interest and suffering the decline in real purchasing power of the returning principal, holders of U.S. Treasury bills lost 5-6 percent.

The costs and benefits of inflation are distributed throughout
society in an arbitrary and capricious manner that is unjust and un-
dermines social values. The frugal and conservative lose. The
shrewd and merely lucky win. The poor and middle classes probably suffer most of all. The poor, in a constant race to survive,
find that prices rise faster than wages if they have employment. And
when employment drops, it is the lower wage groups that suffer the
highest unemployment. The rich are often those most in debt for the
purchase of land and assets of real value, which rise in market
value during inflation. They have an opportunity to select favorable
tax shelters and to obtain better financial advice. The middle income
groups, striving to raise their economic status, often see the value
of their savings decline and their hopes for a better life vanish as
prices race ahead of their ability to accumulate real purchasing
power. Taxed in higher income brackets by progressive taxation,
and taxed on his savings by inflation, it becomes almost impossible
for the average man to improve his economic status by saving and
investing for the future. He becomes dependent upon his employer
or the government for pay/welfare increases to maintain or modestly
advance his economic position. If economic freedom is unobtainable,
is political freedom maintainable?

Since World War II, Western nations have been influenced uni-
versally by the economic theories of John Keynes. In fact, it was
government spending for armaments and mobilization for the war
that pulled the world economy from the depth of the Great Depression
and seemed to prove Keynes's theories. In 1946, Congress passed
the Full Employment Act, which established the Council of Economic
Advisors and set three national economic goals for the United States:
full employment, maximum growth, and maintenance of purchasing
power. Whenever employment sagged in the postwar period,
Keynesian economists advised economic stimulation by fiscal and
monetary means to restore employment and growth. Keynesian economics was taught increasingly in nearly every university economics
course in the country. During the 1950s the rate of growth was unsatisfactory from some viewpoints, although inflation was very mild.
John Kennedy was elected President on the pledge to get the country
moving. Walter Heller, Chairman of the Council of Economic Advisors, recommended a tax cut that did spur employment and

economic growth. It was the golden age of Keynesian economics: all
the charts looked good in the mid-1960s and prosperity was back. It
was just like the 1920s, when everyone believed the business cycle
had been conquered and prosperity would last forever because everyone was getting richer and richer.

But Vietnam, like all wars, was not pay-as-you-go. To a
large extent, it was fought on credit, with the cost to be paid later,
in the form of inflation. Much of the credit was obtained from foreign governments that absorbed dollars under the fixed exchange-
rate system rather than allow their currencies to appreciate relative
to the dollar. For the United States this appeared to be free credit,
since fiat money flowed out to purchase real goods and services in
the international marketplace and remained unredeemed in real goods
and services. But the Bretton Woods system was destroyed in the
process, when the dollar was no longer exchangeable for gold and
became an international fiat money whose only value was what it
could earn in interest or what it could buy. Like any fiat money, its
ultimate value rested on the limitation of the supply or upon its
scarcity. But the dollar was not scarce, and from 1970 to 1973 the
effective dollar devaluation was 20 percent.

The surge of world inflation that accompanied the devaluation
of the dollar crested in 1974 and began to moderate in 1975 as the
world boom subsided and world trade declined in real terms. As unemployment rose in every nation in the West, there was an almost
immediate cry for Keynesian economic solutions to the old problem
of slow growth and unemployment. But inflation was not dead. West
Germany and Japan, suffering from the effect of appreciated currencies, saw their trade surpluses declining. Along with other nations
of the West, they asked the United States to begin the reflationary
process to prevent a deepening of the world recession. The risk that
economic mismanagement by the United States and by other nations
of the West would trigger renewed inflation was great, as was the
risk that recession and economic stagnation would spread. Hope lay
in the coordinated management of the world economy by the major nations of the West, to find together the proper moderate middle ground
between the two unacceptable extremes. The United States has a
pivotal position.

The experience of the 1970s has raised new questions in economics, which is undergoing a severe reassessment as the evolution
of economic theory continues. The areas of monetary theory and international economics are particularly undeveloped to deal with the
current problem. Questions that arise include the following: Is a
world of floating exchange rates and fiat money inherently inflationary
and unstable? Where will new debt creation arise, bringing a resurgence of world trade and employment, now that U.S. balance-of-

payments deficits no longer fill that role? Is the world economy
doomed to another depression and period of debt liquidation, as nation after nation attempts to increase exports and reduce imports in
an effort to lessen domestic unemployment--a major force in increasing the length and creating the depth of the Great Depression of the
1930s? Has our generation been led by the theories of Lord Keynes
into a monetary trap where the solution to unemployment generates
more inflation, followed by even higher unemployment? Are democratic governments capable of making and enforcing the hard decisions necessary to maintain economic stability? Is capitalism
doomed, as the Communist Party believes? Have we met the enemy,
and is he, as Pogo observes, us?

ALTERNATIVE STRATEGIES

These are obviously not simple questions, and certainly there
are no simple answers. The domestic issues remain ones of social
and political values and of risk assessment. The international issues
are nationalism vs. interdependence and risk assessment. I emphasize risk assessment because I believe we are near a critical point
in domestic and world economic evolution when economic mismanagement may be disastrous for those values our nation has held dear for
two hundred years. Like Arthur Burns, I fear for our economic and
political freedom. By economic mismanagement I mean the misallocation of resources and excessive reliance on credit. This economic
mismanagement threatens the credit structure and the value of
money, which is the life blood of the economic system. It threatens
the credit structure because wasted resources or unwise investments
will not repay the debt.
        Economic mismanagement, excessive debt creation, and the
resultant inflation have contributed to the loss of faith in fiat money.
The United States invested large quantities of world product in a
fruitless attempt to influence events in Southeast Asia, and much of
it was purchased on credit. Victims of our own rhetoric, we believed
in the late 1960s that we were the richest nation on earth and that the
cost of the war was only a small portion of our gross national product.
U.S. multinational corporations invested heavily overseas in assets
that are increasingly insecure, and much of that investment was on
credit. New York City increased payrolls, welfare payments, and
retirement benefits--and much of that was done on credit. Debt expansion, both public and private since 1960, has been phenomenal.
(See Table 14.3.) In the United States total private debt in 1973 was
over three times higher than in 1960, and corporate debt was nearly
four times higher. The expansion of public debt has not been as rapid,

TABLE 14.3

Net Public and Private Debt, 1929-73
(billions of dollars)

End of Year		Public			Private							
	Total	Federal Government	Federal Financial Agencies	State and Local Governments	Total	Corporate	Individual and Noncorporate					
							Total	Farm	Nonfarm			
									Total	Mortgage	Commercial and Financial	Consumer
1929	191.9	16.5	--	13.6	161.8	88.9	72.9	12.2	60.7	31.2	22.4	7.1
1933	168.5	24.3	--	16.3	127.9	76.9	51.0	9.1	41.9	26.3	11.7	3.9
1939	183.3	42.6	--	16.4	124.3	73.5	50.8	8.8	42.0	25.0	9.8	7.2
1940	189.8	44.8	--	16.4	128.6	75.6	53.0	9.1	43.9	26.1	9.5	8.3
1941	211.4	56.3	--	16.1	139.0	83.4	55.6	9.3	46.3	27.1	10.0	9.2
1942	258.6	101.7	--	16.4	141.5	91.6	49.9	9.0	48.9	26.8	8.1	6.0
1943	513.2	154.4	--	14.5	144.3	95.5	48.8	8.2	40.5	26.1	9.5	4.9
1944	370.6	211.9	--	13.9	144.8	94.1	50.7	7.7	42.9	26.0	11.8	5.1
1945	405.9	252.5	--	13.4	140.0	85.3	54.7	7.3	47.4	27.0	14.7	5.7
1946	396.6	229.5	--	13.7	153.4	93.5	59.9	7.6	52.3	31.8	12.1	8.4
1947	415.7	221.7	0.7	15.0	178.3	108.9	69.4	8.6	60.7	37.2	11.9	11.6
1948	431.3	215.3	.6	17.0	193.4	117.8	80.6	10.8	69.7	42.4	12.9	14.4
1949	445.8	217.6	.7	19.1	208.4	118.0	90.4	12.0	73.4	47.1	13.9	17.4
1950	486.2	217.4	.7	21.7	246.4	142.1	104.3	12.3	92.0	54.8	15.8	21.5

Year												
1951	519.2	216.9	1.3	24.2	276.8	162.5	114.3	13.7	100.6	61.7	16.2	22.7
1952	550.2	221.5	1.3	27.0	300.4	171.0	129.4	15.2	114.2	68.9	17.8	27.5
1953	581.6	226.8	1.4	30.7	322.7	179.5	143.2	16.8	196.4	76.7	18.4	31.4
1954	605.9	229.1	1.3	39.5	340.0	182.8	157.2	17.5	139.7	86.4	20.8	32.5
1955	665.8	229.6	2.9	41.1	392.2	212.1	180.1	18.7	161.4	98.7	24.0	38.8
1956	698.4	224.3	2.4	44.5	427.2	231.7	195.5	19.4	176.1	109.4	24.4	42.3
1957	728.3	223.0	2.4	48.6	454.3	246.7	207.6	20.2	187.4	119.1	24.3	45.0
1958	769.6	231.0	2.5	53.7	482.4	259.5	232.9	23.2	199.7	128.1	26.5	45.1
1959	833.0	241.4	3.7	59.6	528.3	283.3	245.0	23.8	221.1	141.0	28.7	51.5
1960	874.2	239.8	3.5	64.9	565.1	302.8	263.3	25.1	233.2	151.3	30.8	56.1
1961	930.3	246.7	4.0	70.5	609.1	324.3	284.8	27.5	257.3	164.5	34.8	58.0
1962	995.0	293.6	5.3	77.0	690.1	348.2	311.9	30.2	281.7	180.3	37.6	63.8
1963	1,070.9	257.5	7.2	83.9	722.3	376.4	345.8	33.2	342.6	193.6	42.3	71.7
1964	1,151.6	264.0	7.5	90.4	789.7	409.6	380.1	36.0	344.1	218.9	45.0	80.3
1965	1,243.6	265.4	8.9	98.3	870.0	454.3	415.7	39.3	378.4	236.8	49.7	89.9
1966	1,388.7	271.8	11.2	104.8	950.8	506.6	444.2	42.4	401.8	251.6	53.9	98.2
1967	1,433.7	286.5	9.0	113.4	1,029.9	553.7	476.2	48.3	427.9	266.9	60.2	100.8
1968	1,582.5	291.9	21.4	123.9	1,145.4	631.5	513.9	51.8	462.1	284.9	66.4	110.8
1969	1,735.0	289.3	30.6	133.3	1,282.0	734.2	548.7	55.5	493.2	303.9	68.1	121.1
1970	1,868.9	301.1	38.8	145.0	1,384.0	797.7	586.3	58.7	527.6	332.1	68.3	127.2
1971	2,045.8	325.9	39.9	162.4	1,517.6	888.3	648.3	63.2	585.1	373.4	73.4	138.4
1972	2,270.2	341.2	41.4	175.0	1,712.7	978.3	734.4	67.8	666.6	480.0	82.9	157.6
1973	2,525.8	349.1	59.8	184.5	1,932.4	1,111.1	821.3	77.3	741.0	480.1	83.4	180.5

Source: _Economic Report of the President_ (Washington, D.C.: U.S. Government Printing Office, February 1975), p. 323.

but nevertheless is substantial. The degree to which the credit structure has been weakened by economic mismanagement is impossible to
determine and depends on the future course of the domestic and world
economy. The avoidance of a severe collapse of the debt structure is
one of the major problems facing policy-makers. It is difficult to
deflate a balloon slowly and safely.

In the United States, economic policy is established within the
broad parameters of the two-party system, which was early personi-
fied by the ideological differences between Thomas Jefferson and
Alexander Hamilton. Historians and educators have been kinder to
Jefferson by far. Hamilton has often been cast as a profiteer and
spokesman for the wealthy elite. Jeffersonians probably outnumber
Hamiltonians even more than Democrats outnumber Republicans. I
deeply admire, respect, and wish I could be the equal of Thomas
Jefferson. But I hold no less respect for Hamilton, who secured
the confidence of foreign bankers and merchants in the solvency of
the new nation by acknowledging its just debts and demonstrating its
capacity to collect taxes. He established the public credit, on which,
Hamilton said, ". . . depends the character, security and prosperity
of the nation." And prosperity we have had in abundance.

The credit of the United States is not suspect. No one doubts
that U.S. Treasury bills will be redeemed in dollars when they come
due. It is the purchasing power of dollars or their future real value
that is questioned. A just debt entails not merely repayment of the
agreed quantity of money, but of the real value borrowed. The "character, security and prosperity of the nation" still depend upon a faith
in credit, both public and private.

It has been the tendency of liberal economists and politicians
guided by Jeffersonian ideals to compassionately observe the economic plight of the poor and unemployed, and to recommend Keynesian
economic solutions. When first adopted in the 1960s, their recommendations for an increase in government deficit spending and an increase
in the money supply appeared to work: real incomes rose and unemployment declined. But excessive use of these stimulants has generated inflation and increased unemployment, and has created human
suffering in a degree perhaps greater than otherwise would have been
the case. The Keynesian theories probably are valid; and the United
States and the world may be able to use them, eventually, to prevent
widespread unemployment, poverty, and depression. But economic
stability must be restored first. Its restoration will require time
and, above all, moderation in economic policy. In this time of moderation, higher unemployment than desired may be unavoidable, just
as higher inflation than desired may persist.

Sidney L. Jones, Assistant Secretary of the Treasury for Economic Policy, addressed this problem at Tucson on August 19, 1975,

when he said that economic policies "must guard against fiscal and monetary excesses which would disrupt the current expansion and complicate the problems of a more stable economy." He added that in the next few months "those who advocate more stable economic policies will be considered naive at best and insensitive at worst."[4] If these character traits are essential, let us hope we have enough government officials who are willing to be perceived naive and insensitive. It is not the time for economic extremism.

In 1964, at a national political convention a nominee for President said in his acceptance address: "Extremism in the defense of liberty is no vice! Moderation in the pursuit of justice is no virtue!" Both statements are untrue. Now is the time for moderation in national and international economic policy. Now is the time for healing the wounds that world inflation and recession have inflicted on all of us. Now is the time to restore faith in management.

Vermont Royster, writing for the Wall Street Journal, observed in Europe

> . . . cynicism about democratic governments' ability to grapple with inflation. Everyone from minister to shopkeeper, thinks inflation is a fearful monster. But the shopkeeper is cynical about the minister's willingness to do anything about it, and the minister cynical about the shopkeeper's willingness to accept the remedy. Both sigh and shrug their shoulders. Andre Malraux, that thoughtful Frenchman, describes it as a loss of faith in the very basis of Western civilization.[5]

Now is the time to restore faith in management. Our national security may depend on it.

NOTES

1. Theodore H. White, Breach of Faith: The Fall of Richard Nixon (New York: Atheneum Publishers, Reader's Digest Press, 1975), p. 185.

2. Robert A. Mundell, "Inflation from an International Viewpoint," in The Phenomenon of Worldwide Inflation, ed. David Meiselman and Arthur Laffer (Washington, D.C.: American Enterprise Institute for Public Policy Research, 1975), p. 141.

3. Joyce Kolko, America and the Crisis of World Capitalism (Boston: Beacon Press, 1974), p. 180.

4. New York Times, August 20, 1975, p. 53.

5. Wall Street Journal, August 13, 1975, p. 10.

15

INTELLIGENCE:
THE PROBLEM OF
ACCURATE ASSESSMENT
Ray Cline

THE ISSUE

It is essential for the United States to decide by 1977 whether it needs a central intelligence coordination system and, if so, what kind. Many months of press and television criticisms, exposes of alleged wrongdoing, and revelations of official investigations have brought the Central Intelligence Agency (CIA) into public and Congressional disrepute. The effectiveness of the whole central system for collecting and analyzing foreign intelligence has been drastically reduced. The CIA and the entire community of agencies it coordinates are slowly being sliced to death by charges, many of them exaggerated or unfounded, that are destroying the credibility of American intelligence both at home and abroad. The more passionate hostile commentators have called for the abolition of the CIA, while others suggest eliminating some parts of the system and retaining others. In the sour Washington political climate following the Watergate crisis, the worst seems always to be suspected of government. Congress and public are understandably confused and uneasy. A clear finding must soon be reached on what to do about the system for satisfying the intelligence needs of the nation, or the system will collapse.

BACKGROUND OF THE ISSUE

Prior to World War II, the United States never had a peacetime intelligence system worthy of the name. George Washington personally supervised espionage during the American Revolution; and every time this country became involved in military hostilities, it improvised some sort of temporary intelligence program. Between wars, support always waned for costly secret activities.

The Pearl Harbor attack found this country virtually naked. The cryptanalysis staffs in the Army and Navy were small, and there was no effective coordination of their work with the State Department's Foreign Service analysts. The FBI worried only about subversion and sabotage. There was nothing else in operation. The bits and pieces of information that might have warned of the Japanese attack never got put together in the right places at the right time. The elaborate Congressional inquiry on Pearl Harbor at the end of the war provided a fine case history on the inadequacy of the U.S. peacetime intelligence system in 1941, as well as the lack of a peacetime machinery for decision-making in national security affairs.[1]

In 1945, political confusion and interagency squabbling in Washington caused the wartime structure of intelligence agencies to fall apart, particularly the Office of Strategic Services (OSS), which had marked out a central coordinating role for itself in peacetime but failed to get the concept approved. It is impressive, however, that the function of a coordinating central agency was so clearly articulated by "Wild Bill" Donovan, the head of OSS, from the very beginning of his work in intelligence. His first directive from President Roosevelt in 1941, even before Pearl Harbor and the establishment of OSS, authorized him

> . . . to collect and analyze all information and data, which may bear upon national security; to correlate such information and data, and to make such information and data available to the President and to such departments and officials of the Government as the President may determine; and to carry out, when requested by the President, such supplementary activities as may facilitate the securing of information important for national security not now available to the Government.[2]

This central concept carried over into the legislation that finally established the first American peacetime intelligence structure, the National Security Act of 1947. One of the truly creative innovations in the American governing process in our time, it established the National Security Council (NSC) under the chairmanship of the President, with the Secretary of State and the Secretary of Defense as key members. A crucial element in this structure was the provision that the Joint Chiefs of Staff report directly to the NSC on military policy and that the Central Intelligence Agency report directly to the NSC on foreign situations, trends, threats, and opportunities.

Truman considered the building of the NSC system one of his great accomplishments, and Eisenhower used it systematically.

Kennedy streamlined its staff and its procedures but maintained the essentials of the NSC system as established in the preceding decade. [3]

The provisions of the National Security Act defending the functions of CIA read as follows:

> For the purpose of coordinating the intelligence activities of the several Government departments and agencies in the interest of national security, it shall be the duty of the Agency, under the direction of the National Security Council--
>
> (1) to advise the National Security Council in matters concerning such intelligence activities of the Government departments and agencies as relate to national security;
>
> (2) to make recommendations to the National Security Council for the coordination of such intelligence activities of the departments and agencies of the Government as relate to the national security;
>
> (3) to correlate and evaluate intelligence relating to the national security, and provide for the appropriate dissemination of such intelligence within the Government using where appropriate existing agencies and facilities. Provided, That the Agency shall have no police, subpoena, law-enforcement powers, or internal security functions: Provided further. That the departments and other agencies of the Government shall continue to collect, evaluate, correlate, and disseminate departmental intelligence: And provided further. That the Director of Central Intelligence shall be responsible for protecting intelligence sources and methods from unauthorized disclosure;
>
> (4) to perform for the benefit of the existing intelligence agencies, such additional services of common concern as the National Security Council determines can be more efficiently accomplished centrally;
>
> (5) to perform such other functions and duties related to intelligence affecting the national security as the National Security Council may from time to time direct.

This description of duties is very broadly phrased--deliberately so--and calculated to make the CIA an instrument of the President and his National Security Council advisers. The CIA was plainly intended to be the central mechanism for insuring that all intelligence-collecting agencies worked sensibly together, sharing tasks according to capability and need, and also for putting all the pieces together in an analytical whole for the benefit of the NSC and the President.

While the law does not mention espionage, it was clearly understood by the architects of this new intelligence community that extraordinary measures would be taken secretly to get information that was deliberately concealed by foreign nations, particularly by the Soviet Union, where virtually all facts are considered military secrets. The NSC took advantage of the elastic subclause (5) in the law to "direct" (in a formal NSC directive) the CIA to conduct clandestine foreign intelligence-collection activities and to be responsible for foreign counterintelligence and counterespionage. The latter tasks involve collecting information about what the Soviet secret intelligence services and any other foreign intelligence agencies are doing, and how to prevent them from harming U.S. interests.

In addition, from time to time the NSC (the President) has directed the CIA to carry out covert actions intended to support moderate groups favoring friendly relations with the United States and to resist Soviet efforts through the KGB, their foreign political-intelligence action agency, to subvert parliamentary and electoral processes in order to establish pro-Soviet regimes.

To carry out its responsibilities, the CIA has been obliged to do a number of things inside the United States. Its purpose initially was oriented entirely toward managing intelligence operations abroad, involving such tasks as recruiting and training personnel, providing cover positions for them in U.S. institutions with foreign facilities, establishing appropriate communications with its agents, caring for defectors from foreign intelligence agencies who settle in the United States, and collecting (on a confidential basis) useful information acquired in an overt, legal manner by Americans living or traveling abroad. Finally, because of the statutory injunction on "protecting intelligence sources and methods," the CIA has monitored the security of intelligence installations, operations, and personnel, including checking on the loyalty of the latter. All of these things involve taking actions inside the borders of the United States.

The CIA does not, and never was intended to, exercise police powers in the style of the Gestapo or KGB. The law setting it up expressly prohibited the CIA from having "police, subpoena, law-enforcement powers or internal security functions." Every intelligence officer of any standing and experience was sternly indoctrinated

to the effect that only the FBI operated in the domestic arena, except
for overt and managerial tasks of the kind mentioned above.

In December 1974 one of the great metropolitan newspapers
started a major publicity campaign charging that the CIA, in violation of its "charter," conducted a "massive" illegal domestic intelligence operation against the anti-war movement and other dissident
groups. Since then a Presidential Commission headed by Vice-
President Rockefeller has issued a report on these charges.[4] At the
same time Congress has launched separate investigations of the CIA,
one in the Senate and one in the House, to look into every aspect of
intelligence work. These show signs of going on for a long time,
and seem to be oriented mainly toward critiquing the CIA's covert
political operations.

In the meantime a separate prestigious Commission on the
Organization of the Government for the Conduct of Foreign Policy,
chaired by Ambassador Robert D. Murphy, has issued a report with
a section on intelligence that stresses the importance for effective
foreign policy of "intelligence capabilities of the highest competence."[5]

URGENCY OF THE ISSUE

Criticisms, innuendos, and total condemnations of the U.S.
intelligence system have constituted the television and press sensa-
tion of 1975. Fantasists and fabricators have had their days in the
limelight. On the domestic operations side of the attacks on the
CIA, the Rockefeller Commission reported:

> A detailed analysis of the facts has convinced the
> Commission that the great majority of the CIA's
> domestic activities comply with its statutory
> authority.
>
> Nevertheless, over the 28 years of its his-
> tory, the CIA has engaged in some activities
> that should be criticized and not permitted to
> happen again--both in light of the limits im-
> posed on the Agency by law and as a matter of
> public policy.
>
> Some of these activities were initiated or
> ordered by Presidents, either directly or in-
> directly.
>
> Some of them fall within the doubtful area
> between responsibilities delegated to the CIA
> by Congress and the National Security Council
> on the one hand and activities specifically pro-
> hibited to the Agency on the other.

> Some of them were plainly unlawful and
> constituted improper invasions upon the rights
> of Americans. [6]

The Commission recommended a number of statutory and administrative correctives to prevent repetitions of the improper acts. It pointed out that the role of secret intelligence work in an open society is difficult to define, especially since individual liberties are safe only in a society that has adequate information to protect itself "against external aggression and internal subversion." The Commission put the dilemma thus:

> Individual freedoms and privacy are fundamental
> in our society. Constitutional government must
> be maintained. An effective and efficient intelli-
> gence system is necessary; and to be effective,
> many of its activities must be conducted in
> secrecy. . . .
>   The preservation of the United States re-
> quires an effective intelligence capability, but
> the preservation of individual liberties within
> the United States requires limitations or re-
> strictions on gathering of intelligence. The
> drawing of reasonable lines--where legitimate
> intelligence needs end and erosion of Constitu-
> tional government begins--is difficult. . . .
>   In the final analysis, public safety and in-
> dividual liberty sustain each other. [7]

It was to be hoped that the disclosures in the Rockefeller Commission's report would permit an enlightened Congressional discussion on what kind of intelligence system the United States needs to deal with its security and foreign relations in a world of conflict and turbulence. Inevitably, perhaps, subsequent discussion has focused on the specific instances where the CIA clearly overstepped the bounds of propriety or legality in its twenty-eight years of existence.

The prolongation of the Congressional inquires means that the CIA and, to a certain extent, the intelligence agencies associated with it are winding down to a low speed and, in some areas, to a complete halt. Foreign governments that used to provide invaluable supplementary data relating to U.S. security and foreign agents who used to risk their lives in espionage are breaking off or limiting their connections with U.S. intelligence because they doubt that secrecy can be preserved. Morale in most parts of the CIA is low because of the uproar, much of it out of proportion to the facts, and even the scholarly analytical and estimative components of the intelligence system are meeting public hostility arising from confusion between overt and clandestine functions.

Many experienced intelligence agents fear that the CIA operational capability will be completely destroyed if this trend persists. Certainly the maintenance of high-class, experienced talent in all parts of the intelligence community will become next to impossible unless a consensus forms between the President and Congress on what kind of intelligence work is essential and this view is conveyed persuasively to the American people. This process is unlikely to be completed soon and, even if a solution is worked out in 1976, it must be confirmed by whatever administration and Congressional leadership is in office in 1977. If the problem is not solved promptly in 1977, it will become academic, because the United States will not have a peacetime coordinating system for intelligence in a world that is at least as dangerous as it was in 1941--and a great deal more complicated to observe and understand.

ALTERNATIVE STRATEGIES

The simplest alternative that could be adopted to resolve the unsatisfactory state of affairs in intelligence is to abolish the CIA or let it die of budgetary starvation. A number of young journalists have proposed abolition, on the grounds that foreign dangers are either nonexistent or unimportant, secrecy is incompatible with freedom, and entering into clandestine conflicts abroad is incompatible with morality. Political optimists find covert actions to shore up the center and democratic left in friendly states being swept toward Communist-dominated one-party dictatorships damaging to detente. Neo-isolationists find such actions costly and entangling. All could be settled if the United States could return to the atmosphere of 1920-30, years of neutrality, peace pacts, disarmament, and gentlemen not reading other people's mail--as Secretary of State Stimson said when he closed out the U.S. cryptanalytic effort in the early 1930s.

The trouble is that at least some conflict in international affairs is endemic, both Moscow and Peking say it will continue indefinitely despite detente, and even the disarmament pact enthusiasts want to know whether agreements are being violated. Some kind of central coordinating system seems to be required for monitoring disarmament performance and compliance.

Furthermore, foreign intrusions into the privacy and security of American citizens continues on a large scale. Soviet, Chinese, Polish, Czech, East German, and Cuban intelligence agencies work diligently in the United States as well as in the territories of the principal U.S. allies. The Rockefeller Commission felt obliged, in order to create some perspective in which to view CIA's activities, to comment on this intrusion:

> This Commission is devoted to analyzing the domestic activities of the CIA in the interest of protecting the privacy and security rights of American citizens. But we cannot ignore the invasion of the privacy and security rights of Americans by foreign countries or their agents. This is the other side of the coin--it merits attention here in the interest of perspective.
>
> Witnesses with responsibilities for counterintelligence have told the Commission that the United States remains the principal intelligence target of the communist bloc.
>
> The communists invest large sums of money, personnel and sophisticated technology in collecting information--within the United States--on our military capabilities, our weapons systems, our defense structure and our social divisions. The communists seek to penetrate our intelligence services, to compromise our law enforcement agencies and to recruit as their agents United States citizens holding sensitive government and industry jobs. In addition, it is a common practice in communist bloc countries to inspect and open mail coming from or going to the United States.
>
> In an open society such as ours, the intelligence opportunities for our adversaries are immeasurably greater than they are for us in their closed societies. Our society must remain an open one, with our traditional freedoms unimpaired. But when the intelligence activities of other countries are flourishing in the free environment we afford them, it is all the more essential that the foreign intelligence activities of the CIA and our other intelligence agencies, as well as the domestic counterintelligence activities of the FBI, be given the support necessary to protect our national security and to shield the privacy and rights of American citizens from foreign intrusion. [8]

It is hard to accept the idea that these hostile intelligence activities should go unimpeded. If they are to be monitored and, if possible, circumscribed, it is clear that an internal security service like the FBI is needed and that it can operate effectively only with the benefit of tips, leads, and solid identifications from counterespionage abroad. Looking for agents who are planning to infiltrate the United States is easier and safer than digging them out once they are here. Sophisticated counterespionage requires great secrecy, excellent liaison with foreign governments, and highly motivated agents. The CIA has had all these in the past. Another agency would take years to build capacities that are now in jeopardy. If the FBI were given a charter to operate abroad, the United States would have turned to the KGB-like solution, whereby a secret intelligence agency operating overseas would have police powers at home.

Finally, if the CIA were abolished or allowed to wither on the vine, as it is now doing, the remaining intelligence and analysis capability would exist in the State Department, where commitment to current foreign policies makes it hard to criticize diplomatic progress forthrightly on the basis of new intelligence, and in the Defense Department, where estimates of foreign military threats tend to be magnified lest U.S. budgets be reduced. The analytical and estimative record of the triad of the CIA, the State Department, and the Defense Department expert analytical staffs has not been perfect, but it has been good. It developed techniques of estimating Soviet and Chinese military strength so reliable since about 1960 that our entire strategic plans and security system are based on these findings, as are arms limitation understandings. Much of the reliability and objectivity of this sophisticated analytical machine derive from the planned redundancy of research by intelligence officers reflecting a foreign policy point of view, a military point of view, and--in the CIA--no viewpoint except the best evidence available for all sources. This system of checks and balances in research and analysis at its peak performance provided the U.S. government with the most competent, honest, and objective intelligence reports produced anywhere in the world.

The second alternative is to let the CIA and the other agencies in the intelligence community weather the storm and pull themselves together as best they can whenever Congress and the public lose interest in the details of clandestine practices. In effect, something close to this alternative is what the Rockefeller Commission recommended: improved Congressional oversight in the form of a Joint Committee on Intelligence, express legislative provision that all of the CIA's activities must be related to foreign intelligence, Presidential instructions clarifying the guidelines for domestic activities-- to include counterintelligence and counterespionage when properly coordinated with the FBI, and appointment of a man "of stature, independence and integrity" as Director of the CIA, plus a long list of administrative devices to insure that the intelligence agencies complied with injunctions to avoid improper and illegal domestic activities. [9]

These recommendations are all good ones, and in most cases will improve CIA performance or at least make it more demonstrably related to its foreign intelligence tasks. The objection to this alternative is that it does not eliminate the damage done to the CIA's prestige, credibility, and public esteem. In the full perspective of the CIA's millions of actions over twenty-eight years, the specific instances of illegal or unwise intrusions into domestic security are comparatively few and easily corrected. What is needed is Congressional and public confidence that what the CIA is doing in its proper role is sensibly planned and effectively carried out.

The third, and preferable, alternative is to adopt the major recommendations of the Rockefeller Commission but to go further in reorganizing the basic components of the U.S. intelligence community in a fashion comprehensible to serious-minded observers in Congress, the news media, and the public. Some of the ideas in the Murphy Commission Report should be picked up and promoted. At some point in 1976 the Congressional inquiries should be closed down, since they have already exposed everything that needs exposing and are doing irreparable damage to CIA intelligence operations. The Ford administration should develop a plan emphasizing the positive intelligence needs of the nation and organizing appropriate elements of the CIA and the rest of the intelligence community to concentrate on these hard tasks rather than devoting energy to fending off criticism. This plan probably cannot be finally approved and new legislation passed until 1977, but every effort should be made to educate and inform everybody about what a good central intelligence system should do and what it should not do. My recommendations would run along the following lines:

1. The crucial task in the CIA and the other elements of the intelligence community is to make objective analytical studies of world trends in strategic relationships and foreign affairs, in support of national decision-making in the United States. This work, contributing to an enlightened, sophisticated international outlook for American policy-makers, must continue.

2. To preserve this essential function and maintain a professional staff adequate to the nation's needs, we should now establish by law an Institute of Foreign Affairs Research (IFAR) with a Director who is by training a scholar in the social sciences, preferably one who also has wide experience in government. IFAR should

exercise operational and budgetary control over the analytical elements of all intelligence agencies, no matter where--in State and Defense, mainly--they are physically located.

3. IFAR would establish requirements for intelligence collection by agencies not under the operational command of the Director of IFAR, but receiving assignments from him.

4. IFAR would prepare current intelligence reports and strategic estimates for the NSC and other Executive officials, as CIA does now; and in addition it would prepare reports for whatever Joint Committee of Congress emerges from the present controversy on Congressional oversight of intelligence. It also should be instructed to make as much of its findings as possible available for public use.

5. Other agencies of government should not duplicate IFAR facilities, although all the agencies represented in the intelligence community probably would set up small liaison and coordination staffs. In Defense, DIA would continue to operate the attache system and provide the intelligence link between the Joint Chiefs of Staff and the individual service staffs at headquarters and overseas command levels. For national research and analysis, the Secretary of Defense and the Secretary of State should rely upon IFAR, including its military component in what is now DIA (the Defense Intelligence Agency).

6. The rest of the intelligence community would consist of collection services receiving intelligence assignments from IFAR through the NSC. These collection services would include the present signals and reconnaissance organizations under Defense administration and supervision.

7. The policy guidance and coordination of the intelligence community agencies thus organized and assigned would be worked out in a Cabinet-level National Security Intelligence Committee (NSIC), which should subsume the responsibilities and duties of the 40 Committee, now largely anachronistic because no important covert political or paramilitary operations are feasible in the present Washington climate. The membership of the NSIC should include the Director of IFAR and the present members of the NSC Intelligence Committee, which should be deactivated.

8. The President should appoint a Chairman and Coordinator for the NSIC at the Cabinet level, with responsibility for budgetary control and policy supervision of the entire intelligence community. His staff should be small and should be set up in the White House.

9. Clandestine collection activities would have to be authorized by NSIC and carried out in response to IFAR intelligence requirements and priorities. Operational responsibility and control would be exercised by a small professional staff set up at the White House, working closely with the State Department, the Defense Department, and IFAR.

This staff would assign collection tasks to special groups to be set up in various departments represented on NSC for designated program purposes. These programs would be limited in number, and the special groups would be specifically assigned to procure information not available from all the other sources available to IFAR. They would change in title and area of responsibility from time to time, in accordance with directives evolved under NSIC-IFAR procedures. The aim would be to deflect and diffuse public and journalistic curiosity by scattering these clandestine units. This is a costly and administratively wasteful system of doing business, but essential secrecy could be maintained.

10. The Chairman of NSIC would be responsible for reviewing at the Cabinet level, on behalf of the President, all proposals for covert action abroad. No permanent organization for covert political and paramilitary actions would be established. Programs of support to groups abroad whose existence is vital to U.S. security and foreign policy aims should be small, exceptional, and carried out covertly only when the President makes a formal finding that secret rather than open support is essential to success.

11. Congressional oversight of this whole intelligence structure and program would be exercised by a Joint Committee of the Congress. The Joint Committee would establish procedures whereby it would receive restricted data reports from NSIC on policies governing intelligence programs and operations, as well as restricted data briefings by the Director of IFAR on the effectiveness of the intelligence programs and the information derived from them. The Committee would have to establish rules to protect the security of information provided by the NSIC and IFAR.

12. The Joint Committee of the Congress would hold closed hearings on a single program budget for intelligence, to be presented by the Chairman of NSIC annually and supported in substantive terms by the Director of IFAR. Its findings and recommendations would be made available, with adequate provisions for secrecy, to the Chairmen and ranking minority members of the Senate Finance Committee, the House Appropriations Committee, the Senate and House Armed Services Committees, the Senate Committee on Foreign Relations, and the House Committee on International Relations.

CONCLUSION

The complexities and conflicts that are almost inevitable in the 1970s and 1980s require a resolution of the issue of what kind of intelligence system the United States needs on lines comparable with the sophisticated intelligence community sketched in above. The

Ford administration in 1976 and the administration of 1977, whatever it may be, owe the nation a full and patient explication of what the world situation demands. With a careful explanation of the checks and balances outlined as the third alternative, the administrative prohibitions and guidelines recommended under the second alternative would be adequate to guarantee public and Congress against serious illegal or harmful action in the domestic security area where civil rights are involved. The issue of the proper function of a central coordinating intelligence system can best be settled in this way.

NOTES

1. U.S. Congress, Report of the Joint Committee on the Investigation of the Pearl Harbor Attack (Washington, D.C.: U.S. Government Printing Office, 1946); Roberta Wohlstetter, Pearl Harbor: Warning and Decision (Stanford, Calif.: Stanford University Press, 1962).

2. Order Designating a Coordination of Information, The White House, July 11, 1941.

3. For the decline in the use of intelligence by the NSC under President Nixon, see my article, "Policy Without Intelligence," Foreign Policy, no. 17 (1974/1975), pp. 121-35.

4. Report to the President by the Commission on CIA Activities Within the United States (Washington, D.C.: Government Printing Office, June 1975), p. 9.

5. Report by the Commission on the Organization of the Government for the Conduct of Foreign Policy (Washington, D.C.: Government Printing Office, June 1975), p. 9.

6. Report to the President . . . , p. 10.

7. Ibid., p. 5.

8. Ibid., p. 7.

9. Ibid., Ch. 3.

CHAPTER

16

STRATEGIC ARMS LIMITATION:
THE PROBLEM OF
MUTUAL DETERRENCE
Richard T. Ackley

THE ISSUE

1976 marks the seventh year of the Soviet-American Strategic
Arms Limitation Talks (SALT). Both sides proclaim a commitment
to negotiate a permanent treaty, but to date it hasn't happened. In
fact, following the disappointment of the 1974 Moscow summit meeting even to agree on the principles for a treaty, Secretary of State
Henry Kissinger called for a national debate on strategic policy.
This debate has come to center on the issue of former Secretary of
Defense James R. Schlesinger's new targeting doctrine, associated
force modernization, and their relationship to the prospects for a
successful strategic arms treaty.

BACKGROUND OF THE ISSUE

SALT-1

In the latter 1950s, the Soviet Union developed the capability to
deliver nuclear weapons on the territory of the United States. From
that moment, the essence of U.S. strategic policy has been to deter
a nuclear strike on American soil. Deterrence, then, as the basis
for strategic planning has remained unchanged in principle; however,
strategic doctrine and accompanying force structure have varied to
meet what has been perceived as the principal threat.
Few would dispute that the United States maintained a clear-cut
strategic offensive nuclear superiority over the Soviet Union until
about 1969. But, with Soviet strategic forces growing, many U.S.

strategists focused on the probability that the Soviet Union felt compelled, but was hard-pressed, to compete economically in an arms race. Accordingly, it seemed only logical for the USSR to strive for nuclear parity with the United States; then, with its safety assured, to negotiate a sensible arms limitation treaty that might even result in arms reduction. It was this type of thinking that set the stage for the United States purposely to restrain strategic-weapons deployments in hope of setting a good example for Soviet moderation--meaning the ready acceptance of numerical nuclear parity by the Soviets.

There were those, however, who viewed Soviet strategic development in the 1960s with alarm. This group noted spectacular expansion and deployment of Soviet strategic forces on land and at sea. Additionally, it seemed to them that a Russian multiple independently targeted reentry vehicle (MIRV) capability was only a short time away. From this perspective, the U.S. motivation behind SALT-1 was to curtail Soviet strategic momentum before a major threat to the United States developed. An overriding American objective was, however, "cooling" the arms race in order to arrive at a position of strategic stability.

Early American visions of SALT-1 encompassed far-reaching agreements on both offensive and defensive weapons systems. Establishing agreed-upon ceilings was thought to be a realizable goal, while possible mutual reduction in numbers was held up as a glittering hope. As it turned out, asymmetries in the accords--although approved by the Congress--became the subject of heated debate. Table 16.1 shows the results of the five-year "Interim Agreement of Certain Measures with Respect to the Limitation of Strategic Offensive Arms," arrived at on May 26, 1972.

The numerical ceilings were supposed to equal actual missile deployments, plus the number of missiles being built for deployment at the time the accord was signed. Additionally, there are allowable variations to account for substitutions of certain new weapons for older ones. In sum and substance, however, the U.S. ceilings equale actual deployments--a figure that has remained unaltered since 1967. On the other hand, the ceiling for the USSR was substantially higher than the strategic missiles actually deployed on May 26, 1972--and for the long term the Soviets were permitted nearly half again more missiles than the United States: 2,359 missiles to 1,710 for the United States, a numerical advantage of 649.[1] The agreement placed no prohibition on qualitative improvements, nor did it consider manned bombers on both sides, medium- and intermediate-range ballistic missiles (M/IRBMs) on the Soviet side, submarine launched

TABLE 16.1

U.S. and Soviet Strategic Offensive Missile Launchers Associated with
Interim Strategic Arms Limitation Agreement
(operational and under construction or conversion)

United States			Soviet Union			
Titan II	54	5–10 mt. ea.	SS-7, 8	209	5 mt. ea.	
Minuteman I	260	1 mt. ea.	SS-9	313	25 mt. ea.	(+ new silos)
Minuteman II	510	1–2 mt. ea.	SS-11/13	1,096	1–2 mt. ea.	(+ new silos)
Minuteman III	220	3 x 180 kt. ea.				
Total ICBMs	1,054		Total ICBMs	1,618		
Polaris A-2	128	800 kt. ea.	SLBMs on modern SSBNs	710	mt. range	
Polaris A-3	208	3 x 200 kt. ea.	SLBMs on older SSBNs	30	mt. range	
Poseidon	320	10 x 50 kt. ea.				
Total SLBMs	656		Total SLBMs	740		
Total launchers	1,710		Total launchers	2,358		

mt. = megaton.
kt. = kiloton.

Sources: Commanders Digest, November 15, 1973; International Institute for Strategic Studies, The Military Balance 1973–1974 (London: the Institute, 1973).

ballistic missiles (SLBMs) in Soviet diesel submarines, and existing Soviet submarine-launched cruise missiles (SLCMs). *

Critics of SALT-1 maintain that the USSR acquired advantages in missile "throw-weight" payload (about four to one), and in the numbers of intercontinental ballistic missile (ICBM) launchers (about two to one). On the other hand, supporters of the executive agreement claim the foregoing are offset by U.S. advantages in numbers of re-entry vehicles (RVs), greater accuracy, and MIRV technology.†

Another facet of SALT-1 was the Anti-Ballistic Missile (ABM) Treaty, which in essence limited each party to 100 ABMs at each of two sites, one protecting part of the nation's offensive strategic forces. (Subsequently, an executive agreement signed in Moscow in 1973 reduced the number of ABM sites from two to one each.)‡ When the treaty was signed, however, the USSR had an operational ABM system defending the Moscow area consisting of some sixty-four launchers with supporting radars and command and control equipment. On the other hand, the United States had <u>planned</u> to deploy some 200 ABMs to protect its Minuteman ICBM sites.

-----

*In terms of "heavy" bombers--a maximum range of over 6,000 miles--the United States holds numerical advantage (457 to 140) over the Soviets. However, when one considers medium bombers, the USSR has about 800 and the United States 74. (Soviet medium bombers are capable of striking the continental United States if they are refueled in the air, fly a one-way mission, or are staged from Arctic bases.) Also, there were about 66 Soviet SLBMs in the 350-750-mile range with warheads of megaton yields that are not considered, as well as some 338 SLCMs in the 450-mile range with warheads of kiloton yields. See International Institute for Strategic Studies, <u>The Military Balance 1973-1974</u> (London: the Institute, 1973), pp. 69-71.

†According to New York <u>Times</u> reports on May 29 and July 5, 1974, with nearly 2,600 launchers and an estimated 10-12 million tons of power protected by the agreement, the USSR could, if it decided, put something like 17,000 warheads into the skies, enough to threaten the entire U.S. land-based missile force. Against that, the United States could field about 2 million tons of power in 10,000 warheads.

‡Donald Brennan, Director of Strategic Studies at the Hudson Institute, opposes the SALT-1 agreements. He argues that SALT, by cutting back on ballistic missile defense, insures that nuclear weapons can be used only for city-busting. This, according to Brennan, is immoral. See Donald G. Brennan, "When the SALT Hit the Fan," <u>National Review</u>, June 23, 1972, pp. 685-92.

Critics of the ABM Treaty maintain that the USSR was anxious to sign the agreement in order to preclude deployment of the U.S. Safeguard ABM system, which would have been more advanced, and consequently more effective, than the Soviet Galosh ABM system. Also, it is claimed that the traditional logic of relating the defensive to the offensive threat was broken by the ABM Treaty. That is, setting ABMs at low levels, while theoretically permitting high levels of offensive weapons makes no sense at all. Yet defenders of the ABM Treaty see a conceptual advantage in institutionalizing "mutual vulnerability." That is, mutual assured destruction is seen by some as the only real deterrent to all-out nuclear war. Others say this concept is best described by its acronym "MAD," for any doctrine that deliberately places one's own population in a hostage relationship is indeed mad. After all, we have a Department of Defense to protect and defend our vital interests, not to offer up the population as a sacrifice in the event deterrence fails.[2]

SOVIET STRATEGIC BUILDUP

Table 16.2 provides an overview of quantitative increases in the Soviet central strategic offensive missile force. Between signing the SALT-1 agreement in May 1972, and mid-1975, the USSR deployed an additional 63 ICBMs and 200 SLBMs. In the same time period, the United States maintained a constant force level of 1,710 missiles--640 fewer than the Soviets fielded in mid-1975. (Figure 16.1 shows comparative 1973 dollar-value expenditures for the U.S. and Soviet national defense.) Considering a five- to fifteen-year lead time between the conception of a new strategic system and its initial operational capability (IOC), it becomes apparent that in 1972 the Soviets had no intention of sizing their strategic forces at parity with the United States. In other words, during SALT-1 negotiations the USSR was building new strategic systems as well as deploying more of its existing hardware.

Soviet security, it would seem, rests more upon numerical superiority than upon parity. Since signing SALT-1, the USSR has developed four entirely new types of ICBMs with warheads ranging from one-half to 25 megatons, along with an improved submarine missile, the SS-N-8, that has been test fired over a range of some 4,900 miles. The Soviets are working on new RVs, apparently terminally guided for maximum accuracy, as well as MIRVs. The new Russian SS-19 ICBM can carry six fully MIRVed warheads yielding about 340 kt. each, as compared to the three 190-kt. RVs in Minuteman III. The largest of the new Soviet missiles is the SS-18, carrying eight RVs even larger than those of the SS-19. Additionally,

the SS-18 has an estimated circular error probable (CEP) of about
one-quarter mile. * On the other hand, the new SS-17 appears to be
a city-buster, with four very large RVs; and the SS-16 is the first
Soviet solid-fueled ICBM that has a fixed or land-mobile capability.
In addition to the above, the USSR has been testing sophisticated warheads with yields in the three-four-megaton range. This could make
its MIRVed warheads about twenty times more powerful than those of
the United States.[3] There is also information strongly suggesting
that the Russians are working on advanced reentry vehicles, terminal
maneuvering, and homing guidance.

TABLE 16.2

Historical Changes in U.S.-Soviet Strategic
Offensive Force Levels, 1967-75
(midyears)

	ICBMs	SLBMs	Total
1967			
United States	1,054	656	1,710
USSR	460	130	590
1968			
United States	1,054	656	1,710
USSR	800	130	930
1970			
United States	1,054	656	1,710
USSR	1,300	280	1,580
1972			
United States	1,054	656	1,710
USSR	1,527	560	2,087
1974			
United States	1,054	656	1,710
USSR	1,575	720	2,295
1975			
United States	1,054	656	1,710
USSR	1,590	760	2,350

Note: Soviet SLBM figures include launchers on diesel-
powered submarines.

Sources: International Institute for Strategic Studies, The
Military Balance 1974-1975 (London: The Institute, 1974); Annual
Defense Department Report FY 1976 and FY 197T.

---

*CEP is defined as the radius of a circle in which half of all
RVs fired land.

FIGURE 16.1

Dollar Cost of Soviet Programs as a Percent of U.S. Defense Expenditures

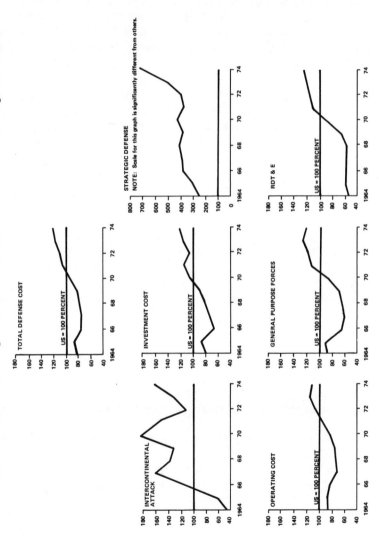

Secretary of Defense James R. Schlesinger announced on June 20, 1975, that the USSR had actually deployed some sixty of these new ICBMs armed with MIRVs. This includes ten SS-18s, the USSR's largest intercontinental missile, and fifty SS-19s--a relatively large ICBM with six MIRVs of considerable accuracy. [4] It seems, then, that Soviet technological (qualitative) development has moved from the drawing board and test range to operational deployment.

Dr. Malcom R. Currie, the Department of Defense Director of Research and Engineering, has termed the Soviets' new missile development "simply staggering":

> The concentration of R & D effort needed for development of four all new missiles, new bus-type dispensing systems, new MIRVed payloads, new guidance, new type silos, new launch techniques, and new warheads exceeds anything seen previously in history. . . . They will gain expanded target coverage, plus improved prelaunch survivability, plus a substantial added hard-target kill capability. [5]

Although the USSR had made technological advances and deployments that increase the threat to American strategic forces, some individuals seek consolation in the fact that a growing Soviet counterforce capability makes a "city-avoidance" doctrine at least a possibility. This point played no small role in the development of Secretary Schlesinger's "new targeting doctrine."

THE NEW TARGETING DOCTRINE

Secretary of Defense Schlesinger saw three goals associated with the USSR's new strategic program advances:

- Expanded target coverage (particularly countermilitary) with MIRV
- Improved prelaunch survivability with new hardened silos
- Attainment of a significant hard-target capability. [6]

Moreover, he made it clear that he did not see Soviet improvements as approximating a first-strike disarming attack against the United States. In part, this is because of the mobility inherent in our manned bomber and SLBM forces. Nevertheless, the Soviets have acquired new capabilities and strategic options that must not be ignored.

If American strategic forces are to fulfill their primary objective of a credible deterrence across the entire spectrum of potential threats, these forces must be

- Able to absorb a first strike and respond with devastating effectiveness (a survivable force that can be withheld)
- Prepared to execute a range of appropriate attacks, including those limited in terms of targets and numbers of weapons (targeting flexibility)
- Perceived as equal in overall capability to the forces of any opponent or combination of opponents, so that no one could hope to use a nuclear threat to gain diplomatic or military advantage over the United States (essential equivalence)
- Equivalent to the forces and programs of any other nations in payload, accuracy, and reliability (essential equivalence). [7]

To obtain and maintain forces with the above capabilities requires a complex force structure today, in contrast with forces required in the 1950s for a massive retaliation response, or in the 1960s for an assured destruction strategy. As John M. Collins observed, "If a nuclear war should erupt, concerted efforts to the contrary, we lack credible means to: contain the conflict quickly, control escalation, protect our population and production base, or facilitate a salutary settlement."[8] It is precisely this type of concern that prompted the Secretary of Defense to reexamine our defense posture in general, and our targeting doctrine in particular.

Beginning in news conferences on January 10 and 24, 1974, Secretary Schlesinger announced an American intention to develop a wider range of strategic targeting options (increased flexibility), and to maintain rough symmetry in counterforce capabilities with the Soviet Union, including the ability to attack "hard" targets like ICBM silos. The rapid development of Soviet strategic force capabilities undoubtedly triggered the proposed U.S. changes in order to avoid the dilemma of "suicide" or "surrender" if deterrence should fail.

The essence of the new targeting doctrine rests on the belief that it is highly unlikely the USSR will launch a preemptive, first-strike disarming attack on the United States, although retaliatory forces will be maintained to hedge against this eventuality. Rather, it is more likely that conventional or tactical nuclear wars might escalate to a strategic exchange if uncontrolled. Indeed, no graduated control of escalation is possible if our major responsive option is one of city-busting in an all-out retaliatory attack. Accordingly, with the USSR's increased capability for flexible, accurate targeting, the United States should be capable of controlled attack options in response. The new doctrine, then, emphasizes measured use of strategic forces for "interwar" deterrence versus automatic uncontrolled escalation. That is, the United States will maintain the flexibility of inflicting punishment commensurate with the deed. The objective is to make war termination a real possibility before an embryonic nuclear conflict races out of control. Such a targeting doctrine, in reaction to known Soviet initiatives, can hardly be termed destabilizing in Russian eyes.

A problem with the new targeting doctrine arises for those who believe the United States already possesses a flexible response. After all, flexible response was the strategic doctrine of the Kennedy-Johnson administrations from 1961 to 1968, and the realistic deterrence of the Nixon years suggested target selectivity and flexibility. The difference, however, is one of degree. Previous flexible-response options involved "withholding" certain targets (countries) in the course of a preprogrammed retaliatory launch. This was within the context of a coordinated strategic attack by all elements. In other words, earlier versions of flexible response were large-scale rather than minimal selective attacks.

The "hard target" or counterforce capabilities referred to by Secretary Schlesinger do fit into the framework of selectivity and flexibility, rather than into a major first-strike capability. Contrary to popular belief, a counterforce capability is not a revolutionary shift for the United States. Our strategy over the years has been to target military airfields, radar installations, submarine bases, and such. What is now suggested, however, is a refined capability to attack, with discretion and minimal collateral damage to populations, certain military targets, including some that are "hardened" for protection against existing U.S. weapons. The new targeting doctrine, one might note, is independent of force size or the acquisition of new capabilities. However, in order to have "forces and programs equivalent to other nations in payload, accuracy and reliability," new capabilities are required and will be subject to change in response to an adversary's weaponry.

An advantage claimed for the new targeting doctrine is its deterrent effect on an adversary that previously might have been willing to engage the United States in a limited nuclear war, believing it would not be worth an American response with massive nuclear retaliation. Conversely, with the new targeting doctrine an adversary would be well advised to exercise due caution. It is this point that is made for American security commitments in Europe--that is, an American President is more likely to consider employment of a lesser strategic option in reply to a Soviet attack in Europe than he is a large-scale strike. [9]

In terms of the effect of the new targeting doctrine on SALT, it can be said that the doctrine's announcement in early 1974 did not preclude the Brezhnev-Ford Vladivostok accords of November 1974. Without doubt, most qualitative improvements increase verification problems; however, this does not seem to be the major stumbling block to SALT. As Dr. William R. Van Cleave pointed out, improving targeting flexibility has nothing to do with SALT or with any attempt to coerce or influence the Soviet Union. It is "essential equivalence" of strategic forces that is directly related to SALT. [10]

The Commander-in-Chief of the Strategic Command (SAC), General Russell E. Dougherty, perhaps most clearly defined the meaning of the new targeting doctrine when he stated, "We at SAC and the Joint Target Planning Staff are engaged in planning that will provide for a range of preplanned choices for consideration in responding to a range of potential provocations less than major nuclear attack." This means the use of nuclear power in "a wider variety of discrete and discriminating ways in order to resolve conflicts without resort to the ultimate nuclear sanctions" by communicating U.S. intentions to an enemy as unmistakably as possible. [11]

STRATEGIC FORCES' MODERNIZATION
AND IMPROVEMENT PROGRAM

In considering the relationship of strategic force modernization and improvements to SALT, our emphasis is on strategic offensive forces. Certainly research and development on strategic defensive systems will continue; however, assuming no deployments outside those permitted by the 1972 ABM Treaty, the R&D aspects of ABM systems should have minimal impact on SALT (offensive weapons) decisions. Additionally, Command and Control and Civil Defense improvements should, at the most, be peripheral issues to the offensive-weapons aspects of SALT.

Secretary Schlesinger recommended retention of our strategic offensive forces of both ICBMs and bombers as well as SLBMs. He stated that we must move forward in an orderly and deliberate manner, with qualitative improvements if essential equivalence in strategic power between the United States and USSR is to be preserved. [12] Secretary Schlesinger has proposed the following ongoing modernization and improvements programs: [13]

ICBMs

In the near term (through the early 1980s) major improvements in the areas of expanded options and maintaining pace with growing Soviet hard-target kill capabilities will be through modification of the Minuteman III. The Mark 12A reentry vehicle, having a refined guidance system and a new, higher-yield warhead, will replace the MK12. The warhead has been credited with twice the power of our present MIRVs, and is planned for deployment on 600 Minuteman III missiles. Along with refinements in accuracy, each warhead will gain the capacity to destroy present Soviet silos with high confidence.[14]

Another improvement to Minuteman III will be the installation of several smaller RVs. This will provide an option to expand target coverage of relatively soft point targets, such as airfields and radar sites that are not located near population.

Beyond the early 1980s, an entirely new missile, the MX, is in the planning stage. Current development work on it is in the three problem areas of selection of a preferred basing mode (air-launched or ground-launched), the unique guidance requirements for the mobile missile, and the technology required for more efficient rocket motors. The mobility option is in response to the probability that fixed ICBMs will become more and more vulnerable to Soviet attack. And, with a mobile launch system, midcourse position-fixing or terminal homing is required to establish high degrees of accuracy. Finally, improved rocket motors will allow weight to be shifted from propulsion stages to the payload package.

Associated with ICBM development is the advanced ballistic reentry systems program (ABRES). This program involves research on the maneuvering reentry vehicles (MaRV), terminal guidance, a large advanced ballistic reentry vehicle, and penetration aids.

SLBMs

In order to ensure the future survivability of the SLBM force, both a quieter submarine and a longer-range missile are deemed necessary. The Trident submarine is designed to meet the first requirement and the Trident I missile (4,000-mile range) the second. Beyond the mid-1980s, the Trident II missile, with about a 6,000-mile range and MaRV, should become available. The Trident submarine will have a submerged displacement of about 18,700 tons, compared with 8,250 tons for the Poseidon submarine. It will carry twenty-four missiles, compared with sixteen for the Polaris/Poseidon, and be considerably quieter than Polaris/Poseidon, as well as having a more efficient command and control system, and a more capable sonar suit.

Bombers

The B-1 bomber is programmed to strengthen and modernize the bomber force sometime in the 1980s. The aging B-52 force may be replaced in part with the B-1, an advanced-technology aircraft. The short-range attack missile (SRAM) and the strategic cruise

missile (both air- and submarine-launched) are also in production
and development stages, respectively.

THE 1974 VLADIVOSTOK ACCORDS AND SALT-2

The accords drawn up at Vladivostok in November 1974 between President Ford and Secretary General Brezhnev have been
said to mark the first real breakthrough in strategic arms limitations since the signing of the 1972 SALT agreements. The Vladivostok meeting provided a framework for subsequent ones, incorporating
several new principles: SALT-2 agreements are to be effective until
December 31, 1985; they embody a common ceiling of 2,400 offensive
delivery vehicles (not launchers, as in SALT-1) for each side; and
no more than 1,320 strategic missiles on each side can be MIRV-
equipped. Additionally, American-theater nuclear forces, called
forward-based systems (FBS) by the USSR, would not be counted
against U.S. totals, nor would the nuclear forces of France and
Britain.
      Quantitatively, this framework opens an option for the United
States to reach the 2,400 ceiling by adding some 200 delivery vehicles,
as well as scrapping some clearly obsolete bombers. On the other
hand, the Soviet Union is at about the agreed-upon force level.
      The major advantage for the United States in the Vladivostok
accords is that they correct the numerical imbalances of SALT-1.
That is, the Jackson amendment was adhered to in that both sides
agreed to numerical parity. Additionally, it has been claimed that
the Soviet Union made a major concession in its decision not to include FBS in the American totals. This argument is less than convincing to many, because during the course of SALT-1, the Soviets
defined a strategic system as any system capable of delivering nuclear weapons on the territory of the USSR. This, of course, included almost all U.S. tactical (theater) nuclear forces in Europe
and strike aircraft on Sixth Fleet carriers. On the other hand,
some six hundred Soviet M/IRBMs and sixty-six missiles in diesel-
powered submarines were not called strategic, supposedly because
they could not reach the United States--but certainly they could reach
U.S. European Theater forces and most NATO nations. It seems
clear that if the Soviets wanted any agreement at all, they would have
to include their "excluded" systems or drop their demand to include
FBS.
      Criticisms often heard of the Vladivostok accord include the
suggestion that the Soviets rushed into the negotiations just prior to
Congressional action on the U.S.-Soviet trade bill. This was in the
hope of securing economic advantages without being saddled with a

binding arms agreement. Others have argued that by setting limits
on strategic delivery systems, the United States must include a sizable number of obsolete American bombers (about 400 B-52s) while
only a few (about 140) comparable Soviet long-range bombers count.
The ongoing problem is that the B-1 bomber, by definition, is a long-
range (6,000 miles plus) aircraft intended to replace at least some of
the aging B-52s. On the other hand, the known Soviet bomber in production, the Backfire, by definition is a medium bomber and is not
counted in the 2,400 total. (Medium bombers are capable of striking
the United States by air-to-air refueling, one-way missions, or Arctic staging.) Critics of the American B-1 program have suggested
that a shift to the FB-111--particularly the (H) or "stretch" version--
would give the United States a "free" system like the Backfire, and
still retain a significant intercontinental attack capability at a lower
cost.

Senator Jackson and others have criticized the high level of
strategic offensive forces agreed to at Vladivostok, on the ground
that it is hardly a step toward arms limitations. Secretary Kissinger,
on the other hand, believes that talks can get under way as early as
1980 (rather than 1981, as specified in the Vladivostok agreement),
with the aim of a mutual reduction of force levels. Others maintain
that the Vladivostok accord failed to limit Soviet missile throw-weight
and to deal effectively with qualitative improvements. The result,
more than likely, will be increased expenditures by both sides in a
technological arms race, driven in part by fear of developing counterforce capabilities.

It follows that if qualitative improvements continue, counterforce capabilities will increase and fixed missile silos will become
more vulnerable. Hence, the conversion to mobile missiles moves
nearer to reality. Perhaps the main reason for success in Vladivostok was that the agreement did not restrict the freedom of both sides
to continue their current strategic programs. [15]

It's not surprising that the SALT talks have been delayed by
problems of verification and defining what is and isn't a strategic
nuclear weapon system. For instance, is the submarine-launched
cruise missile (SLCM) a strategic delivery system? A New York
Times article on June 16, 1975, suggested that the cruise missile
now under development by the Defense Department may be a snag in
SALT. This missile, submarine- or air-launched, would be able to
fly some 1,500 miles at low altitude and carry a nuclear warhead.
Since the weapon is being designed to fit a standard torpedo tube,
would that make every attack submarine a strategic delivery vehicle? [16]
The New York Times article seems to imply that the SLCM is a problem the United States introduced into SALT. What is not said, however, is that the Soviet Union has had cruise missiles deployed in

submarines since the early 1960s. For example, the SS-N-3
(Shaddock) cruise missile has a 450-mile range, a nuclear warhead,
and can do as much damage to coastal targets (cities) as a strategic
weapon. Yet is this system really and only tactical? The International Institute of Strategic Studies in London reports that the USSR
had 314 cruise missiles deployed as of mid-1974--not to mention 48
other Shaddock missiles in Russian surface ships. [17]

  To compound the confusion, the Soviet Union reportedly has a
SS-N-13 short-range (400 miles) ballistic missile that may well be
termed (by the Soviets) an anti-shipping missile and not considered
in the SALT accords. Again, the capabilities of such a weapon include strategic as well as tactical implications. [18]

  Turning to the issue of verification, it is well known that the
Soviets consistently have rejected "on the ground" inspection. And
as it developed, SALT-1 incorporated inspection by "national means"
(satellites). Now, with MIRVed missiles in the accord, how does
one isolate MIRVed from non-MIRVed missiles? Additionally, if
mobile missiles come into the inventory, how does one verify the
number of wheeled or tracked vehicles (transporters) with or without missiles? Moreover, what does one do about reloads? A mobile
launcher with a "cold" launch capability can travel between storage
sheds firing numerous ICBMs.* A possible solution to mobile missile verification is to consider all missile types flight-tested with
MIRV as being deployed with MIRV. If this reasoning is extended to
include all submarines as strategic delivery vehicles, because of an
inherent SLCM capability, the Soviets would likely balk, since they
have about four times more attack submarines than the United States.
It becomes more and more apparent that the Vladivostok accord represents progress in some instances, but has unearthed serious problems in other areas.

URGENCY OF THE ISSUE

  Decisions concerning U.S. strategic doctrine and force modernization in 1977 could have an impact on the successful negotiation of a

_____

  *A "cold" launch refers to a missile ejected from its launcher
by gas rather than thrust developed from first-stage burn. In other
words, it's much like the Polaris system, whereby the missile is
ejected by compressed gas and ignites after clearing the ocean's surface. The significance of the cold launch for ICBMs is that the
launching silo is not destroyed--meaning a capability for multiple
firings from a single launcher. An additional benefit is that the
weight of fuel consumed in a conventional lift-off can be redirected
to increased throw-weight.

strategic arms limitation treaty, if there is a coupling between American force posture and arms limitations. Such decisions might best be considered within the framework of Soviet actions and available U.S. responses, followed by an analysis of American policy alternatives relative to the risks incurred.

Soviet Actions

If Soviet negotiators were under instructions to avoid a SALT-2 agreement until the new generation of Soviet strategic missiles--the SS-16, -17, -18, and -19 and the SS-N-8--were operational, and could justifiably be regarded as part of the Soviet Union's inventory, then they have succeeded.[19] As indicated earlier, the new generation of Soviet strategic offensive missiles has been tested with modern MIRV technology and with considerably more throw-weight than the older systems they are to replace. In fact, "the new ICBM systems entering the Soviet inventory can throw a payload of 16,000 to 20,000 pounds (the SS-18) and 4,500-6,000 pounds (the SS-19), whereas the current throw-weight of the MINUTEMAN III is 2,000."[20] Although the ratio of Soviet to U.S. ICBM throw-weight would increase only from four-to-one to five-or six-to-one if these new missiles were fully deployed, the combination of the available payload with onboard computer guidance has counterforce implications not present in the earlier systems.[21]

Additionally, all of the new Soviet strategic systems have RVs with higher accuracy, and warheads with a probable improved weight-to-yield ratio. The SS-16 system also is a candidate for a mobile "pop-up" or "cold" launch. At sea, the SS-N-8 is being deployed on the new Delta class ballistic missile submarine. Overall, the aggregate throw-weight of deployed Soviet offensive missile systems promises to exceed ten million pounds and could go to fifteen million pounds or higher.[22]

Improvements in Soviet strategic forces exceed what Defense Department analysts consider necessary, if the Russian goal is equivalence and stability. In fact, a careful examination of Soviet strategic literature in the nuclear age clearly indicates their belief in a war-winning strategy through nuclear superiority as the best possible deterrent. There is a fundamental uncertainty, according to Soviet military writings, as to who would start a nuclear war, and there is every indication that the Russians would launch a preemptive strike if they believed the United States endangers them.[23] As Uri Ra'anan has noted, the concept of parity has been rejected, implicitly and explicitly, by Soviet spokesmen on strategic affairs. Soviet literature has almost unanimously called for military superiority.[24]

It appears that the Soviets have an answer to Secretary Kissinger's now famous quote after the unsuccessful 1974 Moscow summit, when he asked, "What in the name of God is strategic superiority? What is the significance of it politically, militarily, operationally at these levels numbers? What do you do with it?"

Soviet actions and words, then, can be interpreted as other than benign. There may be danger in a presumption that the USSR recognizes the necessity of arms limitation and arms reduction, if in fact it is acquiring a strategic force capable of destroying U.S. ICBMs in their silos with only a small proportion of the Soviet force. As Colin S. Gray observed, "On the basis of all known great-power political performances, the danger lies in the foreign policy utility Soviet leaders may perceive in a condition of unprecedented Soviet strategic advantage."[25] The issue of urgency is most simply an appreciation of what the Soviets are doing, and reacting early enough not to have important options closed by default.

U.S. Reactions

Considering the growing Soviet strategic threat just described, U.S. decision-makers find three basic choices that are tied directly to alternative perceptions of Soviet capabilities and intentions, adequate American deterrence, and the prospects for a successful SAL treaty. In the broadest possible categories, basic American strategic options are the following:

• Maintain existing strategic forces and rely on a strategy of assured destruction to dissuade any possible aggressor

• Continue the strategic force modernization and improvement program advocated by the Defense Department

• Opt for a lower-cost Triad. That is, continue some of the Defense Department-recommended programs and doctrine, but at a decelerated rate with reduced numbers.

Decisions in the area of the new targeting doctrine, force modernization, and SALT, in order to be placed in perspective, must be related first to national security and second to the prospects for a successful arms limitations treaty. Soviet momentum in strategic force development, however, may force an early American decision if one wants the flexibility to choose from a maximum number of options. (It should be recalled that it takes some five to fifteen years between concept and operational deployment of new strategic systems.) In other words, it is possible to find oneself in a position of strategic inferiority without near-term prospects of reversing the situation.

Indeed, there is no consensus on the best course for the United States to follow. In fact, qualified opinion has sometimes shifted

from one position to another. Yet, to come to terms with the issues, each of the major policy thrusts will be dealt with in turn.

ALTERNATIVE STRATEGIES

In terms of U.S. choices or courses of action, relative to
strategic offensive force planning and its possible impact on SALT,
an analysis of each of the three basic alternatives is presented for
consideration.

Maintain Existing Strategic Forces and Strategy

The Soviet throw-weight advantage over U.S. strategic forces,
along with advancing MIRV technology, provides a capability for the
USSR to overwhelm the United States in numbers of RVs. Improvements in yield and accuracy, combined with large throw-weights,
produce kill ratios (counterforce) that can be fatal for fixed U.S.
ICBMs, bomber bases, and command and control facilities. The
question is whether existing U.S. strategic forces and a strategy of
assured destruction will cope adequately with this threat.

Assured destruction, as a doctrine of strategy, means that the
United States can absorb the worst possible attack any aggressor can
mount, and retain enough survivable forces to inflict unacceptable
damage on the aggressor in retaliation. Unacceptable damage is
often defined in terms of some percentage of destruction to the
enemy's population and industry.

Those who deny a Soviet counterforce capability, present or
projected, argue that in terms of calculated hard-point (counterforce) kill capability, the United States holds the lead now and will
continue to hold this lead through the late 1980s. Despite Soviet advantages in throw-weight, a smaller U.S. CEP results in a higher
American counterforce or kill capability. Although the calculations
are mathematically correct, the assumption the United States will
continue to maintain higher RV accuracy is questionable, particularly in view of the technological advances fielded by the USSR at dates
earlier than predicted in the West.

The kill probability (P_k) figure generally is obtained from the
formula

$$P_k = \frac{Y^{2/3}}{CEP} \times RV$$

where Y = yield, CEP = accuracy, and RV = the number of reentry
vehicles. From visual examination of the formula, it can readily be
seen that accuracy is by far the most important factor--it is as

important as the cube of megatonnage.[26] The overkill argument, then, maintains that U.S. strategic forces have more RVs, a higher P_k, and an invulnerable SLBM force that by itself can retaliate, with unacceptable damage (assured destruction) on any would-be aggressor. Therefore, why spend unnecessary funds on the Pentagon's "pet projects" that will only increase an existing overkill capacity?

The response to such arguments is essentially a questioning of overkill and assured destruction as realistic concepts today. That is, will threatening massive destruction of populations be a credible deterrent to conventional war in Europe or Asia, or will it deter escalation of limited wars? Moreover, doesn't overkill deal with today's weapons, not with alert, reliable, survivable, penetrating weapons subject to proper command and control? Additionally, doesn't overkill deal with today's situation rather than the future?[27]

Perhaps assured destruction will deter a preemptive first-strike disarming attack on the United States, and as such should be maintained as an ultimate option. However, a major premeditated strike on the United States is not the only, or even the most likely, threat.

In terms of dollar costs, most certainly a status quo strategic force posture is economical. From Table 16.3, it has been roughly estimated that about $35 million will be required if modernization and upgrading are essentially eliminated in fiscal year 1977. However, the real cost might be a national disaster if the USSR believes it has reached a position of unquestioned superiority. Also, political and social costs could easily erode U.S. credibility among its allies, especially the NATO nations and Japan. On the other hand, monies saved from defense might be reallocated into domestic social services, which is appealing but historically rare. Furthermore, stagnation of U.S. strategic offensive forces should be welcome to the Soviets, and might well tend to reduce Soviet-American tensions. In fact, proponents of a status quo in U.S. strategic forces maintain that the USSR will be far more likely to negotiate a strategic arms treaty with the current U.S. force posture than with upgrading weaponry.

Modernize and Improve Strategic Forces

Behind the Defense Department's programs of strategic force modernization and improvement is the fact that a major nuclear war could happen. Accordingly, an assured destruction capability would be retained and advertised as a credible deterrent to the "worst possible case." On the other hand, there is a realization that although the United States has more or less unconsciously grasped assured

TABLE 16.3

Comparative Costs of Major Strategic Offensive Forces
(millions of dollars)

Strategic Offense	Fiscal 1976 Prop'd. Funding	Trans. Period Prop'd. Funding	Fiscal 1977 Status Quo	Fiscal 1977 Prop'd. Improve and Modernize	Fiscal 1977 Low-Cost Triad
Continued procurement of Minuteman III missiles, Minuteman silo upgrading, and related programs	780	105	--	485	--
Advanced ICBM technology, including MX	41	15	--	70	--
Development of advanced ballistic reentry systems and technology (ABRES)	101	29	--	125	--
Conversion of SSBNs to Poseidon configuration, continued procurement of Poseidon missiles, and associated effort	91	7	35	35	35
Development, procurement, and military construction: Trident submarines and missiles (Trident II not included in total)	2,142 (3)	622 (1)	--	3,438 (10)	2,000 (est.)
SSBN subsystem technology	2	1	--	4	4
B-52D modifications	43	--	--	--	--
B-52/Harpoon modification	10	7	--	18	--
Continued development of new strategic bomber, B-1	749	196	--	1,652	--
Acquisition of short-range attack missile (SRAM)	3	2	--	35	--
Development of the bomber-launched and submarine-launched version of the strategic cruise missile	153	55	--	296	--
Total	4,115	1,039	35	6,158	2,039

Notes: The costs include research, development, test, and evaluation; procurement of the system and initial spares; and directly related military construction; the numbers in parentheses refer to the number of Trident submarines.

The period for transitional period is July 1-September 30, 1976.

Source: From U.S. Department of Defense, "Statement of Secretary of Defense James Schlesinger before the Senate Armed Services Committee," Annual Defense Department Report, FY 1976 and FY 1977 (Washington, D.C.: Government Printing Office, 1975), II-22.

destruction as the sine qua non of deterrence, the Soviet Union hasn't. With the size and mix of Soviet conventional, tactical, and strategic nuclear forces, there are numerous possibilities for the use of Soviet force that would not warrant a massive U.S. nuclear reprisal. Indeed, the threat of a massive attack on Soviet cities and industry is hardly a credible deterrent to lower-level Soviet actions, even including a conventional Soviet attack in Western Europe, for in all probability a U.S. nuclear response would in turn assure the destruction of U.S. cities.

The new targeting doctrine and force improvement program is designed to provide preplanned, limited, discriminating strike options that not only will demonstrate American resolve, but also dissuade escalation at all levels and, it is hoped, encourage war termination before it is too late. These objectives are to be achieved through the hardware and system upgrading discussed earlier. For example, the U.S. Air Force upgraded silo program will increase blast overpressures the silos can withstand from 300 to 1,000 psi.[28] In addition, the new technologies will permit existing silos to launch larger missiles, and attacking missiles to deliver greater weight far more accurately.[29] For instance, the CEP of Minuteman III with the present MK-12 warhead is approximately 1,300 feet. With advanced inertial reference sphere (AIRS), the CEP can be reduced to 700 feet initially and quite possibly to some 400 feet--without benefit of terminal guidance.[30] All this can mean very selective targeting, reduced collateral damage to populations, and, in general, flexibility not presently available.

Defense Department-sponsored programs for strategic offensive force improvement and modernization are estimated in the neighborhood of $6,158 million for fiscal year 1977. However, the long-term costs of improvements that can be related to the new targeting doctrine alone are about $300 million.[31] It seems that the Defense Department program should preclude the possibility of the United States falling into a position of nuclear inferiority; but the crucial question is whether the United States can afford not to accept the Defense Department program. Some have argued that if the United States goes ahead with strategic force modernization and improvement programs, the chance of achieving a SAL treaty will be reduced and the USSR will escalate the arms race. Should this happen, it is claimed, detente will become harder to realize and the Congress will be less likely to provide trade credits to the USSR, which seems to be crucial to detente. The Congress would not put itself in a position of indirectly financing a Russian strategic buildup.[32] Tensions will mount, and further U.S. strategic force proposals and funding will become easier and easier to obtain--and so goes the scenario.

When reduced to their lowest common denominator, criticisms of the Defense Department strategic initiatives generally fall into three categories:

- Destabilization of the strategic balance
- Limited counterforce options make limited nuclear war more credible, and therefore more likely
- Increased options will escalate the arms competition (and make an arms agreement less likely).[33]

Looking at existing Soviet weapon systems and capabilities--the SLCM, SS-N-8 and -13, M/IRBMs, deployed MIRV, Backfire bomber, a hard target capability, to name but a few--one might ask how equivalent U.S. forces can be considered destabilizing? And why will limited nuclear war be more likely if the United States has counterforce options, than if it doesn't while the Russians do? And would a resulting war stay limited? Restraint in the use of nuclear weapons, it seems, is on a par with decreasing the likelihood of nuclear war. One must also ask what the Soviets are going to escalate that they haven't already escalated, if the United States opts to upgrade its forces to obtain strategic equivalence. Furthermore, if an equitable and stable arms agreement is an objective, shouldn't the United States have capabilities essentially equivalent to the USSR when entering into serious negotiations?

A Lower-Cost Triad

Some force improvement, but considerably less than recommended by the Defense Department, is the position held by the Center for Defense Information. It argues that skyrocketing costs of military programs, inflation, unemployment, shortages, and changed international circumstances make it necessary to choose among competing programs and priorities. Spending on weapons and forces that contribute to U.S. strength only marginally can no longer be afforded. The Center suggests that hard choices must be made in order to terminate unneeded, redundant strategic weapons. New bombers and new land-based missile programs are prime candidates for elimination. They maintain, without jeopardizing national defense, that these options for holding down the military budget are available for strategic offensive forces: cancel the B-1 bomber; build one Trident submarine a year instead of three every two years; stop spending on new ICBMs; do not start strategic cruise missile programs; set a ceiling of 10,000 strategic nuclear weapons (the United States could have 20,000 by 1985).[34] Such a program might save some $4,000 million in fiscal year 1977 over the Defense Department request.

Without doubt, such a program would cut defense costs. However, for the most part it would also negate the rationale for force
improvement and modernization, and continue the present reliance
on assured destruction as an effective deterrent. Since the issues
of flexible response and assured destruction are not addressed in
this option, the strongest defense for the lower-cost Triad seems
to be economic rather than theoretical or strategic. However, if it
is true that the USSR is more likely to agree to an arms limitation
at present U.S. force levels, and less likely to agree if U.S. forces
are upgraded as the Defense Department suggests, then the "lower-
cost Triad" concept may strike a happy medium for a successful
SALT.

CONCLUSION

If slowing down or halting the arms race is a major objective
of SALT, then a good starting point might be to examine the term
"arms race" and see if it really applies. Generally, a race is a
competition between two or more contestants expending maximum
effort to achieve an established goal. In the strategic arms race,
one fails to see a maximum effort by all sides; and, furthermore,
the goal is imprecise--parity, sufficiency, equivalence, or whatever. About all one can say with certainty is that no one's goal is
strategic inferiority. Furthermore, there is no convincing historical evidence that leads one to believe that "arms races" have ever
been the cause of a single war.

Accordingly, our focus might best be on the real objective of
national security policy--deterrence of war, at any level of violence.
If a state is to convince others that engagement in armed conflict is
ill-advised, it must clearly convey the capability and credibility to
engage in and prevent an opponent from winning such a conflict. For
these reasons, emphasis should be on a strong defense posture to
deter war, including weapons and weapon systems flexible and selective enough to permit a proper response to almost any armed provo-
cation. In this way, should deterrence fail at any level below a
strategic exchange, maximum options for controlled selective response, and early war termination, would be available.

Although the Defense Department's modernization and improvement program may present problems of high cost, possible increased
tensions, and decreased opportunity for an early comprehensive strategic arms limitation treaty, it seems that the Soviet threat level is
too high, and our margin for survival as a nation is too small, not to
concentrate on self-help first. Once essential equivalence is perceived,

even one involving high force levels, then negotiations on mutual reductions become the next logical priority. Herein the future of SALT may lie.

It is suggested that modernizing and upgrading American forces to a level of essential equivalence with the USSR should be expected by the Soviets and will not be destabilizing--nor, for that matter, will it realistically increase tensions. Additionally, a defense posture of credible deterrence through essential equivalence would bolster, rather than undermine, Western Europe's and Japan's confidence in America's defense commitments. But, most important, a strong, flexible defense, although expensive in the short run, can best deter war in the long run.

NOTES

1. Richard T. Ackley, "What's Left of SALT?," Naval War College Review, May-June 1974, p. 45.

2. Donald G. Brennan, "When the SALT Hit the Fan," National Review, June 23, 1972, pp. 685-92.

3. Edgar Ulsamer, "How Russia is Tipping the Strategic Balance," Air Force, January 1975, pp. 48-59.

4. John W. Finney, "U.S. Says Russians Now Have Deployed 60 MIRV Missiles," New York Times, June 21, 1975, p. 1.

5. Currie, cited in Ulsamer, op. cit., p. 50.

6. Michael Nacht, "The Vladivostok Accord and American Technological Options," Survival, May/June 1975, p. 108.

7. The Budget of the United States Government Fiscal Year 1976 (Washington, D.C.: U.S. Government Printing Office, 1975), pp. 72-73.

8. John M. Collins, "Maneuver Instead of Mass: The Key to Assured Stability," Orbis 18, no. 3 (Fall 1974): 750.

9. International Institute for Strategic Studies, Strategic Survey 1975 (London: the Institute, 1975), p. 68.

10. William R. Van Cleave and Roger W. Barnett, "Strategic Adaptability," Orbis 18, no. 3 (Fall 1974): 672.

11. Dougherty, cited in Ulsamer, op. cit., p. 51.

12. U.S. Department of Defense, "Statement of Secretary of Defense James R. Schlesinger Before the Senate Armed Forces Committee," Annual Defense Department Report FY 1976 and FY 1977 (Washington, D.C.: U.S. Government Printing Office, 1975), p. II-20.

13. Ibid., pp. II-18-57.

14. David Aaron, "A New Concept," Foreign Policy no. 17 (Winter 1974-75): 158-59.

15. Strategic Survey 1974, p. 63.

16. John W. Finney, "New U.S. Missile Snags Arms Talks," New York Times, June 16, 1975, p. 1.

17. International Institute for Strategic Studies, The Military Balance 1974-1975 (London: the Institute, 1974), p. 73.

18. Richard Burt, "Kremlin's New Naval Missile," Christian Science Monitor, August 6, 1974, p. 1.

19. Strategic Survey 1974, p. 59.

20. Ibid., p. 48.

21. Donald R. Westervelt, "The Essence of Armed Futility," Orbis 18, no. 3 (Fall 1974): 693.

22. Paul H. Nitze, "The Strategic Balance Between Hope and Skepticism," Foreign Policy no. 17 (Winter 1974-75): 147-48.

23. Ackley, op. cit., pp. 43-44.

24. Uri Ra'anan, "The Changing American-Soviet Strategic Balance: Some Political Implications," in Great Issues of International Politics (2nd ed.), ed. Morton A. Kaplan (Chicago: Aldine, 1974), p. 501.

25. Colin S. Gray, "Foreign Policy and the Strategic Balance," Orbis 18, no. 3 (Fall 1974): 727.

26. Rep. Robert L. Leggett (D-Ca.), "Two Legs Do Not a Centipede Make," Armed Forces Journal, February 1975, pp. 9-F, 10-F.

27. Nitze, op. cit., p. 138.

28. Strategic Survey 1974, p. 50.

29. Ibid., p. 46.

30. Ibid, pp. 46-47.

31. U.S. Congress, Senate, hearing before the Subcommittee on Arms Control, International Law and Organization of the Committee on Foreign Relations, U.S.-U.S.S.R. Strategic Policies, 93d Cong., 2d sess., March 4, 1974, p. 29.

32. Aaron, op. cit., p. 158.

33. G. W. Rathjens, "Flexible Response Options," Orbis 18, no. 3 (Fall 1974): 683.

34. The Defense Monitor 4, no. 1 (January 1975): 1, 4.

17

THE EAST-WEST
TRADE ISSUE
Charles H. Movit

THE ISSUE

U.S. policy on the expansion of trade with Socialist countries should reflect consideration of three interrelated issues: asymmetries inherent in the interface of two differing economic systems; the impact of expanded economic relations with the East on U.S. national security; and the appropriate role of East-West economic interaction in the national economic strategy of the United States.

The first policy area involves the role and organization of foreign economic relations in the two socioeconomic systems. While the details of the conduct of foreign trade vary to some degree from nation to nation, the primary characteristic of Socialist foreign trade is that it is carried on by state trading monopolies. When individual U.S. firms deal with state traders, they may be at a serious disadvantage in negotiating agreements, given the benefits that can accrue to the monopsonist. This difficulty is compounded because much of the commercial information normally required by Western businessmen to make intelligent decisions on business potential and operations is treated by the Socialist country as a state secret.

The nonconvertibility of the currencies of the Socialist countries involves still other costs and risks for the Western firm engaging in East-West trade. As a result of nonconvertible currencies, the need often arises to engage in barter or complex switch agreements, or to accept repayment on a compensatory basis (deliveries from the production capacity provided by the Western partner), often after a significant period has elapsed. Because domestic prices in the Socialist countries are not related to world market prices and need not reflect production cost, the adherence of Socialist traders to fair trade practices is difficult to ascertain even though antidumping clauses are often a feature of bilateral trade agreements with Western countries.

Socialist foreign trade has traditionally filled short-term gaps in order to ease bottlenecks and has been a source of advanced technology and equipment in industrialization drives. Export has served, then, only to finance imports. However, Socialist foreign trade is also an instrument in the overall orchestation of national purpose. Economic benefit, therefore, is not the sole determinant of foreign trade behavior--it can serve as part of an effort to conform to bilateral agreements, to extend influence in a less-developed country, or to importune a capitalist economy.

In addition to the systemic asymmetries that may circumscribe the economic benefits for U.S. trading partners, the expansion of economic relations with Socialist countries has implications for U.S. national security. By easing resource reallocation pressures through exports of machinery and equipment and grain, transfer of advanced technology, and investment in the development of natural resources, increased Western economic interaction with the Socialist countries contributes to their ability to provide resources for the military. In view of the high priority enjoyed by the defense sector and given the expanding economic relations between these countries and Western Europe and Japan, it is doubtful that a lowered level of U.S. exports would lead to a decrease in the level of military effort in the Socialist nations. The transfer of certain technologies, on the other hand, could contribute directly to the Socialist bloc's military capabilities. Such a contribution might also be made through spillover to the military sector of technology transferred for civilian purposes.

The third set of issues is concerned with the role of expanded economic relations with the Socialist countries in the overall U.S. national economic strategy. In engaging in trade and technology transfer to the Soviet Union and Eastern Europe, the United States may be helping to establish competitors in the world market that will adversely affect U.S. commercial interests. On the other hand, new markets may be established in the Eastern bloc for U.S. goods to support modernization efforts based on transferred technology. An important consideration in evaluating the potential commercial impact is the extent to which the technology needs of the Socialist countries could be met exclusively through trade and exchange with Western Europe and Japan. The benefits of expanded economic interaction must be examined as well, in light of the credit terms often necessary to facilitate expanded trade with the East. Many question whether the extension of credit at less than commercial terms is essential for expanded trade. Lastly, formulation of U.S. commercial policy must include an assessment of whether the centrally planned economies will prove to be reliable suppliers and consistent purchasers in light of short-term gap-filling and periodic modernization campaign roles that have been traditional for foreign trade, particularly in the Soviet Union.

BACKGROUND OF THE ISSUE

In the decade following World War II, after the spread of Soviet influence into Eastern Europe, U.S. trade with the Socialist bloc was discouraged by a series of legislative actions, including the Export Control Act of 1949 and the revocation of "most favored nation" status for these countries in 1951. A coordination committee, COCOM, consisting of the NATO countries, less Iceland and plus Japan, was formed to extend export controls to the trade of U.S. allies with the East.

In the Socialist bloc itself, the emphasis during this period was not on intrabloc trade expansion but, rather, on self-sufficiency and national sovereignty. After Stalin's death, however, Soviet leaders faced slowing rates of growth and the need to increase supplies of consumer goods. Under Khrushchev, the Soviet Union began to look westward for technology and equipment to modernize its industry. The late 1960s witnessed a surge of imports from Western Europe. U.S. allies, in turn, reduced export restrictions significantly. Table 17.1 indicates the volume of U.S. trade with Eastern Europe and the USSR for the period 1958-74.

With the 24th Congress of the Communist Party of the Soviet Union, under Leonid Brezhnev in 1971, came the official endorsement of expanded economic relations with the developed West. Expansion of economic relations was further facilitated by the political accommodations reached with the United States and the Federal Republic of Germany. The "Basic Principles of Relations Between the United States of America and the Union of Soviet Socialist Republics," signed in Moscow on May 29, 1972, states:

> The USA and the USSR regard commercial and
> economic ties as an important and necessary ele-
> ment in the strengthening of their bilateral rela-
> tions and thus will actively promote the growth of
> such ties. They will facilitate cooperation be-
> tween the relevant organizations and enterprises
> of the two countries and the conclusion of appro-
> priate agreements and contracts, including long
> term ones. [1]

Thus, the two nations have agreed that ideological differences should not be a barrier to the normalization of relations and, moreover, that expanded economic relations are an important part of that normalization. Very few, if any, believe that increased commercial ties will ensure peace; yet political benefits are envisioned by U.S. observers, whether through explicit linkage of political, military, and economic accommodations or through more indirect diplomatic channels of negotiation. The Nixon and Ford administrations have, in fact, viewed the national benefits of normalized economic relations as primarily political, leaving the calculation of economic benefit, in general, to the private sector.

TABLE 17.1

U.S. Trade with Eastern Europe and the USSR, 1958-74
(millions of U.S. dollars)

	U.S. Exports		U.S. Imports	
	Eastern Europe	USSR	Eastern Europe	USSR
1958	109.8	3.4	45.1	17.5
1959	81.9	7.4	52.3	28.6
1960	154.9	39.6	58.3	22.6
1961	87.9	45.7	57.9	23.2
1962	105.1	20.2	62.6	16.3
1963	143.9	22.9	60.3	21.2
1964	193.6	146.4	77.8	20.7
1965	94.8	45.2	94.8	42.6
1966	156.0	41.7	129.1	49.6
1967	135.0	60.3	136.1	41.2
1968	157.3	57.7	140.0	58.5
1969	143.7	105.5	144.0	51.5
1970	234.9	118.7	153.5	72.3
1971	222.2	162.0	165.8	57.2
1972	276.9	542.2	225.0	95.5
1973	606.5	1,194.7	306.1	220.1
1974	822.4	609.2	540.5	350.2

Source: International Economic Report of the President (Washington, D.C.: U.S. Government Printing Office, March 1975), p. 136.

Official Soviet observers are careful to assert the contribution of expanded East-West economic relations to world peace, but the economic benefits are given prime importance:

Detente and the material basis for peaceful coexistence between states with different social

systems are greatly helped by the Soviet Union's
active foreign economic policy, consistently
aimed at developing our equal and mutually advantageous trade and economic cooperation with
all countries, the industrial capitalist states in
particular. [2]

The Soviet economic motivation for expanding relations with
the developed West must undoubtedly be attributed to the economic
pressures facing Soviet leaders, pressures that will mount in the
1980s if the current approach to economic development is retained.
They are a result of what amounts to the failure of the traditional
Soviet model of economic growth strategy to perform satisfactorily.
The traditional model relies on the extensive methods of economic
development--increase in factor inputs--to provide a more than proportional growth in product. What the Soviet Union has encountered,
however, is a rising capital/output ratio and little growth in labor
productivity. Should extensive methods be pursued into the 1980s to
provide a rate of growth acceptable to Soviet leaders, the share of
investment in GNP would prove so high as to be politically untenable,
especially given the commitment of Soviet leaders to a rising standard of living. One estimate found that by 1990 investment would be
52 percent of GNP and consumption only 39 percent. [3]

The alternative to the extensive development methods of the
past is rapid technological change. The institutional framework of
the Soviet economy, however, and, to varying degrees, of the Eastern European economies, which also must reevaluate the Soviet
growth model, is biased heavily against technological change. The
Soviet Union has not opted for radical reform of the bureaucratic
economic system; rather, it has based its approach on a broad program of technology and equipment imported from the West. [4]

An examination of Russian and Soviet experience since the days
of Peter the Great reveals a pattern of periodic forays into the international economy to procure an infusion of advanced technology from
the more advanced nations of the West. These programs, under the
principal sponsorship of the government, did not create a self-
sustaining process of technological change; and when the modernization goals had been reached and government pressure abated, the
level of technology rapidly fell behind that of the advanced nations.
Is the current period, then, marked by still another spurt of imports
from the West, which, when it has abated, will give way to the domination of the short-term gap-filling role for foreign trade that is
prescribed by a policy of nondependence on the West? Such a pattern
of economic relations would certainly not fulfill the role envisioned
in the "Basic Principles of Relations."

While the motivation for the current surge of Soviet imports from the West is undoubtedly of the nature described above, the historical Soviet-Russian pattern does not involve a nation at the stage of industrialization in which the USSR now finds itself. Thus, future behavior may not repeat that of the past. There are increasing indications that the USSR is amending the role of foreign trade in its development strategy and thereby seeking (and accepting) greater involvement with the West. Given the current stage of Soviet industrialization, increased interrelatedness with the West does not necessarily involve increased dependence on the West--a condition rejected by past and present Soviet leaders. A pattern of interrelatedness could operate at the margin of the Soviet economy to improve performance, rather than involve the economic core. It is conceivable, then, that a shift in the role of economic relations with the West in the Socialist economy may prove to be a basis for long-term economic interaction on a broader scale.

The economic motivation for U.S. involvement in expanded economic relations with the Socialist bloc countries is somewhat simpler to assess. Decreasing international tension and the demonstration effect of the rapid development of Western Europe-Eastern Europe and Japan-Eastern Europe trade convinced a number of American businessmen that East-West trade should not be treated as trading with the enemy, but as a legitimate response to new market opportunities.

The current role of the U.S. government in the conduct of East-West trade includes the general promotion of U.S. commercial interests abroad via trade fairs and other trade development efforts, the control of strategic and militarily related exports, and the extension of loans and loan guarantees. As a result of the Trade Reform Act of 1974, which placed a number of conditions on the extension of most-favored-nation status and Export-Import Bank credits to non-market economies, government-backed credits above the outstanding amounts are available only for exports to Poland and Rumania. The near-term projects for major revision to the Trade Act appear doubtful, but few question that the explicit linking of emigration and trade has not achieved the desired results.

Table 17.2 presents a summary of U.S.-Soviet trade for the period 1950-75. The gradual increase in U.S. exports predates the 1972 summit, beginning in the mid-1960s. The shipment of grain in 1973 comprised over $800 million of the $1.2 billion in U.S. exports to the Soviet Union.

URGENCY OF THE ISSUE

There are costs in delaying the formulation and execution of new East-West trade policy, given the assessment that increased

TABLE 17.2

U.S.-Soviet Trade, 1950-75

(millions of U.S. dollars)

	Total USSR Imports from the U.S.	USSR Imports of Grain from the U.S.	Total USSR Imports from the U.S. Less Grain Imports	USSR Imports of Food from the U.S.	Total USSR Imports from the U.S. Less Food Imports	Total USSR Exports to the U.S.	Total U.S.-USSR Turnover
1950	0.8	--	--	--	--	38.3	39.1
1951	0.1	--	--	--	--	27.5	27.6
1952	negligible	--	--	--	--	16.8	16.8
1953	negligible	--	--	--	--	10.8	10.8
1954	0.2	--	--	--	--	11.9	12.1
1955	0.3	--	--	--	--	17.1	17.4
1956	3.8	--	--	--	--	24.5	28.3
1957	4.6	--	--	--	--	16.8	21.4
1958	3.4	--	--	--	--	17.5	20.9
1959	7.4	--	--	--	--	28.6	36.0
1960	39.6	--	--	--	--	22.6	62.2
1961	45.7	--	--	--	--	23.2	68.9
1962	20.2	--	--	--	--	16.3	36.5
1963	22.9	--	--	--	--	21.2	44.1
1964	146.4	110.0	36.4	--	--	20.7	167.1
1965	45.2	--	--	--	--	42.6	87.8
1966	41.7	--	--	.1	41.6	49.6	91.3
1967	60.3	--	--	.3	60.0	41.2	101.5
1968	57.7	--	--	.9	56.6	58.5	116.2
1969	105.5	--	--	1.2	104.3	51.5	157.0
1970	118.7	--	--	2.3	116.1	72.3	191.0
1971	162.0	14.3	147.7	16.9	145.1	57.2	219.2
1972	542.2	334.1	208.1	365.8	176.4	95.5	637.7
1973	1,190.0	836.4	353.6	842.7	347.3	214.8	1,406.1
1974	609.2	--	--	242.3	366.9	350.2	959.4
(Jan.-June)	(315.6)	--	--	--	--	(187.7)	(503.3)
1975	521.2	--	--	--	--	133.8	655.0
(Jan.-June)							

Note: Values have been rounded.

Sources: International Economic Report of the President, February 1974, p. 101; IMF, Direction of Trade, November 1974; U.S. Department of Commerce, East-West Trade, Export Administration Report, Apr.-June 1973, Jan.-Mar. 1974, Oct. - Dec. 1974; U.S. House of Representatives, Defense Hearings before the Subcommittees on Europe of the Committee of Foreign Affairs, May-July 1974, p. 248.

economic interdependence is occurring and that trade will expand. Economic costs are incurred either via loss of expanded markets or as a result of ineffective mechanisms for the conduct of economic relations now ongoing. There also may be a political cost in the failure to effectively pursue appropriate linkage of political/military/ economic issues in U.S. relations with the East.

ALTERNATIVE STRATEGIES

An evaluation of U.S. policy alternatives in East-West trade must be based on one's view of key political-strategic and political-economic factors in the medium and long term. First, there are the value of detente and the role of economics in detente for improving political relations with the Socialist countries. Will detente lead to meaningful change in the Soviet Union, or is it a tactic to obtain political concessions and trade benefits? Second, what is the nature of economic interdependence that is deemed to ensue from expanded economic relations for the United States and the Socialist countries? Will it create interdependence in the interest of political stability or unilateral vulnerability? Lastly, the future role of U.S. economic relations with the Socialist countries must be viewed in the context of formulating an overall international economic strategy for the United States--whether this will be a free-trade or a protectionist strategy, and what will be the interaction of this East-West strategy for market development with the U.S. pattern of alliances. Any realistic view of the future role of the United States and the Socialist countries in these areas of political and economic concern must proceed from the premise that in the industrial development of the world economy, it is inevitable that the interrelatedness of both the United States and the Socialist countries with the world economy will increase.

What, then, are the policy alternatives that face the United States in approaching economic relations with the East? The first of these, based on an assumption that economic embargo by one nation or a small number of nations is an effective weapon in assuring the ultimate victory of a political, economic, and social system, would be a return to the policies pursued by the United States at the height of the Cold War, following the Korean conflict. This alternative should be rejected out of hand, since its utility was not demonstrated then and would be even more inappropriate today, given the level of development of the Socialist bloc and its economic relations with the other major industrial nations.

The second policy alternative is also restrictive in regard to the development of U.S. economic relations with the East. This alternative is to retain the legislation as it stood at the end of 1974. Such an approach would assume that economic benefit should be pursued on a strictly commercial basis by the private sector, and that the political benefit that might be expected from permitting normal commercial relations to be carried out can best be obtained through explicit linking of political-strategic and political-economic issues in trade legislation.

A third policy alternative suggests itself. This approach would involve amending the Trade Reform Act of 1974 and reconsidering amendments to the Export-Import Bank Act in order to facilitate implicit linkage of political and economic issues by coupling the legislative channel with others, such as the diplomatic, that may prove more fruitful. Thus, a new trade act could provide for an annual review mechanism not linked to specific issues for most-favored-nation status and credit ceilings, and would allow, as a provision of the Trade Act, for expansion of relations over time. Leverage could thus be extended forward through scheduled reevaluations of the interaction between economic, political/military, and foreign policy factors.

A last alternative is suggested by accepting the assumption that explicit economic-to-political linkage is not the most effective approach to political considerations and rejecting the notion that the U.S. private sector, facing the problems of East-West trade alone, can most effectively extract the economic benefits of this interaction. The fourth policy approach would subsume the third plan of action and would, in addition, include major initiatives to expand relations through alterations in the existing mechanism that implement international monetary and trade policy. These new initiatives should be aimed in three directions: to minimize the cost and risk to the private sector of doing business with Socialist countries; to provide government institutions that would facilitate public-private sector coordination to overcome the asymmetries of information flow and state trading; and to provide for increased coordination of government policies toward private sector interaction with Socialist countries by the United States and its allies. Two of the institutional changes that could flow from the above initiatives are the establishment of a government-sponsored facility for East-West trade--a sort of Board of Trade that would be particularly effective in helping small and medium-size firms defray the costs and risks associated with trade--and a financial facility to handle the intricacies of current conversion.

CONCLUSIONS

Several conclusions for policy-makers are suggested from the review of East-West trade.

First, while much of the foregoing analysis was concerned with the potential political benefit to the United States from expanded economic relations with the Socialist countries, a quick consideration of historical experience will confirm that good trade relations do not ensure peace. Political benefits from expanded economic relations will not be automatic, and will require careful orchestration of diplomatic and legislative initiatives in the foreign trade and foreign policy arenas.

Secondly, while an initial consideration of policy on East-West trade issues may regard the Socialist countries as a monolithic bloc, this does not reflect the self-perceptions of these nations, nor does it accurately portray the significantly varied organization they employ to conduct foreign economic relations. U.S. policy should reflect these differences in the approach of the Socialist trade partner when formulating the conditions under which economic relations can be expected to expand to the mutual advantage of the two nations.

The rejection of the conditions of the Trade Reform Act of 1974 by the Soviet Union confirms a third implication for policymakers. Explicit linkage, especially through legislative rather than executive action, of political and economic issues in East-West relations is not likely to prove effective. Implicit efforts via diplomatic channels may well prove to be the most effective mechanism for coordinating the two areas of policy toward the Socialist countries.

A consideration of the problems facing individual U.S. firms in selling to and buying from the Socialist economies and of the need for incorporating U.S. economic relations with the East into an overall U.S. economic strategy indicates that an approach relying solely on the private sector to manage these relations is inadequate. A significant increase in the coordination of private sector and public sector activities would both help to reduce the asymmetry inherent in dealing with Socialist state traders and would provide a firm base from which to orchestrate U.S. policy.

Lastly, the political conditions of the 1970s have produced a reevaluated but firm reliance on a carefully nurtured relationship with the NATO allies and the realization of the importance of the trilateral relationship between Western Europe, the United States, and Japan. While no united front exists in economic areas of concern any more than in the political/military arena, policies could be developed that express the mutual concerns of the allied nations. It was obvious from the tensions in the alliance brought about by the oil embargo of 1973 that the economic interests of U.S. allies are a significant force in their foreign policies and that coordination of these interests can strengthen the internal cohesion of requisite alliances.

NOTES

1. Weekly Compilation of Presidential Documents (June 5, 1972), p. 943.

2. N. Patolichev, "An Important Factor for Peace and Progress: The Present Stage of Trade and Economic Relations Between the Soviet Union and the West," Foreign Trade no. 5 (1975): 2.

3. D. Green, The SRI-WEFA Econometric Model of the Soviet Union: Structure, Policy Applications and Long-Run Projections, SSC-IN-75.34 (Washington, D.C.: Stanford Research Institute, October 1975), p. 30.

4. An excellent assessment of the systemic factors that inhibit absorption of new technology is David Granick, Soviet Introduction of New Technology: A Depiction of the Process, SSC TN-2625-7 (Washington, D.C.: Stanford Research Institute, January 1975).

18

NUCLEAR PROLIFERATION: THE PROBLEM OF IRRESPONSIBILITY
Phillip Karber

THE ISSUE

Large-scale proliferation of nuclear weapons is an immediate possibility. Questions associated with this problem are central to debate over U.S. security policy, yet have received little attention since 1968. Time is running out for the United States to play a major creative role in controlling the spread of nuclear weapons. What is the most responsible approach to this challenge?

BACKGROUND OF THE ISSUE

Nuclear nonproliferation--stopping the spread of nuclear weapons to other nations--has been a prime U.S. foreign policy and national security objective since the end of World War II. U.S. actions to prevent nuclear proliferation include the Baruch Plan of 1946, the Atoms for Peace Program of 1954, the debates over general and complete disarmament in the early 1960s, and the 1963 Limited Nuclear-Test Ban. The culmination of over two decades of American arms control efforts, the Nuclear Non-Proliferation Treaty (NPT), was signed in 1968 and entered into force in 1970.

Even compared with SALT, the NPT represented a breakthrough in arms control. Consummated after almost a decade of negotiation, it was a superpower agreement in an area, intra-alliance politics, where no treaty before or since has been able to penetrate. Unlike bilateral SALT, the treaty is multinational--signed by 106 countries; and unlike the limited test-ban treaty, it imposed significant constraints on nonnuclear nations in exchange for the superpowers' taking on explicit obligations.

Despite three decades of publicity and enormous effort, nuclear proliferation has seldom figured as a national security issue. True, hardly a foreign policy publication or a national security monograph is released that does not mention (and often detail) the problem of nuclear proliferation. Nonetheless, there has been very little real public debate over American proliferation policy; there has been no public controversy where sides are drawn, alternative arguments presented, and a clear choice presented to the American electorate. In seven presidential campaigns, the issue of proliferation has been noticeable only by its absence.

The closest one can come to finding a semblance of conflict was in 1968, when Richard Nixon wanted to delay American ratification of the NPT as a sign of American displeasure over the Soviet invasion of Czechoslovakia. Hubert Humphrey counterattacked with the warning that unless the NPT was signed immediately, Fidel Castro would get the bomb. Ironically, within four months of his taking office, Nixon submitted the NPT to Congress; to date Cuba has neither acquired nuclear weapons nor signed the treaty that was supposed to stop it from doing so.

Despite its history of benign neglect, nuclear proliferation has every sign of being a national security issue in the 1976 presidential campaign. Since May 1974, several events have significantly increased the salience of nuclear proliferation as an impending international problem.

First, India broke a ten-year moratorium to become the sixth state to construct and detonate a nuclear device. This was especially disconcerting because of India's position as a developing nation with a modest technological capability and trouble feeding its own population--a position that made it a prime target of the NPT.

Second, several other states seem close behind India. Three of India's regional neighbors--Iran, Pakistan, and Turkey--announced their initiation of nuclear development programs oriented to a weapons option. In Latin America, nationalistic competition between Argentina and Brazil over nuclear technology threatens to develop into a full-scale arms race.

Third, the U.S. government has offered nuclear technology as a political carrot to the prime Middle East belligerents, Egypt and Israel, thus sparking a major domestic debate regarding U.S. reactor export policy.

Fourth, the worldwide energy crisis and the promotion of reactors being generated by competitive suppliers have created a consumer market demanding access to nuclear-generated electrical power.

Fifth, the five-year review conference of the NPT held in May 1975 resulted in a significant confrontation between the nuclear haves

and have-nots, calling into question the long-term viability of the
NPT as an inhibitor of proliferation.

While each of these issues in itself presents a potential point
of policy debate, cumulatively they create an environment surrounding the question of proliferation that is unique in the post-World War
II world in its potential for politicalization.

Many factors could result in the politicalization of proliferation. One is an international event occurring prior to the 1976 presidential election--for example, overt steps by an American ally such
as West Germany, Japan, South Korea, or Israel to acquire a nuclear capability. Another catalyst would be the crossing of the
threshold by any of several other potential nuclear weapon states--
for instance, Argentina, Brazil, South Africa, Pakistan, or Taiwan--
and the resulting regional instability. Still another would be the attempt by a transnational group such as a terrorist organization
covertly to acquire or steal a nuclear device or initiate a blackmail
campaign with nuclear weapons. Finally, politicalization would occur if there should be a major nuclear disaster, either with a weapon
or at a commercial facility, that resulted in nuclear contamination.

In these cases the United States, if not bearing the brunt of
criticism for having contributed in some way to nuclear instability,
would nonetheless be drawn in and would be expected to take sides
in the ensuing international uproar.

PAST STRATEGIES: DEMOCRATIC OPTIMISM
AND REPUBLICAN "BENIGN NEGLECT"

Even in the absence of an apocalyptic disaster, another factor
that might lead to the politicalization of proliferation is the last
eight years of benign neglect. Prohibition of nuclear proliferation
was a keystone of foreign policy in the Kennedy and Johnson administrations. It was used as a major justification for the U.S. role of
world policeman. The threat of nuclear proliferation was cited repeatedly in justifying foreign commitments: it was argued that the
loss of Vietnam might force Japan over the brink, and that American
troops had to remain in Europe lest the West Germans go nuclear.
The Nuclear Non-Proliferation Treaty was touted as a major success
of the Democratic Party's foreign policy.

In contrast, the Nixonian revolution in foreign policy involved
the acceptance of a multipolar world: Rather than decrying the nuclear capabilities of France and China, the Nixon administration
courted both De Gaulle and Mao. The Nuclear Non-Proliferation
Treaty fell under the shadow of SALT. The signing of the NPT by
two key states, Germany and Japan, and the treaties' coming into

force in 1970 went almost unnoticed. The Nixon administration tilted against India in 1971, but made no attempt at sanctions once the Indians had detonated their nuclear device. In fact, Washington seemed to cater to the new nuclear India; for example, within six months of the detonation, not only did India receive a significantly increased foreign aid package, but its nuclear status was acknowledged by a visit from the American secretary of state--the first visit since the Republicans had gained power.

Rather than reinforce the NPT through the strict regulation of American exports of nuclear material and technology, the Nixon administration based some of its major foreign policy successes upon an increase in the dissemination of nuclear-related technology. In bringing "peace" to the Middle East, the United States offered both Israel and Egypt nuclear reactors; Israel was also offered American delivery systems (the Lance and Pershing missiles) whose only military value to Israel would be in a nuclear role.

Another factor that must be taken into account is the attitudes of the personalities involved. The national security establishment of the Kennedy and Johnson administrations made no secret of its strong personal commitment to the nuclear nonproliferation crusade. William Foster, the head of the Arms Control and Disarmament Agency, considered the successful negotiation of the NPT a personal triumph and the high point of his career. Both Secretary of State Dean Rusk and Secretary of Defense Robert McNamara preached the nonproliferation gospel--warning that a world of nuclear powers would lead to a fiery conflict that could be avoided only through the grace of the NPT.

In contrast, the leading national security personalities of the Nixon administration spoke relatively little on the issue of proliferation. An analysis of speeches and official statements shows a 90 percent reduction in the frequency with which proliferation as a national security threat and nonproliferation as a foreign policy objective were mentioned.

To a certain extent the situation in 1975 not only mirrors presidential concern, but also reflects personal predisposition. For example, in the early 1960s an analyst of the RAND Corporation, in one of the classic articles on nuclear proliferation, argued that the spread of nuclear weapons was not imminent and would not occur as fast as was generally thought.[1] Today that analyst, Fred Ikle, is director of the Arms Control and Disarmament Agency. In 1967, another RAND analyst argued that the potential threats of nuclear power had been exaggerated.[2] That analyst was James Schlesinger, until recently secretary of defense. Throughout the 1960s, a Harvard professor argued not only that multipolarity had its advantages, but that the United States had overemphasized its anti-proliferation policy

at the expense of its relationship with its allies.[3] That professor
was Henry Kissinger, now Secretary of State. To the extent that
the past opinions of decision-makers influence their future decisions,
the predisposition of these personalities may significantly influence
the degree to which nuclear proliferation becomes an issue of debate
in the 1976 presidential election.

ALTERNATIVE OPTIONS

To date, while these issues have received growing attention
and the administration position has been criticized, the development
of the issue has not yet reached the stage of a debate in which alternative options or counterprograms have been formulated--let alone
put forward in the political battles of policy debate. Nevertheless,
a wide range of potentially debatable issues is surfacing. Because
the issue of proliferation is still in its embryonic stages, these issues are being discussed incrementally. A coherent and combined
program linking various issues has not yet surfaced. Nevertheless
the wide range of alternative policy options can generally be divided
into two categories. One is the category of U.S. actions to slow or
stop dissemination of nuclear material and technology; the other is
the category of actions that the United States could take to enforce
or sustain the NPT.

Policy Option One: Limited Export
of Nuclear Materials

Time is running out; the rate of dissemination of reactor technology will quadruple four times in the next fifteen years over what
it was in the last thirty. By 1975, six countries had demonstrated
the capability to develop a nuclear explosive device. Ten countries
have the in-place technological capability to go nuclear almost immediately. Twenty-three other countries will be in a position to ex-
plode a nuclear device with less than ten years of intensive effort.
Today there are over 300 research and power reactors in countries
other than the current nuclear powers. There are twenty-five countries, some of them notoriously underdeveloped, currently mining
or possessing significant uranium reserves. By 1990, eighty-three
countries are projected to have operating nuclear power reactors.
Control of the nuclear genie is beyond the grasp of unilateral
action, or even of combined action by the two superpowers. There
are currently nine states disseminating nuclear reactor technology.
Prior to 1968, the United States was unquestionably the world's

major proliferator of nuclear technology. Since then, however, American exports have been surpassed by other states developing indigenous technology or acquiring nuclear assistance from second- or third-generation nuclear states. For example, in 1975 Germany negotiated a major reactor program with Brazil. Brazil had undertaken a massive nuclear energy program in order to catch up to Argentina's ten-year lead. Argentina, having started with U.S. help, has received most of its assistance from Canada or Canada's major nuclear client, India. Argentina itself is now helping Iran initiate a program--and Iran has just negotiated to purchase a reactor from France. Iran in turn is reported to be underwriting Pakistan's attempt to build a counterpart to India's nuclear explosive. It becomes quite obvious from the second-, third-, and fourth-level patterns of nuclear dissemination that the nuclear genie is out of the bottle, and that there is an exponential growth in the number of Aladdins.

It is important to note that while the United States consciously attempted to inhibit the proliferation potential of its nuclear technology transfer by emphasizing light-water reactors (which require highly enriched uranium) when it was the world's sole supplier of commercial enriched uranium, the technology transferred by other countries has not been so limited. For example, Canada has widely promoted its natural uranium reactors. These, since they permit the use of local fuel, require much less sophistication in the user country, and they are high producers of plutonium. Both factors significantly increase the capability of a recipient to develop a weapon. Thus, the United States (even in the Free World) has exclusive control neither over the atom nor over the kind of technology that is being disseminated by others.

The United States is currently committed to providing nuclear reactors to over twenty states by 1980; fourteen of these have not had a power reactor before. This raises the question of whether the United States should attempt to cut back, restrict, or stop its export of nuclear technology and materials. An interesting case illustrating the problem of cutting back supply in the face of large demand and growing supplier competition is the U.S. experience with enriched uranium. For years, the United States was the major supplier of enriched uranium for over 90 percent of the noncommunist world's reactors. Since 1973, the United States has had to restrict its sales because of reduced production and increased demand. The shortfall between American delivery and world requirements, however, has been completely absorbed by new producing states. The Soviet Union has made enriched uranium agreements not only with many Third World countries, but also with many U.S. allies and domestic reactor operators as well.

There is an anomaly in being a major source of nuclear material and technology in an era of competitive supply. On the one hand, supplying nuclear reactors and material increases the number of countries with a proliferative capability and contributes to the worldwide growth of nuclear energy. On the other hand, by being a major supplier, the United States retains some leverage for promoting safeguard procedures and for discouraging overt weapons development.

Given the lucrative nature of the uranium market, it is very likely that in the case of a partial or complete withdrawal of U.S.-supplied technology and material, supply would simply be taken up by competitors. Such a withdrawal would probably delay some countries' power programs, but would not cancel them. (Those it would most affect would be countries traditionally close to the United States, particularly Japan and South Korea.) Thus, the short-run gain would have to be weighed against the enormous political consequences of an American-induced "nuclear shock." There would also be the long-run probability that it would be ineffective as a proliferation inhibitor and that it might actually force some countries currently dependent on the United States to strive for self-sufficiency.

Five of the eleven international suppliers of nuclear material have refused to sign the NPT and two others, Italy and West Germany, have not ratified the treaty. Exporters of nuclear material and reactor technology have not discriminated against NPT holdouts, and in fact over half of the current recipients either have not signed or have delayed ratification of the NPT.

Policy Option Two: U.S. Enforcement of the NPT

The NPT was designed as a political instrument to slow the spread of nuclear weapons--that is, it was essentially a mechanism through which nonnuclear states would publicly renounce a weapons program. To the extent that the treaty was technically enforced, it required inspection by the International Atomic Energy Agency (IAEA) to insure that a country was not covertly diverting nuclear material from its civilian sector into a military weapons program.

As a political instrument the treaty had several weaknesses. First, several of the countries most likely to go nuclear refused to sign it (these were Argentina, Brazil, India, Israel, South Africa, and Spain). Other states signed but refused to ratify the treaty--the most significant being states very close to an immediate weapons option (Belgium, Italy, West Germany, Japan, Netherlands, and Switzerland) or reportedly seeking a weapons capability (South Korea, Pakistan, and Taiwan). This behavior affords them the illusion of adherence without a formal commitment. Second, the treaty permits withdrawal. Third, in order to encourage states to sign the treaty, every effort was made by the superpowers (during negotiations) and the IAEA (since the treaty went into effect) to insure signatory access to "peaceful" nuclear technology. This actually promoted and accelerated the worldwide spread of nuclear energy.

Thus, in exchange for a political commitment, many countries have had the technological door opened. A result of this promotional activity has been a heightening of nuclear "consciousness"; the growth of great expectations has actually raised the status of nuclear power. Since nuclear power has become an issue of status and reciprocity, many states have been given an added incentive for acquiring at least a peaceful nuclear option.

Lastly, the treaty contained no mechanism for punishing a violation of its covenant; therefore, in the case of detection of an illegal diversion, the only risk a violator runs is the clamor of "world public opinion."

The NPT contains several weaknesses on the technical level as well. By focusing on diversion, it ignores the problems of environmental impact, radiological safety, and security from nonnational diversion. By focusing on power reactors as a source of nuclear fissionable material, it ignores key elements of the fuel cycle--particularly in the case of the reprocessing of plutonium from spent fuel rods. At least eight countries already have large reprocessing facilities, and many others have the minimum technology (such as hot cells) to reprocess plutonium into weapons-grade material.

One option that has been proposed to bolster the technical safeguards is that the United States should develop and promote further safeguard procedures by underwriting multinational development of the fuel cycle, specifically in the design and operation of regional reprocessing centers to be shared and utilized by states not having nuclear weapons. This proposal has all the appearances of schizophrenia. On the one hand, it suggests significant progress in the control of and accountability for nuclear material. On the other hand, U.S. funding and development of regional reprocessing facilities is fraught with danger. First, there is the problem of deciding which country will be the host. One can hardly envision the various states of the Middle East ever agreeing on a designated recipient, let alone accountability procedures and cost sharing. Nor would the prospects be bright in Africa, Latin America, or Asia. Even worse would be the incipient threat of the host country's nationalizing the reprocessing center, thus acquiring not only a major means of bomb production but also a large stockpile of fissionable material.

The major political problem in increasing safeguards, however, is the increasing resentment of the nonnuclear signatories of the NPT.

At the five-year review conference in Geneva, the nonnuclear states emphasized the imbalance of obligations between themselves and the superpowers. The price of the treaty's acceptance by nonnuclear states was the superpowers' pledge in Article 6 to pursue effective measures to end the arms race "at an early date" and to pursue nuclear disarmament. The nonnuclear states have consistently viewed the treaty as inherently discriminatory, since it required nonnuclear states to renounce weapons they did not possess, while the nuclear states could retain them. Even more disturbing, it imposed inspection on the nonnuclear states' peaceful facilities, but not on those of the nuclear powers. Thus, as Lincoln Bloomfield noted, the questions of prestige and nondiscrimination are fundamental to the success of the multilateral agreement on nonproliferation:

> In an era dominated by demands for identity, respect, equity, and participation, it seems reasonable to ask whether with the best will in the world, the present NPT system of discrimination, denial, and second-class citizenship will in fact achieve its aim of preventing the further spread of nuclear weapons. [4]

Nonnuclear states have pointed out that in the seven years since the signing of the NPT, the arsenals of the superpowers have increased rather than decreased. Many states are therefore increasingly concerned over the threat of nuclear blackmail. Others focus on what is perceived as a breach of faith by the superpowers. This is reflected in the comments of one of the participants at the NPT review conference:

> It is the view of my delegation that the most valid test of progress is simply to ask whether or not there are fewer nuclear weapons now than there were in 1970; whether or not there has been any significant abatement in nuclear weapons testing during that period; and whether or not there has been any halt in the further refinement and sophistication of those weapons of mass destruction. The answer to all three questions is patently no. [5]

In exchange for continued adherence to the NPT, over thirty of the nonnuclear signatories participating in the NPT review conference demanded immediate "good faith" arms control measures by the superpowers. Three specific measures were identified:

1. A U.S.-Soviet agreement to sign a comprehensive test ban in the immediate future or, agreement failing, a U.S. test moratorium for a definite and substantial period;

2. An announced schedule for a significant reduction of strategic nuclear weapons;

3. A pledge never to use, or threaten to use, nuclear weapons against nonnuclear states party to the NPT.

Should nuclear proliferation become a national political issue in 1976, it is likely to revolve around these three issues. At the review conference, both the Soviet Union and the United States refused to accede to even one, let alone all three, of these requests. It is interesting to note that while the review conference was in progress, three potential Democratic presidential candidates endorsed these measures. Senators Hubert Humphrey and George McGovern inserted a call for these measures in the Congressional Record, and Senator Edward M. Kennedy, in a speech before an unofficial session attended by several hundred of the conference participants at Geneva, called for a test ban and reduction of the superpowers' strategic nuclear weapons as a means of coping with the problem of strengthening the NPT. He argued that the administration's approach of relying on functional and technical safeguards obscured the essentially political reasons impelling nations to acquire nuclear weapons. Kennedy argued that the superpowers must "play down the importance of nuclear weapons in assessments and assertions of their own national power. No one can ask nuclear have-not nations to foreswear these weapons--for whatever reason--if the superpowers continue to overplay the bombs' importance for political power and prestige."[6]

As a potential political issue, it is important to note that Kennedy's remarks came at the same time the Ford administration was calling for an increase in strategic arms, had announced a new strategic doctrine calling for limited strikes, and, through the secretary of defense, had reaffirmed that the United States would not rule out a first use of nuclear weapons in either Korea or Europe.

To keep our perspective, it is important to examine the issue of proliferation in a broader context than the specific issues related to the NPT. Nuclear proliferation has long been perceived as threatening to U.S. national security. Three threats have generally been identified.

One threat, as expressed by former Secretary of Defense Robert McNamara, is that an increase in the number of nuclear powers is an increase in the possibility of a nuclear war. "The more nuclear powers there are, the more there are likely to be. . . . The addition of each nuclear power to the number of nuclear powers gives other nations reasons that they did not previously have to

acquire nuclear weapons."[7] The more states that have nuclear
weapons, the greater the chance that they will be used in a conflict;
that an irrational or threatened decision-maker will push the button;
that a nuclear accident will occur; that nuclear weapons might be
used in a domestic power struggle; and that terrorists may obtain
access to a bomb. In all of these cases the direct threat of mass
casualties to the United States is relatively low; nonetheless it is
not viewed as in America's interest to have nuclear weapons going
off anywhere.

A second, and much more direct, threat is that with proliferation there is a greater likelihood that nuclear weapons might be employed against U.S. forces overseas, or that the introduction of nuclear weapons in a zone of U.S.-Soviet confrontation (such as the
Middle East) might escalate to a strategic exchange between the
superpowers. Thus a mere 1 percent increase in the likelihood of
killing over 100 million people (in just the first half hour of a strategic nuclear war) becomes a massive threat.

A third, and more general, threat is that the spread of nuclear
weapons will greatly inhibit America's freedom of action throughout
the world. It is this last threat that many of the nonnuclear signatories to the NPT wish to increase. They want neither the United
States nor the Soviet Union to be superpowers with the capability of
coercing the Third World. They are demanding not only a cessation
of the arms race but also a reduction in the superpowers' nuclear
stockpiles--aimed at their eventual elimination. The nuclear have-
nots want the nuclear haves to join them.

This raises a fundamental question regarding nuclear proliferation and national security. If the superpowers begin a nuclear disarmament program, not only will they become increasingly vulnerable to the other nuclear powers (such as Great Britain, France, and
China), but they will also actually increase the incentives for industrial nonnuclear powers to join the nuclear club, because their
smaller arsenals would then have relatively more impact. With a
greatly reduced nuclear arsenal, the superpowers would no longer
be "super."

It is questionable whether this option is acceptable within the
United States; it is clearly not in the Soviet Union. This is, however,
the condition for continued adherence to the NPT by many of the nonnuclear states. "The 'haves' must now pay the price they should have
paid from the beginning in order to make the rest of the world satisfied with being 'have-nots'."[8]

The second major policy dilemma raised by nuclear proliferation is the question of U.S. involvement in the international arena.
If the United States were willing to police the NPT through overt
coercion or intervention, nuclear proliferation probably could be

physically prevented. But with four other nuclear powers already in existence, the problems of joint operations with the Soviet Union, including the enormous costs and onerous tasks of policing the world, it would seem that this option has been foreclosed.

On the other side of the coin, the United States could withdraw from its overseas involvement and let proliferation take its course. This would reduce the threat of escalation or of U.S. forces being the target of another country. Because of the limited capabilities of potential nuclear countries, the threat of strategic attack against the continental United States would be relatively small--at least initially. [9] Still, precipitous withdrawal from our forward bases probably would send our allies, some of the most sophisticated and capable nonnuclear states, into a mad dash for self-sufficiency.

CONCLUSIONS

In looking forward to 1976 and beyond, it is important to remember that while recent Republican administrations were culpable of "benign neglect" and callousness to the increasingly vocal demands of the Third World, the proposed panaceas of the opposition should be examined very critically. Many of those that have been offered to date are incredibly naive. Even short of the ultimate answer of world government, we do not lack solutions. The problem is in devising a political means of implementing them.

There seems to be a tendency for Americans to assume that the generous application of good will packaged in idealistic prose and accompanied by unilateral U.S. action can stem the proliferation tide. Nothing could be further from the truth. The currency of our "good will" has gone into recession, our rhetoric is not believed, and time has passed for a unilateral approach. The United States can not stop the dissemination of nuclear technology alone because too many other states have too much to gain by refusing to cooperate. The very people who now call out for unilateral U.S. political acquiescence to keep the NPT alive are the same ones who in 1968 argued that the NPT would solve the proliferation threat. It did not then and it will not now, because too many sovereign states refuse to surrender sovereignty.

A unilateral U.S. test ban, reduction in strategic forces, and a pledge not to threaten to use nuclear weapons would be superfluous to the problem of stopping nuclear proliferation. It would be meaningless unless all other nuclear powers also agreed--and China, France, and India have consistently refused. It would create serious strains among our allies (who depend upon a U.S. nuclear shield) and perhaps even stimulate them to go for their own independent option.

It would contribute nothing to the safeguarding and reduction of the worldwide dissemination of nuclear technology.

The proliferation problem goes much deeper than a debate over options. It depends ultimately on what role the United States is to play in global affairs. We could have stopped proliferation in the mid-1960s by creating a bipolar hegemony with the Soviet Union and policing it with military force. Today, we could reduce our vulnerability by going into isolation. Or we could launch a moral crusade against nuclear power, attempting to deny much of the underdeveloped world its only long-term hope of electrification and industrialization. This ethic lacks both efficacy and equity. In all probability we will just continue debating options--all the way to Armageddon.

Nuclear proliferation penetrated to the very core of U.S. national security and foreign policy. To date, neither the issues of proliferation nor its horrendous consequences have been brought before the American electorate. Even if there is no solution, the American public ought to know--it's their future.

NOTES

1. Charles Fred Ikle, "Nth Countries and Disarmament," in Arms and Arms Control, ed. Ernest W. Lefever (New York: Praeger, 1963).

2. James R. Schlesinger, "The Strategic Consequence of Nuclear Proliferation," in American Defense Policy, second edition, ed. Mark E. Smith and Claude J. Johns, Jr. (Baltimore: Johns Hopkins Press, 1968).

3. Henry A. Kissinger, The Troubled Partnership: A Reappraisal of the Atlantic Alliance (New York: Doubleday & Co., 1965).

4. Lincoln Bloomfield, "Nuclear Spread and World Order," Foreign Affairs, July 1975.

5. Ambassador H. V. Roberts of New Zealand, May 1975. Cited in Allan Geyer, "The Nuclear Question Explodes," World View 53, no. 4 (September 1975). Council on Foreign Relations, Inc., 1975.

6. Cited in ibid.

7. Robert McNamara to the U.S. Congress, Joint Committee on Atomic Energy, "Nonproliferation of Nuclear Weapons," hearings on Senate Resolution 179, 89th Congress, 2nd Session, 1966, pp. 91-92.

8. Alva Myrdal, "The High Price of Nuclear Arms Monopoly," Foreign Policy 18 (Spring 1975).

9. For a discussion of the relationship between isolationism and nuclear proliferation see Philip Karber and R. W. Mengel, "In Defense of Fortress America," in Isolation or Interdependence?, ed. Morton Kaplan (New York: Free Press, 1975).

CHAPTER 10

INTERNATIONAL ARMS TRADE:
THE PROBLEM OF CONTROLLING
CONVENTIONAL WAR
Robert Harkavy

THE ISSUE

The issue of American conventional arms sales and aid policies has acquired a degree of urgency in a climate of enhanced Congressional concern. The United States has reasserted itself as the
world's leading purveyor of arms in the immediate wake of a dis-
illusioning period in which it attempted somewhat to pursue unilateral
control measures. Fueled by massive deals in the Persian Gulf
area, most notably with Iran and Saudi Arabia, U.S. arms sales
have now climbed to an unprecedented level of about $9 billion a year
(with actual deliveries lagging behind, near $5 billion), several times
the volume of just a few years ago. Arms sales now dwarf a relatively insignificant arms aid program, with the phasing out of the Vietnam conflict and the increased ability of many recipients to finance
their own arms purchases. All this has occurred amid a startling
rise in the overall level of worldwide arms transfers, with Soviet,
British, and French competitors also achieving large increases in
sales in an increasingly buyer's market. With an oligopolistic but
still somewhat dispersed supplier market, restraints by one supplier
normally lead merely to a shift of purchases to others.

These events have encouraged serious soul-searching in Congress. Important sets of hearings were held in 1975 by both the
Senate Foreign Relations Committee and the House Foreign Affairs
Committee. They took place in the wake of a major increase in
American arms sales and in the midst of serious scandals involving
massive bribery in the Middle East, Europe, and Latin America by
arms-selling corporations. At the same time as the investigations
of the CIA, these hearings brought a recrudescence of themes familiar from the "merchants of death" days of the Nye Committee in the

mid-1930s and, to a lesser extent, from the hearings of the late 1960s on the role of the Eximbank in financing Pentagon arms deals. In this second wave of post-Vietnam focus on the arms trade issue, there were calls for new policies, new international initiatives, and, most critically, for a shifting of the locus of decision-making away from a harried Executive branch.

The development of a coherent global doctrine to guide U.S. arms sales is no easy matter, nor are the specific, single-country issues. Policies in this area interface with, or exist within the context of, a range of crucial economic and political foreign policy matters. There are costs and benefits to any approach, with very serious trade-offs an inherent given. For example, arms control initiatives are being sought in a period of increasingly serious balance-of-payments problems, caused by massive outflows of currency required to finance imports of expensive oil and other raw materials. Arms sales have acted as a counterbalance to these outflows. Indeed, the heaviest sales, to OPEC members, have helped to absorb their petrodollar surpluses during a period of an increased trend toward broad government-to-government barter deals. Currency matters aside, arms increasingly are being used to assure continuing supplies of critical raw materials, with the French now leading the way in a free-for-all competition for quid pro quo deals.

Aside from the balance-of-payments factor, there remain questions about how far the United States should move from its alliance and security commitments, how far it should allow its credibility to erode, amid obvious, though unannounced, movement toward a form of neo-isolationism. To the extent that commitments remain, arms transfers are part and parcel of a broader effort at military assistance, which includes military training activities and assistance to overseas arms production. Still, there are serious questions about an alleged "slippery slope," a la Vietnam, said to lead from arms supplying and training, through supply of spare parts and resupply during crises, the prestige implications of the supplier's weapons, and hence to the possibility of overt intervention. Aside from these problems as applied to relations with the Third World, within NATO there are questions surrounding the continued progress of weapons standardization and commonality programs as an integral underpinning of the Atlantic defense structure, however politically eroded.

One other issue, obscured until very recently, has now begun seriously to surface in connection with arms sales: the linkage of security commitments to the proliferation of nuclear weapons. The United States has been--and remains--adamantly supportive of the Non-Proliferation Treaty, but with that treaty's omission of security guarantees against conventional aggression, and with the drawing down of American defense commitments and the degradation of the

American weapons production base, doubts have arisen in some nations accustomed to the U.S. umbrella. As a hedge, some of these
nations are now making the first moves toward the nuclear option.
Such moves--first by Israel but now, apparently, also by Pakistan,
South Korea, and Taiwan, and perhaps later by Iran, Turkey, and
still others--indicate at least one possible indirect cost of a policy
of unilateral conventional arms controls and withdrawals from prior
commitments.

There are also other economic issues: the loss of domestic
jobs dependent on arms sales; the maintenance of a viable U.S. arms
production base; and the amortization of weapons research and development costs to achieve economies of scale.

In short, U.S. policy has become mired in a traditional dilemma, one not easily solved in the past. There is the basic question of
what can be done unilaterally to stanch the worldwide flow of arms
in the face of the continuing futility of efforts toward international
controls, through either supplier or recipient agreements. There
is the continuing evident unwillingness of other suppliers, some with
more pressing economic (if not political) rationales, to collaborate
in controls, along with the attitude of almost all Third World arms-
dependent nations, who perceive any hint of coordinated big power
controls as a discriminatory, thinly veiled attempt at maintaining
big power hegemony. There is an apt analogy here with the distinction between vertical and horizontal proliferation as applied to nuclear weapons.

For some U.S. policy-makers, then, bent upon control initiatives both overall and in specific cases, there is the basic question
of how to combat the time-worn rationale, "If we don't sell them,
someone else will"--which empirically, if not morally, is almost
always an irrefutable argument, the quality of weapons aside. Critics
of the U.S. role in the arms trade raise the charge of "merchants of
death." Its defenders claim, often with no little sadness, that unilateral control efforts can achieve little more than a fleeting sense
of rectitude, and point out that in specific cases, it may actually hurt
friends and allies with no other easily available source of supply.
Hence, an impasse, historically solved by a discernible rhythm of
policy ebbs and flows between the nether poles.

Thus, for the administration in 1977 the basic conundrum remains the search for an overall doctrine or general policy guide to
cope with a mixture of moral, pragmatic, political, and economic
concerns. Where, it is being asked, can U.S. policy be pegged
along a continuum running from an all-out, no controls, commercially oriented emphasis--perhaps with periodic adherence to embargoes for compelling reasons--to a moralistically inspired policy
of selective arms sales, still minimally aimed at maintaining regional

balances and to helping selected, deserving clients. Development
of a coherent doctrine does not, of course, preclude the inevitable
need for ad hoc decision-making in selected and sometimes anoma-
lous cases, where conflicting rationales may be apparent. Few general doctrines might have handled the 1974-75 dilemmas over arms
sales to Jordan, Israel, Turkey, Greece, and Saudi Arabia.

BACKGROUND OF THE ISSUE

The current debate over American arms sales policies, despite its contemporary veneer, hardly represents anything new.
Rather, one receives the distinct impression of old wine in new
bottles, a sense of deja vu. In almost every respect, roles in the
present debate have been played out before, with identifiable cycles
discernible over several decades, with one side or the other temporarily prevailing.

Before the 1930s and the Nye Committee hearings, the issue
was somewhat simpler. Prior to the era of government control and
licensing, inaugurated in the mid-1930s, arms trading was, in the
United States as elsewhere, essentially the province of private manufacturing and trading corporations. This harked back to the outset
of the era of laissez-faire early in the 1800s, which reached a zenith
in the late nineteenth and early twentieth centuries. True, there was
some assistance to arms-trading activities by military attaches and
diplomats; but in the most basic sense, arms trading was rarely utilized as a purposive instrument of diplomacy. Essentially, what was
involved was a rather free-wheeling, often corrupt trade, almost in-
explicable in juxtaposition to the prevailing patterns of alliance diplomacy, and often--surprisingly--involving the sale of arms to rivals
or even enemies, spawning the term "anti-national trade in arms."
The few exceptions for the United States were cases where the American government attempted to embargo arms sales to revolutionary
groups or civil war factions in Latin America, where American business interests were at stake.

In line with this traditional laissez-faire policy, the U.S. government virtually ignored some serious but ultimately futile efforts
at controlling the arms trade subsequent to World War I, refusing to
participate in the St. Germain and Geneva agreements of 1919 and
1925, respectively, because they conflicted with laissez-faire principles as well as with the Monroe Doctrine. Attempts to participate
in the embargoes against China and the participants in the Chaco War
were easily obviated by arms-selling corporations through trans-
shipment via overseas subsidiaries.

The first serious break in America's traditional policy came in the wake of the China and Chaco situations, with their attendant scandals--at a time when the very legitimacy of the capitalist system was under fire after the Great Depression. In the mid-1930s, the Nye Committee hearings brought "merchants of death" accusations, resulting in the neutrality acts, the establishment of the licensing machinery embodied in the Munitions Control Board, and, overall, the beginnings of some governmental controls over the destinations and volume of arms sales. Basically, the controls then instituted involved denying arms to all participants in conflicts-- "quarantining"--which, as it turned out, could mean denying arms to victims as well as aggressors. That was the lesson of Ethiopia and Spain.

There was then a new swing of the pendulum, with neutrality replaced by 1940 with cash-and-carry and lend lease, when it became evident that American arms-sales restrictions were merely hurting the embattled Western allies in their desperate struggle against the Nazis. Some interesting precedents were set here, germane to contemporary issues. It was demonstrated that it is not easy to formulate an overall doctrine toward arms selling that can encompass both morality and pragmatism, both controls and the assisting of the deserving and the dependent. These reversals, a dialectic between morality and cynicism, were repeated in new phases after the war.

In the postwar period, U.S. arms sales and aid policies have undergone several discernible phases. In the first decade or so of the postwar period, and until about 1960, there were the massive giveaways--also by Great Britain--of mountains of World War II surplus stocks, as a backup to the Marshall Plan, the Truman Doctrine, and the numerous bilateral and multilateral alliances set up around the periphery of the Sino-Soviet bloc. Arms aid greatly exceeded arms sales in an era of dollar surplus, with the United States maintaining its role as "armorer of the free world." Aid was concentrated in a number of key "forward" nations in the alliance structure--South Korea, Taiwan, Greece, Turkey, Pakistan, and Iran-- in addition to the NATO nations, whose arms industries were still crucially dependent upon American licenses for most major weapons systems.

Until the mid-1950s the Soviet Union was not a serious factor. It was relatively quiescent in the arms markets, absorbing most arms production internally or within the Warsaw Pact group. Further, what was to become the Third World was not yet a significant market for sophisticated arms, with a host of newly independent nations still in the midst of the decolonization process.

In 1955, huge initial Soviet bloc arms transfers to Egypt and
Syria, and subsequent ones to Indonesia, Iraq, Cuba, Ghana, North
Korea, and North Vietnam, signaled the beginnings of the bipolar
competition for influence through arms sales, with each of the superpowers arming its ideological adherents. There was little competition for sales within given nations; but the competition gradually became broader, with the advent of a host of newer nations, some
hungry for arms if not yet able to foot the bill. Arms sales and aid
now became primary instruments for the extension of influence and
the cementing of bloc alliances.

By the early 1960s, the U.S. World War II surplus was expended or obsolete for the most part; and with Europe on its feet,
the earlier dollar surplus was reversing. At that point, the incom-
ing Democratic administration, under Kennedy and McNamara, with
Henry Kuss as the Pentagon's chief arms salesman, embarked on a
new effort to expand cash arms sales. Improved balance of payments
was as important as the rationale binding recipients to the American
security orbit. Despite this relative shift to a more commercial
policy, however, some political restrictions on transfers were maintained or inaugurated. Other Western nations were persuaded to act
as surrogate arms suppliers to Israel, while a moralistically inspired embargo was placed on both India and Pakistan after the 1965
war, driving them into the arms of the USSR and China, respectively.
The United States adhered to the UN-sponsored embargo on South
Africa, and itself placed partial embargoes on a number of nations
as a manifestation of Congressional discouragement with internal
political developments.

Generally, however, there was extensive bipartisan consensus
on arms sales and aid policies, with merely a few muted Congressional laments, and an almost total absence of outside critical literature or even much press attention to these matters. The arms trade
remained an esoteric domain, an aspect of "closed politics," familiar
only to the readers of the London Institute for Strategic Studies' publications and the military journals. And, despite the more openly
commercial nature of American arms sales during the early 1960s,
the volume of transfers was but a shadow of what it would become in
the 1970s, reflecting burgeoning OPEC purchasing power.

In 1967-68, in the midst of the Vietnam War controversies,
there were the first stirrings of a fundamental debate over U.S.
arms sales policies since the 1930s; this was one aspect of the
breakdown of the postwar foreign policy consensus, along the fault
line running between traditionalism and revisionism. Arms-trading
policies were put under close scrutiny during the onslaught against
an alleged American "imperialism" and its instruments in the
"military-industrial complex," particularly since it was now alleged,

on the basis of the Vietnam example, that military aid was the first
step on the road to military involvement. There were extensive
hearings by the Senate Foreign Relations and Banking and Currency
Committees, with the latter investigating the newly unearthed role
of the Eximbank in financing the Pentagon's revolving credit account
for arms. As in the earlier Nye Committee hearings, American involvement as a supplier on both sides of conflicts--in the Middle
East and in South Asia--drew particular notice.

At the same time as the Congressional hearings of the mid-
1960s, there was a flowering of critical muckraking and illustrative
literature on the arms trade, some of it a throwback to the 1930s.
These adumbrated more serious efforts initiated at the MIT Center
for International Studies, the London Institute for Strategic Studies,
and the Stockholm International Peace Research Institute, the three
centers that in combination were to become the focus for nongovernmental inquiries on this subject.

The result of the furor over arms transfers in the mid and late
1960s was a tightening of American sales and aid policies, with Congress bludgeoning a recalcitrant Executive branch into moderate controls. The Eximbank's role was curtailed; there was increased Congressional scrutiny at least of aid and credit sale transfers--most
stringently applied to allegedly repressive regimes; and regional
ceilings (in dollar amounts) were placed on annual transfers to Africa
and Latin America.

During this period, the primary rationale for controls, other
than that relating to conflict control itself, revolved about an assumed
causal relationship between economic development and arms acquisitions by developing nations. In an era of optimism about the future of
economic and political development, the United States took upon itself
the task of attempting to force reallocations of resources, at least indirectly, using the economic aid program as a lever, and recognizing
that economic aid often merely amounted to an indirect financing of
arms acquisitions. Later, in the burst of controls efforts in the mid-
1970s, political criteria came to outweigh economic ones in determining aid. Besides, the tying of arms sales to economic development
had been largely rejected by developing countries as paternalistic and
demeaning.

The late 1960s and early 1970s, marked by optimism, reform-
ism, and unilateral control efforts, were to lead to still another volte-
face around 1972. This shift partly reflected attempts to implement
the Nixon Doctrine in the post-Vietnam period, the doctrine asserting that if the United States was unwilling to be dragged into other
Vietnams, it would at least try to maintain its world role and some
of its accumulated security commitments by helping others to defend
themselves through arms shipments and other forms of military aid.

Moreover, there were still other forces acting to move the
United States away from its unilateral control efforts. For one thing,
the expanding European arms export industry, forced into a competitive commercial policy in order to achieve economies of scale, as
well as to maintain balances of payment, began to fill in the gaps
where the United States had backed off as a supplier. In country after country--South Africa, Rhodesia, Libya, Greece, Portugal,
Spain, Pakistan, India, Peru, Brazil, Argentina--where the United
States had attempted to limit arms transfers, the French and other
Western Europeans moved in. Backed by a militantly pragmatic
arms sales doctrine that was related to a nuclear proliferation doctrine, and oddly immune from the criticism regularly leveled at the
United States by Third World nations, the French flooded the markets
with Mirage jets, AMX tanks, Alouette helicopters, Panhard armored
cars, and a variety of missiles. Other Western European nations,
now on the way to recovery, filled still other gaps, as did the Soviets
in some areas where U.S. and Soviet interests intersected or com-
peted directly. In Latin America particularly, the U.S. share of the
arms market dropped precipitously; and over all, the U.S. control
effort did not result in a discernible decrease anywhere in the flow of
arms.

In addition, American participation in the lucrative European
arms market began to wane, as numerous European codevelopment
consortia sprouted to provide key major weapons systems. These
resulted in projects such as the Jaguar, MRCA, and Alpha jet fighters, the Roland and HOT missiles, and the Transall transport. At
the same time, the previous U.S. control over retransfer of European arms licensed from the United States through end-use restrictions began to evaporate. In a buyer's market for arms, unilateral
efforts at controls seemed to have no practical impact other than to
shift export advantages elsewhere. It is not an exaggeration to state
that U.S. control efforts during this period were made altogether
futile by an absence of European cooperation. Hence, when the rise
of OPEC further worsened European balance-of-payment problems,
and the trend of selling arms for oil developed, the United States,
along with other suppliers, was virtually forced to abandon its efforts
at controls and to join the scramble for OPEC petrodollars.

The wheel had turned again; and the result, because of absolutely massive American arms sales to the Persian Gulf area in 1973-75,
was a new wave of Congressional concern. This led to a new look,
in a Congress dominated by liberal Democrats after the 1974 election.
Hence, the Congressional-Executive impasse of 1975, hearings in
both houses of Congress, and the broaching of important new legislation aimed at controlling and monitoring America's role in the arms
markets. Basic policy issues, however, were enmeshed in the

squabble over the specifics of policies toward Jordan, Turkey, and Israel; bribery scandals surrounding dealings by Northrop and Lockheed; and the massive movement of American technicians and mercenaries to accompany arms shipments to Saudi Arabia and Iran at the very time at least some Americans seemed to contemplate invasions of the very countries being assisted.

In a context broader than the confines of U.S. policy, and amid a welter of detail describing the intricacies of the arms trade, a few generalizations may be offered about emerging patterns and trends. In combination, they form the decision-making environment for the present and future of American arms transfer policy.

The changing context is a function of emerging structural and attitudinal alterations in the global system. As noted in Chapter 1, there has been a discernible shift away from the rigid bipolar system of the immediate postwar period and its concomitantly narrow ideological basis of conflict and alliances. With the rise of new power centers, in economic if not military terms--in Western Europe, Japan, and China, and now among the wealthier OPEC nations--diplomatic relationships have become more flexible and less predictable than they were during the Cold War. Simultaneously, changes in the patterns of the arms trade have emerged that can be discussed briefly under the headings of supplier markets, donor-recipient patterns (who sells to whom), regional arms acquisition patterns, trends toward partial weapons-producing independence by some developing nations, the emergence of a definable "pariah" class of nations with low leverage in the arms markets, and profound changes in conventional arms--highlighted by the 1973 war--that augur basic alterations in the nature of conventional warfare and its associated military doctrines. These, in combination, have produced increasingly complex and serious dilemmas for the formulation of U.S. arms transfer policies. Let us examine each area a little more closely.

Table 19.1 on arms exports to Third World countries only, up to 1974, illustrates the continuation of a still somewhat narrowly oligopolistic supplier market, dominated by the two superpowers. These markets would be shown, if the data were disaggregated by weapons systems, to be more narrowly concentrated for the most sophisticated and expensive classes of military equipment--that is, modern strike aircraft and advanced missiles. Here, the Soviet role may be somewhat understated relative to the American role, because of the lower comparative unit costs of weapons systems, essentially the result of far lower labor costs. Data comparing supplier market shares to the numbers of discretely transferred weapons systems would portray a somewhat altered picture.

Although the arms markets continue to be dominated by the two superpowers, it should be pointed out that increased inroads

TABLE 19.1

Arms Supplier Markets Broken Down by Recipient Blocs
(in millions of current dollars)

	World Total	Developed	Developing	NATO	Warsaw Pact	OPEC
United States	29,688	9,480	20,208	9,806	--	1,993
Soviet Union	15,678	4,783	10,895	--	4,989	1,760
France	2,409	788	1,621	675	--	439
United Kingdom	1,770	714	1,056	431	--	446
Czechoslovakia	1,295	770	491	--	809	128
People's Republic of China	1,608	5	1,603	--	5	--
Canada	1,344	1,288	90	--	1,278	3
Poland	1,144	902	242	892	--	41
Federal Republic of Germany	1,184	567	617	829	--	68
All others	1,816	515	1,301	476	40	452
Total	57,936	19,812	38,124	13,109	7,121	5,330

Source: World Military Expenditures and Arms Trade: 1963–73, U.S. Arms Control and Disarmament Agency (Washington, D.C.: Government Printing Office, 1974), p. 67.

have been made in recent years by a growing host of other nations across the whole spectrum of weapons systems. France and the United Kingdom in particular have seriously begun to compete all over the globe, with the former's arms being successfully sold in areas where political and economic factors have inhibited the maintenance of a primary role for the United States or the Soviet Union. Meanwhile, German and Swiss manufacturers have succeeded in breaching markets for armored equipment, missiles, and anti-aircraft cannon, and--in the case of the former--with a variety of naval systems. Italy has lately enjoyed a great increase in arms sales, much of it through retransfer of aircraft and tanks originally licensed from the United States, but including indigenously designed jet trainer aircraft and naval equipment. Even Sweden, earlier engaged only in limited arms sales in areas relatively free of political tensions, has begun to move toward a more serious competitive stance, now vying for some NATO markets with its advanced Saab Viggen fighter aircraft. China, still producing relatively obsolete copies of Soviet equipment licensed over a decade ago, has become a significant supplier to Pakistan, Albania, North Korea, North Vietnam, and several sub-Sahara states.

Meanwhile, several heretofore essentially dependent states in the Middle East have become significant retransferrers of arms, as their own inventories have progressively been upgraded. Israel and Egypt have supplied countries in Africa, while even Jordan has transferred tanks and surface-to-air missiles to South Africa. Secondary retransfers among dependent nations are growing rapidly, and presumably will grow further, particularly given the vast arsenals now being built up in the Middle East that are subject to rapid obsolescence

Still, the arms markets remain relatively oligopolistic; and with the advent of newer technological developments, they may narrow further in some areas, as new supplier aspirants may not be able to keep pace with the research and development efforts of the United States and USSR in supplying the new "electronic battlefield." Nevertheless, the existence of a finite but significant number of suppliers in most weapons categories renders control efforts difficult, on a qualitative if not a quantitative basis. Almost all dependent nations, with the exception of a few with low leverage (usually right-wing regimes out of favor with the Third World) are able to shift purchases elsewhere, assuming cash is available, if dissatisfied with or cut off from an existing source of supply. The history of the subject scarcely lends itself to optimism about present efforts to achieve supplier agreements on controls.

As previously indicated, the patterns of global arms sales were earlier determined by the bipolar and ideological nature of the international system, with most dependent nations then tied to either

of the superpowers by tight client relationships, often backed up by
military training and security commitments, with or without formal
alliances. Until the 1960s, only a few of the Third World nations
were able to play off both sides, rarely simultaneously but, rather,
in time segments indicating subtle back-and-forth changes of bloc
allegiances. India, Indonesia, Morocco, Yugoslavia, Finland, and
Austria were, until fairly recently, about the only nations in the
world receiving simultaneous arms shipments from the East and the
West.

Now, with the decline of bipolar ideological global alignments,
an array of nations has moved into cross-bloc arms acquisitions.
Among these are Libya, Egypt, Iraq, Syria, North Yemen, Pakistan,
Sri Lanka, Burma, Uruguay, Peru, Nigeria, Zaire, and a host of
smaller nations, particularly in Africa, in addition to those mentioned earlier. In the Middle East, recent events in Libya, Egypt,
Jordan, and Iran have well illustrated this pattern, so crucial to the
controls question. Libya, until recently primarily a French client,
has turned to the USSR for massive equipment purchases, in apparent exchange for basing rights and a nuclear reactor sale, while
still maintaining its Western options. Egypt, still primarily reliant
on the Soviets, has entered into a massive arms deal with France
while beginning to build an indigenous arms production base by
licensing additional systems from Great Britain, most notably aircraft and helicopters. Iran earlier threatened the United States with
some small purchases of armored personnel carriers and other
equipment from the USSR, indicating its potential flexibility and
hence insuring a vastly increased flow of arms from all of the Western powers. Jordan, temporarily thwarted by the U.S. Congress in
its efforts to obtain advanced surface-to-air missiles, immediately
threatened to turn to the USSR for equivalent equipment, hence putting more pressure on the United States to forestall such a turn by
keeping its pipeline open. Pakistan, once a formal member of the
U.S.-led alliance system, had earlier been forced to turn to China
when embargoed by the United States after the 1965 war with India.
The result of all of this activity has been a buyer's market in most
cases, the futility of almost all efforts at controls, and an increasing tendency, even for the United States, toward preemptive selling,
under the assumption that "if we don't sell them, someone else will."

Maintenance of an existing supplier relationship at least keeps
one's hand on the pipeline for spare parts and follow-on sales, allowing the seller some leverage in crisis or conflict situations. Ironically, though, multipolarization and the deemphasis of ideological
ties have led to less control and influence over arms supplies by the
superpowers, have shifted the leverage to most recipients, and perhaps have exacerbated a number of regional and dyadic cockpits of

contention. There are now very few "unthinkable" arms supplier relationships, as recently highlighted by impending French sales of Mirage jets to China.

On a broad regional basis, there have been some important shifts in recent years, reflecting the trends mentioned earlier. There has been a marked erosion of U.S. supplier market shares in Latin America, once almost a monopoly, with Western European sales making inroads in most areas, the Soviets in Peru and Uruguay, and even Israel in several countries with STOL transports and ship-to-ship missiles. The Middle East has become a complicated free-for-all supplier competition, with little of it now predictable on an ideological basis. Soviet dominance in Egypt and Iraq has been eroded by European sales, while the Soviets in turn have replaced France as the major supplier to Libya and now threaten to move into Jordan to replace U.S. and British influence. The United States, meanwhile, is moving into North Yemen and continues to make vast sales in Saudi Arabia, Iran, and Kuwait, formerly a British client. More and more, arms sales in the Middle East have become tied to economic deals in other areas, to government-to-government oil agreements, investment commitments, and nuclear reactor sales. The exception is in Israel, with its precarious, virtually sole dependence upon American arms.

Also on a regional basis, it is noteworthy that until recently, American arms firms had gradually been pushed out of their traditional role as purveyors of licensed equipment by burgeoning Western European codevelopment schemes within the NATO area. There was a political as well as an economic component to this trend, with the Europeans striving to free themselves from onerous American restrictions on retransfer of arms elsewhere. The recent winning, however, of the "arms deal of the century" by General Dynamics for the YF-16 fighter may represent a reversal, indicating the limits of European willingness to adhere to French policies, which thrust toward regional hegemony under cover of the embryonic European union.

Amid an overall buyer's market, there is a small but identifiable group of nations that, because of their diplomatic isolation or absence of leverage relative to regional adversaries, consistently have had difficulties in acquiring arms. These nations--Israel and South Africa most notably, but also Pakistan--have all been on the receiving end of quasi-international, multilateral, or unilateral embargoes, explicitly or indirectly enforced.

The cases differ according to the residual leverage held by the pariahs. Israel is now virtually unable to receive any significant volume of arms from any source other than the United States. South Africa has had a similar dependence upon France, perhaps now weakened by a recently announced partial French embargo, though it has

also bought Belgian, Italian, and Israeli arms. Pakistan, until recently embargoed by the United States and Great Britain for major
items of equipment, has been somewhat able to rely on China,
France, and West Germany.

In each of these cases, powerful adversaries have been able to
achieve not only leverage for obtaining their own arms, but also that
for denying them to pariahs. One important corollary effect here,
however, at least in the cases of Israel and South Africa, is a thrust
toward independent arms development and production in the face of
possibilities for further cut-offs from remaining suppliers. The embargoed then become new factors in the supplier markets, often trading arms with each other. Further, the pariah nations as a group
now threaten to crack open the heretofore somewhat stabilized nuclear
proliferation situation. Each fears the consequences of overwhelming
conventional weapons inferiority, and their insecurities breed the desire for an equalizer. For U.S. policy, with each of these situations
containing serious political trade-offs with respect to rivals of the
pariahs, some very serious dilemmas have been created, in which
little if any succor can be expected from NATO allies.

Israel and South Africa are not, however, alone among the
smaller or middle-range powers now striving for increased independence in conventional arms development and production. India in
particular, but also Brazil, Argentina, Iran, Saudi Arabia, Egypt,
Turkey, Taiwan, South Korea, and North Korea, among others, are
all moving along the route that leads from license production of major
weapons systems through increased manufacturing capability, to actual development of indigenous arms. Israel, under great pressure,
has gone the furthest, at least in a qualitative sense, now building
its own jet aircraft--albeit with U.S. engines--and its own tanks with
American transmissions, plus a range of missiles and other equipment. Among the Third World nations, India probably has gone the
furthest in the range of foreign systems built on license, including
Soviet MIG-21s, British tanks and aircraft, and French helicopters.

With the present pace of technological development, however,
it remains to be seen whether there will be a long-term trend toward
more of nations' achieving substantial degrees of indepedence in arms
manufacture. As the 1973 war so well demonstrated for Israel, independence also involves the volume of production achievable.

As pointed out in the massive literature commenting upon the
lessons of the 1973 war, vast changes in the nature of conventional
warfare have been heralded, the impact of which upon the future of
the international arms trade is not yet clear. There is perhaps a
parallel here with the Spanish Civil War of the mid-1930s, which
demonstrated the efficacy of combined armor and tactical airpower
techniques, presaging the early Blitzkriegs of World War II.

With specific application to the trade in arms, one can specu-
late at several levels. To begin with, mere measurement and monitoring of the trade will be rendered more difficult. Whereas up to
now, the usually easily verified movements of aircraft, armored
equipment, and ships allowed for easy observation, by both public
and private entities, the contemporary transnational movement of
complex radars, stand-off missiles, electronic gear, computers,
and laser-guided weapons will be harder to follow. For the layman--
but also for those relatively well versed in the subject--reading contemporary military journals is now a painful trip into the arcane.

One major result is a newer emphasis on the qualitative aspects of the arms trade, as aircraft, tanks, and ships have become
mere launching platforms for expensive and deadly new missiles. In
a period of rapidly changing technology, the efficacy of the launching
platform becomes extremely dependent upon its electronic accesso-
ries. As indicated in the 1973 war, for instance, a modern jet strike
aircraft is next to useless without them, and regional balances will
come increasingly to depend on a fine tuning of the level of sophistication of electronic and other equipment.

Serious policy problems are raised here for the United States
and other arms suppliers, not the least of which concerns the extent
to which they will be willing to part with new weapons secrets hot off
the drawing boards, in an era when the level of modernity of weapons
being transferred seems constantly to be escalating. The Soviets, of
late, have begun to transfer equipment to the Middle East even before
similarly equipping Warsaw Pact forces. Iran has ordered a startling
proportion of new U.S. F-14 fighters and British Chieftain tanks, and
Israel is requesting the most modern U.S. electronic warfare gear.

It is not yet clear how these developments will affect the levels
of oligopoly in the supplier markets and, hence, the prospects for
controls. So far, the United States appears to have a considerable
qualitative lead in many areas of modern weaponry, with some exceptions, such as tactical surface-to-air missiles. However, it is
noteworthy that European manufacturers are also more or less keeping pace, particularly in surface-to-air missiles (French Crotale and
British Rapier), in anti-tank missiles (the codeveloped Roland and
HOT missiles, British Swingfire), and in air-to-air missiles (particularly the French Matra Magic).

These newer developments also appear to have created broader
changes in the very nature of warfare, pointing to an impending reversal of the advantage held by offensive over defensive tactics for
the past half century, with some analysts predicting that in the near
future, conflicts will be wars of attrition reminiscent of World War
I--materialschlacten, to use Lagueno's term.[1] Also, the 1973 war
seems to have demonstrated some new economic considerations to

warfare, particularly the extent to which relatively inexpensive "one-shot, one-kill" weapons were able to knock out far more expensive systems at an impressive rate.

Some analysts have further predicted a newer era where the advantage may well pass to those able to field mass infantries armed with newer missiles. If so, one can point to several possible impacts on the arms trade: more intense, qualitatively based arms races among dependent clients; the need for much greater volumes of weapons to anticipate wars of attrition; and the need for massive resupply if wars occur. Overall, there is the potential for still further surprise in a rapidly changing military-technological environment.

Meanwhile, the interface between American arms sales and nuclear proliferation policies appears to be becoming one of growing urgency. Though in some cases the impetus for acquiring nuclear arms may hinge primarily upon prestige and the striving for great-power status in the wake of the long colonial era, the bulk of the most likely proliferation candidates are those threatened by the ebbing of American power and credibility relative to the USSR in the aftermath of Vietnam. Here too, there is the related question of America's defense production base, only recently found insufficient even to supply Israel for three weeks of war without drawing down the inventories of front-line units in Europe. The contrast with the Soviet production base, particularly in armor and aircraft, is striking, as indicated by the latter's ability simultaneously to supply the Arabs, North Korea, North Vietnam, India, and others, as well as itself and Eastern Europe.

A related problem for U.S. arms supply policy is that of controlling the transfer of potential nuclear delivery systems, often where systems can alternatively be used for conventional or nuclear delivery. The imbroglio over sales of Pershing missiles to Israel may be a hint of things to come.

ALTERNATIVE STRATEGIES

In formulating arms transfer policies, American decision-makers must take into account a number of actors, both external and internal. Concerning the former, a neat two-way categorization can initially be made between suppliers and recipients, with some further subcategorization possible. Internally, a major fault line can be delineated between those forces in favor of a permissive arms trading policy, and those putting heavier weight on efforts both at unilateral and international controls. This latter line of cleavage can be portrayed as a question of ideological perspective within both Congress and the Executive.

We have previously described the competitive nature of the contemporary arms trade rendering controls, collaboration or cartelization very difficult in theory, and almost nonexistent in practice. Further, present world economic conditions in possibly other raw materials cartels militate against any immediate hope for increased controls with the increasingly competitive arms market.

Yet, as pointed out in a major volume on the arms trade by the Stockholm International Peace Research Institute (SIPRI), supplier behavior is still not to be described as altogether monolithic, though there is perhaps a trend toward convergence. The SIPRI group has devised a somewhat primitive typology to differentiate supplier behavior, utilizing three identifiable supplier types: hegemonic, commercial, and restrictive.[2] Hegemonic behavior, with the USSR considered closest to an ideal type, is defined in terms of primary emphasis in arms selling on extending political influence, sometimes at an economic "cost." Political leverage, bases, trade, alliances, and U.N. votes might be seen variously as returns for arms trading relationships. The commercial policy represented in the recent past most clearly by Britain and France, is one in which the primary focus is economic, variously to achieve increased exports for balance-of-payments purposes, favorable consideration in raw materials barter arrangements, or tie-ins with other commercial arrangements (for instance, with nuclear reactor sales). A secondary purpose is to achieve economies of scale for one's own arms industries, pay off research and development costs, and perhaps also achieve greater independence for one's own arms-selling efforts by getting out from under the end-use restrictions attached to license production. Finally, a restrictive policy, one normally thought to describe Sweden and Switzerland, refers to a rather controlled strategy on selling arms only in special situations, where relative assurance exists that the arms will not be used in conflict.

Needless to say, in dealing with such ideal types it is difficult to fit any nation's policy at any given point so easily into this Procrustean bed. Some nations can perhaps be described as exhibiting amalgams of these behavior types (France, for instance, would appear to be pursuing a mixed commercial-hegemonic policy), while in some cases one can discern at least subtle alterations from time to time. American policy in recent years has appeared to vacillate among all three points of the triangle.

One other division of those on the supplier side may be useful; it utilizes the hoary distinction between status quo and revisionist powers and their associated behavior. It is a distinction useful in analyzing arms supplier market behavior in historical focus. In the interwar period, while the Western powers did not go all-out in utilizing arms transfers as an instrument of diplomacy, the Axis

powers gradually made inroads in previous Western arms client relationships all over the world. Likewise, since 1945 it has been
easy to discern a long-term secular trend in which first the Soviets,
and then the French, have edged into arms markets previously dominated by the United States and Great Britain.

If one were to generalize here on an admittedly very complex
matter, one might perhaps point out that revisionist powers, bent on
upsetting the prevailing world order or balance of power, are not
normally reluctant to use arms sales as a device for stirring up
trouble. It is the status quo power that has the most interest in controls, in stabilizing existing relationships. For this reason, as well
as those deriving from the very structure of the supplier markets,
U.S. efforts at control have, up to now, often appeared as little more
than idealistic exercises in futility.

Overall, however, with the breakdown of the postwar blocs,
supplier behavior is mostly explicable as a commercial and political
competition between supplier entities acting independently and with
only marginally different motives and methods.

It is not easy to categorize dependent nations in terms of differential perspectives on arms acquisitions. Basically, they can
usually be said to resist general efforts at controls, while seeking
in a more specific way to have arms denied to adversaries. Beyond
that, some narrow distinctions can be made between nations, depending upon whether their strivings for arms are based primarily on
security or military rationales or, rather, are primarily for prestige or status. At least until recently, the relatively subdued arms
races in Latin America were habitually described as status-oriented,
with little prospect for actual conflict. In other areas, particularly
the Middle East, Far East, and South Asia, it was easier to describe
recipient behavior as maximizing defense capability to prepare for
conflict.

Hence, it is not surprising that in Latin America alone, some
tentative efforts to achieve controls, initiated by the region's nations
themselves, have been made. At present, there are purportedly
serious negotiations, following the recent Ayachuco accords, on limiting acquisitions of sophisticated offensive weapons in the area--
initiated by Peru in the wake of its heavy arms purchases from the
USSR under President Velasco. It is too early to tell whether this
initiative will result in the first serious regional effort to control the
inflow of arms. Elsewhere, in regions where conflict has been endemic and remains imminent, such regional arrangements would appear to be out of the question.

As noted, U.S. domestic conflict over arms transfer policies
can basically be perceived as existing on two separate but overlapping
levels: a growing rift between Congress and the Executive and, over-

all, a split along partisan and ideological lines. In addition, there are important differences in perspective, not very visible to the outside observer, between various institutional elements in the decision-making strata of the federal bureaucracy.

Most important is the growing struggle between the two branches over arms sales. Actually this is just one element of a growing battle over the control of foreign policy that has been building since the Vietnam conflict. Some observers, moreover, pointing to the serious impasses over arms sales to Turkey and Jordan, have claimed that the battle over the control of arms sales policies has become the single most serious foreign policy problem faced by the Ford administration. It is a conflict that extends across the issues of the War Powers Act, foreign aid and military spending, the sale of nuclear equipment and materials, intelligence operations, and foreign intervention in general.

The basis of the Congressional onslaught against present arms sales policies can be described on three levels: the introduction of new legislation emerging from recent hearings that, if passed, would seriously hamper the independence of Executive decision-making; votes on specific issues, such as on sales to Jordan, Turkey, and Israel; and a crescendo of public utterances, including some novel proposals, that increasingly have brought the issue into the limelight.

Until recently, the Executive branch was able to act virtually without the hindrance of tight legal restrictions in the arms selling area, though somewhat constrained by pro forma legislative resolutions setting up a conceptual underpinning for control efforts. This was the case anyway for outright cash sales. Military grant aid and credit sales have had to pass through the appropriations process. Earlier, Congress had put an end to the role of the Eximbank in financing arms sales. Otherwise, the Congress merely monitored cash arms sales post hoc, occasionally prodding the administration, as with the Jackson Amendments to the Defense Procurement Authorization Acts, giving the President authority to transfer military equipment to Israel.

With America having expanded its role as arms seller, Congress in 1974 passed the Nelson Arms Sales Amendment, now perceived as perhaps a prelude to tight legislative controls. Under the Nelson Amendment, which was enacted with little opposition, the President was required to give notice of "all letters of offer to sell any defense articles or services" in excess of $25 million. Congress was then to have twenty calendar days for both houses to disapprove a proposed sale.

By mid-1975, amid new hearings before the Humphrey subcommittee of the Senate Foreign Relations Committee, it was apparent that some Senators were not satisfied by the impact of the Nelson

Amendment in curbing Executive discretion on arms sales. There were problems about access to classified data. Some members complained that the twenty calendar days did not provide enough time to react amid the press of daily business. Then, the $25 million minimum allowed, at least hypothetically, for circumvention by a series of sales in smaller amounts. Generally, it was reported that Congress had made few inquiries about specific arms deals. There had been no attempts to veto transfers--that is, up to the point of the Turkey and Jordan imbroglios.

Disappointed at the impact of the Nelson Amendment, still newer legislation was being proposed by mid-1975. Senator Edward Kennedy proposed banning all arms sales to the Persian Gulf area for six months, pending a comprehensive policy review, in the light of massive sales to Iran, Saudi Arabia, and Kuwait. Representative Les Aspin, a leading critic of the military, introduced a bill requiring Congressional approval of sales on a country-by-country basis, amounting virtually to placing arms sales decisions on a par with appropriations. If passed, future decisions would be forced into the limelight, with all that might entail for serious controversies.

Though it appeared that both the Kennedy and Aspin proposals would have rough sledding in Congress because of their drastic implications, more attention was being paid to newer amendments by Senator Gaylord Nelson, aimed at tightening Congressional controls intended in his original legislation.

One new amendment would require the President to submit to Congress any arms sales causing the total amount to a given country to exceed $50 million in a given year. This would replace the present requirement specifying a $25 million limit for an individual arms deal. This would close one obvious loophole.

Still another amendment would lengthen the Congressional review period for arms sales from the present twenty calendar days to thirty working days. The amendment would also authorize a member to move to discharge a resolution of disapproval if the committee considering it has not reported it out after ten calendar days. Altogether, the proposed legislation would give Congress more time to react, and make more difficult the possibility of administration allies in Congress bottling up articles of disapproval in committee.

Perhaps the most important aspect of the new proposed legislation, however, and a variant of Congressman Aspin's proposal, is one that would require the President to submit to Congress an annual report containing a forecast of the dollar amounts of foreign military sales proposed to be made to each country during the next fiscal year, including the types and numbers of major weapons systems, and major defense services to be transferred. Further, Congress would be charged with authorizing a maximum amount of sales for each country involved but would be free, after setting a dollar ceiling, to allow the President some flexibility in exceeding this amount. Still another proposal would require the Executive to report on the impact of sales upon the readiness of U.S. forces. The ideological and partisan basis of the proposed legislation could be gauged by noting its cosponsorship: Senators George McGovern, Mark Hatfield, P. J. Leahy, Adlai Stevenson, Edward Kennedy, W. D. Hathaway, Harrison Williams, Quentin Burdick, Walter Mondale, F. K. Haskell, Philip Hart, Alan Cranston, and Mike Gravel.

While considering the new legislation, in the midst of wide-ranging hearings on arms trade matters, both in the Humphrey subcommittee and in its House equivalent under Representative Lee Hamilton, Congress voted down proposed arms sales to Turkey and Jordan. Both cases created major furors, with some dissenters accusing supporters of sabotaging important elements of the nation's foreign policy. The Turkish issue raised serious questions about the impact of ethnic politics upon the nation's conduct of foreign policy, and between those seeking a "principled" foreign policy and others more willing to be flexible on behalf of the national interest. In the aftermath, even some supporters of the Turkish embargo confessed they had perhaps gone too far when it became clear that American basing and intelligence capabilities were being seriously damaged, and that the impact of Congressional action was being vitiated by French and German arms sales to Turkey.

In the Jordan case, threats by King Hussein to turn to the USSR and the concurrent drawing together of the Jordanian and Syrian militaries, demonstrated anew the pitfalls of unilateral embargoes where other willing suppliers were waiting anxiously in the wings. Congress here was perceived by some as acting irrationally on behalf of Israeli interests, under the cover of arms control and morality.

With a bit of caution appearing in the aftermath of the Jordanian and Turkish cases, it remained to be seen whether Congress would oppose proposed arms sales in still other cases, and whether the anticipation of such blockages might introduce a newer degree of caution into administration moves in this area.

During the period 1974-75, the press was full of declaratory statements on arms trade matters, many more than a little reminiscent of the days of the Nye hearings. Altogether, these statements formed the context for the Nelson Amendments, the Jordan and Turkey arms blockages, and the Congressional hearings. Picked up almost daily by the press, the impression was rendered of a serious move toward controls in this area, political and economic trade-offs to the contrary.

Senator Nelson was quoted as saying that "the hope is to put ourselves into a moral position to argue against world arms sales."

Asked whether this would simply divert the business to other arms suppliers, he answered, "At least we shouldn't lead the world in arms sales. We should cut back to the level of the Soviet Union."[3] In a related area, Senator Nelson averred that "recent revelations that Northrop and other big arms dealers have engaged in systematic bribery of foreign officials in order to peddle their wares is shocking evidence that sales decisions are based not so much on careful rational considerations of U.S. national interest or allied defense needs, but rather on bribery and corruption, pure and simple."[4]

Still others were vocally active in Congress. Senator William Proxmire, a leader with Nelson in the attack against arms sellers, called for a reduction, charging that such armaments are often used "to prop up dictatorships" and end up "encouraging regional arms races which often break out in open warfare." He rejected the argument that others will sell the equipment if America does not, stating that this country "hands out more military aid than the rest of the world combined . . . every year, we supply more than 50% of the world's total military exports."[5] Proxmire also charged that the arms sales deprive smaller nations of the critical resources needed for self-development; are often used for domestic repression; are a drain on critical and scarce commodities here at home; and are, in fact, subsidized by the American taxpayers by granting favorable financing terms or price. Further toward the center of the political spectrum, Senator Hubert Humphrey echoed approximately the same theme, concentrating on the issue of Congressional controls, while Representative Aspin was perhaps the leading voice requesting a drastic cutback in the American sales effort. Throughout it all, there was the irony of procontrols Senators and Congressmen continuing to support large-scale military aid and sales to Israel, often overriding an administration striving to assert a more "even-handed" policy in the Middle East.

A further irony emerged, with Senator Humphrey and others calling for a reduction of the government's role in arms sales, seemingly advocating a return to the more laissez-faire approach that had been assailed in the 1930s. Such a change was seconded by some administration spokesmen, apparently eager to remove some of the onus of decisions on arms trading from the bureaucracy, thus allowing a lower profile behind the facade of allegedly pure commercial dealings.

Because of the sensitive nature of the issue, there were few voices in Congress and elsewhere willing to match the fervor of procontrols Congressmen in defending administration arms sales policies. No one, it appeared, wished to be tarred as an advocate of an American "merchants of death" role, though there were many dissenting voices on Jordan and Turkey, on the ground of overriding

national interest. For the most part, rebuttals to Congressional
liberals in the hearings came from Pentagon and State Department
officials in charge of arms sales policies. They agreed on the need
for restraints, spoke defensively, but also presented in muted tones
the traditional rationales of security commitments, bases, credibility in foreign policy, balance of payments, domestic jobs, and, of
course, the futility of controls in the absence of multilateral supplier agreements.

During the hearings, a somewhat forceful statement was made
by Thomas Stern, Deputy Director of the State Department's Bureau
of Political-Military Affairs, who took issue with those who think
that U.S. foreign military sales "are intrinsically destabilizing and
eventually lead to conflict." In contrast, Stern suggested that an
arms balance in areas of tension has, in most cases, inhibited the
occurrence of conflict. Further, he suggested that "a good case can
and should be made that the risk of wars is increased in situations
where a power imbalance exists."[6] At bottom, what was involved
was the classic debate between the balance of power and the utopian-
normative approaches to the conduct of foreign policy.

Not to be underestimated in an analysis of domestic conflict in
arms transfer decision-making is the "closed politics" of the several
national security bureaucracies, with their horizontal and vertical
bargaining patterns. There are dimly discernible bureaucratic perspectives, somewhat predictable on the basis of organizational roles
or missions. As with Congress, here too, one must often disaggre-
gate perspectives at the levels of overall policies or doctrines and
of stands on arms trading with given nations.

Contrary to assumptions widely held by the press and the public, the Pentagon is not now considered to be the key actor in arms
trading decision-making. Rather, the balance of bureaucratic power
is thought to have shifted markedly to the State Department since the
departure of former arms supersalesman Henry Kuss from the Pentagon. Partly this has been a result of Congressional pressures
leading to a shift of decision-making domain and partly a function of
the shift in power associated with Kissinger's move to the State Department. The Defense Department, while still a key factor in inter-
departmental committees dealing with this subject, is now considered more an implementor than a formulator or coordinator of policy in this area. The final word has been with Kissinger, who has a
veto on all arms sales not formally matched by the Secretary of
Defense.

Below the level of the National Security Council and the Secretary of State on the decision-making pyramid for arms transfers,
is the Office of the Undersecretary of State for Security Assistance.
Indirectly under this office, and the ultimate hub of decision

formulation on this subject, is the crucial Bureau of Political-Military Affairs in the State Department. In turn, under its wing the Offices of Security Assistance and Sales and of Munitions Control are at the center of the action. At the Pentagon, there are important inputs from the Joint Chiefs of Staff, the Office of International Security Affairs, and, specifically in the arms sales area, from the Pentagon's Defense Security Assistance Agency. These Pentagon organizations implement arms sales, deal with defense contractors and customers, and act as conduits for information and advocacy stemming from overseas military assistance groups and military attaches.

Little, if anything, is publicly known about specific bureaucratic conflicts over arms sales doctrine of policies among these organizations. For the Middle East, there was formerly a widely held assumption about the State Department's pro-Arab bias, thought to have been somewhat countered by the military's traditionally close ties with the Israelis. Again, little of this is public, and it may be that the differences in perspective have been merely those of nuance. It is interesting to note that in testimony in 1975 before the Senate Foreign Relations Committee concerning arms sales policies, representatives from the Departments of Defense and State presented rather congruent views, defending a pragmatic and somewhat permissive arms sales doctrine on the traditional basis of national interest and security commitments. There are some indications, moreover, that the Pentagon has been disproportionately upset by the drawing down of U.S. military stocks in Europe and elsewhere by heavy shipments to Israel, as well as by the sophisticated level of arms transfers to the Middle East.

It further remains to be seen whether a future change of administration or conflicts created by events will bring bureaucratic infighting into the open in this area, as it has been brought out on SALT and the strategic balance, and over nuclear proliferation and commercial nuclear reactor sales. The election of a liberal Democratic President, and the accompanying installation of a like-minded Secretary of State, would at least have the potential for opening overt conflict between the State and Defense Departments in this area to an extent not evidenced during the recent Republican administrations.

As an addendum to a discussion of the internal governmental actors fighting over arms sales policies, a few words are warranted about the nongovernmental milieu, as constituted by interest groups and public opinion. Mostly, the positions of key nongovernmental actors are almost too obvious to require extensive discussion; in most respects, interest group behavior with respect to arms trade policies has been altogether pro forma. What is perhaps more important is a discerning of their real impact, and whether this might be predicted to change as the issues themselves--and the balance of governmental power--alter.

Probably the most significant interest group behavior on this issue has not come from associational interest groups, forced to operate almost sub rosa, but from ethnic groups, with their extensive influence deriving from the pressure of potential votes. Jewish voting potential, real or imagined, has up to now kept some arms flowing to Israel, though not without interruptions, as in the Ford administration's Middle Eastern "reassessment." Pressures from the Greek-American community, channeled into Congress by a handful of supporters, have been instrumental in the formulation of American policy toward Turkish arms acquisitions in the wake of the Cyprus conflict. Likewise, the latent power of the black vote has ensured America's remaining clear of a potentially lucrative arms market in South Africa and adhering to the UN-sponsored embargo. More and more in the future, Congressional behavior on this issue may come to be explicable in terms of ethnic log-rolling, with key groups trading off votes to ensure compliance with their own arms trading policy preferences. It is noteworthy that pro-Israeli Congressmen, as a bloc, voted against continued arms sales to Turkey, despite the possible injurious effect of such a policy on Israel, no doubt fearing the consequences of a backlash vote on Israeli arms requests by those members more concerned with Cyprus.

Further removed from the center of decision-making in Washington is the role of public opinion on arms trading. It has often been pointed out, backed by numerous studies, that public knowledge on most foreign policy issues is quite low, far lower than with domestic issues, at least until overseas events are made very dramatic, as in the later stages of the Vietnam War. Further, it has been indicated that mood shifts from isolationism to interventionism (introverted and extroverted phases of foreign policy), or vice versa, often originate with key elites, followed (with a time lag) by public opinion. Thus it is not surprising that by the mid-1970s, with some liberal Congressmen beginning to back off from the extremes of the post-Vietnam mood of pacifism and isolationism, that public opinion, as reflected in the polls, seemed to remain essentially isolationist, if only in a confused and nebulous way. The few polls that tapped attitudes on military aid issues demonstrated surprisingly shallow support for arms transfers of any sort, even to allies--no doubt reflecting fears of possible subsequent military involvement.

Because of the low salience and the complexity of this issue, which places it well outside the cognitive map of most of the public, the administration has felt free to pursue a relatively aggressive arms trading effort in defiance of the subdued public mood. Whether

a continuation of this mood would serve to constrain arms sales is
not entirely clear, just as it is hard to say whether these matters,
aside from the specifics of the Middle Eastern and Greco-Turkish
situations, could become significant campaign issues. On the basis
of past experience, it would appear unlikely. Such matters more
probably will remain merely a shadowy subset of broader foreign
policy questions in the public's perspective, leaving policy-makers
a wide range of discretion on specific issues.

URGENCY OF THE ISSUE

It is difficult to judge the extent to which arms trading issues
ought to be perceived as an urgent matter for a new administration
or for an extension of the present one. Degrees of urgency could be
perceived on different aspects of these issues, depending upon one's
point of view. Perhaps the most cogent arguments for urgency could
be made with respect to dyadic or regional sales issues. In these
cases crises could erupt as a result of American arms sales policies,
and the outcomes could be vitally affected by American decisions on
arms resupply.

On an overall basis, many liberals see some urgency in curbing the size of American arms sales, perceived as potentially destabilizing and exacerbating of existing tensions. The theme of economic development and misallocation of resources is now perceived
as less important or urgent, as it is recognized that the bulk of
American arms sales are now going to the currency-bloated OPEC
states. Fears about American involvement are part of a sense of
urgency in some areas--for instance, Korea and the Middle East.
Finally, there is some feeling of urgency by some about the increasingly asymmetric arms acquisitions by the Arabs relative to Israel--
which in conjunction with the Middle Eastern "reassessment" is seen
by some as increasing the chances for another war.

On the other side, conservatives--self-professed pragmatists
on the arms trade issue--see some urgency to the extent that moralistically inspired American control policies seem gradually but crucially to be whittling away at the American security commitment system. Perceiving the cutoff of arms to Turkey as against the national
interest, they fear that further such actions will erode the nation's
overseas position. Anti-control forces also see as urgent the maintenance of American credibility as an arms supplier, fearing that
lost markets will irretrievably be taken over by others, with ramifications stretching across alliance ties, balance of payments, and
political influence in general.

There is the underlying theme, previously muted but now growing, of the connection between U.S. arms sales policies and nuclear proliferation. Ironically, it is Congressional liberals who voice the most concern about proliferation in regard to conventional arms sales, though they are not alone. The concerns of conservatives in this area tend to be balanced by worries parallel to those regarding conventional arms: commercial implications in an area where unilateral restraint is habitually frustrated by the activities of competitors.

Most of all, however, a new administration, particularly if it is a continuation of the present one, will experience urgency in dealing with Congress. It will have to find a way of allowing Congress a real voice in arms trading matters while maintaining a semblance of coherence in its relations with the rest of the world. In recent years, that has not been an easy matter, leading many increasingly to question the future viability of a foreign policy conducted on the basis of bargaining between two branches of government, when the two are at loggerheads over the very basics of foreign policy issues.

CONCLUSION

Looking forward to 1977 and beyond, various options on arms trading policies may be set forth, both on the level of overall doctrine and with respect to specific countries or areas. We shall briefly set out the options at the general level of policy, while indicating in the interstices some dilemmas presented for specific cases. We shall deliberately present the options somewhat at the extremes of what is foreseeable to illustrate the issues more vividly, simultaneously recognizing the incremental nature of the foreign-policy decision-making process that tends to maintain policies in a state of drift from the past, barring shocking and altogether destabilizing events. From left to right, from isolationist to interventionist, from moralistic to amoralistic, the major lines of the options would appear as described below.

Option 1

This is a liberal-moralist-isolationist perspective.

The United States must cut back as drastically as possible from the present $9 billion a year level of American arms sales, with cuts primarily in areas where there is a likelihood of arms sales, in connection with military training assistance, resupply during conflicts, and the prestige of American arms, leading to actual

involvement by American forces; massive past American arms sales
have allegedly created dangerous instabilities, as in the Persian
Gulf; and American arms sales can be construed as contradicting
the nation's pretensions to moral leadership in propping up repressive, authoritarian regimes, usually defined as right-wing military
governments such as those now in power in South Korea, Brazil,
and Chile.

Pros

The United States can attempt spearheading of worldwide efforts at controls, having set an example by unilaterally restraining
its own arms shipments. A corollary is the hope for convening international and regional diplomatic efforts to achieving such controls, at the Committee for the Conference on Disarmament in
Geneva, or in various regional settings--for instance, in Latin
America.

The probability of American involvement in actual conflict--
in Korea, Southeast Asia, the Middle East, Latin America--is reduced, assuming the nexus between arms sales and eventual military involvement, as was alleged in the Vietnam example.

The proportion of the American economy involved in defense
production is lowered and, it is assumed, results in a reallocation
of domestic resources to social services, urban rehabilitation, and
such.

Insofar as arms sales policy conflicts now exacerbate ethnic
political conflicts within the U.S. polity, and insofar as these policies could otherwise be formulated on a coherent and consistent
basis, this issue is removed somewhat from the political arena.

The possibilities decrease for corruption in this area, considered to have a baneful impact upon the body politic, already rent by
Watergate and much else.

The bulk of U.S. defense production can be utilized by U.S.
forces; hence, this option lends itself to a strong, self-sufficient
military posture, albeit somewhat isolationist.

Insofar as many U.S. arms recipients are alleged to be repressive, right-wing military regimes, this option removes the onus
from the United States of propping up such political structures, and
hence perhaps allows for the betterment of the U.S. image in the
eyes of the now hostile Third World, with possible practical implications in the economic sphere.

Cons

Depending upon how far U.S. arms sales efforts are reduced,
a rather large dent in the nation's overall exports picture is created.

Though the present $9 billion in arms exports is relatively small in proportion to overall exports of well over $100 billion, several billion dollars less in arms exports could exacerbate a now precarious balance-of-payments situation under pressure from staggering and growing oil imports requirements, relieved somewhat by massive agricultural shipments to the Soviet bloc. In addition, there would be the loss of a proportion of an estimated 350,000 jobs related to arms exports sales, in a period of already high unemployment (every $1 billion in arms sales is considered to create about 47,000 jobs in American industry).

America's defense production base will be lowered, as research and development costs will not, to the extent now possible, be paid off in part by export sales. This may result in higher marginal costs for equipping U.S. forces.

There may be a serious erosion in the credibility of U.S. defense commitments, jeopardizing the security of some U.S. allies. Reactions may include, for some nations, diplomatic movement toward rivals or "neutralization." There may be costs in U.S. defense capability vis-a-vis the USSR in terms of basing rights, overflight privileges, communications, intelligence-gathering capabilities, and, in some cases, access to raw materials. These benefits will almost automatically pass to newer suppliers.

In cases such as Israel, South Korea, Taiwan, Pakistan, and perhaps Turkey, where loss of optimism about acquiring U.S. arms is matched by the uncertainty of other sources, and where serious conventional imbalances threaten national security, an inevitable further impetus toward the development of nuclear options will be created. If the United States, given its stringent views on proliferation, withdraws still further from commitments, the probability of the actual use of nuclear weapons may well become more serious.

Insofar as there is no agreement by other suppliers to match U.S. control efforts, there are merely shifts of supplier sources elsewhere, mostly to Western European nations, allowing them balance-of-payments and raw materials access advantages and diplomatic influence. Also, further impetus to indigenous development of arms will be created, thereby reducing U.S. leverage in some cases and, incidentally, exacerbating control problems, in that additional centers of arms supply are thereby created. Israel and South Africa have already begun to serve as models for this syndrome.

U.S. leverage in crisis situations, heretofore obtaining where the United States has had a hand on the spare-parts pipelines, has been removed. This may allow the United States to control outcomes and to foreshorten conflicts, as with the 1973 war and in the earlier conflict between Honduras and El Salvador.

Option 2

This is an all-out, commercially oriented policy, selling virtually to all comers, perhaps with occasional exceptions made where moral, economic, or political reasons for abstaining from arms supplying are overriding.

Pros

The United States can compete fully and unhindered for export sales, utilizing its advantages as a producer of high-quality, advanced-technology arms and as a provider of first-rate training and maintenance. If pushed to extremes, this could allow for a great increase in the present level of arms sales, perhaps altogether ameliorating the present U.S. payments problems. Such a policy would create hundreds of thousands of extra jobs and allow for a substantial buildup of the U.S. defense production base, important in maintaining a high state of readiness.

The United States could fully maintain credibility as an ally and protector, perhaps forestalling movement of client nations away from the U.S. political and economic orbit and, in the process, assuring access to bases, overflight rights, and raw materials.

The option would mitigate the thrust toward nuclear proliferation in some cases, or at least slow it down, thus buying time on this issue. Further, there would be less impetus toward the development of indigenous conventional arms production bases in some dependent nations, thus holding down the expansion of the arms supplier market base.

The United States can maintain regional balances of power where it is in the national interest, hence forestalling conflicts in some cases where, otherwise, destabilization might result from the policies of other arms suppliers. South Korea and Israel are two examples.

By cutting into the arms sales of other suppliers, the United States keeps their arms production bases from expanding, in some cases allowing for greater U.S. arms sales. An indirect spinoff may be an increased ability of the United States to maintain hegemony in the Western European arms markets.

Cons

The option increases the probability of U.S. involvement in local conflicts, particularly if advisers are involved in training and to the extent that the prestige of U.S. arms is involved and becomes a psychological issue.

The United States is partly precluded from taking initiatives, based on a moralistic stance, in international forums on arms trade issues, though such hypocrisy is virtually an international norm and does not normally restrain other suppliers.

If the challenge is taken by other suppliers, dangerous and escalating arms races may result in some regions, and perhaps conflicts in some cases where the United States is supplier to both sides. Previous situations in the Middle East and in South Asia are noted.

There may be some distortion of the U.S. economy, to the extent that more personnel and resources are devoted to the production of arms. The extent of this distortion, and its meaning, are much argued.

In some cases, the option may allow authoritarian regimes to further suppress legitimate political groups that, if they achieve power, will resent the United States as the supporter of the fallen regime. Most relevant here is the supply of arms usable for counterinsurgency purposes.

These are the options at the extremes. A more realistic and complex set of options might have been set out in between, for the most part amounting to variations on the themes of current policy, with left- and right-leaning nuances. A watered-down version of option 1, for instance, might allow greater flexibility in dealing with cases that are difficult to pigeon-hole on an ad hoc basis. Policymakers then would pick and choose where commitments would be made, on the grounds of security, economic advantage, or morals and sentiment. Likewise, a weaker version of option 2 would involve some narrowing of the eligibility requirements for U.S. arms supply, at least to cover cases such as South Africa and Chile, where significant segments of the U.S. public might object to any form of military dealings.

Ad hoc decision-making between the extremes would allow for greater flexibility in dealing with specific cases; but there are drawbacks, in that the policy then presents a picture of incoherence, confusion, indecision, and often hypocrisy, to the public and Congress, and also to foreign governments. Further, such a policy, characterized somewhat by stealth and indirection, at times requires tight controls, secrecy, and the relative absence of public debate, all increasingly difficult.

It is hard to predict how these issues will be handled in the near future by a new administration, of whatever political coloration. Quite probably, the options at the extremes will not be regarded as viable, or will be precluded by the nature of incremental decision-making, the installation of a McGovern-type administration aside, if backed by a like-minded Congress. It is still more difficult to imagine the United States going back to option 2, essentially an

anachronistic throwback to the pre-1935 era and a carbon copy of
present French policy, though continued frustration in getting cooperation from other suppliers to assist in controls may yet push
U.S. policy in that direction, particularly if there is a further downgrading of the role of ideology in world affairs.

In closing, it ought to be stressed that development of a coherent arms sales policy is an altogether difficult matter, for the very
reason that the United States has an only marginal unilateral capability to affect the overall volume of arms absorbed by dependent nations. It is not just an idle cliche that "if we don't sell them, someone else will." So long as this continues to be the case--and there
are few auguries of change in that basic condition--U.S. policy is
most likely to oscillate in a gray area between the poles of a
commercial-hegemonic orientation, and a more moralistically inspired direction. In that gray area, hard decisions will have to be
made on immediate and specific situations, such as Turkey, Israel,
Jordan, and Pakistan. It is not clear whether the development of a
solid doctrine to encompass these matters is either possible or desirable. In the absence of international agreements, which of necessity would first require a considerable reduction in international tensions, the problem bids fair to remain an intractable one.

NOTES

1. See Walter Lagueno, Confrontation: The Middle East and
World Politics (New York: Quadrangle Books, 1974).

2. See The Arms Trade and The Third World (New York:
Humanities Press, 1971), pp. 17-41.

3. See "Congress is Slow to Exercise Arms-Sales Controls,"
New York Times, June 14, 1975, p. 3.

4. Quoted in "Nelson Supports Legislation to Monitor Arms
Sales," Defense and Space Business Daily 80, no. 34 (June 18,
1975): 267-68.

5. Quoted in "Proxmire Calls for Cutback of Foreign Military
Sales," Defense and Space Business Daily 80, no. 4 (May 6, 1975):
29.

6. Quoted in "Administration Defends Foreign Military Sales
Program," Defense and Space Business Daily 80, no. 35 (June 19,
1975): 275-77.

MUTUAL AND BALANCED
FORCE REDUCTIONS:
THE PROBLEM OF "BALANCE"
Kenneth H. Jacobson

THE ISSUE

In October 1975, the East-West talks in Vienna on military force reductions in Europe that had begun in 1972 remained deadlocked. The talks, known by the formidable title "Mutual Reduction of Forces and Armaments and Associated Measures in Central Europe," are related to the ongoing Strategic Arms Limitation Talks (SALT) and the recently concluded Conference on Security and Cooperation in Europe (CSCE) in the overall context of arms control and detente diplomacy.

The central issue in conflict at Vienna is and has been the question of balanced force reductions. NATO has sought asymmetrical cuts to bring force levels down to a common troop ceiling for both military pacts. The Warsaw Pact, on the other hand, denies that any imbalance presently exists, and seeks equal percentage cuts in men and weapons to preserve the current East-West force ratio at lower levels. Related to this question is the issue of stationed (U.S. and Soviet) and national (European) forces. The West wants the first cuts to be absorbed by the former; the East seeks to include other national--especially West German--forces.

The areas of agreement that have been reached were concluded during the preliminary talks that began in February 1972. Both sides agree that reductions should take place on a step-by-step basis, and that military maneuvers and reinforcements must be subject to some controls. The Central Front, from which forces are to be removed, has been defined to include Belgium, the Netherlands, Luxembourg, and the Federal Republic of Germany on the NATO side, and the German Democratic Republic, Poland, and Czechoslovakia on the Warsaw Pact side. The status of Hungary remains in dispute.

NATO holds that forces stationed there should be included, while the
Warsaw Pact insists that the country is part of the Southern Front.
Talks have proceeded despite this fundamental difference.

Negotiations are closed and confidential, and the negotiating
positions taken are joint ones, with the NATO participants on one
side and their Warsaw Pact counterparts on the other. All the states
in the Central Zone are participants, as are those having forces stationed there--the United States, Canada, and Great Britain for NATO
and the Soviet Union for the Warsaw Pact. France does not participate in the talks and refuses to reduce her forces, but the 58,000
French service personnel are included in the NATO total.[1] Special
status has been given five countries from NATO's flanks--Norway,
Denmark, Italy, Greece, and Turkey--and to Hungary, Rumania,
and Bulgaria on the other side.

When formal talks opened in November 1973, the Warsaw Pact
proposed a three-stage plan for proportionally reducing ground troops,
air forces, and nuclear weapons. The reductions were phased over a
three-year period. Each side would reduce its forces in designated
units by 20,000 men and supporting equipment by 1975. Forces in the
reduction zone would then be cut by an additional 5 percent in 1976
and 10 percent in 1977. West German units would be subject to initial cuts.

The NATO counterplan, of American origin, would reduce only
ground force personnel, which in November 1973 totaled 770,000 for
NATO and 925,000 for the Warsaw Pact, to a common ceiling of
700,000 men, and would designate the Soviet units to be removed. In
the first phase of the plan, the United States would withdraw 20,000
and the Soviet Union 68,000, the latter from tank units. No national
forces would be involved. After agreement on the first phase, both
sides would reduce to the common ceiling of 700,000 in the second.
Follow-on cuts would include national forces. The second phase
would also restrict maneuvers and reinforcements in the Central Zone.

BACKGROUND OF THE ISSUE

Origins

Although the concept of mutual and balanced force reductions
(MBFR) derives from NATO proposals, the original idea of East-
West force reductions in Europe is a time-honored Soviet foreign
policy objective and propaganda theme. The many variations of the
Rapacki Plan, proposed by the Poles with Soviet support in the late
1950s and 1960s, advocated a nuclear-free zone in Central Europe,
and held out the prospect of an eventual drawdown of conventional

forces as well. Western leaders, however, invariably treated such proposals with skepticism--noting that the West would be required to surrender its tactical nuclear advantage without assurances that the large conventional forces of the Warsaw Pact would be reduced.

What might be termed the CSCE/MBFR dialogue began in July 1966 when the Warsaw Pact proposed an all-European security conference, simultaneous liquidation of both military pacts, and complete withdrawal of all foreign bases from Europe. The proposal was, of course, a rather obvious attempt to drive a wedge between the United States and its European allies, but the NATO ministers-- mindful of the popular hopes aroused by detente, their own manpower and budgetary constraints, and particularly by political pressures in the United States for unilateral force reductions--responded with the Harmel Report in December 1967, which raised the possibility of MBFR. The NATO Council followed up this initiative in its June 1968 meeting at Reykjavik, where a "Declaration on Mutual and Balanced Force Reductions" was issued that called for East-West talks on force reductions in Europe. [2] Two months later, Warsaw Pact forces invaded Czechoslovakia.

The invasion of Czechoslovakia and the subsequent proclamation of the Brezhnev Doctrine declaring the Soviet Union's right to intervene anywhere in the Socialist commonwealth chilled the winds of detente. It also brought more Soviet troops to the Central Front. Yet a year had not elapsed before the Warsaw Pact issued a March 1969 appeal for European security negotiations. One month later, the NATO Council reiterated the Reykjavik Declaration. Throughout this period, neither the Soviet Union nor the Warsaw Pact addressed the specific issue of MBFR. Instead, they pressed for more general discussions on European security. In June 1970, however, the Pact's Political and Consultative Committee did issue a communique stating that reductions of "foreign troops in Europe" might be discussed-- but only by a special study group of a European security conference.

The first serious indication of Soviet interest in force reduction talks came in the spring of 1971. Secretary-General Brezhnev referred to the possibility of a "reduction of armed forces and armaments in Central Europe" in a May 14 speech at Tbilisi to the XXIV Congress of the Communist Party of the Soviet Union. In response to Brezhnev's invitation for NATO to "taste the wine" of negotiations, the Western Alliance appointed Manlio Brosio, former Secretary-General of NATO, to explore Soviet views on MBFR and report to the December meeting of the Ministerial Council. Brosio, however, was not invited to Moscow; and for a few months the East made no further references to force reductions as an integral part of a European security conference.

In January 1972, the Warsaw Pact issued the "Prague Declaration on Peace, Security, and Cooperation," which called for disarmament but made no mention of MBFR. It was not until then Presidential adviser Henry Kissinger visited Moscow in mid-September 1972 that an agreement was reached to begin preliminary CSCE talks in November 1972, with separate but parallel force reduction talks to begin in early 1973. Two points bear emphasis in this brief chronology. First, it was the United States that sought to keep MBFR separate from CSCE. Second, both sets of negotiations were clearly a product of detente.

Western Motivations

Western motivations for MBFR are varied. There is, of course, the natural interest all NATO countries have in reducing the risk of war growing out of a European crisis. The hope of reducing heavy defense expenditures is another incentive for exploring the possibility of troop cuts. In addition, there are undoubtedly some who see in reduction of tensions that has accompanied detente diplomacy the hope that the Soviets might renounce the Brezhnev Doctrine or at least that direct Soviet military intervention, as in Czechoslovakia, will become less likely.

Perhaps the strongest motivation, however, has been to neutralize U.S. domestic pressures for unilateral force reductions in Europe. The perennial Mansfield Amendment, which seeks to cut by half the number of American servicemen stationed abroad, began to gather heavier Senate support in the United States as disillusion with the war in Indochina increased. Many Americans also began to ask why some 300,000 U.S. servicemen still were needed to defend an economically resurgent Western Europe that seemed perfectly capable of providing for its own security.

Western European governments have never showed much enthusiasm for force reduction talks, which they tend to view either as a cover for withdrawing the U.S. security guarantee to Europe in an era of strategic nuclear parity, or as an omen of eventual superpower collusion. France is unalterably opposed to MBFR. British and Western support for the idea has been unenthusiastic. In the United States, the Nixon administration and its allies in the U.S. national security community originally supported the MBFR idea chiefly—though by no means entirely—to reduce the appeal of unilateral force reductions that was perceived to be growing in the United States. The argument made in the early 1970s by opponents of unilateral force cuts was that there was no reason to give away what might be surrendered in exchange for other Soviet concessions.

Soviet Motivations

Despite changing styles of national leadership politics, Soviet foreign policy in Western Europe appears to have been consistently directed toward the following goals:
- Military superiority in Eurasia against any combination of opponents
- The legitimization of the Soviet position in Eastern Europe
- The fragmentation of the NATO alliance as the first step toward the reduction and eventual elimination of U.S. power and influence in Europe
- The permanent division of Germany, the prevention of West German acquisition of nuclear weapons, and the neutralization of West Germany within the larger European community
- The prevention of political unification and military and economic integration in Western Europe.

In the light of these objectives, the early 1970s must have seemed a propitious time to Moscow to press for CSCE/MBFR talks. While the growth of the Chinese nuclear arsenal renewed the old Russian fear of a two-front threat, the opportunities presented in Europe by a climate of detente suggested that perhaps the military danger from the West might be permanently neutralized. Detente and Ostpolitik had already led to the West German accords with the USSR and Poland, accords that went far toward recognizing the Soviet position in Eastern Europe. The prospects of increased trade, technology transfer from the West, and perhaps even NATO acceptance of a Soviet voice in establishing Western European defense ceilings were appealing. In addition, the Soviets--like their Western counterparts--undoubtedly sought some reduction in their defense expenditures to free badly needed investment capital for development of other sectors of the economy.

MBFR IN THE CURRENT STRATEGIC ENVIRONMENT

The agreement to hold force reduction talks came within a few months of the 1972 Moscow Summit at which President Nixon and Secretary-General Brezhnev signed the SALT accords. This was a period of great expectations for detente and the future of Soviet-American relations. Much has happened since then, however, to scale down these expectations.

One source of tension has been the Middle East. Soviet behavior during the October 1973 Arab-Israeli War--arms deliveries to Egypt and Syria on the eve of the war, the threat to intervene to prevent an Egyptian defeat in the Sinai, and encouragement of the

Arab oil embargo of the United States--angered Washington. On the other hand, the Soviet Union has been resentful of the new U.S. - Egyptian tie, which threatens its hard-won position in the Middle East. Events in Southeast Asia have also contributed to doubts about detente, with the United States protesting the heavy Soviet arms support for Hanoi's final drive against Saigon. The SALT-2 negotiations remain stalemated over a range of issues, such as limiting cruise missiles and whether the Soviet Backfire bomber should be counted as a strategic weapon. Moreover, the SALT atmosphere has been chilled by continuing Soviet tests of new missiles and allegations of Soviet SALT-1 violations in recent months.

None of this means an imminent return to the Cold War. What is suggested, however, is that the present strategic environment is very different from the one prevailing in the fall of 1972. The new climate is also far less encouraging to substantial agreements on mutual force reductions.

Problems Within NATO

Consensus on an appropriate alliance position on MBFR has always been difficult to achieve in a coalition of fifteen sovereign nations. (See Chapter 5 for a detailed discussion of central issues in NATO.) There are natural splits in NATO born of major differences in strategic positions and outlook. Naturally, the North American perspective differs from the European. There are also differences between continental and maritime countries, nuclear and nonnuclear countries, and countries of the Central Front and those on NATO's flanks. Given such a diversity of outlook, consensus has always been difficult.

One important difference in the alliance centers on the need for U.S. troops. Western European governments have historically attached great importance to a sizable U.S. presence. As a 1970 West German Defense White Paper noted, the presence of some 300,000 American servicemen in Europe "plays an indispensable role in the defense of Europe. At the same time, these troops constitute the link between Europe and the U.S. nuclear deterrent."[3] As a symbol of American commitment, the troops are of inestimable value to NATO. In the European view, ground forces from other NATO countries are no substitute for U.S. ground forces.

In addition, the presence of U.S. forces serves to link Europe's three security zones (Northern Europe, Central Europe, and the Mediterranean) into a single system. This theater-integrating function is important, since its links are both military and political.

Just as the Europeans attach great value to the presence of
U.S. troops and have come to regard unilateral force reductions by
the United States as a major security threat, so a high value is placed
on U.S. forward-based systems (FBS). These NATO-committed nuclear delivery systems, which are capable of striking the homeland of
the Soviet Union, are also viewed as visible links in the chain of deterrence that binds U.S. strategic forces to Europe's defense. A
nagging fear in Europe has been that MBFR--or a combination of
MBFR and SALT--could lead not only to a reduction of American
conventional forces but also to an elimination of FBS.

The alliance is also in the throes of an internal debate as to its
role in a new strategic environment. Some of the questions raised
are fundamental, and require satisfactory answers before any commitment is made to accept qualitative and quantitative limitations:[4]

● Does the growth and modernization of Warsaw Pact theater
forces preclude the possibility of the conventional defense of
Europe and require NATO to adopt a tactical nuclear weapon defense posture?

● Will rising defense costs, smaller defense budgets, and the
unpopularity of military service in Western Europe mean that
NATO will eventually have to rely on reserves in time of war?

● What measures can be taken to reduce duplication in national weapons procurement programs and promote greater military standardization within the alliance?

● Does the comparative success enjoyed in the October 1973
War by new weapon systems (antitank missiles, antiaircraft missiles, and precision-guided munitions) suggest a "revolution in
tactics" that might neutralize the effectiveness of the aircraft-
tank combination in coming wars? If so, can NATO adopt a reliable "defense-only" strategy for its own defense?

Against this background of serious debate over fundamental
questions about deterrence and defense, new political strains have
developed within and between NATO countries. Unsettled political
conditions in Portugal, the continuing friction between Greece and
Turkey, the 1975 Communist success in Italy's local elections, the
mounting economic crisis in Great Britain, and the uncertain political futures of Spain and Yugoslavia are only the most obvious problems threatening alliance cohesion.

The theater military posture of the Warsaw Pact has been
strengthened through the addition of tanks, artillery, and antitank
weapons, and modernized through the introduction of high-performance
aircraft, mobile air defenses, and new airlift capabilities. In addition, Soviet naval strength has grown along NATO's flanks to the point
that allied wartime control of the sea-lanes across the Atlantic can
not be reasonably assured.

Another aspect of the deteriorating security position of the alliance is the unwillingness of NATO governments to shoulder a greater share of the burden of Europe's defense. In general, national defense budgets have not kept pace with inflation rates. In some countries, forthcoming unilateral force reductions have been announced.[5] This European willingness to reduce forces, even in the face of a mounting security threat, probably reflects continuing hopes for detente, a sense of dependence on the United States to take the lead in defense matters, and a sense of fatalism about the capacity of Western European governments--even acting in concert--to offset current Warsaw Pact military gains.

Problems Between East and West

From the outset of preliminary discussion about possible troop reductions, Western analysts repeatedly assessed NATO's conventional forces as inferior to those of the Warsaw Pact. Most of these analysts reckoned that in any conventional conflict in Central Europe, the Warsaw Pact forces would be victorious within a matter of days. They hastened to add, however, that the combination of NATO conventional forces, tactical nuclear weapons in the theater, and U.S. strategic offensive forces were sufficient to deter an attack of this kind. In the main, these analysts agreed that NATO's ability to deter insured a balance of forces in the theater. The critical question for many of them was that if present trends continued (for instance, quantitative and qualitative improvements to Warsaw Pact forces), at what point would the Western Europeans come to regard NATO's defense posture as incapable of deterring an attack?

There are fundamental geostrategic asymmetries between the Soviet Union and Warsaw Pact, on the one hand, and NATO on the other. These include the following:

● A preponderance of Warsaw Pact theater nuclear forces--numerous and varied--for which NATO has no direct force equivalent, including 700 intermediate- and medium-range ballistic missiles (I-MRBMs) and 800 medium-range bombers

● Larger conventional forces in being (see Table 20.1) that use common weapons, equipment, and tactics, and have undergone common training

● Large enough concentration of force in East Germany (including twenty-one of the thirty-one Soviet divisions on the Central Front) to launch a surprise attack against the "layer cake" NATO force deployments in West Germany

● The capability for rapid reinforcement of ground combat operations owing to the geographical proximity of the Soviet Union and shorter and more secure lines of communication, and

● Special bilateral status-of-force arrangements between the
Soviet Union and its Warsaw Pact allies that would permit the
former to reenter any of the latter, regardless of the outcome of
pact-to-pact agreements about force ceilings, reinforcement, or
peacetime training maneuvers.

TABLE 20.1

Force Levels on the Central Front

	Manpower (1,000)	Tanks	Aircraft
NATO			
United States	190	2,100	240
Great Britain	55	600	130
Canada	3	30	40
Belgium	65	375	140
Netherlands	77	500	160
West Germany	340	2,950	600
Subtotal	730	6,555	1,310
France	58	325	400
Total	788	6,880	1,710
Warsaw Pact			
USSR	460	7,850	1,250
Czechoslovakia	155	2,900	500
East Germany	100	1,650	330
Poland	220	3,100	730
Total	935	15,500	2,810

Source: International Institute for Strategic Studies.

In addition to the above geostrategic advantages favoring the
Warsaw Pact, there are peculiar features of force deployment in
NATO that contribute to its vulnerability to a conventional surprise
attack spearheaded from East Germany. First, the firepower-
intensive U.S. forces are stationed in the south of the NATO Central
European Command, in a part of West Germany that is comparatively
easy to defend. It is the North German Plain, however, that is the
most likely invasion route, given the absence of natural obstacles.
It is this vital region that is defended by the less well-armed and
-equipped NATO forces from five countries. In addition, the

comparatively large Italian ground forces are stationed in Italy and, in the event of a conflict, would be geographically removed from the central arena of combat.

These maldeployments are well-known to those concerned with problems of European security. Less well-known, but hardly surprising, is the conclusion of a Western European Union (a defense forum for seven of the nine countries forming the European Community) study that warns of a maldeployment of U.S. tactical nuclear weapons and their overconcentration in a few storage sites. [6]

Another difference between East and West is that whereas U.S. forces perform both a military and a political function within NATO, Soviet forces perform these two functions plus a policing function within the Warsaw Pact. As has been noted, the size of the Soviet deployment in Eastern Europe is not only larger than required for regional defense, but also larger than required for strictly policing duties. This suggests some reservations in Moscow about the reliability of the armies of its Warsaw Pact allies. [7] Clearly, the policing function performed by Soviet forces is one unstated justification for the deployment of some thirty-two divisions in Eastern Europe.

In the final analysis, however, the greatest difference between East and West from the standpoint of mutual force reductions is that NATO is fundamentally a defensive alliance. The Warsaw Pact, too, claims a defensive mission; but its concentrated deployment in East Germany and its military doctrine, which calls for the rapid assumption of the offensive following the outbreak of hostilities, suggests a somewhat different orientation. It is the size and deployment of Warsaw Pact forces that have led to the NATO deployment of some 7,000 tactical nuclear warheads in Western Europe, an arsenal roughly twice that of the Warsaw Pact.

In the past few years, both sides have moved to improve their general-purpose forces. The momentum of the Soviet Union in broadening the combat roles of its units has been impressive, and additional changes may be anticipated in the next few years. On the quantitative scale, the Warsaw Pact has increased the artillery of its combat units, and added newer T-62 tanks to the armored inventory without withdrawing the older T-54 and T-55 models. Air transport, road transport, and engineer heavy-bridging capabilities also have been expanded. Qualitatively, the Soviets have introduced improved armored personnel carriers, mobile air defense systems, and high-performance aircraft, such as the SU-20, SU-19, and MIG 25. [8]

There have, of course, been NATO force improvements as well, though most of these have been on the qualitative side. In related moves intended to strengthen the links between U.S. strategic offensive forces and theater forces, the United States deployed FB-111 bombers to Great Britain and later shifted more submarine-

launched Poseidon missiles to Western European defense. Honest
John and Sergeant ground-to-ground missiles were replaced with the
newer Lance. Air defenses have been improved, and new antitank
weapons--notably the modified Cobra helicopter with TOW--have entered the NATO inventory. In two highly symbolic but unrelated developments, one U.S. Army brigade was deployed to the vulnerable
North German Plain region, and the French added their Pluton
ground-to-ground missile to French forces station in West Germany.
The significance of the shift of a token U.S. force north is that it is
the first commitment of U.S. ground forces to this part of Germany.
The Pluton, a missile with a range of seventy-five miles, is the first
tactical nuclear system introduced to the Central Front that is not
under NATO command.

From the NATO perspective, the most menacing aspect of the
theater balance is the Warsaw Pact's force of 15,500 tanks located
in East Germany, Poland, and Czechoslovakia. Approximately half
of these are the more modern T-62s. NATO's total tank force on the
central front is 6,555, excluding some 325 French tanks deployed in
West Germany. It is a mixed force of many models of American,
British, and German tanks.

A NEW DIRECTION FOR MBFR?

As noted previously, the talks that resumed in Vienna in late
September 1975 remained deadlocked on the issue of balanced reductions. After two years of negotiations, no formula had been found
capable of getting the talks moving. As the latest round of negotiations began, however, there were clear signs that the United States,
with support from its NATO allies, was prepared to offer to withdraw a significant number (perhaps 1,000) of its tactical nuclear
weapons in exchange for reductions in Soviet conventional (and particularly) armored forces. The most frequently cited scenario en-
visions a withdrawal of 1,000 tactical nuclear weapons to the United
States and a simultaneous withdrawal of a Soviet tank army to European Russia.

The United States apparently views such an offer as a means
of getting the talks off dead center. It also has other reasons for
reducing the size of its nuclear stockpile in Europe. In some circles
of the U.S. defense community, there are those who wish to replace
some of the older, larger, and less discriminate weapons with lower-
yield "clean" weapons that might be used against military targets.
On the other hand, many in government have become concerned about
the physical security of so many nuclear weapons all over Europe.
(See Chapter 4 for an analysis of terrorism as a new factor in the
international security environment.)

European support for the reported American initiative has been grudging. The figure of 7,000 nuclear weapons has become symbolic, like the figure of 300,000 U.S. servicemen. Europeans have tended to equate both with security. At the same time, there is a recognition that the alliance has deterred attack for a long time, despite its political and military weaknesses. There is a natural inclination to distrust abstract formulas for calculating the respective effectiveness of the two military pacts.

URGENCY OF THE ISSUE

Force reductions in Europe are not a high-priority item on the agenda of national security issues. Congressional and public pressure to unilaterally reduce U.S. troop commitments has receded in the wake of the debacle in Indochina and continuing tensions in the Middle East. Moreover, the winds of detente that blew warmly following the Moscow Summit of 1972 have chilled in recent months. Momentum is gone from SALT and MBFR, and more public figures have begun to express concern about further concessions to the Soviets. In the months following the Conference on Security and Cooperation in Europe, which ended in July 1975, all the signatories had an opportunity to evaluate Soviet adherence to the agreements reached in Helsinki, particularly the so-called Basket 1 agreements that renounce the use of force, call for a respect for sovereignty and the inviolability of existing borders, and promise to give advance notice of military maneuvers.

While a period of "watchful waiting" appears a desirable approach to force reduction talks by the United States, the condition of the NATO alliance, presently so troubled, should be the principal focus of U.S. concern. The United States should guard against even the appearance of being willing to compromise European security in order to obtain Soviet agreement on arms control initiatives.

CONCLUSION

No significant breakthrough is likely at the force reduction talks at Vienna. A growing Western disenchantment with detente, conflicting views within the NATO alliance itself as to what constitutes an appropriate alliance position on European force reductions, and the slow and unsatisfactory progress at SALT militate against general East-West agreement. At the same time, neither side will wish to be accused of sabotaging troop cut talks. Negotiations will continue, but gradually diminish in importance.

NOTES

1. All figures on force levels in Europe are taken from The International Institute for Strategic Studies, The Military Balance 1974-1975 (London: the Institute, September 1974).

2. The NATO and Warsaw Pact background documents described in this section can be found in Wolfgang Klaiber, Laszlo Hadik, et al., Era of Negotiations (Lexington, Mass.: D. C. Heath, 1973), pp. 99-142.

3. Federal Republic of Germany, White Paper 1970 on the Security of the Federal Republic of Germany and the State of the German Federal Armed Forces (Bonn: Press and International Office, May 20, 1970), p. 30.

4. These topics are addressed in four excellent monographs published as Adelphi Papers by the International Institute for Strategic Studies, London: Wolfgang Heisenberg, The Alliance and Europe: Part I: Crisis Stability in Europe and Theater Nuclear Weapons (Summer 1973); Kenneth Hunt, The Alliance and Europe: Part II: Defense with Fewer Men (Summer 1973); Roger Facer, The Alliance and Europe: Part III: Weapons Procurement in Europe-- Capabilities and Choices (1975); Stephen Canby, The Alliance and Europe: Part IV: Military Doctrine and Technology (Winter 1974/ 1975).

5. See, for example, the British "Statement on the Defense Estimates, 19 March 1975," which outlines a phased withdrawal of British air and naval forces from the eastern Mediterranean. Reprinted in Survival 17 (May/June 1975): 141-45.

6. See Anthony Murray, "NATO Deployment Weakness Found," Baltimore Sun, June 3, 1975, p. 2.

7. Thomas W. Wolfe, Role of the Warsaw Pact in Soviet Policy (Santa Monica, Calif.: RAND Corporation, 1973), p. 5; also see Wolfe, Soviet Attitudes Toward MBFR and the USSR's Military Presence in Europe (Santa Monica, Calif.: RAND Corporation, April 1972), pp. 4-5.

8. For a thoughtful rundown on theater force developments, see John Erickson, "Soviet Military Capabilities in Europe," RUSI-- Journal of the Royal United Services Institute for Defense Studies 120 (March 1975): 65-69.

21

R&D STRATEGY:
THE PROBLEM OF VISION
Douglas N. Beatty

Spending for the military budget becomes a central point of discussion in any matter involving U.S. national security. Funds approved each year are largely determined by the size and composition of the current forces and procurements for the operations of those current forces. Of critical impact for the future are those funds allocated to the research, development, test, and evaluation (RDT&E) portion of the budget, for the current RDT&E determines the character of tomorrow's military equipment. Therefore such activities supported by the budget materially impact the nature and utility of forces for the next five to ten years. As a result, all the basic issues of the military budget are reflected in a consideration of the RDT&E budget, with the additional consideration that RDT&E activities have high leverage for the future of military forces and thus our vision of what U.S. national security should be.

THE ISSUE

The RDT&E portion of the military budget accounts for about 10 percent of the total for the fiscal year 1976. However, its importance lies in the fact that this portion of the budget funds the next generation of weapons and provides a basis for the creation of future weapons options and future U.S. military initiatives. In addition, it provides for the creation of basic understanding of military hardware that may be used now and in the future. While the investment is current, the impact on military forces is delayed. As such, current spending on RDT&E can have great impact on the character of future forces as well as influence the current perception that others have of the future nature of U.S. forces.

315

The primary issue associated with the RDT&E budget concerns its size and character. While recognizing that this cannot be addressed totally independent of a consideration of the full military budget, the issue is particularly important because the sum of what is spent for current weapons (procurement) and future weapons (RDT&E) is about one-third the total military budget. Hence a small percentage (as a function of the total military budget) change between these funding categories can have a large impact. This occurs because the expenditures in the RDT&E budget can heavily influence the type of forces and size of forces, and thus the manpower required for the future.

Within this context, the major issues are the following:

● How large should the RDT&E budget be?

● What major new systems developments should it support? (Currently about 60 percent of the RDT&E budget is associated with this category.)

● How much should be allocated to sustain the technology base (research, exploratory development, and some parts of advanced development activities for creation and demonstration of options)? (Currently this is about 40 percent of the RDT&E budget.)

In considering these issues, answers to three major questions must be considered:

● What is the role of military forces in the future?

● What is the nature of the emerging and future threat, and, a corollary, do programs undertaken in RDT&E influence adversary, allied, or neutral responses?

● How can we make judgments regarding the issue of quality versus quantity of equipment?

BACKGROUND OF THE ISSUE

The debate over the RDT&E budget has, in the past, not focused on the issue of size per se but, rather, on the merits of individual major system development programs. The dialogue is usually between the RDT&E leaders within the Department of Defense, both civilian and military, and the members of Congress. Occasionally, as in the case of the anti-ballistic missile (ABM) development, the discussion escalates to include other groups. In the main, however, the points of discussion will primarily be between members of Congress and officials of the Defense Department.

The case presented by the Defense Department is usually contained in various yearly posture statements, while that of the critique is more fragmented. Current discussion is mainly found in articles in the New York Times or the Washington Post. Reports of Congressional committee testimony or committee reports represent the next

best source, although the discussion is still in a somewhat fragmented form due to the manner in which testimony is presented.

Complicating the explicit discussion of the basic issue is the
apparent implicit policy that equipment of U.S. military forces
should be qualitatively superior to that of an enemy. Given this
premise, the discussion then usually centers on the advantages, disadvantages, costs, and effectiveness of proposed individual new systems. The only major discussion relating to basic technology has
been in reference to whether programs to support improvements in
intercontinental ballistic missiles should be funded. With the discussion focused on the characteristics of individual weapons performance, the larger issue has rarely been addressed.

In the discussion, the individuals involved are easily categor-
ized, since the Defense Department officials and military officers
are proponents of the budget. They are confronted by an ever-
changing set of opponents, depending on the particular views concerning each weapon system by specific individuals. However, there
seems to be a core group of Representatives and Senators who consistently present the strongest case against the Defense Department
requests.

The most comprehensive statements are by some members of
the House Armed Services Committee. Although the initial discussion often begins to address the problem from the overall point of
view, the final rationale for budget reductions (about 15 percent in
RDT&E) is usually based on a series of isolated considerations of
individual weapons systems.

Despite the character of past discussions, there has been a
change in the budget decision-making process in Congress that can
now provide the forum for debate over basic issues. This change is
the creation of the Budget Committees, whose function is to assign
overall funding levels. In their phase of the budget process, the
Budget Committees focus on aggregate totals and thus have an opportunity to address the total size of the RDT&E budget and what determines it. Admittedly the discussion is complicated by the difficulty
of projecting the future threat, but there should be enough unclassi-
fied data to permit an intelligent public discussion.

URGENCY OF THE ISSUE

In light of the current economic picture and increasing demands
for the provision of social services by the national government, there
are severe pressures on the military budget. Because of the large
impact that a current small increase (or decrease) in RDT&E funds
can have on the requirements in future budgets, it is important to address the issue of the size and purpose of the RDT&E budget now.

The size of the RDT&E budget is also important, considering that portion of the Defense Department funds allocated to current procurement or future (RDT&E) weapons hardware. Of the total military budget allocated for fiscal year 1976 to the provision of hardware, the RDT&E budget is about one-third ($10 billion) and the procurement is about two-thirds ($25 billion). This has been true for the past several fiscal years. The issue of whether the RDT&E budget is the appropriate size in comparison with procurement should be addressed.

POLICY ALTERNATIVES

In regard to the size of the military RDT&E budget there are essentially three alternatives:
- Reduce the budget substantially (more than 20 percent)
- Maintain status quo
- Significantly increase the budget (by more than 10 percent, to provide a real increase in spending).

Each of these actions implies certain views about the answers to the three major questions presented earlier. Moreover, considering the complexity of any discussion about major federal funding, the discussion that follows is focused on the larger issues. This is not to deny the complexity of other factors, such as impact on other economic conditions, or the efficiency with which the funds are spent, or the details of the type of weapons or procurement practices; but our purpose here is to highlight major policy alternatives.

Reduction in Budget

This implies that in the future, both the immediate and the long-term, the United States will have a lesser need either to employ military power in international conflict resolution or to furnish its forces with advanced, quality equipment. Additionally, such a decision would imply that military forces will be relatively less important than in the past, at least in certain areas, and that the threat will not be so severe. Marginal improvements to national security may occur because of the higher-quality equipment that enters the inventory.

In favor of this course of action is the fact that the restriction of the RDT&E budget could reduce U.S. military budgets in the future. The reduction in technology levels and the elimination of future developments will mean that in the future, procurements of some high-priced systems will be avoided. This cut initiates a reduction in the military budget that over time can provide for the transfer of funds that can substantially improve the economic situation of other, more productive parts of the economy.

A major reduction in the budget tends to highlight the arguments about the purpose of the activities, and thereby would force decision-makers to address the more critical and basic issues. The resulting debate could clarify the nature of national policy in this area. In addition, the cut would demonstrate dramatically the trends that have been inherent in the budget for some time as the real purchasing power has decreased. Also, the reduction could serve as a signal to our adversaries that they too could reduce their budgets and thus move away from arms competition.

The unfavorable aspects of a decision to substantially reduce the budget would be that an adverse signal may be given to others. The action could be interpreted as an indication that current U.S. military commitments may not be supported in the future. It may also signal a retrenchment in U.S. positions that would cause others to take initiatives inimical to U.S. interests. Finally, it would also signal abrogation of the technological initiative now held by the United States in several areas.

The elimination of development programs caused by a reduction would force a major future readjustment in U.S. forces as weapons became obsolete and modernization was slowed. The reduction in RDT&E also removes some options and initiatives, thus encouraging U.S. security policy into a more reactive military mode.

The amount of funds made available for federal outlays by the magnitude of a substantial reduction of the RDT&E budget (say about $2 billion) is marginal when compared with the amount of the annual incremental growth of the aggregate of non-Defense Department programs. Therefore, while an individual program may be somewhat improved, the total impact on a yearly basis is small. Thus the advantages obtained by non-Defense Department programs could be offset by the larger impact such a cut would have on the military security posture.

The reduction could be accomplished through emphasis on cuts to the technology base. This would affect the far future and could be configured to have little impact in the near term (say over five years) on new forces available for modernization of forces. On the other hand, the budget could be reduced through elimination of major development programs, which could have an immediate impact, depending on their status of development. Force modernization would be severely influenced, and the opponents of the Defense Department budget and U.S. military policies probably would approve of such actions.

Status Quo

The maintenance of the status quo assumes that the RDT&E budget holds fairly constant, in terms of real dollars, and that the assumptions inherent in the current budget will prevail for the next several years. Current funding trends and inflation trends would indicate a gradual erosion of the buying power of the RDT&E programs. The general assumption is that the threat declines or does not change materially in the future, and that our policies concerning the use of military forces are much the same as in the past.

The advantage to the maintenance of the status quo is that no major changes or decisions have to be made. Implicit are past policies and the continuance of current procedures for evaluation of the budget. Such an action avoids the political controversy associated with decisions concerning a major change. The successful character of our military forces, which has been demonstrated in the past, is maintained. The planned modernization programs would be continued about as presently conceived.

The major disadvantage of the status quo alternative is that it is the course of action least likely to raise, and force to be addressed, the basic issues and questions regarding U.S. military forces and developments. Considering the nature of the threat, such an action implicitly, over time, decreases U.S. capability relative to the projected threat.

The continuance of current trends promises a major readjustment of U.S. responses in a future crisis. This is because the gradual erosion of real power may deprive the United States of options for future initiatives. Because of the gradual nature of this impact, the full awareness of the situation may not be apparent to decision-makers until the crisis situation occurs, thus complicating future actions and inhibiting the U.S. ability to sustain a course of action favorable to U.S. security interests.

Finally, the status quo means that the programs of the Defense Department will consume significant resources, and therefore the pressures on the military budget from domestic programs will be maintained. Since the major issues are not likely to be addressed, the resolution of some basic dilemmas will not occur.

Increase of Budget

This implies that the United States believes that the military forces will likely play an important role in national security in the future and that the threat against those forces will increase. The commitment to technological leadership and force quality is judged to be important.

One of the advantages of a substantial increase in the RDT&E budget is that it signals a long-term U.S. commitment to quality military forces, and technological initiatives and leadership. In addition, such actions would indicate that the United States has a long-term commitment to military assistance to her allies. Also, the increase in funding would provide a more vigorous technological base and create more technological options to deal with crises and uncertainties in the future. It would give the United States the ability for certain initiatives and capabilities (national verification schemes) to enhance its future security posture. The strong RDT&E program can provide opportunities for the United States to provide material that can be used by allies to support their military security posture by developing items suitable to their needs and budgets.

One of the pressures for the future is caused by the actions that a potential adversary may take. These actions are made possible by his spending for military R&D programs. To the extent that major imbalances occur, instabilities develop. Increases in U.S. RDT&E spending would provide levels that more nearly match the threat. Thus the likelihood of surprises is diminished and a better understanding of enemy RDT&E activities is permitted. A better match of adversary RDT&E activities also means that U.S. leadership in individual areas can be maintained.

The disadvantages of an increase in the RDT&E budget lie in several areas. Certainly, funds are denied that potentially could be applied to other federal programs. This removes an opportunity for growth in some non-Defense Department areas. The impact on future budgets has already been noted. Thus an increase in spending will require further increases in the defense budget over the long term, to procure and field what is developed. Alternatively, some developments would not be fielded; but such a conscious action could be interpreted as a waste of RDT&E funds, since one of the purposes of RDT&E activities is to field militarily effective systems.

Finally, the increase in RDT&E funds may complicate current disarmament negotiations such as the Strategic Arms Limitation Talks and the Mutual and Balanced Force Reductions. The development (or potential development) of new weapons could raise issues concerning their inclusion or might evoke an adverse reaction on the part of other negotiating parties.

This increase in RDT&E funding, because of its leverage and potential impact on the total Defense Department budget, undoubtedly would increase tensions between Defense Department supporters and those in Congress who oppose larger appropriations. In terms of addressing the basic issues, however, an increase in the budget would probably draw criticism only of major new programs. Thus, while exacerbating differences between adversary groups on the

defense budget, an increase probably would not force debate over
the basic issues.

CONCLUSION

The basic security issue relating to the RDT&E military budget is to force the discussion to center on the fundamental, driving
factors regarding the projected role of U.S. military forces and the
projected security environment in which they must operate. Insofar
as defense issues at the national level focus on the merits of individual weapons systems, there can be nothing other than a fragmented discussion, peripheral to basic issues of role and environment.

Since in their posture statements of 1975 the Secretary of Defense and the Director of Defense research and Engineering spoke to
the basic issues and requested approval of their views, the opportunity for discussion at that level appears to be available. Also,
there is sufficient material available to provide an open, objective
discussion of the issues. As a result, this is a legitimate issue
for consideration in 1977.

The pressures on the RDT&E budget will continue to cause a
reassessment of the component activities. The selection of projects
that were possible in the past due to the availability of funds and
cheaper materials and labor cannot now be permitted. There must
be an improved means for defining and selecting new weapons systems. This cannot be solely based on quality, because the fundamental issue is the relevance to the security environment five to
ten years in the future.

There are trends that should tend to improve the ability of the
dialogue on the RDT&E budget to focus on the basic issues. One, as
was mentioned earlier, is the creation of the Budget Committees in
Congress. Another is the policy emerging from the Office of Federal
Procurement Policy (OFPP) and supported by the Office of Management and Budget.

The OFPP actions do not materially affect the technology base,
and the basic exploratory research programs not oriented toward
specific military missions are not addressed. However, prior to
approval for advanced development of a new weapons system, the
Congress must be assured by the Secretary of Defense that there is
a valid requirement for the system to meet a deficiency in a recognized military mission, or that the development is necessary to
achieve a mission goal. 'The need is to be expressed in mission,
not equipment, terms. However, the mission needs may be the result of deficiencies (caused by a change in threat, for example) or

of an opportunity to exploit a technologically feasible opportunity. Additionally, major hardware systems must be related to military mission. This will focus discussion on the missions of military forces (as opposed to equipment performance), and this broader discussion should develop an environment in which the more basic issues (such as purpose of military forces, and threat) can be discussed.

The basic issues must be confronted and a position taken before an intelligent assessment of the military RDT&E program can be made. The impact on the national security is too large to continue the piecemeal, system-by-system critique of the budget. The assumptions not made explicit cloud our vision, and can lead to short-term actions inimical to our long-term security.

Idealism has been a strong motivating factor in twentieth-century American foreign policy. A positive vision of the future is a powerful tool in the formulation of policy and the generation of support. In this concluding chapter the roots of optimism are reviewed, with the goal of developing new organizing ideas to guide U.S. policy in the near term. Moving out of the era of the Cold War, and the disappointments of the last few years, requires a sense of direction that is lacking in the current period of flux. Three elements of a new direction are explored: manifest environmental concern, creative internationalism, and strength to share. These factors are examined as they can be reflected in new organizing ideas for future American policy.

22

TOWARD NEW
ORGANIZING IDEAS
Lewis S. Sorley III

That effective national action in a complex and dangerous world requires a governing image is beyond doubt. Secretary of Defense James Schlesinger, in his initial testimony before the Congress, quoted Proverbs: "Where there is no vision, the people perish."[1] The American character, mercurial and often baffling though it may be, undeniably contains elements of a strong ethical consciousness. And while pragmatism, practicality, and hardheadedness are much admired virtues in this country, no conception of the American role in world affairs can long be satisfying and capable of capturing the imagination and energies of the people if it lacks an ethical appeal.

American foreign policy has consistently been informed by a philanthropical as well as a practical sense. While some would argue this point, or at least that the latter element has not always had the intended effect, it seems clear that Americans in general have strongly supported foreign policy initiatives that not only advanced U.S. interests but also were of benefit to other peaceful nations.

Undoubtedly many Americans feel the strongest pride in their country's foreign policy and its implementation when they contemplate the events of World War II and the immediate postwar period. A large-scale aggression that was on the way to subjugating all of Europe was stopped, and then defeated, when American men and arms joined the conflict. National unity and support for this endeavor were strong. Following the war General Eisenhower, having commanded the victorious forces, could, with no touch of irony, term the campaign a crusade and find general agreement with his outlook. Soon thereafter this popular esteem for a successful wartime commander was translated into his election as President.

But even more than the battlefield successes in defeating aggression, it was the nation's role in the postwar period that gratified the American philanthropic sense. The magnanimous feelings for distressed European nations that were given outlet through the Marshall Plan may well have been unique. As has often been pointed out, not only wartime allies, but also defeated enemies, were given generous assistance. In contrast with the crippling reparations, institutionalized looting, or even (in Biblical times) sacking, salting, and plowing under that had often been visited upon defeated nations, the United States and her allies enabled Germany and Japan to rebuild themselves economically, to regain their self-sufficiency, and, most important, to resume a responsible role in world affairs in a remarkably short time. In contrast with some other, perhaps equally well-intentioned, programs of later years, it is important to point out that the Marshall Plan proved both achievable and effective. It worked, and that is key. Reflection on this remarkable period of national unity and morale is appropriate in attempting to identify the essential aspects of workable organizing ideas.

THE TASKS

Foremost among the attributes of useful organizing themes is that they be capable of engaging the national imagination and energies. The altruistic element, as well as practical considerations of efficacy and relevance, must be presented in a meaningful way if a positive consensus is to be obtained. Along with satisfaction of idealistic instincts, there must be real promise of perceptible progress.

Next, the proffered vision must be seen to serve legitimate national self-interest. Several elements form the heart of perceived self-interest, and the dynamic search for a working balance among their competing claims upon our energies and resources provides much of the political and social excitement of American life. My instinct is to cite national security as first among equals, on the premise that it is the essential element in maintaining an environment within which other goals may be sought. Surely a desirable standard of living must also be recognized as a priority aspect of national self-interest, and concern in this area increasingly involves not only achievement of the good life but equitable access to it for all. Last--and we may hope that the increased attention directed to this aspect of national self-interest by our youth in recent years will prove to have lasting impact--is the quality of life.

Related to the quality of life--and this is the most contemporary aspect of meaningful organizing ideas--is that organizing ideas must be seen as promoting a viable international environment. This entails addressing a whole range of the most perplexing and urgent problems of our time, from the search for workable commercial

institutions and means of equitable distribution of resources through
the promotion of nonviolent interaction among peoples. An important
element of this environment is that it provide scope for energy and
creativity of nations, institutions, and individuals alike.

THE CONTEMPORARY SETTING: A REPRISE

As a nation we are faced with the problems of indecision, lack
of direction, and blurred sense of purpose that are typical of periods
of transition. These result from the declining utility of the post-
World War II governing image. That image was responsive to the
realities of the time. It was also highly successful in fulfilling the
tasks of a successful organizing idea. The central element in this
governing image was that of bipolar confrontation between the United
States and the Soviet Union. Deriving from this concern were the
subsidiary ideas of containment and collective security. The resultant
world view underpinned notions of national identity, direction, and
purpose. It led to creation of the unprecedentedly extensive and en-
during alliance system still largely intact today, and it provided a
magnetic field that exerted powerful, if little visible, force upon the
proliferation of states set adrift in the world by the dissolution of
empires. Alliances historically have been of short duration, forged
by expediency under threat of shared danger. The exceptions have
been alliances imposed by imperial domination. Those that the
United States entered into following World War II, and that continue
in existence today, have thus been strikingly untypical.

Much has happened to erode the utility of the former governing
image in the intervening years, and most of it predates recent concern with the matter of detente. Most significant, particularly in
national security terms, has been the impact of nuclear technology.
Beyond the simple fact of the existence of nuclear weapons systems
of colossal destructive power, the key element has been the acquisition of arsenals of such weapons by the two nations known as superpowers. Indeed, possession of military power of this magnitude has
been the distinction that set "superpowers" apart from other powerful nations.

The evolution of a state of nuclear parity between the United
States and the Soviet Union is of utmost importance. The impact of
the technology is that, between the two superpowers, a strategic defense is impossible; either can absorb a massive attack by the other
without losing its capacity to retaliate (its "second-strike" capability); and either can inflict an unacceptable level of damage upon the
other, regardless of which strikes first.

This is an unprecedented situation in the history of mankind, truly a revolutionary development, and its implications are still only beginning to be realized (not only by Americans and Soviets, but by others as well). An important result strategically, and one that seems likely to have extremely far-reaching and increasing effects in other realms as well, is the dominance of deterrence as a strategic concern. Prevention of war has come to be, in light of the probable results of nuclear conflict, more important than the uses of war (at least for the superpowers in their relations with one another). The historian Russell Weigley has called this shift in focus from the object of war to deterrence of war "a revolution in the history of American military policy."[2]

This does not mean, of course, that there will not be future conflict. It may even mean an increase in conflict stemming, in part, from the condition that Alastair Buchan has pointed out: "a characteristic of the present state system which differentiates it sharply from that of the late nineteenth or early twentieth centuries, namely the ability of the small to defy the great."[3] This condition, when combined with further nuclear proliferation, may well prove to be intolerable to the superpowers, with significant results for the future of the alliance system. Driven by the imperative of avoiding strategic nuclear war, and the central uncertainty of whether lesser conflicts will escalate to that level, the superpowers have been severely constrained in damping or resolving conflicts that involve the prospect of confrontation with one another. Various ploys--including use of a proxy, provision of arms, and advisory efforts--have been resorted to by the Soviet Union and the United States in efforts to retain influence in conflicts without risking war with one another.

The proliferation of new states, many having accidental boundaries or based on resources of questionable viability, coupled with diminished direction and control resulting from the end of the Western colonial empires, seems likely to produce many more occasions for resort to warfare in an attempt to resolve differences. In this transitional period, the impact of nuclear weapons on the superpowers continues to be a perplexingly inhibiting one.

Compounding these problems are a host of other contemporary limitations on self-determination. No state, such is the interdependence of the modern world, is truly capable of self-determination. As Fernand Braudel has illustrated for the Mediterranean zone in the sixteenth century,[4] so for the global zone today: essential unity in terms of economics and communications decrees that none shall be wholly independent. Understanding the implications of this reality, in terms of options genuinely available and opportunities to have beneficial influence, and also in terms of those things not possible of accomplishment, may well be the central determinant of a nation's ability to act meaningfully in the contemporary context.

We have described some aspects of the impossibility of complete security, those inherent in mutual possession of a "second-strike" nuclear capability. This relatively invulnerable retaliatory capacity is, paradoxically, the primary sanction for superpower restraint. It brings about a kind of enforced interdependence. The prospective acquisition of nuclear weapons and the means of delivering them by other states, perhaps many other states, illustrates even further the violent limitations on self-determination that states must be prepared to contemplate. Should this proliferation continue, as seems likely in the absence of concerted action by the major powers to control it, and perhaps even extend to subgovernmental terrorist or criminal elements, the problems will be severely compounded.

Many peaceful limitations on self-determination are operative as well, including the state of world commerce and its differing but interrelated impacts on various nations. Resource requirements, need for markets, distribution problems, inflation, and development all cut across national and regional boundaries, and dictate that failure to cooperate internationally shall bear an increasingly high penalty. With the diminished control that derives from interdependence with others there comes increased uncertainty, the adjustment to which is particularly difficult for nations accustomed to dominance. Efforts on their part to retain a differential influence are inevitable.

Before leaving the matter of limitations on self-determination, it should be pointed out that for the foreseeable future the nation-state appears to be the level at which interaction will occur. Many have hopefully predicted the evolution of the macrostate as a regional force. But, even in regions with as much cultural and historical commonality as Western Europe, political affiliation, let alone union, has been slow to evolve. Whether current security and economic ties can involve political aspects as well is problematical, particularly in light of a diminishing perception of threat on the part of some member nations. Elsewhere, given less homogeneity, greater geographical dispersion, and more diversity of political structure, evolution of an effective regional governance seems even more remote.

Some mention should be made of the influence of historiography upon contemporary concerns. [5] There is a school of thought that holds that the world view that has shaped the underlying assumptions of historians for several centuries is, or soon will be, undergoing very substantial modification. The prevailing outlook has been characterized, it is said, by a set of voluntarist assumptions deriving from the impact of the scientific method, burgeoning technology, and belief in progress (in spiritual and psychological as well as material and intellectual terms). This has led, among other things, to diminished concern for natural forces, an attitude engendered by increasing confidence in man's ability to control those forces as he has learned through industrialization to multiply his own strength and reach.

We may well anticipate the impending decline of this outlook. The increasing complexity of modern life, coupled with an accelerating rate of change and the philosophical and ethical challenges that often accompany new technology, has already diminished the confidence of many in man's ability to order his own affairs. While this chastened outlook may not be entirely welcome, it may have beneficial impacts, such as decreasing the gap between aspiration and achievement that has done so much to undercut the effectiveness of leaders and governments. If expectations are not unlimited, if some problems are seen as susceptible of amelioration but not solution, and if modest improvement is seen as worthwhile achievement rather than miserable failure to attain the ideal, then it might be possible to take comfort from such successes as may be grasped while preserving enough goodwill to try for more. We might even satisfy the plaintive hope of the poet Robert Frost, who once wrote: "If you have the kind of a mind that can't help looking for something or someone in heaven or earth to blame, you will write life ugly like a lot of Americans lately; but if you take it naturally as it comes, you will write it simply sad some of the time."[6]

A cluster of additional factors contributing to the contemporary setting should also be recalled. They relate to proliferation of destructive capacity (especially nuclear weaponry) and the increase in the number of nation-states interacting with one another. One that must be squarely faced is the essential weakness, perhaps even failure, of international organizations. While concern in the United States has been increasing over the perversion of the purposes of the United Nations by what has been called a "tyranny of the majority,"[7] one need not adopt a judgmental or blame-fixing approach to the phenomenon. But it does seem useful simply to observe that, whether for good or for ill, the international institutions in existence today lack sanctions, lack strength, lack all but those powers voluntarily conceded to them at the moment by individual member states, and thus are negligible influences on the course of international events.

Whether this situation will be changed in the long run may in part depend upon what some believe is a current decline of ideology. While such a trend is extremely difficult to verify, and well may be subject to rapid and radical alteration, some hold that it may be expected to lead to increased rationality and, therefore, greater susceptibility to peaceful influences.

CONSIDERATIONS OF CHANGE

Here (and in Chapter 1) it is suggested that the present is a period of flux, an unsettled interim between adherence to an organizing idea whose foundations have eroded and the articulation of a successor vision capable of providing purpose and direction for the period ahead. Two aspects of change are of surpassing importance for our purposes: the security implications of change and the ethics of change.

Change is a threatening and frightening thing. Even change that leads to improvement is often resisted through fear of the unknown or the unpredictable. Inertia plays a part as well. In economic terms, so do sunk costs. Sometimes it turns out to be literally true that "you can't get there from here."

The risks of change are felt most keenly by those concerned with national security. Stability and security are often thought to be closely related--indeed, sometimes are even equated. Thus the security implications of this era of change are of special interest and concern.

First it may be appropriate to consider the phenomenon of force as an escape from the consequences of choice. We are coming, I believe, to a more mature understanding of the "frontier mentality" as it has operated in the American experience. Balancing the real, if often romanticized, elements of independence, self-reliance, curiosity, adventuresomeness, hardiness, and like virtues attributed to those who were on the leading edge of westward expansion are other elements. These include understandable, if less admirable, impulses to avoid accommodation of differences in outlook and life style, social adaptation with a structure of law, and acceptance of a share of community responsibility. Just as relatively unbridled use of force provided an outlet for some early settlers that permitted them to avoid consequences (by moving onto new and unspoiled land rather than wisely tending what they had already acquired, for example), so nations have sought to use force in this way. Acquisition of territory, of raw materials, of strategic positions, and of additional population have all motivated expansionist movements. We are accustomed to speak now of space as the last frontier. Short of that outlet, forcible expansion seems likely to yield more and more ambiguous results in an era of inescapable and increasing interdependence.

Similarly, population has recently acquired far different security implications. Historically, a large and growing population has been viewed as an element of national power to be encouraged. In the USSR, depleted especially of young men by the staggering losses of World War II, state policy was to recognize and grant special privileges to the "Hero Mother of the Soviet Union" who bore ten or more children. Many other states sought large populations to man agricultural and industrial enterprises, which had equally important contributions to make to security.

Contemporary realization of the burdensome aspects of uncontrolled population growth is one of the elements of change with important security implications. Those implications are, however, ambiguous at best. Industrialized states, devoting little of their population to now highly mechanized agriculture, are faced with massive economic and social problems of rapid urbanization, problems exacerbated by population growth. Increasingly complex and expensive life-support systems are becoming more and more overburdened and vulnerable. Increased mechanization of warfare has diminished (but not eliminated) the importance of large masses of men as elements of military power. These are among the factors bearing on the interrelationship of population and security in an era of change. States have yet to deal with them in any coherent manner in policy and programs.

Much has been said of the realities of interdependence among nations today. The search for security has usually led states to seek the opposite, the greatest amount of self-sufficiency possible. Inasmuch as total self-sufficiency has been both too difficult and too costly even for those who theoretically could attain it, compromise solutions have sought relative self-sufficiency, at least within alliances or spheres of influence. Heightened awareness of the vulnerabilities of interdependence, especially for industrialized nations, followed the recent Arab oil embargo. Some, such as the United States, were led at least to talk of attaining oil self-sufficiency by means of "Project Independence." Whatever the merits of a plan for using one's own oil resources for fear of the possibility that foreign sources could be cut off, this would do little to relieve the derivative vulnerability stemming from the far greater reliance of America's allies in Western Europe and Japan on oil from the Middle East. Once again the point to be illustrated is that the change abroad, in this case change to greater interdependence and less self-sufficiency, has important implications for security.

Force has often been used to induce change. Both domestically and internationally, states have sought to impose conditions (or orderliness, discipline, noninterference, or whatever) that would permit change to occur, ranging from collectivization of agriculture to unpopular alliances. This is of particular interest as one contemplates the shifting relations among states. If the organizing image of a bipolar confrontation, arraying lesser states about the contending poles like some great global magnet, has lost much of its power over the imagination, it is still unclear what the results will be in days ahead. One may be sure that the temptation will remain for states to use force to control, resist, or induce change. Realignments of blocs seem inevitable, though their nature and influence are not yet discernible.

What is clear, however, is that if erosion of the growth ethic continues, under the influence of increased awareness of the finite

supply of natural resources, developed nations will be tempted to
dampen industrialization of developing nations so as to conserve the
remaining resources and thereby maintain their industrialized economies and life styles for as long as possible. It is also clear that
this would engender explosive reactions from emerging states thus
thwarted, and that the reactions need not be proportional to the resources of the states in an age of nuclear proliferation. Again the
security implications, and especially the potential impact on current
alliance structures, are sobering.

What, then, of the ethics of change? Surely controversy over
change of the growth image will be at the heart of it. Those who not
only view the earth's resources as finite, but are motivated to move
rapidly to conserve what is left of them, face inevitable opposition
from those who either discount the danger of continued expansionism
or are determined to get their share before the supply runs out.
Difficult, perhaps insuperable, domestic difficulties confront societies determined to take effective action to manage change creatively.
Limitations on the possibilities of individual choice appear essential,
but imposing them in an acceptably nonauthoritarian manner may
prove to be impossible in democratic states.

Protection of the environment, the total life-support system of
the planet, would seem logically to be of overriding importance. In-
dividualistic nations and men have often insisted on the freedom to
accept the consequences of their acts. Should the latter now be, in
an increasingly interdependent physical and social system, no longer
an affordable freedom, very traumatic periods of adjustment may be
expected to follow, with violent threats to both domestic and international security likely.

ASPECTS OF A NEW AMERICAN VISION

I suggest three elements that could combine to produce a new
American vision for the period ahead: manifest environmental concern, creative internationalism, and strength to share. Clearly
formulated and competently translated into action, I believe they
could serve to promote a viable international environment, serve
the legitimate national self-interest, and engage the national imagination and energies. There could result a reawakening of that sense of
purpose so essential to the morale and effective functioning of the
American people.

Manifest Environmental Concern

It will not do to selfishly perpetuate propagation of the growth
ethic. There is no real debate as to the finite nature of the earth's

resources. The only arguable question relates to how long they will
last at a given level of exploitation, and speculative consideration of
what alternatives may be developed within that time. Thus modification of the growth ethic is inevitable. The choice lies between conscious, planned, and creative accommodation to the necessity for
change, on the one hand, and inescapable and potentially devastating
change that occurs when resources run out or are savagely scrambled
for in their dwindling deposits.

Obviously the United States, the prototype of the highly industrialized state, will by its example have great influence on other nations and how they accommodate to the necessity for change in the
growth ethic. If changes in laws, economy, social custom, and
philosophy can be brought about quietly, calmly, and creatively, this
will present a model of enormous usefulness to other nations. Such
change need not depend on an unattainably idealistic and altruistic
conversion on the part of Americans. Quite the contrary. The
philosophy that contemplates the consumption of fewer resources as
inevitably a reduction in the standard of living may be a root cause
of the problem. There is little evidence that material superabun-
dance promotes happiness and, in fact some cause to think that it
interferes with it. Beyond a certain decent level of well-being, happiness is derived from self-acceptance, a sense of purpose, and
meaningful interpersonal relationships. A dehumanizing quest for
ever more material gain is fatally destructive of the environment in
which such nourishing relationships can flourish.

A key element of concern for the environment is that of population growth. The dispiriting experience of achieving increases in
productivity and infrastructure, only to fall further behind as population increases overtake all gains and cause the increased resources
to be spread even more thinly, is known in many nations today. Yet
men have seldom dealt with control of population; and the overwhelming need to do so is often most pressing in Third and Fourth World
nations where governmental stability, authority, and technical competence are least able to deal with the problem.

The more prosperous nations have found more or less natural
solutions to population increase, as educated people trade off family
size for increased material well-being. I suggest that they can assist
less prosperous nations in restricting population growth by attaching
provisions to generous assistance programs. Conditional food assistance may serve as an example. By stipulating that eligibility for
food assistance depends upon specified success in controlling population growth, donor nations (or international organizations) can provide incentives, shift some of the onus for instituting control measures from the governments concerned, and reinforce success in
population control by providing discernible increases in the standard

of living. No element of coercion would be involved, as it would be entirely up to recipient nations whether they wished to meet the conditions attached to receiving assistance.

Controls and sanctions of other kinds, particularly those of an economic nature, could be used to persuade nations to act responsibly toward the environment. These could be applied in cases ranging from depletion of world fishing resources to manipulation of the weather. In extreme cases of disregard for the environment, such as radioactive pollution of the atmosphere, nations or groups of nations would no doubt contemplate use of force to control irresponsible behavior.

Creative Internationalism

This element of a new governing image includes and goes beyond manifest environmental concern. It contemplates a leadership role that develops innovative solutions to perplexing problems of international affairs, and can provide the wise and skillful diplomacy to gain their acceptance by other concerned nations. Foremost is the need for an improved world commerce apparatus. Bearing in mind a modified growth ethic, such an apparatus would entail meaningful arrangements for interaction of capital, raw materials, and labor in ways that are both fair and efficient, and for assistance on a systematic and effective bases to nations requiring it. A reformed international monetary system and appropriate controls over multinational corporations would be sought.

Leadership by example would be an important aspect of creative internationalism, and would entail the search for fairness and mutual advantage in commercial transactions, rather than maximizing profit, as a first principle. This concern would stem from informed self-interest rather than altruism, since it would recognize the important contribution such an approach would make to national security.

Finally, stipulated foreign aid, an aspect of which was cited in discussing conditional food assistance, could be employed. The circumstances might differ from case to case; but it is possible to think of instances where control of corruption within the recipient government, thereby assuring that the aid provided did indeed help the people rather than merely enriching certain officials, might be a precondition, with an independent auditing agency to monitor compliance. It should be reemphasized that this constitutes no interference with the prerogatives of the recipient government, which is free to refuse the aid if it deems the stipulations to be unreasonable.

Strength to Share

The third and final element of a new American vision must be strength to share. Lest it be objected that this is a dangerous world, and that the preceding elements are overly optimistic and idealistic, let it be emphasized that the several elements together are what make the vision a practical one, and strength to share is an essential element. What this entails, as I view it, is simply this: a strong national defense; the will to use it in appropriate situations; the ability to project power; a balanced capacity to apply military, economic, and diplomatic power; and a resultant control of violence.

A strong national defense is, I would argue, an obvious necessity in a world so filled with turmoil, conflict, uncertainty, and change. As a steadying and restraining force during an era of dangerous turbulence, it is essential not only for our own security, but also for constructive and responsible influence over events elsewhere in the world. Even great strength, however, is of no value without the will to use it and the means to bring it to bear; and thus national will (a demonstrable function, I believe, of an operative national vision) and the ability to project power are indispensable aspects of having strength to share.

The threats to international peace and prosperity are today more convoluted, more complex, and more ambiguous than we are accustomed to dealing with. Manipulation of a critical raw material, stimulation of an inflationary trend, undermining of a shaky currency, or tolerance of terrorist acts can be threats to security as great as overt military action. Thus an important (and as yet little realized) element of a strong national defense is development of effective means for coordination and appropriate application of balanced military, economic, and diplomatic power. In a world faced with further proliferation of nuclear weapons, and the assurance of even more terrifying technology in years to come, control of violence will become a primary objective. Not all violence, of course, will be of concern to the major powers; but that which threatens the environment, or interferes in a substantial way with international commerce, or tends to involve the major powers in confrontation with one another, should not and must not be tolerated.

The turbulent times of the last decade, and especially of the last few years, have, in the words of one observer, "left American power and international standing astonishingly intact."[8] But we have undeniably reached a time of change, too--of reassessment of American goals, strengths, and vulnerabilities, and of the world and the role we can and should play in its affairs. Meaningful change is preceded by the recognition of the need for it. That precondition has essentially been met. While the achievement of some consensus as

to what goals and values shall inform national actions in the period
ahead will take time to evolve, the dialogue from which it will
emerge is in full vigor, and gives promise of being a central issue
in the bicentennial Presidential campaign.

What role should we seek? I have suggested some of the possibilities. It is important to emphasize that we seek, not choose,
since none can guarantee success in the quest. Even partial success
results from the interaction of a complex of social, political, psychological, economic, and military factors. Some we can control,
others influence; but many are beyond our reach entirely, either
subject to the control of others or merely functions of chance. Thus
it is possible to say only what we will try to do, and hope that with
our best efforts it will turn out that we are able to do it. In making
our choices, the essence of judgment lies not only in selecting
courses that are best in terms of national interests, but also in
choosing those that are reasonably attainable, and at a price we are
willing to pay.

In many ways the choices to be made in security issues that
are delineated elsewhere in this volume are derivative from this
central choice of an organizing idea. Essential to the success of
any choice involving a creative, constructive role for the United
States in future years is leadership with competence, integrity, and
vision. I believe the American people can still be relied upon to
respond with loyal and willing support to such leadership. This response can be tapped by those with heart, spirit, intellect, and ability to do so, and ability to meaningfully articulate a new and persuasive governing image for the days ahead, perhaps based on such
elements as manifest environmental concern, creative internationalism, and strength to share.

Consider this assessment:

> America is now sauntering through her resources
> and through the mazes of her politics with easy
> nonchalance; but presently there will come a time
> when she will be surprised to find herself grown
> old, --a country crowded, strained, perplexed, --
> when she will be obliged to fall back upon her
> conservatism, obliged to pull herself together,
> adopt a new regimen of life, husband her re-
> sources, concentrate her strength, steady her
> methods, sober her views, restrict her vagaries,
> trust her best, not her average, members. That
> will be the time of change.[9]
>
> Woodrow Wilson
> 31 January 1889

The prescience of Woodrow Wilson was focused on a time that has come. In that realization is both an exciting challenge to leadership and a splendid opportunity to exercise it creatively.

NOTES

1. Annual Defense Department Report, FY1975, p. 1.

2. R. F. Weigley, The American Way of War (New York: Macmillan, 1973), p. 368.

3. Alastair Buchan, The End of the Postwar Era (New York: Dutton, 1974), p. 130.

4. Fernand Braudel, The Mediterranean and the Mediterranean World in the Age of Philip II (New York: Harper & Row, 1972), passim.

5. I am indebted for these insights to Richard Mowery Andrews' brilliant review of Braudel's The Mediterranean in New York Times Book Review, May 18, 1975, pp. 1-3, 42-45.

6. Robert Frost, The Letters of Robert Frost to Louis Untermeyer (New York: Holt, Rinehart and Winston, 1963), p. 233.

7. Chief U.S. Delegate John A. Scali, "Address to the United Nations General Assembly, 6 December 1974," as quoted in New York Times, December 7, 1974, p. 15.

8. The International Institute for Strategic Studies, Strategic Survey 1974, p. 3.

9. Arthur S. Link et al., eds., The Papers of Woodrow Wilson, 1888-1890 (Princeton, N.J.: Princeton University Press, 1969), p. 72.

SELECTED BIBLIOGRAPHY

CHAPTER 2

Bergsten, C. Fred. "The Response to the Third World." Foreign Policy 17 (Winter 1974-75): 3-34.

Gelb, Leslie H., and Anthony Lake. "Washington Dateline: Less Food, More Politics." Foreign Policy 17 (Winter 1974-75): 176-89.

Knight, Virginia C. "Readings on Food and Energy: Parts I and II." Current History, June 1975, pp. 271-72, and July 1975, p. 42.

Moynihan, Daniel P. "United States in Opposition." Commentary 59 (March 1975): 31-44.

Poleman, Thomas T. "World Food: A Perspective." Science, May 9, 1975, pp. 510-18.

Sanderson, Fred H. "The Great Food Fumble." Science, May 9, 1975, pp. 503-09.

_____. "The World Problem: Possibilities of International Action." Current History, June 1975, pp. 265-70, 276-78.

U.S. Department of Agriculture. The World Food Situation and Prospects to 1985. Foreign Agricultural Economic Report, No. 98, 90 pp.

Walters, Harry. "Difficult Issues Underlying Food Problems." Science, May 9, 1975, pp. 524-30.

(For special issues on the world food problem, see the following: Current History, June 1975; Mosaic, May-June 1975; and Science, May 9, 1975.)

CHAPTER 3

The Conference Board. Information Technology: Some Critical Implications for Decision Makers. New York, 1971.

Ginzberg, E. Technology and Social Change. New York: Columbia
    University Press, 1964.

U.S. Department of Commerce. "Factors Affecting the International
    Transfer of Technology Among Developed Countries." Report
    of Panel on International Transfer of Technology to Commerce
    Technology Advisory Board. Washington, D.C., 1970.

Vernon, Raymond. The Economic and Political Consequences of
    Multinational Enterprises: An Anthology. Cambridge, Mass.:
    Harvard University Press, 1972.

                            CHAPTER 4

Edwards, Lyford P. The Natural History of Revolution. New York:
    Russell and Russell, 1965.

Fanon, Franz. The Wretched of the Earth. New York: Grove
    Press, 1963.

Lenin, V. I. What is to be Done? New York: International Pub-
    lishers, 1969.

Masaryk, Thomas G. Spirit of Russia. London: George Allen and
    Unwin, 1919.

Neiburg, H. L. "The Threat of Violence and Social Change."
    American Political Science Review 61, no. 4 (December 1962).

Weber, Max. Politics as a Vocation. Philadelphia: Fortress Press,
    1965.

The President's Commission on the Causes and Prevention of Violence
    Report. Washington, D.C., 1970.

                            CHAPTER 5

Ball, Robert. "NATO Needs a Fresh Breeze." Fortune, February
    1974.

Barclay, Brig. C. N. "What Happens to Europe If the Americans
    Leave?" Army, November 1973, pp. 7-11.

Beaufre, Gen. Andre. L'O.T.A.N. et l'Europe. Paris: Calmann-
    Levy, 1966.

Bowman, Brig. Gen. Richard C. "NATO in a Time of Crisis." Air
    Force Magazine, April 1975, pp. 49-54.

Buchan, Alastair. Europe and America: From Alliance to Coalition.
    Farnborough, England: Saxon House, 1973.

_____. Power and Equilibrium in the 1970s. New York: Praeger,
    1973.

Callahan, Thomas A., Jr. U.S./European Economic Cooperation in
    Military and Civil Technology. Revised edition. Washington,
    D.C.: Center for Strategic and International Studies, George-
    town University, September 1975.

Calleo, David P. "The European Coalition in a Fragmenting World."
    Foreign Affairs 54 (October 1975).

Canby, Stephen L. "NATO Muscle: More Shadow Than Substance."
    Foreign Policy 8 (Fall 1972): 38-49.

Coffey, J. L. Strategic Power and National Security. Pittsburgh:
    University of Pittsburgh Press, 1971.

Cummings, Lawrence B. "The Obsolete Alliance? NATO at the
    Crossroads." Harvard Political Review, Winter 1974, pp.
    18-20.

Dials, G., and D. Larsen. "NATO: Two Views." Army, February
    1975, pp. 10-19.

Enthoven, Alain C. "U.S. Forces in Europe: How Many? Doing
    What?" Foreign Affairs 53 (April 1975): 513-32.

Geiger, Theodore. The Fortunes of the West: The Future of the
    Atlantic Nations. Bloomington, Ind.: Indiana University
    Press, 1973.

Gilmour, I. H. J. "The Prospects for NATO." NATO's Fifteen
    Nations 19 (February-March 1974): 22-25.

Goodpaster, Gen. Andrew J. "NATO and U.S. Forces: Challenges
    and Prospects." Strategic Review 2 (Winter 1974): 6-17.

Gray, Colin S. "Deterrence and Defense in Europe: Revising
    NATO's Theater Nuclear Posture." Journal of the Royal
    United Services Institute for Defense Studies 119 (December
    1974): 3-11.

Hammond, Paul Y. Changing Bargaining Relations in the NATO
    Alliance. Santa Monica: RAND Corporation, 1973.

Hunt, Kenneth. The Alliance and Europe: Part II: Defense with
    Fewer Men. London: International Institute for Strategic
    Studies (Adelphi Papers No. 98), 1973.

Ismay, Lord. NATO: The First Five Years, 1949-1954. Nether-
    lands: NATO, 1955.

Kaiser, Karl. "Europe and America: A Critical Phase." Foreign
    Affairs 52 (July 1974): 725-41.

Klein, Jean. "Arms Control, Desarmement, Regional et Securité
    en Europe." Defense Nationale, 30e annee, August-September
    1974, pp. 53-67.

Knorr, Klauss. The Atlantic Alliance: A Reappraisal. New York:
    Foreign Policy Association, 1974.

Komer, R. W. "Treating NATO's Self-inflicted Wound." Foreign
    Policy 13 (Winter 1973-74): 34-48.

Korbel, Josef. Detente in Europe: Real or Imaginary? Princeton:
    Princeton University Press, 1972.

Lawrence, Richard D., and Jeffrey Record. U.S. Force Structure
    in NATO: An Alternative. Washington, D.C.: Brookings In-
    stitution, 1974.

Longworth, Richard C. "NATO: Trouble at Twenty-Five." Saturday
    Review World, April 6, 1974, pp. 12-15.

Mally, Gerhard. The European Community in Perspective: The New
    Europe, the United States, and the World. Lexington, Mass.:
    D. C. Heath & Co., 1973.

Merkl, Peter H. "The German Janus: From Westpolitik to Ost-
    politik." Political Science Quarterly 7 (Winter 1974-75):
    803-24.

Milton, Gen. T. R. "NATO and the Aging Process." Strategic Review 2 (Winter 1974): 39-43.

Newhouse, John. U.S. Troops in Europe: Issues, Costs, and Choices. Washington, D.C.: Brookings Institution, 1971.

Osgood, Robert E. NATO: The Entangling Alliance. Chicago: University of Chicago Press, 1962.

Pfaltzgraff, Robert L., Jr. "The United States and Europe: Partners in a Multipolar World." Orbis 17 (Spring 1973): 31-50.

Pierre, Andrew J. "Can Europe's Security Be Decoupled from America?" Foreign Affairs 51 (July 1973): 761-77.

Record, Jeffrey. "To Nuke or Not to Nuke? A Critique of Rationales for a Tactical Nuclear Defense of Europe." Military Review 54 (October 1974): 3-13.

Rostow, Eugene V. "America, Europe, and the Middle East." Commentary 57 (February 1974): 40-55.

Ruhl, Lothar. "NATO's Political Limitations." Atlantic Community Quarterly 12 (Winter 1974-75): 463-69.

_____. The Nine and NATO: The Alliance and the Community: An Uncertain Relationship. Paris: Atlantic Institute for International Affairs, 1974.

Spaak, Paul Henri. Why NATO? London: Penguin Books, 1959.

Staercke, Andre de. "Where Does the Atlantic Alliance Stand Today?" Atlantic Community Quarterly 11 (Winter 1973-74): 448-55.

Steinhoff, Johannes. "NATO Enters Crucial Phase." Armed Forces Journal International 3 (June 1974): 32-34.

U.S. Congress. House of Representatives. Committee on Armed Services. U.S. Military Commitments to Europe. Report of the Ad Hoc Committee, 93rd Congress, 2nd Session, April 9, 1974.

U.S. Congress. House of Representatives. Committee on Foreign Affairs. Detente. Hearings before the Subcommittee on Europe, 93rd Congress, 2nd Session, May-July 1974.

U.S. Congress. Senate. Committee on Armed Services. Policy, Troops, and the NATO Alliance. Report of Senator Sam Nunn, 93rd Congress, 2nd Session, April 2, 1974.

U.S. Congress. Senate. Committee on Foreign Relations. U.S. Security Issues in Europe: Burden Sharing and Offset, MBFR and Nuclear Weapons. A Staff Report Prepared for the Use of the Subcommittee on U.S. Security Interests Abroad. 93rd Congress, 1st Session, December 2, 1973.

Windsor, Philip. "NATO's Twenty-Five Years." World Today 30 (May 1974): 181-87.

Wohlstetter, Albert. "Threats and Promises of Peace: Europe and America in the New Era." Orbis 17 (Winter 1974): 1107-44.

Yochelson, John. "MBFR: The Search for an American Approach." Orbis 17 (Spring 1973): 155-74.

Zumwalt, Elmo R. "The Lessons for NATO of Recent Military Experience." Atlantic Community Quarterly 12 (Winter 1974-75): 448-62.

CHAPTER 6

Barker, A. J. The Yom Kippur War. London: Ballantine Books, 1974.

Binder, Leonard. The Middle East Crisis: Background and Issues. Chicago: University of Chicago Center for Policy Study, 1967.

Carpenter, William M., and Stephen P. Gilbert. Great Power Interests and Conflicting Objectives in the Mediterranean-Middle East-Persian Gulf Region. Arlington, Va.: Stanford Research Institute, 1974.

Hammond, Paul Y., and Sidney S. Alexander, eds. Political Dynamics in the Middle East. New York: American Elsevier Publishing Company, 1972.

Journal of Conflict Resolution 16, no. 2 (June 1972). Special Issue on the Arab-Israeli Conflict.

Keer, Malcolm. The Arab Cold War. Third edition. Oxford: Oxford University Press, 1971.

Monroe, Elizabeth, and A. H. Farrar-Hockley. The Arab-Israel War, October 1973: Background and Events (Adelphi Papers No. 111). London: International Institute for Strategic Studies, 1975.

U.S. Department of State. Bureau of Public Affairs. Special Report: U.S. Policy in the Middle East December 1973-November 1974. Washington, D.C.: Department of State.

CHAPTER 7

African Development. London.

Africa Report. New York: African-American Institute.

Bell, J. Bowyer. The Horn of Africa: Strategic Magnet in the Seventies. New York: Crane, Russak & Company, Inc., 1973.

Cottrell, Alvin J., and R. M. Burrell, eds. The Indian Ocean: Its Political, Economic and Military Importance. New York: Praeger, 1972.

Grundy, Kenneth W. Confrontation and Accommodation in Southern Africa. Berkeley: University of California Press, 1973.

Gurtov, Melvin. The United States Against the Third World: Anti-nationalism and Intervention. New York: Praeger, 1974.

Kanet, Roger E., ed. The Soviet Union and the Developing Nations. Baltimore: Johns Hopkins University Press, 1974.

Legum, Colin. Africa Contemporary Record.

McHenry, Donald. United States Firms in South Africa. Bloomington: Indiana University African Studies Program, 1975.

Potholm, Christian, and Richard Dale, eds. Southern Africa in Perspective. New York: Free Press, 1971.

Spence, J. E. The Strategic Significance of Southern Africa. London: Royal United Service Institution, 1970.

Survey of Race Relations in South Africa. Institute of Race Relations, Johannesburg.

Weinstein, Warren, ed. Chinese and Soviet Aid to Africa. New
York: Praeger, 1975.

Yu, George T. China's African Policy: A Study of Tanzania. New
York: Praeger, 1975.

CHAPTER 8

General

U.S. Congress. House. Committee on Foreign Affairs. The Indian
Ocean, Political and Strategic Future. Hearings before the
Subcommittee on National Security Policy and Scientific Devel-
opments. 92nd Congress, 1st Session.

_____. New Perspectives on the Persian Gulf. Hearing before
the Subcommittee on the Near East and South Asia. 93rd Congress, 1st Session.

Bendra, A. P. S. "The Indian Ocean as Seen by an Indian." U.S.
Naval Institute Proceedings, May 1970, pp. 178-203.

Coye, Beth et al. "An Evaluation of the U.S. Naval Presence in the
Indian Ocean." Naval War College Review, October 1970, pp.
34-52.

Engelhardt, Tom. "The Indian Ocean Defence Club." Far Eastern
Economic Review, May 27, 1974, pp. 30-34.

Misra, K. P. "International Politics in the Indian Ocean." Orbis,
Winter 1975, pp. 1088-1108.

Spence, Jack. "Naval Armaments in the Indian Ocean." In Sea
Power in the 1970's, ed. George Quester. New York:
Dunellen, 1975, pp. 117-57.

Minimalist Viewpoint

Blechman, Barry. The Control of Naval Armaments. Washington,
D.C.: Brookings Institution, 1975, Chapter 5.

Jukes, Geoffrey. "Soviet Policy in the Indian Ocean." In Soviet
Naval Policy: Objectives and Constraints, ed. Michael
MacGuire et al. New York: Praeger, 1975, pp. 307-18.

Peiris, Denzil. "The Strategy of Brinkmanship." Far Eastern
Economic Review, May 6, 1974, pp. 30-34.

Wriggins, Howard. "Heading Off a New Arms Race: Let's Try to
Neutralize the Indian Ocean." War/Peace Reports, August-
September 1971, pp. 7-11.

Maximalist Viewpoint

Cottrell, Alvin J., and R. M. Burrell. "Soviet-U.S. Naval Competition in the Indian Ocean." Orbis, Winter 1975, pp. 1109-28.

Harrigan, Anthony. "Security Interests in the Persian Gulf and
Western Indian Ocean." Strategic Review, Fall 1973, pp. 13-22.

Paone, Rocco M. "The Soviet Threat in the Indian Ocean." Military
Review, December 1970, pp. 48-55.

CHAPTERS 9-12

Abramowitz, Morton. Moving the Glacier: The Two Koreas and
the Powers (Adelphi Papers No. 80). London: International
Institute for Strategic Studies, 1971.

Buck, James H., ed. The Modern Japanese Military System.
Sage, 1975.

_____. "The Japanese Self-Defense Force." Naval War College
Review, January-February 1974, pp. 42-52.

Brzesinski, Zbigniew K. The Fragile Blossom: Crisis and Change
in Japan. New York: Harper and Row, 1972.

Buhite, Russell, ed. The Far East. Vol. IV in The Dynamic of
World Power: A Documentary History of United States Foreign
Policy 1945-1973, gen. ed. Arthur M. Schlesinger, Jr. New
York: Chelsea House, 1973.

Clough, Ralph H. East Asia and U.S. Security. Washington, D.C.:
The Brookings Institution, 1975.

East Asia and the World System (Adelphi Papers Nos. 91-92).
London: International Institute for Strategic Studies, 1972.

Greene, Fred. Stresses in U.S.-Japanese Security Relations. Washington, D.C.: The Brookings Institution, 1975.

Harrison, Selig. "One Korea." Foreign Policy 17 (Winter 1974-75): 35-62.

Hinton, Harold C. Three and a Half Powers: The New Balance in Asia. Bloomington: Indiana University Press, 1974.

Japan Defense Agency. The Defense of Japan. English translation. Tokyo: October 1970.

Kosaka, Masataka. Options for Japan's Foreign Policy (Adelphi Paper No. 97). London: International Institute for Strategic Studies, 1973.

Matsueda, Tsukasa, and George Moore. "Japan's Shifting Attitudes Toward the Military: Mitsuya Kenkyu and the Self-Defense Force." Asian Survey 7, no. 9 (September 1967): 614-25.

Muraoka, Kunio. Japanese Security and the United States (Adelphi Papers No. 95). London: International Institute for Strategic Studies, 1973.

Okimoto, David. "Japan's Non-Nuclear Policy: The Problem of the NPT." Asian Survey 15, no. 4 (April 1975): 313-27.

Pillsbury, Michael. "U.S.-Chinese Military Ties?" Foreign Policy 20 (Fall 1975).

Robinson, Thomas W. "The Border Negotiations and the Future of Sino-Soviet-American Relations." Santa Monica: RAND Corporation, 1971.

Saeki, Kiichi. "Japan's Security in a Multipolar World." In East Asia and the World System Part II: The Regional Powers (Adelphi Paper No. 92). London: International Institute for Strategic Studies, November 1972, pp. 21-29.

Scalapino, Robert. Asia and the Major Powers: Implications for the Order. Washington, D.C.: American Enterprise Institute, 1972.

Thornton, Richard. China: The Struggle for Power, 1917-1972. Bloomington: Indiana University Press, 1973.

CHAPTER 13

Adie, Robert F., and Guy Poitras. Latin America: The Politics of Immobility. Englewood Cliffs, N.J.: Prentice-Hall, 1974.

Commission on U.S.-Latin American Relations. "The Americas in a Changing World." New York: Center for Inter-American Relations, 1974.

Harris, Louis, and Victor Alba. The Political Culture and Behavior of Latin America. Kent, Ohio: KSU Press, 1974.

Kohl, James, and John Litt, eds. Urban Guerrilla Warfare in Latin America. Cambridge: MIT Press, 1974.

Sklar, Barry, and Virginia Hagen, comps. Inter-American Relations: A Collection of Documents. Washington, D.C.: Government Printing Office, 1973.

Therberge, James D. The Soviet Presence in Latin America. New York: Crane, Russak, 1974.

U.S. Congress. Senate. Committee on Foreign Relations. Subcommittee on Western Hemisphere Affairs. "Rockefeller Report on Latin America." 91st Congress, 1st Session. Washington, D.C.: Government Printing Office, 1970.

Wiarda, Howard J., ed. Politics and Social Change in Latin America. Amherst: University of Massachusetts Press, 1974.

CHAPTER 14

Aliber, Robert Z. The International Money Game. New York: Basic Books, Inc., 1973.

Brown, Lester R. World Without Borders. New York: Random House, 1972.

Bundy, William P. The World Economic Crisis. New York: W. W. Norton & Co. Inc., 1975.

Corbet, Hugh, and Robert Jackson. In Search of a New World Economic Order. New York: Halsted Press, John Wiley & Sons, 1974.

The Economist. London, England.

Friedman, Irving S. Inflation, A World-Wide Disaster. Boston:
    Houghton Mifflin Company, 1973.

Glyn, Andrew, and Bob Sutcliffe. Capitalism in Crisis. New York:
    Pantheon Books, 1973.

International Economic Report of the President. Washington, D.C.:
    Government Printing Office, February 1974.

Kindleberger, Charles P. The World in Depression 1929-1939.
    Berkeley and Los Angeles: University of California Press,
    1973.

Knorr, Klaus. Power and Wealth. New York: Basic Books, Inc.,
    1973.

Kolko, Joyce. America and the Crisis of World Capitalism. Boston:
    Beacon Press, 1974.

Little, Jane Sneddon. Eurodollars, The Money Market Gypsies.
    New York: Harper and Row, 1975.

Meiselman, David I., and Arthur B. Laffer. The Phenomenon of
    Worldwide Inflation. Washington, D.C.: American Enter-
    prise Institute of Public Policy Research, 1975.

Parsson, Jens O. Dying of Money, Lessons of the Great German
    and American Inflations. Boston: Wellspring Press, 1974.

Rolfe, Sidney E., and James Burtle. The Great Wheel: The World
    Monetary System. New York: Quadrangle-The New York
    Times Book Co., 1973.

Rosen, Sumner M. Economic Power Failure: The Current American
    Crisis. New York: McGraw-Hill Book Company, 1975.

Wall, David. The Charity of Nations. New York: Basic Books,
    Inc., 1973.

Wiegand, G. C. Inflation and Monetary Crisis. Washington, D.C.:
    Public Affairs Press, 1975.

CHAPTER 16

Aaron, David. "A New Concept." Foreign Policy 17 (Winter 1974-75): 157-65.

Ackley, Richard T. "What's Left of SALT?" Naval War College Review, May-June 1974, pp. 43-49.

Collins, John M. "Maneuver Instead of Mass: The Key to Assured Stability." Orbis 18 (Fall 1974): 750-62.

Garthoff, Raymond L. "Salt and the Soviet Military." Problems of Communism, January-February 1975, pp. 21-37.

Nacht, Michael. "The Vladivostok Accord and American Technological Options." Survival, May-June 1975, pp. 106-13.

Nitze, Paul H. "The Strategic Balance Between Hope and Skepticism." Foreign Policy 17 (Winter 1974-75): 136-56.

Rathjens, G. W. "Flexible Response Options." Orbis 18 (Fall 1974): 677-88.

Strategic Survey 1974. London: The International Institute for Strategic Studies, 1975.

Ulsamer, Edgar. "How Russia is Tipping the Strategic Balance." Air Force, January 1975, pp. 48-53.

U.S. Congress. Senate. Committee on Foreign Relations. Hearing before the Subcommittee on Arms Control, International Law and Organization. U.S.-U.S.S.R. Strategic Policies. 93rd Congress, 2nd Session, March 4, 1974.

U.S. Department of Defense. Statement of Secretary of Defense James R. Schlesinger before the Senate Armed Forces Committee. Annual Defense Department Report FY 1976 and FY 1977. Washington, D.C.: Government Printing Office, 1975.

Van Cleave, William R., and Roger W. Barnett. "Strategic Adaptability." Orbis 18 (Fall 1974): 655-76.

Westervalt, Donald R. "The Essence of Armed Futility." Orbis 18 (Fall 1974): 689-705.

CHAPTER 18

American Regulation of Arms Exports. New York: Carnegie En-
dowment for International Peace, 1941.

Einaudi, L. et al. Arms Transfers to Latin America: Toward a
Policy of Mutual Respect. Report prepared for the Department of State. Santa Monica: RAND Corporation, 1973.

Frank, Lewis. The Arms Trade in International Relations. New
York: Praeger, 1969.

Hanifhen, Frank C. Merchants of Death: A Study of the International
Armaments Industry. New York: Dodd, Mead and Co., 1934.

Hovey, Harold A. United States Military Assistance: A Study of
Policies and Practices. New York: Praeger, 1965.

Harkavy, Robert E. The Arms Trade and International Systems.
Cambridge, Mass.: Ballinger, 1975.

Joshua, W., and S. Gilbert. Arms for the Third World: Soviet
Military Aid Diplomacy. Baltimore: Johns Hopkins Press,
1969.

Leiss et al. Arms Transfers to Less Developed Countries.
Cambridge, Mass.: MIT Center for International Studies,
1970.

Noel-Baker, P. The Private Manufacture of Armaments. London:
V. Gollancz, 1936.

Ra'anan, Uri. The U.S.S.R. Arms the Third World. Cambridge,
Mass.: MIT Press, 1969.

Stockholm International Peace Research Institute (SIPRI). The Arms
Trade and the Third World. New York: Humanities Press,
1971.

_____. SIPRI Yearbook of World Armaments and Disarmament.
New York: Humanities Press.

_____. Arms Trade Registers: The Arms Trade with the Third
World. Cambridge, Mass.: MIT Press, 1975.

Stanley, John, and Maurice Pearton. The International Trade in
    Arms. International Institute for Strategic Studies. London:
    Chatto and Windus, 1972.

Thayer, George. The War Business. New York: Simon and
    Schuster, 1969.

USACDA. World Military Expenditures and Arms Trade, 1963-1973
    and The International Transfer of Conventional Arms. Report
    to the Congress by USACDA. Washington, D.C.: Government
    Printing Office, 1974.

                        CHAPTER 19

Atlantic Council of the United States. Conference of Security and
    Cooperation in Europe and Negotiations on Mutual and Balanced
    Force Reductions. Washington, D.C., November 23, 1972.

Ball, Robert. "Rethinking the Defense of Europe." Fortune 87
    (February 1973): 60-65, 138, 142-44.

Bertram, Christoph. Mutual Force Reductions in Europe (Adelphi
    Paper No. 84). London: International Institute for Strategic
    Studies, January 1972.

Brown, Neville. European Security 1972-1980. London: Royal
    United Services Institute for Defense Studies, 1972.

Canby, Steven. The Alliance and Europe: Part IV: Military Doc-
    trine and Technology (Adelphi Paper No. 109). London: Inter-
    national Institute of Strategic Studies, 1975.

Coffey, Joseph I. "Arms Control and the Military Balance in
    Europe." Orbis 16 (Summer 1973): 132-54.

_____. New Approaches to Arms Reduction in Europe (Adelphi
    Paper No. 105). London: International Institute for Strategic
    Studies, 1974.

Cliffe, Trevor. Military Technology and the European Balance
    (Adelphi Paper No. 89). London: International Institute for
    Strategic Studies, November 1972.

Erickson, John. "MBFR: Force Levels and Security Requirements." Strategic Review 1 (Summer 1973): 28-43.

_____. "Soviet Military Capabilities in Europe." RUSI--Journal of the Royal United Services Institute for Defense Studies 120 (March 1975): 65-69.

Facer, Roger. The Alliance and Europe: Part III: Weapons Procurement in Europe--Capabilities and Choices (Adelphi Paper No. 108). London: International Institute for Strategic Studies, 1975.

Hahn, Walter F. "Nuclear Balance in Europe." Foreign Affairs 50 (April 1972): 501-16.

Heisenberg, Wolfgang. The Alliance and Europe: Part I: Crisis Stability in Europe and Theater Nuclear Weapons (Adelphi Paper No. 96). London: International Institute for Strategic Studies, Summer 1973.

Hunt, Kenneth. The Alliance and Europe: Part II: Defense with Fewer Men (Adelphi Paper No. 98). London: International Institute for Strategic Studies, Summer 1973.

Klaiber, Wolfgang, Laszlo Hadik et al. Era of Negotiations. Lexington, Mass.: D. C. Heath & Co., 1973.

Lawrence, Richard D., and Jeffrey Record. U.S. Force Structure: An Alternative. Washington, D.C.: The Brookings Institution, 1974.

Newhouse, John et al. U.S. Troops in Europe: Issues, Costs, and Choices. Washington, D.C.: The Brookings Institution, 1971.

Pierre, Andrew J. "Can Europe's Security Be Decoupled from America?" Foreign Affairs 51 (July 1973): 761-77.

_____. "Limiting Soviet and American Conventional Forces." Survival, Summer 1973, pp. 59-69.

Stanley, Timothy. A Conference on European Security? Problems, Prospects, and Pitfalls. Washington, D.C.: The Atlantic Council of the United States, 1970.

Stockholm International Peace Research Institute. Force Reductions in Europe. New York: Humanities Press, 1974.

Ullman, Richard H. "No First Use of Nuclear Weapons." Foreign
    Affairs 50 (July 1972): 669-83.

U.S. Congress. House. Committee on Armed Services. U.S. Mili-
    tary Commitments to Europe. Hearings February 15, 26;
    March 5, 6, and 8, 1974. Washington, D.C.: Government
    Printing Office, 1974.

U.S. Congress. House. Committee on Foreign Affairs. Subcom-
    mittee on Europe. Conference on European Security. Hear-
    ings April 25; May 10; August 10, 17; September 7, 27, 1972.
    Washington, D.C.: Government Printing Office, 1972.

U.S. Congress. House. Committee on Foreign Affairs. Subcom-
    mittee on Europe. U.S. Forces in NATO. Hearings June 18,
    19, 25, 26; July 10, 11, 12, 17, 1973. Washington, D.C.:
    Government Printing Office, 1973.

U.S. Congress. Senate. Committee on Foreign Relations. Subcom-
    mittee on Arms Control, International Law, and Organization.
    U.S. Forces in Europe. Hearings July 25 and 27, 1973.
    Washington, D.C.: Government Printing Office, 1973.

CHAPTER 20

Belchman, B. M., E. M. Gramlich, and R. M. Martman. "Setting
    National Priorities--The 1975 Budget." Washington, D.C.:
    The Brookings Institution, 1974.

Binken, Martin. "Support Costs in the Defense Budget: The Sub-
    merged One-Third." Washington, D.C.: Brookings Institu-
    tion Staff Paper, 1972.

Braudel, Fernand. The Mediterranean and the Mediterranean World
    in the Age of Philip II. 2 vols. New York: Harper and Row,
    1972-74.

Brzezinski, Zbigniew. Between Two Ages: America's Role in the
    Technetronic Era. New York: Viking, 1970.

Buchan, Alastair. The End of the Postwar Era: A New Balance of
    World Power. New York: Dutton, 1974.

Cobbledick, James R. Choice in American Foreign Policy: Options
    for the Future. New York: Crowell, 1973.

Enthoven, Alain C., and K. Wayne Smith.   How Much is Enough?
New York: Harper and Row, 1971.

Mansfield, Edwin. Defense, Science and Public Policy. New York:
W. W. Norton and Company, 1968.

Melman, Seymour. The Permanent War Economy. New York:
Simon and Schuster, 1974.

Schlesinger, James R. "Annual Defense Department Report FY 1976
and FY 1977." Department of Defense.

U.S. Department of Defense. "Program of Research, Development,
Test, and Evaluation, FY 1976." Statement of the Directors
of Defense Research and Engineering to the 94th Congress,
1st Session, 1975.

CHAPTER 21

Frost, Robert. The Letters of Robert Frost to Louis Untermeyer.
New York: Holt, Rinehart and Winston, 1963.

International Institute for Strategic Studies. Strategic Survey 1974.
London: IISS, 1975.

Laszlo, Ervin. A Strategy for the Future: The Systems Approach
to World Order. New York: Braziller, 1974.

Lefever, Ernest. Ethics and United States Foreign Policy. New
York: Meridian, 1957.

Link, Arthur S. et al., eds. The Papers of Woodrow Wilson, Volume
6: 1880-1890. Princeton: Princeton University Press, 1969.

Middleton, Drew. Can America Win the Next War? New York:
Scribner's, 1975.

Tucker, Robert W., and William Watts, eds. Beyond Containment:
U.S. Foreign Policy in Transition. Washington, D.C.:
Potomac Associates, 1973.

U.S. Department of Defense. Annual Defense Department Report:
FY 1975.

Weigley, Russell F. The American Way of War: A History of United
States Military Strategy and Policy. New York: Macmillan, 1973.

ABOUT THE EDITOR
AND CONTRIBUTORS

DR. WILLIAM W. WHITSON is the Director of Policy Research at the BDM Corporation in Vienna, Virginia. He holds a B.S. from the U.S. Military Academy at West Point, and a Ph.D. in International Relations from the Fletcher School of Law and Diplomacy. He has served as Director of Asian Studies at the Rand Corporation; is a frequent lecturer on U.S. security policy issues at war colleges, service schools, and universities; is the author of The Chinese High Command: A History of Communist Military Politics, 1927-1971, and has edited several other Praeger books, including The Military and Political Power in China in the 1970s, and Doing Business with China: American Trade Opportunities in the 1970s.

DR. RICHARD ACKLEY, Associate Dean of Academic Administration and Assistant Professor of Political Science at the San Bernadino campus of California State College, is involved in defense-related analytical systems planning. He holds a B.A. in History from the University of Southern California, an M.A. in Political Science from the University of Hawaii, and a Ph.D. in International Relations from the University of Southern California. He is a graduate of the Naval Intelligence Postgraduate School, has served as Assistant Naval Attache in Moscow, and is the author of many articles in the field of international security and defense strategy.

JOHN AMOS is an Assistant Professor of Political Science at the Naval Postgraduate School. He holds a B.A. in Political Science from Occidental College in Los Angeles, an M.A. from the University of California at Berkeley, and has studied at the American University in Cairo. He served in Turkey as an Air Force officer, and has authored several articles on Middle East affairs.

DR. DOUGLAS BEATTY is Assistant Vice President, Applied Sciences, at the BDM Corporation in Vienna, Virginia. He holds a B.S.E. and a MS.E. in Aeronautical Engineering from Princeton University. He has extensive experience in research and development program analysis management, having served for several years in the office of the Secretary of Defense and the Institute for Defense Analysis.

DR. JAMES BUCK is Coordinator of Graduate Programs in History at the University of Georgia. He holds an A.B. in Far East Affairs from the University of Washington, an A.M. in History from Stanford University, and a Ph.D. in History from the American University. He has had extensive military experience in Japan, including participation in the Foreign Area Specialist Training Program; was the first American officer to serve in a Japanese self-defense course; and has authored several articles on Japanese military history and defense policy, recently editing a book on the "Modern Japanese Military System."

COL. ROBERT CHENOWETH is an Associate Professor in the Department of Social Sciences at the U.S. Military Academy at West Point. He holds a B.S. in Agriculture from Purdue University, and an M.B.A. from the Harvard University Business School. His specialty is international economics, and he has served in France, Thailand, Korea, and Vietnam.

DR. RAY CLINE is the Executive Director of Studies at the Georgetown Center for Strategic and International Studies. He holds a B.A., an M.A., and a Ph.D. in History and International Relations from Harvard University, where he was elected to the Harvard Society of Fellows; and he was a Henry Prize Fellow at Balliol Oxford University. He has served as Deputy Director (Intelligence) at the Central Intelligence Agency; as Special Advisor to the American Embassy in Bonn, Germany; as Director of the Bureau of Intelligence and Research in the Department of State; as the State Department member of the U.S. Intelligence Board; and as Chairman of the National Security Council Subcommittee on Foreign Affairs Research.

DR. DONALD DANIEL is an Assistant Professor of Political Science at the Naval Postgraduate School. He holds a B.A. in Political Science from Holy Cross, and a Ph.D. in Political Science from Georgetown University. He has published several articles concerning research on general Naval affairs, focused particularly on Soviet Naval affairs.

DR. ROBERT DELANEY is Adjunct Professor of International Management at Soave Regina College in Newport. He holds a Bachelor of Naval Science from Holy Cross University, an M.A. in Political Science from Boston University, and a Ph.D. in Political Sociology from the Catholic University. He served in the Foreign Service in Panama and El Salvador, and is a former Public Affairs Advisor for Esso-Standard, S.A.

EDWARD GUDE is an independent consultant on international security affairs. He holds an A.B. from Dartmouth College and has studied at the London School of Economics and Political Science, and at the Massachusetts Institute of Technology where he has held both Reynolds and NDEA fellowships. He has worked extensively with a number of U.S. government organizations, and has authored several publications dealing with domestic and international violence.

DR. ROBERT HARKAVY, as Professor of Political Science at Kalamazoo College, has written a book on the arms trade, and is currently completing a monograph for the Denver World Affairs Monograph Series on the Israeli Nuclear Weapons Program. He holds an M.A. in Political Science from the University of California at Berkeley, and a Ph.D. in International Relations from Yale University. He has served at the Atomic Energy Commission, and is presently working on problems of proliferation and transfer at the International Relations Bureau of the Arms Control Agency.

JACK H. HARRIS, manager of the BDM Corporation's Foreign Area Studies Department, is a specialist on international security affairs. He holds a B.A. in Economics and Chinese History from the University of Chicago, and is currently completing a Ph.D. in International Politics and Asian Affairs at the George Washington University. He is an authority on Chinese military and foreign affairs, has served as the principal China analyst for one of the U.S. intelligence organizations, and has authored a number of works on Sino-Soviet-U.S. strategic concerns.

MARC J. HERSH is a specialist on international business and the multinational corporation. He holds a law degree from New York University, and a graduate degree in East Asian Studies from Harvard University. He recently conducted a major study for the Department of Defense concerning the impact of multinational corporations on U.S. national security interests.

KENNETH JACOBSON is a political scientist at the Stanford Research Institute. He holds a B.A. in Political Science from LaSalle College; an M.A. and an M. Phil. in International Relations from George Washington University; and is a Ph.D. candidate in International Relations at George Washington University. While at the Institute, he has' been involved in the analysis of political implications of SALT and MBFR negotiations for the U.S. Atomic Energy Commission, and in an analysis of MBFR European Security Conference and OST POLIK for the U.S. Army Deputy Chief of Staff for Military Operations.

PHILIP KARBER is Director, Strategic Studies and Force Assessment, at the BDM Corporation in Vienna, Virginia. He holds a B.A. in Political Science from Pepperdine University, an M.A. in Government, and a Ph.D. in International Relations from Georgetown University. He has extensive experience in the study of nuclear proliferation and terrorism, served as Congressional Consultant on National Security Policy, worked at the Center for Strategic and International Studies, and was a member of the CBS Television News team.

COL. WILLIAM KENNEDY is a research analyst with the Strategic Studies Institute at the U.S. Army War College. He holds a degree in Journalism from Marquette University. He has served in Japan and China, as an intelligence officer in the Strategic Air Command; as an Army public affairs officer in the National Guard Bureau, Washington, D.C.; and has authored several publications concerned with the analysis and reporting of military affairs.

DR. PHILIP MORGAN is a Senior Associate in the International Development Research Center at Indiana University. He holds a B.A. in Economics from Southern Methodist University, an M.A. in Political Science from the University of Illinois, and a Ph.D. in Political Science from Syracuse University. His experience in Africa as a Fulbright Lecturer at the University of Botswana, Lesotho, and Swaziland, includes assistance in the establishment of an Institute in Development Management, designed to serve the higher level training requirements of African countries; extensive consultation with public and private officials; and he served as a Statistical Training Officer and Field Survey Supervisor at the National Statistical Office, Ministry of Development and Planning of the Malawi government.

CHARLES MOVIT is an economist with Stanford Research Institute's Strategic Studies Center. He received his undergraduate education at the Massachusetts Institute of Technology, and did his graduate work at the University of Pennsylvania. At the Strategic Studies Center his research has focused on the economics of technology transfer and East-West trade, and other areas of Soviet and comparative economics. He is currently engaged in research on the Soviet construction industry.

COL. GEORGE OSBORN is an Associate Professor in the Department of Social Sciences at the U.S. Military Academy at West Point. He holds a B.A., an M.A., and a Ph.D. in Modern Chinese History from Stanford University. His Southeast Asian experience includes research in both Vietnam and Thailand, and he was assigned to the U.S. Embassy in Bangkok.

DR. HERBERT SCHANDLER is a specialist in National Defense for the Congressional Research Service at the Library of Congress. He holds a B.S. from the U.S. Military Academy, an M.P.A. from Harvard University, and a Ph.D. in Political Economy and Government from Harvard University. He has served extensively in Europe, in the Office of National Security Affairs, in the Office of the Chief of Staff of the Army, as Director of National Security Policy Studies at the National War College, and as a member of the NATO Policy Branch, Plans and Policy Directorate of the Organization of the Joint Chiefs of Staff.

CHARLES SHIRKEY is Professor of Management at the U.S. Naval War College in Newport, where he concentrates on the management of national security policy. He holds a B.A. in Social Science from Southern Methodist University, and a Master's degree from Oxford University in Philosophy, Politics, and Economics. He has worked as an aide to Representative Les Aspen of Wisconsin, at the Brookings Institution, at the Pentagon, and in the Executive Office complex.

LTC LEWIS SORLEY is military assistant to the Director of Net Assessment, Office of the Secretary of Defense in Washington, D.C. A graduate of West Point, he also holds an M.A. degree in English from the University of Pennsylvania, an M.P.A. degree from Pennsylvania State University, and is a Ph.D. candidate at the Johns Hopkins University. He has served in Germany and Vietnam, on the staff of West Point, in the Office of the Army Chief of Staff, and at the Army War College as Chairman of the Current Affairs Panel.

RELATED TITLES
Published by
Praeger Special Studies

CURRENT ISSUES IN U.S. DEFENSE POLICY
Center for Defense Information

THE CONSTITUTION AND THE CONDUCT OF
FOREIGN POLICY*
edited by Francis O. Wilcox
and Richard A. Frank

FOREIGN TRADE AND U.S. POLICY: The Case for
International Free Trade*
Leland B. Yeager and
David G. Tuerck

PLANNING ALTERNATIVE WORLD FUTURES: Values,
Methods, and Models*
edited by Louis Rene Beres
and Harry R. Targ

QUANTITATIVE INTERNATIONAL POLITICS: An
Appraisal
edited by Francis W. Hoole
and Dina A. Zinnes

QUANTITATIVE TECHNIQUES IN FOREIGN POLICY
ANALYSIS AND FORECASTING
Michael K. O'Leary and
William D. Coplin, with the
assistance of Howard B. Shapiro

THE UNITED STATES AND INTERNATIONAL OIL: A
Report for the Federal Energy Administration on U.S.
Firms and Government Policy*
Robert B. Krueger

U.S. POLICY TOWARD AFRICA*
edited by Frederick S. Arkhurst

*Also available in paperback as PSS Student Editions.